COLERIDGE AND THE
ABYSSINIAN MAID

SAMUEL TAYLOR COLERIDGE

Born, Ottery St Mary   *21 October 1772*
Died, Highgate   *25 July 1834*

COLERIDGE
& *the Abyssinian Maid*

GEOFFREY YARLOTT

METHUEN & CO LTD
11 NEW FETTER LANE EC4P 4EE

First published in Great Britain, 1967
First published as a University Paperback 1971

Hardback SBN 416 07750 1
University Paperback SBN 416 60280 0

© 1967 Geoffrey Yarlott
Printed in Great Britain
by The Broadwater Press Ltd
Welwyn Garden City

Distributed in U.S.A. by
Barnes & Noble Inc.

FOR JENNY

CONTENTS

PREFACE

I wish first to thank the Arts Faculty Board of the University of Nottingham, for the award some years ago of a research grant which enabled me to lay the foundations of this book. My thanks are due also to the Librarians of both Nottingham and Leicester Universities for their assistance in procuring for me texts which would otherwise have been inaccessible, and to the Keepers of the British Museum who kindly gave me access to the original Coleridge manuscripts. My obligations to Miss Kathleen Coburn and Professor E. L. Griggs, on whose editions of the Coleridge Notebooks and Letters I have relied heavily, are inestimable. The influence of many recent critical studies of Coleridge upon my book is everywhere apparent and, I hope, has been adequately acknowledged. To Mr House's excellent study of Coleridge I owe an especial debt of thanks: it was he, I believe, who first pointed out to us that the emotional element in Coleridge's work has received inadequate attention.

In passages printed from the manuscripts and letters an attempt has been made to preserve, as far as possible, the spelling, punctuation, abbreviations, and general living character of the original material. Conjectural, illegible, and explanatory words are indicated in the text by square brackets, and my own italicizations of particular words or phrases are recorded in the footnotes. Notes and references are supplied at the foot of each page, and four Appendices dealing with problems of special interest may be found at the end of the book.

The name 'Sara' is apt to cause confusion in Coleridge's writings since it was the name of his wife (Sara Fricker), of Sara Hutchinson (Wordsworth's sister-in-law), and of his daughter (Sara Coleridge). Throughout this study therefore 'Sara' stands for Coleridge's wife, Sara Hutchinson is referred to as 'Asra' (Coleridge's favourite appellation for her), and the daughter is called 'Young Sara'.

I am grateful to the many friends and colleagues who have helped me with this book, especially Dr G. D. Yeoman, Mr G. Hinchliffe, and Mr V. Houghton. To Professor J. T. Boulton, who has made many invaluable suggestions for its improvement, and who has allowed me to draw freely on his own (unpublished) interpretation of *The Ancient Mariner*, I cannot sufficiently express my thanks.

I am grateful also to Mrs Joyce West, who cheerfully undertook to type a difficult manuscript, and to Miss Margaret Woolliscroft, who assisted her.

The book is dedicated finally to my wife, without whose constant help and encouragement it could never have been written.

GEOFFREY YARLOTT

February 1966

INTRODUCTION

The present 'boom' in Coleridge studies is bound to lead to a
major revaluation of his work. The editing of the Notebooks and
Letters, already far advanced through the heroic labours of Miss
Kathleen Coburn and Earl Leslie Griggs, is now to be supple-
mented by *The Collected Coleridge*, the first volumes of which will
be published shortly by the Bollingen Foundation in the United
States and by Rupert Hart-Davis Limited in the United King-
dom. Not only will the contents of almost seventy of Coleridge's
private notebooks and the records of a lifetime's correspondence
soon be available to the general reader, but the texts of everything he wrote (including marginalia and fragmentary remains)
will also be accessible, while the poetical canon too, it is anticipated, will be established on sounder principles than hitherto.[1]
Coleridge's reputation is sure to be enhanced by these endea-
vours, and critics will rejoice that standard works like *Table Talk*,
Anima Poetae, and E. H. Coleridge's and J. Dykes Campbell's
editions of the *Poems*, valuable though these have been in their
time, may now make way for something better. A fresh biography, more sympathetic to its subject than that of Sir Edmund
Chambers, will doubtless be forthcoming. When all these projects are accomplished and the way lies open to re-assessment,
we shall understand at last perhaps the true grounds of Lamb's
indignation that anyone could even think of patronizing Coleridge.

Meanwhile the business of re-appraisal has begun already and
in recent years our image of Coleridge has changed considerably.
Thus, the Victorian view of Coleridge's poetry as incantatory
magic incapable of analysis has been superseded, and his status
as critic, religious thinker, philosopher, and political theorist has

---

[1] See George Whalley, "Coleridge's Poetical Canon: Selection and
Arrangement", in *A Review of English Literature*, Vol. VII, No. 1, January
1966.

been reconsidered. Because, as Mr Beer remarks, that extraordinary myriad-mindedness cannot be contained within a single volume, it is inevitable that critical attention should focus on restricted areas of Coleridge's activity, advancing by the accumulation and correction of particular insights. It needs to be borne in mind however that to differentiate and isolate these areas too specifically is to offend against that principle of organic unity which Coleridge, more than any English writer before him, so constantly expounded in his writings. While it is true that the preoccupations and achievements of successive phases of his life have each a distinctive tone and colour, they belong nevertheless to an integral pattern of development. Coleridge's own dislike of anything which dislocates the organic pattern might be inferred from his strong preference (expressed in *Table Talk*) for chronological arrangements of a poet's work:

> All your divisions are in particular instances inadequate, and they destroy the interest which arises from watching the progress, maturity, and even the decay of genius.

The living quality of Coleridge's own inner mental history may best be presented by a chronological approach which, with the help of biographical data, treats the poems not as individual set-pieces but as parts of an organic sequence.

The extent to which biographical information may be adduced in support of the poem upon the page is, rightly, a matter for critical dispute. Where a poem is explicitly autobiographical (as many of Coleridge's were) biographical commentary is clearly legitimate, but in cases where the personal element is not established—or has been objectified and transcended—a confrontation with the poem itself is called for. Hence, in my treatment of *Kubla Khan, The Ancient Mariner*, and *Christabel*, biographical commentary is preceded by an objective analysis of the poems themselves. Mr House's statement of the point at issue here expresses the matter succinctly: 'Even the more impersonal poems,' he wrote, '*The Ancient Mariner* above all, though not by any means to be primarily interpreted or valued by biographical reference, can yet have their meaning enhanced by the most terrible details of biographical knowledge.' It *is* relevant to a full understanding of *The Ancient Mariner* that the life-as-voyage image at its centre had stood as a personal symbol for Coleridge since childhood; it *is* relevant to an appreciation of *Dejection: an Ode*

that the 'dear Lady' for whom the poem invoked 'wings of healing' was Sara Hutchinson, whose sufferings Coleridge himself
had caused. The 'limber elf' who appears in *Christabel* and the
'Abyssinian maid' in *Kubla Khan* may likewise have had deep
personal significance for Coleridge.

So much is now known or knowable about Coleridge's life at
first hand that we *must* use this information: properly handled,
it not only adds to his stature, but it induces also a broader sympathy with his defects. In particular, it enables us to make a more
accurate diagnosis of the very real problem of maladjustment
which clearly needs to be explained in his case. Traditional explanations of his sudden 'failure' as a poet—such as that metaphysics, opium, or ill-health 'killed' the poet in him—can now
be seen to be quite inadequate, descriptive of the symptoms of
his trouble rather than of the cause. As we examine the details of
Coleridge's life during the critical period 1800–2, a tragic story
emerges which not only explains why his poetical ambitions
suddenly collapsed but which has an important bearing on the
theory of poetry he subsequently developed. The famous principle, interminably propounded—that creativity requires a spontaneous exertion of all the poet's powers in harmony—was a sad
commentary perhaps on the actual dissociation of Coleridge's
own personality, described in *Dejection: an Ode*. His insistence
that poetry necessitates an utter *aloofness* of the poet's own feelings may likewise have sprung from a recognition that he could
no longer prevent his private feelings from intruding into his own
poetical work. All the new evidence to which we now have access
points to the fact that this later critical theory evolved out of the
real-life experiences of 1802.

This book seeks to show the causes which led to Coleridge's
breakdown in 1802 and to indicate how his views on poetry
changed as a result of it. The approach is selective in that it
focuses attention on only one part of Coleridge's life (roughly
from 1793 to 1810) while it allows little autonomy to the religious, philosophical, and political preoccupations. Within these
limits however it attempts to relate a number of different areas
of Coleridge's activity and to trace his emotional and moral development more closely than might be possible in a full-scale
biography. The account terminates in 1810, about the time when
Coleridge's relationships with Asra and Wordsworth, the two key

figures in his life, were ruptured. Until the contents of the remaining volumes of the Notebooks are available it would be pre-
mature to continue the story further.

ABBREVIATIONS

AP   *Anima Poetae*, From the Unpublished Note-Books of Samuel Taylor Coleridge, Edited by Ernest Hartley Coleridge, 1895.

AR   *Aids to Reflection*, by S. T. Coleridge, 1825.

Baker   J. V. Baker, *The Sacred River*—Coleridge's Theory of the Imagination, Louisiana State University Press, 1957.

Beer   J. B. Beer, *Coleridge the Visionary*, 1959.

BL   *Biographia Literaria*, by S. T. Coleridge, Edited by J. Shawcross, 2 vols., 1907.

Boulger   J. D. Boulger, *Coleridge as Religious Thinker*, Yale University Press, 1961.

CF   *Coleridge Fille*, a Biography of Sara Coleridge, E. L. Griggs, 1940.

CL   *Collected Letters of Samuel Taylor Coleridge*, Edited by E. L. Griggs, Vols. I–II, 1956, Vols. III–IV, 1959.

Friend   *The Friend: a series of Essays in Three Volumes*, by S. T. Coleridge, 1818 edition.

HCR   *Blake, Coleridge, Wordsworth, Lamb, etc.—being Selections from the Remains of Henry Crabb Robinson*, Edited by Edith J. Morley, 1932.

HH   H. House, *Coleridge*, the Clark Lectures 1951–2, published 1953.

HL   *Letters of Hartley Coleridge*, Edited by G. E. and E. L. Griggs, 1937.

IH   Maurice Carpenter, *The Indifferent Horseman:* the Divine Comedy of Samuel Taylor Coleridge, 1954.

IS   *Inquiring Spirit*, a New Presentation of Coleridge from his Published and Unpublished Prose Writings, Edited by K. Coburn, 1951.

KC   *The Notebooks of Samuel Taylor Coleridge*, Edited by K. Coburn, Vol. I (two parts) 1957, Vol. II (two parts) 1962.

L   *Letters of Samuel Taylor Coleridge*, Edited by E. H. Coleridge, 2 vols., 1895.

Life   E. K. Chambers, *Samuel Taylor Coleridge*, 1938.

Lowes   J. L. Lowes, *The Road to Xanadu*, revised edition, 1931.

LS   *Essays and Lectures on Shakespeare*, by S. T. Coleridge, 1907 edition.

LSH   *The Letters of Sara Hutchinson, 1800–1835*, Edited by K. Coburn, 1954.

MC   *Coleridge's Miscellaneous Criticism*, Edited by T. M. Raysor, 1936.

PL   *The Philosophical Lectures of Samuel Taylor Coleridge*, Edited by K. Coburn, 1949.

PW   *The Poems of Samuel Taylor Coleridge*, Edited by E. H. Coleridge, 1912.

Sandford Mrs H. Sandford, *Thomas Poole and his Friends*, 2 vols., 1888.

Schulz   M. F. Schulz, *The Poetic Voices of Coleridge*, Detroit, 1963.

Suther   M. Suther, *The Dark Night of Samuel Taylor Coleridge*, New York, 1960.

Warren   "A Poem of Pure Imagination: an Experiment in Reading", in Robert Penn Warren, *Selected Essays* (London 1964).

Whalley   G. Whalley, *Coleridge and Sara Hutchinson and the Asra Poems*, 1955.

Wanted: a Sheet-Anchor

Coleridge spent the evening of 7 January 1807 listening to Wordsworth recite his recently completed *Prelude*, an autobiographical poem describing the growth of a poet's mind, and he spent the remainder of that night composing a tribute to his friend's achievement.[1] A feature of Coleridge's poem was the contrast it contained between Wordsworth's self-sufficiency as an individual and his awareness of the disorganization of his own personality:

> Ah! as I listened with a heart forlorn,
> The pulses of my being beat anew:
> And even as Life returns upon the drowned,
> Life's joy rekindling roused a throng of pains—
> Keen pangs of Love, awakening as a babe
> Turbulent, with an outcry in the heart;
> And fears self-willed, that shunned the eye of Hope;
> And Hope that scarce would know itself from Fear;
> Sense of past Youth, and Manhood come in vain,
> And Genius given, and Knowledge won in vain;
> And all which I had culled in wood-walks wild,
> And all which patient toil had reared, and all,
> Commune with thee had opened out—but flowers
> Strewed on my corse, and borne upon my bier
> In the same coffin, for the self-same grave! (61–75)

Wordsworth's strength of character was emphasized, his 'calm and sure' capacity for facing life squarely 'from the dread watch-tower of man's absolute self'. Though Coleridge intended the poem to be a 'triumphal wreath' in Wordsworth's honour, he could not resist making these embarrassing self-comparisons. Masochistically almost, he abased himself before the other man: 'O Friend, my comforter and guide! / Strong in thyself, and powerful to give strength!' The exhibitionist in Coleridge relished this opportunity for self-exposure, but the self-acknow-

---

[1] "To William Wordsworth", PW 403.

ledged inferiority revealed also a basic temperamental deficiency. Like all exhibitionists, he hated loneliness.

Whereas Wordsworth wrote of the '*bliss* of solitude' with complete self-assurance, as though lonely communion with nature
was an experience to be cherished, something sought deliberately
and rejoiced in when discovered, in Coleridge's case solitude
generally awoke painful 'musings' or even terror. The buoyancy of *I wandered lonely as a cloud* or the self-congratulatory tone
with which Wordsworth spoke of having achieved 'inviolate retirement' suggests that for him sequestration amounted almost
to self-indulgence. Coleridge, too, subscribed for a time to the
romantic convention of seeking inspiration in desolate solitudes,
but dropped this pose once experience taught him loneliness was
unendurable. The dominant theme of his later poetry was not the
bliss but the '*ache* of solitariness'.[1]

It was unlikely that one who even as a schoolboy had written
with apprehensive (almost precognitive) dread of enforced isolation would long embrace the cult of Chattertonian 'outsiderism'.[2]
Years before he wrote *The Ancient Mariner* Coleridge was consistently employing an archetypal image to represent a life deprived
of personal relationships as a fearful 'voyage' or journey, indicating that from the first he valued sympathy and affection above
the 'bliss' of solitude. As a fifteen-year-old he had already experienced enough of emotional deprivation to dread the loneliness of
celibacy:

> . . . without child or tender wife,
> To drive away each care, each sigh,
> Lonely he treads the paths of life
> A stranger to Affection's tye.[3]

---

[1] "The Blossoming of the Solitary Date-Tree", l. 43, PW 396. See H. J. F.
Jones, *The Egotistical Sublime* (1954), 26, 32. Jones argues that whereas Coleridge's philosophy represented a life-long quest and love of the great and
the whole, based on a love of identity, a longing 'to ease the burden of *differentiated* existence', to lose the self in a higher synthesis; Wordsworth, on the
contrary, *exults* in 'inviolate retirement', *seeks* solitude as a means of poetic
grace, and *embraces* differentiated existence as a source of enlightenment and
strength. The difference appears in their poetry: apart from the quest of the
One Life, Coleridge's great poems (Jones points out) 'reflect his dread of
isolation as a state of helplessness and vulnerability', whereas Wordsworth's
best poetry deals with lonely places and solitary people, and in markedly
different manner.

[2] For further discussion of the 'Chatterton cult', see below, pp. 81–2.

[3] "Nil Pejus Est Caelibe Vitâ", PW 4.

Dura Navis, another adolescent poem, employed the voyage image again, this time reflecting his own bitterness perhaps at having been 'exiled' from home while still a child:

> To tempt the dangerous deep, too venturous youth,
> Why does thy breast with fondest wishes glow?
> No tender parent there thy cares shall sooth,
> No much-lov'd Friend shall share thy every woe.
> Why does thy mind with hopes delusive burn?
> Vain are thy Schemes by heated Fancy plann'd:
> Thy promis'd joy thou'lt see to Sorrow turn
> Exil'd from Bliss, and from thy native land.[1]

Conversely, 'love' could disperse the terrors of life's voyage for him;[2] with a 'friend' or, better still, some 'lovely maid' to share it, he could face the voyage confidently:

> So shall my little vessel glide
> With a fair breeze adown the tide.[3]

This life-as-voyage image became engraved from adolescence upon Coleridge's associative memory so that when in 1804 he embarked upon an actual voyage to Malta, deliberately isolating himself from personal contacts, this sea-trip (as his notebooks show) became the living allegory of his earlier forebodings.

Emotionally, he was too insecure to be self-sufficient, and several factors contributed towards this instability. During childhood, for instance, his relationships with his family were emotionally impoverished and it is significant that he showed little wish to return to his home once he had left it. His intellectual endowment, furthermore, was quite exceptional, that of an infant prodigy in fact, and inevitably he experienced some childhood isolation as a result of it. Doubtless, this early deprivation of emotion induced him to marry prematurely, while his very immaturity posed a threat to his marriage. Apart from these considerations there was an inherent instability in his make-up which caused him (rather like Boswell) to seek friendships with 'sheet-anchor'

---

[1] ll. 1–8, PW 2.
[2]
> Unkindly cold and tempest shrill
> In Life's morn oft the traveller chill,
> But soon his path the sun of Love shall warm;
> And each glad scene look brighter for the storm!
> ("Anthem" (1789), ll. 29–32, PW 6)

[3] "Happiness", ll. 100–1, PW 33.

men who possessed the qualities which he himself lacked.[1] Though these friendships were not homosexual (the men were more like father-figures to him) his 'sheet-anchors' were never-less love-objects in a rather special sense.

Coleridge was nine years old when he was packed off to boarding school, to what Wordsworth in the *Prelude* called his 'dreary exile'. Even at the time he felt he had been made an outcast. This removal severed him from his family (he was the youngest of a family of ten) so that he grew up virtually a stranger to them. It was a traumatic experience and for years afterwards he continued to envy his more fortunate brothers who were brought up under the security of the parental roof:

> To me the Eternal Wisdom hath dispens'd
> A different fortune and more different mind—
> Me from the spot where first I sprang to light
> Too soon transplanted, ere my soul had fix'd
> Its first domestic loves; and hence through life
> Chasing chance-started friendships . . .
> My soul is sad, that I have roam'd through life
> Still most a stranger, most with naked heart
> At mine own home and birth-place.[2]

He felt acutely isolated while at school, as *Frost at Midnight* indicates. His father by then was dead and after leaving home Coleridge appears to have had little further contact with his mother except during holiday periods, of which no written record remains. His letters from school and university contain few references to her, and those are mainly curt and off-handed. Her behaviour towards him seems to have been characterized chiefly by inconsistency, alternating between over-indulgence and indifference. There were two periods at least, in his infancy and in the brief interval between his father's death and his going to school, when he was his 'mother's darling' and she delighted in

---

[1] Professor J. T. Boulton points out to me that Boswell, in his relationships with Johnson, Paoli, Sir David Dalrymple, and Sir Alexander Dick, appeared to look for similar qualities to those Coleridge sought in his 'sheet-anchor' men. The special character of Coleridge's male friendships is discussed towards the end of this chapter.

[2] "To the Rev. George Coleridge", ll. 15–20, 40–2, PW 174.

his cleverness,[1] but after he left home he seemed deliberately to shut her out of his life and when she died, in 1810, he neither attended her funeral nor bothered to write home.[2] Clearly, it was an unsatisfactory relationship; hence the diagnostic inference has been made that he tended to seek in his later love-relationships the protective mother-love of which he had been deprived as a child.[3]

There is evidence that he was more closely attached to his father; indeed, the upbringing of his own son, Hartley (described in *The Nightingale*), was perhaps unconsciously modelled on his father's pattern:

> ... my father was fond of me, & used to take me on his knee, and hold long conversations with me. I remember, that at eight years old I walked with him one winter evening from a farmer's house, a mile from Ottery—& he told me the names of the stars—and how Jupiter was a thousand times larger than our world—and that the other twinkling stars were Suns that had worlds rolling round them —& when I came home, he shewed me how they rolled round—/. I heard him with a profound delight & admiration.[4]

Yet such intimate filial revelations are rare in Coleridge's writing, his rather distant attitude to both parents being typified perhaps by the following passage:

> My Father was not a first-rate Genius—he was however a first-rate Christian. I need not detain you with his Character—in learning, good-heartedness, absentness of mind, & excessive ignorance of the world, he was a perfect *Parson Adams*. . . My Mother was an admirable Economist, & managed exclusively.[5]

Soon after his father died he was sent to Christ's Hospital, which for the next few years became his home. We know from Lamb's and Leigh Hunt's reminiscences something of the rigours of that

[1] CL, I, 347, 388. Her excessive favouritism at this time aroused jealousy in Francis, the next youngest, who so persecuted Samuel in consequence that he threatened his tormentor with a knife, then ran away to the river where he slept all night (CL, I, 353).

[2] Life, 227.

[3] See Suther, 64. Deprivation of maternal affection during childhood is regarded by many psychologists as the major cause of emotional maladjustment in later life; see J. Bowlby, *Child Care and the Growth of Love* (Pelican Original, 1953).

[4] CL, I, 354; cf. "The Nightingale", ll. 91–109, PW 266.

[5] CL, I, 310.

life and its effects upon the mind of a sensitive child.[1] Boyer, the headmaster, was scarcely an adequate emotional substitute for any child's parent.

Coleridge had one sister, Anne Coleridge, who died in March 1791, and evidently he turned to her for the affection he craved, using her almost as a mother-substitute:

> I too a Sister *had*, an only Sister—
> She lov'd me dearly, and I doted on her!
> To her I pour'd forth all my puny sorrows
> (As a sick Patient in a Nurse's Arms).[2]

(This sick-room image, incidentally, appeared as frequently in Coleridge's early work as did the life-as-voyage metaphor.) Anne's death occasioned a sonnet, prompted as much by his own desolate sense of isolation perhaps as by genuine grief:

> The tear which mourn'd a brother's fate scarce dry—
> Pain after pain, and woe succeeding woe—
> Is my heart destin'd for another blow?
> O my sweet sister! and must thou too die?
> Ah! how has Disappointment pour'd the tear
> O'er infant Hope destroy'd by early frost!
> How are ye gone, whom most my soul held dear!
> Scarce had I lov'd you ere I mourn'd you lost;
> Say, is this hollow eye, this heartless pain,
> Fated to rove thro' Life's wide cheerless plain—
> Nor father, brother, sister meet its ken—
> My woes, my joys unshared! Ah! long ere then
> On me thy icy dart, stern Death, be prov'd;—
> Better to die, than live and not be lov'd![3]

It is an inferior poem,[4] interesting mainly because its final line contains his earliest premonition perhaps of his acute need for female affection and of what the loss of it meant.

---

[1] See R. B. Johnson, *Christ's Hospital: Recollections of Lamb, Coleridge and Leigh Hunt* (London, 1896).

[2] "To a Friend", ll. 12–15, PW 78.

[3] "On Receiving an Account that his only Sister's Death was Inevitable", PW 20. The 'brother' (l. 1) was Luke Herman Coleridge, who died in 1790.

[4] The 'tear' *poured* over 'infant Hope destroy'd by early frost' is a sadly mixed metaphor, while the 'hollow eye' and 'heartless pain fated to rove Life's plain' is open to similar objections to those Coleridge himself made later against Wordsworth's apostrophe to the child—'thou eye among the blind' (cf. BL, II, 111).

Of the remainder of his family only James, Edward, and George lived to maturity, and it was only with George, the eldest, that he maintained anything like a close relationship. George's influence, until Coleridge met Southey at Cambridge, was formidable: if Anne was a substitute-mother George was equally a father-figure—'I have lov'd thee ever, / Lov'd as a brother, as a son rever'd thee!'[1] After their father's death George assumed paternal responsibility for Samuel and in his testy, curmudgeonly fashion extricated his younger brother from the various difficulties he got into, especially at Cambridge—settling the unpaid tutor's bills, securing his release from the army following the extraordinary enlistment débâcle, and even persuading Mary Evans to use her influence to curb his recklessness.[2] Whether remonstrating about Samuel's atheistical tendencies or his dereliction of personal obligations, George conducted the relationship *de haut en bas*, as Coleridge's lugubrious self-prostrations indicate: 'O that without guilt I might ask of my Maker Annihilation! My Brother—my Brother—pray for me, comfort me, my Brother!'[3] They were epistles rather to a father-confessor than to a brother he loved.

James Coleridge helped in securing the discharge from the army but, because Samuel's misadventures had affronted the family pride, added his voice to the general censure. Coleridge found it particularly galling to be under obligation to James, of whom he had written only a month or two earlier:

> . . . when I first went into the country, I had scarcely seen either James or Edward—they had neither been the companions or the guardians of my Childhood.—To love them therefore was a sensation yet to be learnt. . . Add to this—that both the one and the other

[1] "To the Rev. George Coleridge", ll. 43–51, PW 175.

[2] For details of George Coleridge's generosity in settling Samuel Taylor Coleridge's college debts, see CL 1, 59n, 64n, 81n. On 2 December 1793, Coleridge, distracted by pecuniary difficulties, enlisted as a trooper in the 15th Light Dragoons, under the name of Silas Titus Comberbacke. With the assistance of his brothers, George and James Coleridge, he secured his discharge on 7 April 1794, and by 10 April he was reinstated at Jesus College, Cambridge, the college debts of £132 having been paid by his brothers. See Life, 23–4; and CL, 1, 75n.

Coleridge's love-affair with Mary Evans is discussed more fully in Chapter 2. For George Coleridge's attempt to manipulate his brother through Mary Evans, see CL, 1, 113n.

[3] CL, 1, 64.

exacted a deference, which conscious of few obligations to *them*, aware of no *real* inferiority, and laughing at the artificial claims of primogeniture, I felt myself little inclined to pay.[1]

He had little feeling for his brothers save envy at their close-rootedness. He never thought of theirs as his true home, nor ever knew real affection with them. Laconically he summed them up: 'My Brother George . . . is worth the whole family in a Lump!'[2] There could scarcely be a clearer indication of the extent to which Coleridge was emotionally deprived in his relations with his family. In the years that followed, though often lonely and desperately in need of help and sympathy, he scarcely ever looked towards the family home for comfort.

The childhood experiences of alienation were not wholly the result of emotional deprivation. His isolation was partly the concomitant of his abnormally high intelligence. Living in a remote Devonshire village he suffered the inevitable isolation of the ultra-intelligent confronted with a restricted environment. His second autobiographical letter to Poole affords us insight into what it is like to be a boy genius—the acute sense of separateness, the indeterminate rôle, neither fish nor fowl, where normal relationships can be formed with neither the peer-group nor the older generation:

> —So I became a *dreamer*—and acquired an indisposition to all bodily activity—and I was fretful, and inordinately passionate, and as I could not play at any thing, and was slothful, I was despised & hated by the boys; and because I could read & spell, & had, I may truly say, a memory & understanding forced into almost an unnatural ripeness, I was flattered & wondered at by all the old women—& so I became very vain, and despised most of the boys, that were at all near my own age—and before I was eight years old, I was a *character*—sensibility, imagination, vanity, sloth, & feelings of deep & bitter contempt for almost all who traversed the orbit of my understanding, were even then prominent & manifest.[3]

A further consequence of his exceptional talents was the pressure imposed by the high expectations people held of him. This pres-

---

[1] CL, I, 53–4.   [2] ibid, I, 311.

[3] ibid, I, 347–8; and cf. 388. Samuel Johnson experienced a similar childhood isolation, possibly for similar reasons.

sure tended to produce a severe anxiety depression whenever consciousness of 'wasted talents' overcame him.

Whatever its ultimate cause, whether environmental or congenital, there was undoubtedly a latent *instability* in Coleridge's emotional make-up. He was inclined (more than most of us) to *parade* his feelings, or to act a part according to the mood of the moment. Particularly was this true of his relationships with women:

> Every thing, that has been known or deemed fit to win woman's Love, I have an impulse to make myself—even tho' I should otherwise look down upon it—I cannot endure not to be strong in arms, a daring Soldier— . . . again, I must be the high Intellect, that despises it—& both at once. I must be a graceful & bold Horseman / I must sing & play on the Harp / I must be beautiful instead of what I am, and yet she must love me for what I now am, even for myself & my exceeding Love.[1]

His excess of feeling was sometimes remarked upon. Tom Poole observed: 'He indulges in such tumultuous feelings upon every possible occasion where his wife and children are concerned.'[2] The critic Jeffrey expressed it more tersely—Coleridge suffers from 'hypochondriasis' of the feelings.[3] Crabb Robinson, Lamb, and Dorothy Wordsworth all commented on this emotional imbalance in Coleridge.[4] Was that interminable loquacity of his yet another product of it?

> . . . my eloquence was most commonly excited by the desire of running away and hiding myself from my personal and inward feelings, and not for the expression of them, while doubtless this very effort gave a passion and glow to my thoughts.[5]

It is small wonder then that he found personal relationships difficult.

Looking back over his life in December 1818, he tried to explain to Allsop the nature of this personal problem: 'In Sympathy alone I found at once Nourishment and Stimulus; and for Sympathy alone did my heart crave.'[6] Much as he needed sympathy

---

[1] KC, II, 3148, f. 42.
[2] See R. B. Litchfield, *Tom Wedgwood the First Photographer* (1903), pp. 66–7.
[3] L, II, 534.   [4] See p. 12 below.
[5] T. Allsop, *Letters, Conversations and Recollections of S. T. Coleridge* (1834), II, 134–5.
[6] CL, IV, 888.

though, too often he proved incapable of retaining it, because his demands were so excessively self-centred. He never appeared in worse light than when, lachrymose and self-abasing, he indulged in undignified self-pity. This unfortunate trait, so common in his letters, marred much of his poetry too:

> Kind-hearted stranger! patiently you hear
> A tedious tale: I thank you for that tear.
> May never other tears o'ercloud your eye,
> Than those which gentle Pity can supply![1]

He derived a morbid satisfaction from regaling acquaintances with long and often nauseating accounts of his illnesses. He rather enjoyed the rôle of principal performer in the sick-room scene, because this enabled him to make greater demands upon the sympathy of his friends:

> Yet if any thing can throw a melancholy smile over the pale, wan Face of Illness, it must be the sight and attentions of those, we love. There are one or two Beings, in this planet of our's, whom God has formed in so kindly a mould, that I could almost consent to be ill to be nursed by them.[2]

At such times, no doubt, his friends were solicitous and kindly, deferring to his wishes rather than exhorting him with practical advice, which he hated. In these circumstances he felt secure in their affections:

> Quiet, therefore, a comfortable Bed and Bed room; and that [still] bett[er] Comfort of kind Faces—English Tongues & English Hearts—now and then—this is the Sum Total of my *Wants*. The last article indeed is not so much a *Want*, as it is a Thing, which I *need*.[3]

Such imagined security was, he well knew, a precarious thing, and the general terms in which that passage is couched ('Quiet . . . *a* bed . . . kind *faces* . . . *English hearts'*) are indicative of its remoteness from the possibility of realization.

Coleridge's letters, like his poetry of the early 1790's, revealed often a rhetorical extravagance and false elaboration of sentiment quite foreign to the sincerity of ordinary friendship. The very abjectness of his posturing must have served merely to irritate his sympathizers:

---

[1] "The Old Man of the Alps", ll. 89–92, PW 250.
[2] CL, I, 54–5.   [3] ibid, II, 1021.

Thursday, Nov. 6th 1794.

My dear Brother

Your letter of this morning gave me inexpressible Consolation—I thought, that I perceived in your last the cold and freezing features of alienated affection—Surely—said I—I have trifled with the Spirit of Love, and it has passed away from me!

There is a Vice of such powerful Venom, that one Grain of it will poison the overflowing Goblet of a thousand Virtues. This Vice Constitution seems to have implanted in me, and Habit has made it almost omnipotent. It is INDOLENCE! Hence, whatever Web of Friendship my Presence may have woven, my Absence has seldom failed to unravel. Anxieties that stimulate others, infuse an additional narcotic into my mind. The appeal of Duty to my Judgment, and the pleadings of affection at my Heart—have been heard indeed—and heard with deep regard—Ah! that they had been as constantly obeyed.

By sheer inflation of sentiment, by loquacious bombast or bathos, he sought to command the attention that unaffected spontaneity might have achieved more readily, as in the following letter to George Coleridge:

The anguish of those who love me—of him [George Coleridge], beneath the shade of whose protection I grew up—does it not plant my pillow with thorns, and make my dreams full of terrors? . . .

Alas! my poor Mother! What an intolerable weight of guilt is suspended over my head by a hair on one hand—and if I endure to live—the look ever downward—insult—pity—and hell.—

God or chaos preserve me! What but infinite Wisdom or infinite Confusion can do it![1]

Had he not possessed other and more attractive qualities besides, his self-centredness would probably have vitiated his relationships with even the most patient and charitable of his acquaintances.

His chameleon-like character was unbalanced and insecure, gravitating always towards stronger personalities to whom he clung with embarrassing tenacity. He has freely admitted that he had a 'dog-like' instinct to look up to people he fancied superior to himself. His readiness to stoop to cajolery and flattery was well known among his acquaintances. He told Sir Humphry Davy that 'of all men known to me I could not justly equal any one to you'.[2] When Thelwall criticized some of his poems he pro-

[1] ibid, I, 63.   [2] ibid, III, 28.

mised to 'alter accordingly', since Thelwall's nerves were 'exquisite *electrometers* of Taste'.[1] None knew better than Crabb Robinson this weakness in Coleridge's character:

> Without meaning to impute insincerity to C. I may observe that
> he had a need of sympathy & therefore preferably said what he
> knew would please, not what would displease.[2]

'What he *imagined* would please' might be more accurate, but
Crabb Robinson rightly divined Coleridge's neurotic need of
sympathy. Poets *need* sympathy, said Coleridge; without it they
are powerless as sick men—'the sense of power sinks back on itself, like a sigh heaved up from the tightened chest of a sick man'.[3]

If, as seems probable, Coleridge sought a substitute for mother-
love in sexual relationships, it is no less certain that many of his
male attachments were governed by the search for a father-
figure. A possible strain of homosexuality has been suggested,
which cannot entirely be discounted, despite his assertion that
gifted individuals are frequently androgynous.[4] It was his belief
that it is

> . . . possible that a man may, under certain states of the moral
> feeling, entertain something deserving the name of love towards a
> male object—an affection beyond friendship, and wholly aloof from
> appetite.[5]

Though the possibility of a male love-relationship is acknowledged here, yet the sexual element is quite specifically excluded,
and not, I think, merely out of reticence. The expression 'under
certain states of the moral feeling' points to a special quality in
his male friendships. Even allowing for the fulsome epistolary
style of the period, Coleridge's letters harped constantly on his
friends' moral qualities, while those with whom he quarrelled—
Godwin, Mackintosh, Hazlitt, Lloyd, Montagu (even Southey
and Wordsworth finally)—he invariably attacked in terms of the
severest moral censure.

His relative inability to cope with practical affairs was a further reason for attaching himself to strong male personalities.
Though occasionally, as with the production of *The Friend*, he
revealed an unaccustomed business acumen, generally he ap-

---

[1] CL, I, 307.   [2] HCR, 63, 38.
[3] S. T. Coleridge, *Table Talk*, 10 August 1833.
[4] ibid, 1 September 1832.   [5] ibid, 14 May 1833.

peared almost a naïf in the practicalities of ordinary life. The Susquehanna project, the scheme to subsist by horticulture, the tendency to seek escape from entanglements in flight, the restless wandering and abandonment of family, all suggest an incapacity to grapple with the details of everyday living.[1] In practical affairs he was incapable of making up his mind—'I have so seldom acted right, that in every step I take of my own accord I tremble lest I should be wrong.'[2] Faced with the decision whether to start a school or write for the *Morning Post* he appealed for advice to Cottle, Beddoes, Estlin, Danvers, and Wade in turn and then considered riding two days on horseback to Poole for further suggestions, all in an effort to make up his own mind. He would not have arrived at church for his own wedding had not Southey tracked down his hiding-place and dragged him off to Bristol.[3] Of all decisions he found moral ones the most difficult. This irked his friends:

> ... he neither will nor can execute anything of important benefit to himself, his family, or mankind; [all is] frustrated by a derangement in his intellectual and moral constitution. In fact, he has no voluntary power of mind whatsoever, nor is he capable of acting under any *constraint* of duty or obligation.[4]

Lacking any psychological insight into the real cause of his ineptitude, they found his procrastinatory vacillations inexplicable. Coleridge hinted as much, to Southey—'O ye invincible

[1] In 1793 Coleridge and Robert Southey evolved a scheme, known as Pantisocracy, whereby it was proposed that a new society should be established in America beside the Susquehanna river. It should consist initially of twelve men and twelve women, each man contributing £125 to the common pool, while any member of the society might withdraw at will. Religious opinion was to be free, the marriage contract was to be dissoluble by mutual agreement, though the parties should be married initially. Leisure was to be spent in the cultivation of the mind, Coleridge arguing that the produce of the men's labour for three hours a day would suffice to maintain the colony. The scheme never materialized. For further information, see Life, 26 ff.

Coleridge's scheme to subsist by horticulture at Nether Stowey is discussed more fully towards the end of this chapter.

[2] CL, I, 76.   [3] ibid, I, 148–9.

[4] Written by Wordsworth to Poole; see J. D. Campbell, *Samuel Taylor Coleridge* (1894), 172. Carlyle said, 'His cardinal sin is that he wants *will*' (IH, 344). Crabb Robinson wrote: 'With powers of original thought & real genius both philosophical & poetical such as few men in any age have possessed Coleridge wants certain low & minor qualities wh. render his great powers almost inefficient & useless' (HCR, 131).

Soldiers of Virtue, who arrange yourselves under the General-ship of Fixed Principles—that you would throw up your Fortifi-cations around my Heart!'[1]

His condition, unfortunately, was not susceptible of simple diagnosis—as he found, after repeated attempts to analyse his sense of possessing what he called 'power without strength'. There was, he decided, an inherent weakness in his own nature which required bracing by the moral support of a stronger per-sonality than his own. He several times illustrated this condition by the analogy of tropical vegetation whose growth outstrips its strength:

> There *is* a something, an essential something wanting in me. I feel it, I *know* it—tho' what it is, I can but guess. I have read some-where that in the tropical climates there are Annuals [as lofty] and of as ample girth as forest trees. So by a very dim likeness, I seem to myself to distinguish power from strength & to have only the power. But of this I will speak again: for if it be no reality, if it be no more than a disease of my mind, it is yet deeply rooted & of long standing, & requires help from one who loves me in the Light of knowledge.[2]

There was however no one capable of helping him in the light of the psychiatric knowledge his condition demanded and, rest-lessly, he went on exploring it through sheer power of introspec-tion alone, becoming in the process increasingly sceptical of his self-sufficiency for the rôle of romantic genius:

> My inner Mind does not justify the thought that I possess a Genius—my *Strength* is so small in proportion to my Power—I be-lieve, that I first from internal feeling made, or gave light and im-pulse to this important distinction, between Strength & Power—the Oak, and the tropic Annual, or Biennial, which grows nearly as high and spreads as large, as the Oak,—but the *wood*, the heart of *Oak*, is wanting—*the vital* works vehemently, but the *Immortal* is not with it.[3]

It was in fact precisely out of such searching analysis of his own deficiencies that Coleridge's 'whole man' theory was later to

[1] CL, I, 138.

[2] ibid, II, 1102; see also IS, 40–1, and E. Bostetter, *The Romantic Ventrilo-quists* (Seattle, 1963), 82 ff., where this 'power without strength' theme is further discussed.

[3] cf. AP, 197, KC, II, 2914.

evolve—the theory (to adopt the terminology of an obsolete psychology) by which mental health is regarded as the balanced equilibrium of all the mental faculties. The imbalance implied in the metaphor of tropical growth which so outstrips its resources as to bring about its self-destruction is quite the obverse of the faculty theory of what constituted mental normality. Later, he tended to identify this want of 'strength' with some atrophy or deficiency of the *Will*. It was from these introspective experiences, however, rather than from anything Kant taught him, that he arrived at his belief in the Will as the self-starter of action.[1]

A letter Coleridge wrote to Southey on 1 August 1808 contains a further passage with an important bearing on this 'power without strength' theme. This was written after the major depression had occurred which is described in *Dejection: an Ode*, and it indicates a profound discovery he had made about himself under stress of that crisis. Here, if anywhere, he came closest to the true explanation of his personal inadequacy, to the shattering realization that, though he demanded so much in the way of love and sympathy from others, he never reciprocated this affection to the degree or in the manner necessary to sustain a mutual interchange. The level tone of this auto-diagnosis would suggest either that he now accepted the fact with stoic resignation or, more probably, that he still had not realized its full implications. 'I needed', he told Southey—

> . . . to have my power proved to me by transient evidences, arising from an inward feeling of weakness, both the one & other working in me unconsciously—above all, a faulty delight in the being be-

[1] Wordsworth, Carlyle, and Crabb Robinson over-simplified the matter when they equated Coleridge's 'want of will' with laziness and procrastination. Coleridge's energy and capacity for work was prodigious, as was Samuel Johnson's, yet both men constantly reproached themselves with idleness. Will was, for Coleridge, that principle which *operating through the whole nervous system* summons the forces of personality and directs them to an aim (IS, 47, 131), and whose efficacy may therefore be undermined by physiological or emotional factors (see *Table Talk*, 12 September 1831; IS, 60; also my discussion of Coleridge's notebook entry concerning the associative power of love; pp. 220–1 below). Eventually, Coleridge became neurotically afraid to *will* his personality into action, since this meant making a 'beginning of living feeling' (see p. 279 below). His condition required a psychiatrist rather than a taskmaster, as he himself realized: 'A Gymnastic Medicine is wanting, not a mere recommendation but a system of forcing the Will and *motive faculties* into action' (IS, 36).

loved, without having examined my heart, whether, if beloved, I
had any thing to give in return beyond general kindness & general
Sympathy—both indeed unusually warm, but which, being still
general, were not a return in kind, for that which I was unconsciously desiring to inspire / — . . . A sense of weakness—a haunting
sense, that I was an herbaceous Plant, as large as a large Tree, with
a Trunk of the same Girth, & Branches as large & shadowing—but
with *pith within* the Trunk, not heart of Wood / —that I had *power*
not *strength*—an involuntary Imposter—that I had no real Genius,
no real Depth.[1]

The men with whom his most enduring relationships were formed
—Southey, Poole, Wordsworth, and Gillman—were all, significantly, men who possessed 'strength' rather than 'power' (in *his*
sense of those terms). In contrast to his own rootless existence
their lives were securely planted within a circle of domestic affection. They were men who coped easily with the daily practicalities of living and Coleridge was drawn towards them, as to the
protection of sturdy oaks. He used this tree image to describe his
period of residence beside Poole at Stowey:

> . . . beside one Friend,
> Beneath the impervious covert of one oak,
> I've raised a lowly shed.[2]

Wordsworth he likened to a towering beech tree—'fagus exaltata
sylvatica'.[3] His other favourite emblem of 'strength', the 'sheet-
anchor', may be seen, on the other hand, as a peculiarly appropriate foil to his habitual imaging of his own life as a purposeless
'voyage'.

What these 'sheet-anchor' figures had in common was that, in
contrast to himself, they were virtually 'whole men', emotionally
well-balanced and of formidable integrity. They provided the
moral ballast he himself lacked—'I did not only venerate you
[Southey] for your own Virtues, I prized you as the Sheet-Anchor

[1] CL, II, 959.   [2] "To the Rev. George Coleridge", ll. 32–4, PW 174.
[3] 'The soil is a deep, rich, dark Mould on a deep Stratum of tenacious Clay,
and that on a foundation of Rocks, which often break through both Strata,
lifting their back above the Surface. The Trees, which chiefly grow here, are
the gigantic Black Oak, Magnolia, Fraxinus excelsior, Platane, & a few
stately Tulip Trees—Bart. p. 36 [William Bartram, *Travels through North and
South Carolina*, (Philadelphia, 1791)]. I applied this by a fantastic analogue &
similitude to Wordsworth's Mind. March 26, 1801. Fagus exaltata sylvatica'
(KC, I, 926).

of mine.'[1] They possessed in addition notable father-figure qualities. Each became in his way the rather dominating head of a
close-knit family: the Rev. George Coleridge at Ottery, Southey
at Greta Hall, Wordsworth at Dove Cottage, and Poole, though
unmarried, at Stowey. A further interesting point is that they
succeeded one another in Coleridge's life almost without intercession, Southey replacing George, Poole replacing Southey,
Wordsworth supplanting Poole, and—following the nightmare
nomadic period when he was without any major 'sheet-anchor'
—the succession of Morgan and Gillman.[2] Apart from Mary
Evans, moreover, it is noticeable that all the major *female* figures
in Coleridge's life—Sara Fricker, Sara Hutchinson, Dorothy
Wordsworth, Catherine Clarkson, and Mrs Gillman—were in
some way connected with one or other of the male 'sheet-anchors'.
There is not space in a study of this sort to deal with the 'fatherly'
qualities of John Prior Estlin or Daniel Stuart, nor with the sort
of anchorage Gillman and the still undervalued Morgan provided, except to emphasize that in a lesser degree they stood in
similar relationship to Coleridge.[3] Our concern will be primarily

[1] CL, I, 173.

[2] The Rev. George Coleridge's influence over Coleridge began to wane
from about October 1794, the constant remonstrances of this father-figure
proving unendurable (CL, I, 118). Southey's influence predominated from
about July 1794 until the time of Coleridge's marriage in October 1795, when
they quarrelled (CL, I, 163–73; and cf. pp. 22–3 below). Coleridge met Poole
in December 1793, but his first letter to this new friend 'in whom *first* and in
whom alone, I had felt an *anchor*!' (CL, I, 491) was written just three days after
his marriage, when his resentment towards Southey was at fever-pitch (CL, I,
160–1). Coleridge's friendship with Wordsworth ripened during 1797 (they
had met in the autumn of 1795), continued during their joint tour of Germany
in 1798–9, and on 29 June 1800 Coleridge moved his family north to live at
Keswick. This brought him closer to Wordsworth (and Sara Hutchinson) but
nearly cost him Poole's friendship. After quarrelling with Wordsworth in 1808
and again in 1810, Coleridge lived for the next fifteen months with John
Morgan (Life, 236–7). He stayed with the Morgans again at intervals during
1815–16 but on 15 April 1816 moved to James Gillman's house at Highgate,
his home until his death in 1834 (Life, 268, 275). This last 'sheet-anchor'
possessed similar qualities to those he had looked for in each of the earlier
figures (Life, 289). Despite the quarrels, Coleridge continued to have relationships of differing intensity with all his former 'anchor' men, but after
their periods of major influence their ascendancy over him waned.

[3] John Prior Estlin (1747–1817), a Unitarian minister, the 'fatherly and
brotherly friend' who attempted to secure Coleridge a salaried Unitarian
ministry at Shrewsbury in January 1798 (Life, 86–8). Estlin joined Poole in

with Southey, Poole, and Wordsworth, the most important of the 'sheet-anchors' because their influence so radically affected his whole development. Coleridge's relationships with Southey and Poole are examined in the remainder of this chapter, while Wordsworth's influence is discussed in Chapters 4, 8, and 9.

If Coleridge was indeed wanting in moral fibre, Robert Southey, it appeared, was just the pillar of support he needed— 'truly a man of *perpendicular Virtue*'.[1] Southey possessed in abundance all those qualities in which Coleridge regarded himself as deficient—'Consider the high advantages, which you possess in so eminent a degree—Health, Strength of Mind, and confirmed *Habits* of strict Morality'.[2] As in the tribute to Wordsworth Coleridge again indulged in embarrassing self-comparisons: he was not ashamed, but '*delighted* to feel you superior to me in Genius as in Virtue'.[3] This excess of admiration during the first flush of their acquaintanceship eventually evaporated and in the long run Wordsworth achieved a higher place in Coleridge's moral esteem, though Southey might be supposed the more conventionally respectable. One reason for this reversal was that Southey undoubtedly took advantage of Coleridge's confessed inferiority and exploited it.[4] There was moreover a priggishness in Southey (as indeed in the later Wordsworth) that proved increasingly irritating to Coleridge as time went on. He had turned from father-figure George to Southey expecting comfort after the painful termination of the Mary Evans affair, feeling that his self-denial merited sympathy:

---

a scheme to contribute to Coleridge's financial assistance during 1796–7 (see CL, I, 210, 326).

Daniel Stuart (1766–1846), owner-editor of the *Morning Post* (1795–1803) and of the *Courier* (1796–1822). Coleridge was one of the principal contributors to both papers, and received both financial help and occasional lodgings from Stuart, who was the 'sheet-anchor' man with the best-developed business acumen—'a man of the most consummate knowledge of the world, managed by a thorough strong and sound judgement, and rendered innocuous by a good heart—indeed the wisest, most disinterested and constant Friend I was ever blest with' (Life, 219).

[1] CL, I, 152.   [2] ibid, I, 85.   [3] ibid, I, 104.

[4] See E. L. Griggs, "Robert Southey's Estimate of Samuel Taylor Coleridge", *Huntingdon Lib. Quar.*, Nov. 1945, pp. 61–94; also CL, I, 149n.

I loved her, Southey! almost to madness. Her Image was never absent from me for three Years—for *more* than three Years.—My Resolution [to marry Miss Fricker] has not faltered—but I want a Comforter.[1]

Unfortunately, Southey's unbending rectitude proved as starchy as George's and friendship suffered in consequence. In this tense atmosphere all enthusiasm for the Pantisocratic scheme, for the sake of which alone Coleridge married Sara Fricker, quietly disappeared. In the emotional disturbance produced by these quarrels and by the loss of Mary, Coleridge found that his 'versemaking faculties' suffered—an early experience of the close association between feeling and imagination. He wrote the sonnet *On a Discovery made too late* but it disappointed him. 'When a Man is unhappy, he writes damned bad Poetry, I find.'[2]

What this incident shows is that moral bolstering had to be attended with understanding and sympathy to meet Coleridge's demands, affection being really more important to him than moral example. This explains why Poole was eventually to prove the favourite of his 'sheet-anchors'. In later life Coleridge's own moral equilibrium became more stabilized, but in the frenetic 1790's his prickly insecurity in this sphere gave rise to frequent misunderstandings.

Since this quarrel with Southey was later made up there would seem little point in re-exhuming the acrimonious details of that dreary recital of accusations and counter-accusations. Neither reputation was enhanced by the quarrel. However, it threw a significant light upon Coleridge's motivation such as a study of the peculiarities of his personal relationships may not ignore. The ostensible cause of his disappointment (the overthrow of the Pantisocratic scheme) may be disregarded, since at bottom Coleridge was probably glad to have done with it anyway. The true cause of his distress went deeper, and sprang from the consciousness of his personal inadequacy as compared with Southey's self-sufficiency. There was resentment, too, and some jealousy arising from the discovery that Southey, having perceived the impracticability of the Susquehanna project, had worked out other plans for his own future—'selfish' plans, since they excluded Coleridge. Coleridge seems to have felt that, having made his

---

[1] CL, I, 113. The Mary Evans affair is discussed more fully in Chapter 2.
[2] ibid, I, 115; PW 72.

gesture to 'principle' by marrying Sara Fricker at Southey's insistence, he could virtually leave his problems in Southey's hands
and be entitled to a perpetual lien on the other's support. Did
Southey even now appreciate what sacrifices he had made?

> And was not this your own Plan? The Plan, for the realizing of
> which you invited me to Bristol—the plan, for which I abandoned
> my friends, and every prospect & every certainty, and the Woman
> whom I loved to an excess which you in your warmest dream of
> fancy could never shadow out?

Then, in this important letter of 13 November 1795, followed a
remarkable confession of personal weakness and, in the form of
an analogy, an indication of what Coleridge expected from a
'sheet-anchor'. It was a curious admission from a man just turned
twenty-three:

> How would an honest Man have reasoned in your Case, and how
> acted? Thus. 'Here is a Man who has abandoned all for what I
> believe to be Virtue—But he professed himself an imperfect Being
> when he offered himself an associate to me. He confessed that all
> his valuable Qualities were "sloth-jaundiced"—and in his Letters
> is a bitter self-accuser. This man did not deceive me—I accepted
> of him in the hopes of curing him . . .'

Coleridge's almost total abnegation of personal responsibility induces us to sympathize with Southey for the burden thus gratui-
tously placed upon him. At the same time, one feels for Coleridge
in the nakedness of his exposed vulnerability. He seemed quite
incapable of standing on his own feet, and was already morbidly
neurotic about his personal inadequacy.

The breach with Mary Evans was undoubtedly one of the great
disappointments of his life; it produced 'convulsive Struggles of
Feeling'. Southey should have known, better than anyone, how
much Coleridge had suffered by it: 'You remember what a Fetter
I burst, and that it snapt, as if it had been a Sinew of my Heart.'
Had Coleridge's courtship of Mary ripened into marriage she
might conceivably have provided the home-life he needed, but
Southey forestalled that possibility and convinced Coleridge that
he had a duty to marry Sara. Under Southey's pressure Coleridge
paid court to Miss Fricker—'from Principle, not Feeling'—but
he remained resentfully conscious that he had allowed his feelings
to be manipulated, and all for the sake of a foolhardy scheme that
Southey himself had now abandoned. He felt that his martyrdom

to 'duty' deserved at the very least some recognition or sympathy, but instead he met with recrimination and vilification. His reaction was in the circumstances as might be expected. He turned on his 'sheet-anchor' and discovered he had feet of clay. Whereas previously he had been accustomed to think of Southey 'with almost superstitious Veneration', he now saw him

> . . . as one who had *fallen back into the Ranks*; as a man admirable for his abilities only, strict indeed in the lesser Honesties, but like the majority of men unable to resist a strong Temptation.

Southey had become an ordinary selfish, money-loving man, totally devoid of the boasted '*flocci-nauci-nihili-pilificating* Sense!'

The theme of Coleridge's long indictment was Southey's fall from virtue, recapitulated not without a certain vicarious pleasure from the unaccustomed novelty of believing himself for once in the right, the deliverer rather than the recipient of censorious harangue:

> You were become an Acquaintance, yet one for whom I felt no common tenderness. I could not forget what you had been. Your Sun was set: your Sky was clouded: but those Clouds and that Sky were yet tinged with the recent Sun.

This long letter reveals, for all its tendentious moralizing, an inability to sustain the didactic rôle, and a final collapse into self-pity. Coleridge contrasted Southey's recession from Pantisocratic principles with his own firm consistency, and he highlighted Burnet's incredulous reaction to this act of apostasy—'George sat petrified—gaping at the pigmy Virtue of his supposed Giant'. He reminded Southey of the duplicity of his decision to take holy orders instead of pursuing Pantisocracy, especially in view of the unorthodoxy of Southey's doctrinal standpoint and his former levity on this grave subject. Sanctimoniously, he expressed his belief that 'however foul your Stream may run here' it would ultimately be purified again and redeemed, once Southey reconsidered his ways. The letter abounded in exquisitely turned moral sententiae—'how infinitely more to be valued is Integrity of Heart than effulgence of Intellect'.

But towards the end the threadbare pontifical detachment wears thin, Coleridge's hand begins to 'tremble' and, the language growing more violent, he lapses into more directly personal attack. His own centre of gravity was insufficiently stable for him to sustain the rôle of moral prosecutor. Perhaps as he faced his bride of six weeks across the table, in the knowledge that Southey would in a week or two become his brother-in-law and the circle thus be closed around him, the consciousness deepened of how different this actuality was from his earlier fond illusion of what marriage would be like:

> You have left a large Void in my Heart—I know no man big enough to fill it. Others I may love equally & esteem equally: and some perhaps I may admire as much. But never do I expect to meet another man, who will make me unite attachment for his person with reverence for his heart and admiration of his Genius! I did not only venerate you for your own Virtues, I prized you as the Sheet Anchor of mine!

Fortunately, this 'void' was shortly to be filled by Poole.

As the first of Coleridge's acquired 'sheet-anchors', Southey was in many respects a prototype for all of them. His forceful personality supplied the 'strength' necessary to complement Coleridge's own radical insufficiency, hence the ease with which Southey manipulated him. As early as 1791 the poem *Happiness* had specified friendship and marriage as Coleridge's two primary needs, and both of these Southey had in a sense supplied, though not in a fashion expected or desired. There was a curious paradox in this relationship however (as later in that with Wordsworth), for whereas Coleridge demanded the highest moral integrity in his 'sheet-anchors', as an ideal standard against which he could measure his own shortcomings, yet at the same time he demanded a tolerant and charitable forgiveness of his own infirmities—his habitual procrastination, his emotional imbalance, his sexual irregularities, and, already perhaps, his opium indulgence.[1]

This rupture with Southey was patched up in December 1796 after Southey's return from Lisbon, though never on quite the same terms of familiarity. Coleridge continued still to 'love and esteem' Southey, but the love was 'one fourth, the esteem all the remainder'.[2] Beneath his later testimonies to Southey's virtues there lurked always an unforgiving sense of having been be-

---

[1] See pp. 44–5 below (also Life, 25–6) concerning Coleridge's sexual adventures at Cambridge. He was taking daily quantities of opium early in March 1796 (see CL, I, 188). E. L. Griggs in his introduction to Vol. III of the Collected Letters examines the whole history of Coleridge's opium addiction.

[2] CL, III, 377.

trayed. Southey, for his part, concluded that henceforth 'no dependence could be placed upon Coleridge'.[1]

It is difficult to imagine a personality more generously endowed than Thomas Poole with all the primâ facie qualities requisite in a Coleridgean 'sheet-anchor'. A successful business man, practical and efficient, yet on the whole good-naturedly tolerant of human weakness; radiating from his farm and tannery at Nether Stowey a comforting sense of deep-rooted security; self-educated yet well-read, and sufficiently knowledgeable about politics and the labour problems of the day to be called in by the House of Commons as a consultative expert on the Poor Laws question; a man of attractive personality and rock-like independence of spirit—Poole was the incarnation of the strength which Coleridge needed. They met in 1794, when Pantisocratic enthusiasm and Coleridge's political activity were at their height and, with some intermissions, Poole's friendship endured until Coleridge's death in 1834.

Poole, conscious perhaps of the academic shortcomings in his own education, was captivated from the first by the brilliance of Coleridge's conversation. He was quick to recognize Coleridge's genius and made it his self-appointed duty to encourage and assist Coleridge to produce the '*original* works of genius [which] are your forte'.[2] In succumbing to Coleridge's magnetism he found himself in disagreement often with his own family, especially cousin Charlotte, whose insight was remarkable. 'Tom Poole', she wrote, 'has a friend with him of the name of Coldridge [*sic*]: a young man of brilliant understanding, great eloquence,

---

[1] Life, 44. During 1802–4, however, they became very friendly again, Coleridge reckoning 'Lamb & Southey, the two men, whom next to Wordsworth, I love the best in the world' (CL, II, 1074–5), and Southey regarding Coleridge, Rickman, and William Taylor as his 'Trinity of living greatness' (Life, 184). When Coleridge left England for Malta in April 1804 Southey virtually took over the safeguarding of Coleridge's family for him (CL, II, 1098).

[2] Sandford, I, 122, 125–6. Poole was one of the syndicate of seven or eight friends who pledged themselves to contribute five guineas annually to Coleridge 'as a trifling mark of their esteem, gratitude and admiration'. Payments of £35 or £40 were made in 1796 and 1797, but were discontinued when Coleridge received an annuity from the Wedgwoods in 1798 (see Sandford, I, 142–4).

desperate fortune, democratick principles, and entirely led away by the feelings of the moment.'[1] Poole's neighbours, moreover, regarded Coleridge (and his friends, Wordsworth and Thelwall) as French spies!

After his experience of Southey's duplicity Coleridge found Poole's forthright manner refreshing. It acted as a check, too, on his own over-subtle intellectualizing:

> I love & honor you, Poole! for many things—scarcely for any thing more than that, trusting firmly in the Rectitude & simplicity of your own Heart, and listening with faith to it's revealing Voice, you never suffered either my Subtlety or my Eloquence to proselyte you to the pernicious Doctrine of Necessity.[2]

Both Poole and Mary Evans seemed impervious to Coleridge's casuistry: the same could not always be said of Southey or Wordsworth. Yet, though Poole never shrank from telling Coleridge he was wrong, he did it in a way which bred no resentment. From the commencement of their friendship it became Coleridge's habit to take his problems to Poole: the difficulties of finding subscribers for the *Watchman*; whether to set up a private school or become a dissenting parson; whether to learn German in order to translate Schiller, or take up journalism and abandon poetry and metaphysics. After moving to Stowey so as to be next door to Poole Coleridge had a gate constructed between their two gardens to facilitate this intercourse still further. Having established his home under Poole's wing he dashed off a joyful letter to Cottle, describing the congenial environment and underlining the pleasure Poole's propinquity gave him—'from all this you will conclude *that we are happy*'.[3] Coleridge was then on the brink of his 'annus mirabilis', and the upsurge of creative activity that followed was to some extent facilitated by the propitious circumstances ensuing upon his move to Stowey.

Coleridge's marriage deteriorated rapidly after he parted from Poole and moved his family north to Greta Hall in June 1800. Mrs Coleridge did not want to leave Stowey, which was convenient for Bristol where most of her family and friends lived. Also she disliked the Wordsworths intensely, whereas she was as

---

[1] Sandford, i, 124.   [2] CL, ii, 1037.
[3] ibid, i, 296–7. Joseph Cottle (1770–1853), a bookseller of Bristol, who published works of Southey, Coleridge, and Wordsworth; author of *Early Recollections* (1837), *Reminiscences* (1847), and some indifferent poems.

fond of Poole's company as her husband was. Poole was always solicitous for her welfare and he frequently advised Coleridge to have more consideration for his wife's feelings, especially while Coleridge was away in Germany. Almost twenty years after she had left Stowey Mrs Coleridge was still expressing gratitude for the comfort Poole had been to her in the early years of her marriage:

> I scarcely could have ventured this long and egotistical epistle, if I could ever forget that he whom I address is the same person who, in days long past, made so many and so friendly exertions to render a miserable cottage an abode of comparative comfort.[1]

She maintained a regular correspondence with Poole right through these later years, and he included in many of his letters to Coleridge pages of local gossip intended mainly for her pleasure.

With the possible exception of Gillman, Poole understood the basic neuroticism in Coleridge's temperament better than any of the other 'sheet-anchors'. Recognizing this emotional instability he tried at the same time to protect Mrs Coleridge from it, perceiving that it could destroy their marriage. Very gently he tried to dissuade Coleridge from emotional excesses: 'Only let your *mind* act, and not your *feelings*. Don't conjure up any scenes of distress which never happened.'[2] Or, still more directly, he pointed out to Coleridge the probable consequences of giving way to impetuous feelings:

> Mrs. Coleridge has sent me from Bristol the letter you wrote her. Was it well to indulge in, much less to express, such feelings concerning *any* circumstance which could relate to two infants? I do not mean to check tenderness, for in the *folly* of tenderness I can sympathise—but be *rational*, I implore you—in your present situation, your happiness depends upon it.[3]

But his sympathy and his unwavering belief in Coleridge's genius did more for Coleridge even than the soundness of his advice. Of all Coleridge's acquaintances, it was Poole and Lamb particularly who, ignoring what others said, listened to his bitter self-reproaches, then sought to bolster his self-esteem. If Poole believed that Coleridge's neurosis would eventually destroy him,[4]

---

[1] Sandford, I, 199.   [2] ibid, I, 293.   [3] ibid, I, 285.
[4] Poole's letter to Henrietta Warwick of 6 February 1796 on the ill-effects of over-indulgence in abstruse researches was almost certainly written with Coleridge in mind (see Sandford, I, 133; also I, 279–80).

he was careful to conceal it. Poole's affectionate admiration was balm to Coleridge's vanity; with this 'sheet-anchor' there was never any of that prickly fault-finding which so characterized George Coleridge and Southey:

> My very dear Friend! I send these poems to you with better heart than I should to most others, because I know that you will read them with affection however little you may admire them.[1]

Affection more than anything else cemented the friendship between them. Poole was genuinely interested in Coleridge's well-being and progress, and in no sense could he be considered a rival, as Southey and Wordsworth undoubtedly were.

On the other hand Poole's good-natured indulgence rather invited displays of neuroticism—therapeutic, possibly, but embarrassing. The least suggestion of dyspathy agitated Coleridge unbearably, causing him nakedly to expose his jealous possessiveness:

> My dear, very dear Poole
> The Heart, thoroughly penetrated with the flame of virtuous Friendship, is in a state of glory; but 'lest it should be exalted above measure, there is given it a Thorn in the flesh:'—I mean, that where the friendship of any person forms an essential part of a man's happiness, he will at times be pestered by the little jealousies & solicitudes of imbecil Humanity.—Since we last parted I have been gloomily dreaming, that you did not leave me so affectionately as you were wont to do.—Pardon this littleness of Heart—& do not think the worse of me for it. Indeed my Soul seems so mantled & wrapped round by your Love & Esteem, that even a dream of losing but the smallest fragment of it makes me shiver—as tho' some tender part of my Nature were left uncovered & in nakedness.[2]

It was shortly after writing this that Coleridge decided he would prevent any risk of further misunderstandings by taking up residence next door to Poole. He rationalized this decision by arguing that he could better support his family by horticultural work than by writing, but really he simply wanted to be close to Poole:

> To live in a beautiful country & to inure myself as much as possible to the labors of the field, have been for this year past my dream of the day, my Sigh at midnight—but to enjoy these blessings *near you*, to see you daily, to tell you all my thoughts in their first birth,

[1] CL, I, 204.   [2] ibid, I, 235.

and to hear your's, to be mingling identities with you, as it were;—
the vision-weaving *Fancy* has indeed often pictured such things, but
Hope never dared whisper a promise![1]

'Mingling identities' was perhaps only a curious way of fusing
'power' with 'strength'. There was a lengthy correspondence in
connection with this scheme in which Coleridge revealed his conviction that the full integration of his personality depended absolutely upon a close liaison with his 'sheet-anchor'. 'I so ardently
desire it,' he wrote, 'that any disappointment would chill all my
faculties, like the fingers of death.'[2]

Practical objections against the scheme were raised by both
Charles Lloyd senior, who was then about to send his son to
Coleridge as a private pupil, and Poole, but they were vehement-
ly over-ruled; not by rational counter-argument but by sheer
torrent of feeling—'I will *make* the Cottage do.' Unashamedly
Coleridge played on Poole's good nature, forcing him into the
position where refusal implied heartless indifference to a struggling poet's sufferings. The key letter of 13 December 1796 may
be compared with that to Southey of 13 November 1795, which
we examined earlier, as indicating the profound difference in
these relationships. Whereas with Southey Coleridge was almost
invariably on the defensive, apologetic and placatory, yet spite-
fully rejoicing when Southey exposed a vulnerable heel, with
Poole it was the reverse. Coleridge normally wrote to him from
a position of strength, of acknowledged intellectual superiority
from which he could gracefully condescend or patronize. Having
realized his need of Poole, however, and fearing that this need
was about to be frustrated, he now cajoled and implored with
every art of persuasion at his command, in an attempt to beat
down phlegmatic common sense and win condonation for the
irregularities of genius. Inevitably, Coleridge overdid it; no stop
was left unopened; no device ignored which might serve to wring
Poole's heart. A summary of one part (about a tenth) of it will
convey the tone of this inordinately long epistle:

> *Unkind* so to write to one who is *ill*, subjecting him to *anxieties*
> which might prove *fatal*. To advise him, though *haunted* by the
> spectres of Otway and Chatterton [both conveniently supposed to
> have starved on journalism] to depend on so *precarious* a means of
> livelihood, the while his wife is *broken-hearted* and his *babe bitten with*

[1] ibid, I, 249. [2] ibid, I, 242.

hunger, as *anxieties* and *debts* pile up, and the shadow of *madness* and *Newgate Prison* looms over all.

This, contrasted with the simple, *good life* of husbandry, where industry has its reward in *virtue* and *innocence*.

[Further on] the *threat* [which never failed to evoke a response from Poole] that Literature must henceforth become *a secondary object*.

This is a fair specimen of the specious theatricality. Nowhere did Coleridge attempt to meet the main objection to the scheme, which could best be summed up in Charles Lamb's query, 'Pray, what does your worship know about farming?'[1]

Poole's reservations were wholly reasonable, as was his advice that Coleridge should concentrate on literary work, supplementing his income as and when necessary with free-lance journalism. (The Wedgwood annuity had not yet come his way.) Yet, in a curious way, Coleridge was right to follow his instincts rather than accept Poole's practical advice. The horticulture was only a blind, never seriously entertained by Coleridge, whereas his intuition that Poole could give him that enriching emotional and moral stability his nature needed in fact proved accurate. Within months of moving to Stowey he burgeoned forth into his 'annus mirabilis'. Poole's propinquity may not in itself have been the direct cause of this—Wordsworth's influence was needed too— but it was an indispensable element in it.

Safely established 'beneath the impervious covert' of this *oak*, Coleridge took heart to write a series of autobiographical letters to Poole, to a father-confessor of whose sympathetic understanding he was at last assured:

> . . . it will perhaps make you behold with no unforgiving or impatient eye those weaknesses and defects in my character, which so many untoward circumstances have concurred to plant there.[2]

It was as though his earlier 'sheet-anchor' relationships had never been. Poole, he declared, was 'the man in whom *first* and in whom alone I had felt an *anchor*'. With all previous connections (alluding to the Rev. George Coleridge and Southey) he felt by comparison 'a dim sense of insecurity and uncertainty, terribly uncomfortable'. He felt himself attached to Poole 'beyond all other men'.[3]

[1] Sandford, I, 203.   [2] CL, I, 302.   [3] ibid, I, 491.

Even more satisfactory perhaps, Poole seemed enthusiastic about accepting the rôle required of him:

> By you, Coleridge, I will always stand, in sickness and health, in prosperity and misfortune; nay, in the worst of all misfortunes, in *vice* ... if vice should ever taint thee—but *it cannot*.[1]

While Coleridge was in Germany in 1798–9, Poole cheerfully shouldered responsibility for finding fresh accommodation for Mrs Coleridge and her children (rather as Southey did five years later when Coleridge fled to Malta). Poole's dedication to Coleridge's cause in 1799 was unwavering (or had he sensed that Coleridge was about to throw him over for Wordsworth?)—'*I will not part from you, if you will not part from me;* be assured of that.'[2] Coleridge had experienced nothing like it before: the combination of oak-like protectiveness with genuine, even admiring, affection for his person in full knowledge of all its infirmities, made his days beside Poole the happiest of his life. Poole's placid strength of character lent ballast to a mind adrift on change. Southey may have been the prototype for the 'sheet-anchor', but Poole was undoubtedly the original Coleridgean 'whole man'.

Poole served Coleridge as a pattern of 'wholeness': stable and balanced, self-sufficing and independent; virtuously industrious on his own behalf, yet deeply concerned for the well-being of others. Coleridge expected, he said, to see 'the *whole man* of God and his country' developed in Poole.[3] A note, dated July 1830, appended to the second edition of *On the Constitution of Church and State*, suggests that Poole fulfilled this expectation. After reviewing the many-sidedness of Poole's character Coleridge singled out as his most 'individualising trait' what he called 'the integrity, i.e. *entireness* of his being (*integrum et sine cerâ vas*)'.[4]

---

[1] Sandford, I, 161 (written on 26 September 1796).

[2] ibid, I, 286. In this letter Poole tried to tempt Coleridge to return to Stowey by mentioning a desirable house that was vacant there. He went on to say: 'I can truly say that your society is a principal ingredient of my happiness, a principal source of my improvement.'

[3] CL, III, 130. Coleridge's 'whole man' concept is discussed more fully in Chapter 10.

[4] The full note reads: 'A man whom I have seen now in his harvest field; now in a committee-room with the Rickmans and Ricardos of the age; at another time with Davy, Woolaston, and the Wedgwoods; now with Wordsworth, Southey, and other friends not unheard of in the republic of letters; now in the drawing-rooms of the rich and the noble; and now presiding at

More significant from our present point of view is the integratory effect Poole's friendship appeared to have on Coleridge's personality. Not to live near Poole, he had said, would 'chill all his faculties'. This in effect is what happened, it seems, while Coleridge was isolated in Germany and lonely amid alien faces:

> O my God! how I long to be at home—My *whole Being* so yearns after you, that when I think of the moment of our meeting, I catch the fashion of German Joy, rush into your arms, and embrace you —methinks my *Hand* would swell, if the whole force of my feeling were crowded there.[1]

Years later he wrote, to Poole: 'Love so deep and so domesticated *with the whole being,* as mine was to you, can never cease to be.'[2]

Coleridge's elaboration of his 'whole man' theory came later, however; during the late 1790's he was conscious only of his need for Poole's friendship and support. For a period at Stowey life's 'voyage' seemed suspended, as though his vessel had found secure anchorage. *The Ancient Mariner* was thus a purely *imaginative* exploration of his dreaded presentiment that he must one day set forth again:

> I *love* but few, but those I love as my own Soul; for I feel that without them I should—not indeed cease to be kind and effluent, but by little and little become a soulless fixed Star, receiving no rays nor influences into my Being, a Solitude which I so tremble at, that I cannot attribute it even to the divine nature.[3]

---

the annual dinner of a Village Benefit Society; and in each seeming to be in the very place he was intended for, and taking the part to which his tastes, talents, and attainments gave him an admitted right.

'And yet this is not the most remarkable, not the most individualising trait of our friend's character. It is almost overlooked in the originality and raciness of his intellect; in the life, freshness, and practical value of his remarks and notices, truths plucked as they are growing, and delivered to you with the dew on them, the fair earnings of an observing eye, armed and kept on the watch by thought and meditation; and above all in the integrity, i.e. *entireness* of his being (*integrum et sine cerâ vas*), the steadiness of his attachments, the activity and persistence of a benevolence, which so graciously presses a warm temper into the service of a yet warmer heart, and so lights up the little flaws and imperfections incident to humanity, in its choicest specimens, that were their removal at the option of his friends (and few have, or deserve to have, so many!), not a man among them but would vote for leaving him as he is' (*On the Constitution of Church and State* (1830), Chap. v, p. 115).

  [1] CL, i, 490.   [2] ibid, iii, 435.   [3] Allsop, op. cit., ii, 137.

Not the least of Coleridge's reasons for declining a Unitarian ministry in Shrewsbury in January 1798 was the fact that it meant leaving the friend whose society had become indispensable to his 'ideas of happiness', the friend 'dearer to my understanding and affections unitedly, than all else in this world'. He could not face it. He agreed later to go to Germany because he would be with the Wordsworths but, even so, the wrench at leaving Poole's side was painful.[1]

This departure for Germany marks a watershed in Coleridge's career: it terminated the 'annus mirabilis' and was followed shortly after by the 'Dejection' crisis of 1801–2. To Poole's disappointment (and Lamb's) Coleridge fell under Wordsworth's spell and very soon afterwards decided to leave Stowey and go north. As a result of this move Coleridge was rarely to know peace of mind again for, in leaving Stowey, he left behind not only Poole but a domestic arrangement which, if not ideal, had not been devoid of happiness. At Greta Hall, however, open discord soon broke out between him and his wife and the precarious emotional balance Coleridge had achieved at Stowey rapidly gave way.

We can only speculate what effect continued residence at Stowey might have produced on Coleridge's work. The events of 1800–3 are so complicated that the altering of merely one element in the situation might not radically have changed the pattern as a whole. Certainly Coleridge afterwards regretted the move, and he could not fail to recognize the quality of the work he had done at Poole's side. It was not only Poole's practical assistance and advice which he missed (indeed, Poole's advice was not always sound); it was not simply Poole's belief in his genius (Poole's very expectations were sometimes guilt-inducing); it was chiefly that Coleridge's auto-diagnosis had been accurate—his unstable nature did require a stronger one to support it, and Tom Poole, *integrum et sine cerâ vas*, was in 1797 the man he needed. Southey and Wordsworth, 'invincible Soldiers of Virtue', never so effectively met this need (why indeed should they?)—for they were prone to judge Coleridge by the standards the world uses, whereas the unconventional Poole was magnanimous enough to accord this bizarre genius a special dispensation of his own.

[1] CL, I, 415, 418.

2

Love: the Vital Air

Coleridge's 'sheet-anchor' relationships, abnormal and complex though they were, can be resolved into a fairly straightforward pattern. On the one hand there was his own emotional and moral instability; on the other the sheet-anchor's strength of character, his self-sufficiency as an individual and his capacity for regulating his emotional life evenly. Coleridge's relationships with the opposite sex, however, are much less simple to analyse. Something of the ambivalence of his attitude towards women might be inferred indeed from the variety of his female characterizations. As Geraldine or Life-in-Death he represented Woman as the sort of nightmare apparition that bedevilled his dreams, but he portrayed her also with the naïve innocence of a Christabel or Genevieve. In *Lewti* or *The Picture* she was elusive and unattainable; in the person of the ruthless mother of *The Three Graves* predatory and malevolent. Sometimes her rôle within the same poem seemed indeterminate, as when she both bewailed her demon lover yet, as the visionary Abyssinian maid, became the source of inspiration. She was both the 'Dark Ladie' of Spenserian romance and the 'pure Lady' of *Dejection: an Ode*. Was there a common denominator amid such an assemblage any more than there was among, say, Mary Evans, Sara Fricker, Sara Hutchinson, Dorothy Wordsworth, Catherine Clarkson, Mary Morgan, Charlotte Brent, and Mrs Gillman, the women who, apart from his mother, played the most significant part in Coleridge's life?

It should be stressed that no male 'sheet-anchor' friendship could wholly satisfy Coleridge's emotional needs. He regarded marriage and parenthood as indispensable to the fulfilment of personality:

> We cannot love a friend as a woman; but we may love a woman
> as a friend. Friendship satisfies the highest parts of our nature; but

a wife, who is capable of friendship, satisfies all . . . [helps] to establish *a concord and unity betwixt all parts of our nature*, to give a feeling and a passion to our purer intellect, and to intellectualise our feelings and passions. This a happy marriage blest with children, effectuates in the highest degree.[1]

His deep-felt need for female affection was his constant poetic theme: 'To be beloved is all I need / And whom I love, I love indeed'.[2] In 1810, following the break with Sara Hutchinson (hereafter called 'Asra' to distinguish her from Sara Fricker and from 'Young Sara', his daughter), he wrote:

One human being, *entirely* loving me (this, of course, must have been a Woman) would not only have satisfied all my Hopes, but would have rendered me happy and grateful, even though I had no Friend on earth, herself excepted.[3]

He had a strong *physical* need of woman's love, judging from his claim that he could have lived happily with a servant girl 'had she only in sincerity of heart responded to my affection'.[4]

Yet there was something curiously emasculated about Coleridge's dealings with the other sex, as though he preferred *talking* about love to more positive commitment. He tended to idealize the women with whom he came in contact, appearing sometimes to be in love chiefly with his own idea of love. Deliciously he meditated upon what love must be like, subtly and fastidiously dwelling on its lyrical and even mystical possibilities, refusing to see its more sensual, earthy qualities. Perhaps only Coleridge could have proposed writing a series of love poems—

. . . truly Sapphic, save that they shall have a large Interfusion of moral Sentiment & calm Imagery on Love in all the moods of the mind—Philosophic, fantastic, in moods of high enthusiasm, of simple Feeling, of mysticism, of Religion—[to] comprize in it all the practice, & all the philosophy of Love![5]

Was it in this vein he spoke in his lecture on *Love* on 9 December

[1] MC, 255 (my italics). This passage has some bearing on Coleridge's 'whole man' theory, discussed in Chapter 10.

[2] "The Pains of Sleep", ll. 51–2, PW 391.

[3] Whalley, 86. Derek Stanford traces a resemblance between Coleridge's dependence upon another human being and the characteristic insufficiency of Clare, Hood, Darley, Beddoes, and Rossetti. He mentions Clare's madness, Beddoes' suicide, and Rossetti's use of chloral (D. Stanford, "Coleridge as Poet and Philosopher of Love", in *English*, Vol. XIII, 1960, No. 73, pp. 3–7).

[4] IH, 107.   [5] KC, I, 1064.

D

1811, considered by Crabb Robinson far and away the best lecture Coleridge ever gave on any subject?

In making love something mystical, almost ethereal, did Coleridge in fact mask a lack of genuine passion? Something very like the rhetorical extravagance of his letters to Poole occurred also in his descriptions of heterosexual relationships. Delicately and beautifully as the limpid prose pursues the subtle complexities of his unwinding thoughts, one yet feels something wanting, a sense of unreality. This account of an imagined wedding anniversary may serve as illustration:

> On some delightful day in early spring some of my countrymen hallow the anniversary of their marriage, and with love and fear go over the reckoning of the past and the unknown future. The wife tells with half-renewed modesty all the sweet feelings that she disguised and cherished in the courting-time; the man looks with a tear full in his eye and blesses the hour when for the first time (and oh! let it be the last) he spake deep and solemn to a beloved being— "Thou art mine and I am thine, and henceforward I shield and shelter [thee] against the world, and thy sorrows shall be my sorrows, and though abandoned by all men, we two will abide together in love and duty."
>
> In the holy eloquent solitude where the very stars that twinkle seem to be a *voice*, that suits the dream, a voice of a dream, a voice soundless and yet for the *ear* not the *eye* of the soul, when the winged soul passes over vale and mountain, sinks into glens, and then climbs with the cloud, and passes from cloud to cloud, and thence from sun to sun—never is she alone. Always one, the dearest, accompanies and even when he melts, diffused in the blue sky, she melts at the same moment into union with the beloved.[1]

Or compare the following conception of the love-relationship which, apart from its fragile beauty and its being almost beyond the capacity of mortal woman to realize, is fraught with apprehensiveness as to his own ability to sustain the part:

> The two sweet silences—first in the purpling dawn of love-troth, when the heart of each ripens in the other's looks within the unburst calyx, and fear becomes so sweet that it seems but a fear of losing hope in certainty; the second, when the sun is setting in the calm eve of confident love, and [lovers] in mute recollection enjoy each other. "I fear to speak, I fear to hear you speak, so deeply do I now enjoy your presence, so totally possess you in myself, myself in you.

[1] AP, 216.

The very sound would break the union and separate *you-me* into you and me."[1]

His love-letters, with their extravagant sentiments, were not the effusions of the conventional lover, soon penned and as quickly forgotten. Idealized though his notion of the love-relationship was, Coleridge clung to it obstinately and was deeply hurt when it failed to materialize. Sometimes he even wondered himself whether he did not *sublimate* sex by his mystical rhapsodizing:

> ... I have *loved* so as I should feel no shame to describe to an Angel, and as my experience makes me suspect—to an Angel alone would be intelligible.[2]

It is hardly surprising, in view of such an admission, that some critics suppose Coleridge to have been considerably under-sexed. This is a point I shall return to.

Though the Protean variety of his poetic characterizations of Woman appears to preclude narrow categorization, it is in fact possible to isolate two chief attributes which he valued in her sex above all else. There was Woman the *comforter*, or 'soother of absence', and there was Woman the *inspirer* (whom I shall refer to alternatively as the 'Abyssinian maid'). These two attributes were not of course mutually exclusive: Mary Evans and Asra (possibly Dorothy Wordsworth, too) combined both functions. His first encounter with a woman possessing both potentialities appears to have occurred when as an undergraduate he vied with other young admirers in paying homage to Miss Brunton—Cambridge's early prototype for Zuleika Dobson.[3] Mrs Morgan, Charlotte Brent, and Mrs Gillman may also have exemplified both qualities; it is impossible at this distance to say. Catherine Clarkson certainly possessed them; indeed her relationship with Coleridge throws a special light upon his need for female sympathy.

When in 1804 he decided to leave England in a last attempt to cure himself of his infatuation for Asra, Catherine Clarkson was distressed by his desperate mental state and anxious to do something to restore his faltering genius.[4] During 1808, after his return from Malta, she gave him shelter and with her assistance he made heroic efforts to break free of his addiction to opium.

[1] ibid, 224.   [2] Whalley, 108.   [3] See PW 66–7; Life, 32.
[4] See E. de Selincourt, *The Early Letters of William and Dorothy Wordsworth, 1787–1805* (Oxford, 1935), 358 ff., 374.

This unexpected access of practical sympathy both comforted and strengthened him with the result that he felt a resurgence of creative activity: 'Catherine, I shall soon be a poet again; you will make me a poet.'[1] She, like Poole earlier, was perfectly willing to accept the rôle he designed for her:

> He found in me [she wrote] a being capable of sympathising with him. It wd have made me supremely happy to have been the means of restoring him to myself—My husband wd have valued me the more for having done it.[2]

No poems ensued from this resuscitation of literary ambition, but Coleridge did in the glow of it begin making preparations for *The Friend*. By this time he had become deeply envious of the solace and inspiration Wordsworth derived from Dorothy's self-effacing dedication to the furtherance of his career, and he argued that a similar relationship between Catherine Clarkson and himself might have been the saving of his own genius:

> Had she been my Sister, I should have been a great man. . . But I have never—had any one, in whose Heart and House I could be an Inmate, who loved me enough to take pride and joy in the efforts of my power. . . I never saw a woman yet, whom I could so imagine to have been of one parent with me at my Birth, as Catherine Clarkson.[3]

Yet, though he married and had children and experienced two major love-affairs besides, Coleridge never succeeded in forming a wholly satisfactory relationship with a woman possessing the qualities he desired. Was he incapable of enjoying a normal love-relationship?

It has been remarked that since his religion, philosophy, and

---

[1] Life, 214, 216. Coleridge's closest attachments were formed with women who were sympathetic to his weaknesses. His comment on Mrs Green is revealing: 'I like Mrs J. Green better and better; but feel that in twenty years it would never be above and beyond *liking*. She is good-natured, lively, innocent, but without a *soothingness*, or something I do not know what that is tender' (see L, II, 692).

[2] See Whalley, 74n. As late as 1812 Catherine Clarkson was still anxious to be a *comforter* to Coleridge: 'My path is clear before me—I will show him only love and tenderness, that which is in the depths of my heart—Whenever the opportunity occurs I will seek him out—sooth him with kindness greater than womans—the kindness the compassion of angels when they pity human frailty—I have written to ask him to come hither—I do not expect that he will' (ibid, 96).

[3] ibid, 88–9.

aesthetic all stem ultimately from ideas of love he should be designated the 'Poet and Philosopher of Love'. His importance, it is claimed, consists in his being 'the philosopher of love, sympathy, empathy, and union'.[1] Certainly this is an aspect of Coleridge's myriad-mindedness which has so far escaped serious critical attention. Yet the term 'Philosopher of Love' suggests a certain intellectual detachment from areas of feeling, 'philosophical' perhaps in the sense that Coleridge said Wordsworth was a philosopher—that is, as a *spectator ab extra*. As was mentioned earlier, the sequence of love-poems he planned promised an extremely sophisticated treatment of the subject, an eclectic blend it seemed of Sapphic, quasi-Epicurean, and Neo-Platonic elements. It carried overtones closer perhaps to oriental aestheticism than physical love—a preference for contemplation rather than active engagement.

It is the unreality of this sort of attitude which has led to the suspicion that Coleridge sought from love a religious, mystical experience which was not properly in it to be found. Because love 'never produced any results' for him, it is claimed, his overall problem was basically a religious one. There are, certainly, many indications that he seemed to seek in love a purely religious gratification, as though he used the beloved only to fulfil certain somewhat obscure mystical longings: 'You are the God within me . . . My Love of κθY [Asra] is not so much in my soul, as my soul in it . . . Love, passionate in its deepest tranquillity, Love unutterable, fills my whole Spirit'—and so forth.[2] Such passages suggest not so much a flesh-and-blood relationship as a quest after some mystical experience of the Absolute. Merely human love, it would seem, could not satisfy his longings when, at most, he wanted a lovely maiden only to read his visage in his mind. Love, therefore, the argument runs, was for him virtually devoid of sex, Coleridge being in reality 'passionless and under-sexed'. Thus, the love-affair with Asra failed because it could not produce this union with the Absolute which was what he was really after.[3]

Coleridge's love *was* sometimes 'unreal' in the sense that he idealized it quite impossibly, and the idealization frequently did

[1] See Stanford, op. cit.   [2] See Suther, 26–9.   [3] ibid.

acquire distinctly religious overtones. After 1802 certainly, Coleridge's love for Asra became akin to religious devotion until, finally, he abandoned it altogether and turned wholly to religion for sublimatory (or compensatory) comfort. But in this matter the chronology is particularly important for, though Coleridge came eventually to believe that religion could provide what Asra had not provided, it is a mistake to suppose that Coleridge was seeking a primarily religious gratification at the outset of his affair with her. It will not do to juxtapose his 1810 statements about Asra with the disturbing events of 1801–2. Indeed, this unfortunate practice of utilizing material from Coleridge's middle or later life to 'explain' events in his earlier life has sometimes obfuscated rather than clarified the important issues.

Mr Suther's theory that Coleridge was 'passionless and undersexed' is based, partly, on the following passage from *The Improvisatore*, ignoring the fact that this first appeared in 1827, only seven years before his death and when, presumably, sex had lost much of its attractiveness for him:

> *Friend:* Love, as distinguished from Friendship, on the one hand, and from the passion that too often usurps its name, on the other—
>
> *Lucius* (Eliza's brother, who had just joined the trio, in a whisper to the Friend): But is not Love the union of both?
>
> *Friend* (aside to Lucius): He never loved who thinks so.[1]

Though the 'Friend' here was undoubtedly Coleridge himself, all he has done is to distinguish love from lust (the passion which too often *'usurps'* its name); he has not denied that love may be accompanied by passion. The piece is really saying that 'true love', to endure, must be based upon something more than appetite. Love supposes, he goes on:

> ... a peculiar sensibility and tenderness of nature; a constitutional communicativeness and *utterancy* of heart and soul; a delight in the detail of sympathy, in the outward and visible signs of the sacrament within—to count, as it were, the pulses of the life of love. But above all, it supposes a soul which, even in the pride and summer-tide of life—even in the lustihood of health and strength, had felt oftenest and prized highest that which age cannot take away and which, in all our lovings, is *the* Love;—
>
> ... I mean that *willing* sense of the insufficingness of the *self* for

[1] Suther, 50–4.

itself, which predisposes a generous nature to see, in the total being of another, the supplement and completion of its own.[1]

This is the later Coleridge speaking, safe on Highgate Hill, and (by implication) referring not to Asra, but to his wife from whom he had parted twenty years before. *The Improvisatore* went on in fact to list Mrs Coleridge's shortcomings, though these are not of immediate concern. Between Coleridge and his wife there had been scarcely any 'utterancy of heart and soul' after 1800, no acceptance of the other as the necessary complement to full personal integration. But why turn to 1827 for Coleridge's views on love when material of more immediate relevance is to hand?

When Mr Suther turns to the critical 1802 period, it is to offer interpretations of *Dejection: an Ode* and *The Picture* in support of his contention that love did *not* kill the poet in Coleridge. So far as *The Picture* is concerned he misses surely the whole point of the poem. His interpretation amounts to this: that the lover in the poem, instead of going after the 'real maiden', wastes his time pursuing a reflection. This is said to represent Coleridge's own case—a flight away from actual love to the dream of a higher reality. What the poem actually depicts, however, is a lover try-ing *without success* to 'emancipate himself from Passion' for, when towards the end he discovers that the maid has dropped a picture (deliberately?), he at once forgets his resolution and hastens off after her with this new pretext for *renewing* the relationship. The last lines, in their understanding of the lover's psychological tor-tuousness, reveal an unexpected mastery of dramatic mono-logue:

> My heart,
> Why beats it thus? Through yonder coppice-wood
> Needs must the pathway turn, that leads straightway
> On to her father's house. She is alone!
> The night draws on—such ways are hard to hit—
> And fit it is I should restore this sketch,
> Dropt unawares, no doubt. Why should I yearn
> To keep the relique? 'twill but idly feed
> The passion that consumes me. Let me haste!
> The picture in my hand which she has left;
> She cannot blame me that I followed her:
> And I may be her guide the long wood through. (175–86)

[1] PW 464–5.

The sub-title, *The Lover's Resolution*, is intended actually to be ironic, for the lover's resolution fails utterly, and at the end of the poem he recommits himself more firmly than ever to 'reality'. Even more ironic is E. H. Coleridge's placing of this poem (in Coleridge's collected verses) immediately after *Dejection: an Ode*, which is itself a poem about a lover's resolution. The Ode celebrated Coleridge's own resolve to part from Asra, that she might thereby be assured of the 'Joy' which he himself had lost.[1] Was *The Picture* a satirical comment upon his own frail resolution, on the absurdity of supposing that he *could* simply will himself not to love Asra? In point of fact Coleridge's resolution to break with Asra in 1802 (and again in 1804 when he went to Malta) was not sustained; years of further struggle ensued before their ways finally separated in 1810.

The Picture neither proves nor disproves that Coleridge was under-sexed. We must turn to other poems for information on this point though, because of the conventions of his time, one hardly looks for intimate, private revelations in them. It can at least be said that the recurrence of sexual themes and imagery throughout his poetry was no less marked than in that of his contemporaries. We may recall, in this connection, that the notorious undressing incident in *Christabel* occasioned a furore only paralleled perhaps by the reception given later to Hardy's *Tess*.[2] I am not concerned here, by the way, with the sort of psychoanalytical interpretation of *Kubla Khan* which Mr Graves attempted.[3] Many of Coleridge's poems are sexual on a quite explicit level.

Images of the female breast, for instance, are particularly numerous in his work. He lavished admiration with indiscriminate prodigality on Nesbitt's, Angelina's, Anna's, and Sara's breasts.[4] As a young man he adopted a tender lyrical approach, virginal almost in its delicate sensuousness:

> Fair, as the bosom of the Swan
> That rises graceful o'er the wave,
> I've seen your breast with pity heave,
> And *therefore* love I you, sweet Genevieve.[5]

[1] See Whalley, 126; also Chapter 9, below. The irony in E. H. Coleridge's juxtaposing of these poems was unintentional: he did not know of the second version of "Dejection: an Ode", where the Asra theme is developed.

[2] See pp. 181–2 below.   [3] See Lowes, 595, 400n.   [4] PW 45n.

[5] "Genevieve", ll. 11–14, PW 20.

After he fell in love with Asra and felt the pull of physical desire, the treatment became more tense and sensual, with a corresponding advance from visual delight to pleasures of touch:

> Her bosom heaved—she stepped aside,
> As conscious of my look she stepped—
> Then suddenly, with timorous eye
>   She fled to me and wept.
>
> She half enclosed me with her arms,
> She pressed me with a meek embrace;
> And bending back her head, looked up,
>   And gazed upon my face.
>
> 'Twas partly love, and partly fear,
> And partly 'twas a bashful art,
> That I might rather *feel*, than see,
>   The swelling of her heart.[1]

The sight of his wife suckling their children constantly inflamed erotic impulses, and even religious themes evoked considerable erotic sensuality:

> She gave with joy her virgin breast;
> She hid it not, she bared the breast
> Which suckled that divinest babe!
> Blessed, blessed were the breasts
> Which the Saviour infant kiss'd.[2]

He had protested to Southey that to marry a woman he did not love would degrade her into an 'Instrument of low Desire', the object merely of 'desultory Appetite', yet as their wedding-day approached, sexual excitability grew in him:

> ... give me to the bosom of my Love!
> My gentle Love, caressing and carest,
> With heaving heart shall cradle me to rest![3]

Genuine epithalamial passion occurs in the *Lines written at Shurton Bars* a month before his wedding as, bridegroom-like, he impatiently anticipated the ecstasy of sexual union:

> ... from your heart the sighs that steal
> Shall make your rising bosom feel
>   The answering swell of mine!

[1] PW 334.　　[2] PW 306.
[3] "The Hour When We Shall Meet Again", ll. 4–6, PW 96; and cf. CL, i, 145.

> How oft, my Love! with shapings sweet
> I paint the moment, we shall meet!
>   With eager speed I dart—
> I seize you in the vacant air,
> And fancy, with a husband's care
>   I press you to my heart!
>
> 'Tis said, in Summer's evening hour
> Flashes the golden-colour'd flower
>   A fair electric flame:
> And so shall flash my love-charg'd eye
> When all the heart's big ecstasy
>   Shoots rapid through the frame! (82–96)

The poems he poured forth immediately before and after his wedding testify to the delight and creative stimulus the physical raptures of the honeymoon gave him.

The above description of sexual ecstasy affords as direct a treatment of this subject perhaps as the Augustan conventions of propriety still obtaining in the 1790's permitted. It may be compared with, say, *Vaudracour and Julia*, Wordsworth's prim attempt to deal with a similar subject. Wordsworth contrived to evade altogether the description of physical ecstasy, reserving his more sensuous invention for the outward details of Julia's house and chamber-window!

> I pass the raptures of the pair;—such theme
> Is, by innumerable poets, touched
> In more delightful verse than skill of mine
> Could fashion; chiefly by that darling bard
> Who told of Juliet and her Romeo . . . (87–91)

At the centre of this story is Julia's seduction, an incident with obvious bearing on Wordsworth's own affair with Annette Vallon, but Wordsworth's readers could never have guessed so much. All trace of personal passion is rigorously excluded from the poem, which sags under its weight of sententious moralizing:

> So passed the time, till, whether through effect
> Of some unguarded moment that dissolved
> Virtuous restraint—ah, speak it, think it, not!
> Deem rather that the fervent Youth, who saw
> So many bars between his present state
> And the dear haven where he wished to be
> In honourable wedlock with his Love,

Was in his judgment tempted to decline
To perilous weakness, and entrust his cause
To nature for a happy end of all;
Deem that by such fond hope the Youth was swayed,
And bear with their transgression, when I add
That Julia, wanting yet the name of wife,
Carried about her for a secret grief
The promise of a mother. (54–68)

Compared with such coy circumlocution Coleridge's treatment is refreshingly outspoken.[1]

Yet only with certain reservations may Coleridge be called the 'Poet of Love'. As regards sexual love at least he sang usually with his breast against a thorn, about frustrated love and his own bewildered feelings.[2] *The Blossoming of the Solitary Date-Tree* distilled the anguish of a host of poems into one unforgettable line —perhaps the most poignant he ever wrote: 'Why was I made for Love and Love denied to me?' *The Blossoming of the Solitary Date-Tree*, apart from some isolated felicities, was a failure and was left unfinished. It was an attempt to universalize private feeling into the organized impersonality of a work of art; to attain the representative and generic attributes which ideally poetry demands, exclusive of accident and personal idiosyncrasy, in the manner laid down in *Biographia Literaria*. Here the attempt failed; in *Dejection: an Ode* it nearly succeeded. This is why we must look to Coleridge's private notebooks rather than to his poetry for full insight into the strength of his sexual feelings. Poetry, he always insisted, requires an 'utter *aloofness* of the poet's own feelings, from those of which he is at once the painter and analyst'; the poetic genius always 'modifies the images, thoughts, and emotions of the poet's own mind'.[3] His personal diaries, on the other hand, those 'dear confidantes' of his heart, were the recipient

[1] Professor Bateson suggests that Wordsworth's 'prudishness' is excusable once its 'biographical basis' is understood. He alludes to the incestuous relationship which, he alleges, existed between Wordsworth and his sister. He believes that some of Wordsworth's work was actually 'too outspoken' by Victorian standards (F. W. Bateson, *Wordsworth: A Re-interpretation*, 1954, p. 154).

G. Wilson Knight finds a lack of passion in Coleridge's poetry, which he calls love poetry 'seen in a water-haze' (*The Starlit Dome*, 1959, p. 111).

[2] 'And like the Poet's Philomel, I sing / My Love-song, with my breast against a Thorn' ("Dejection: an Ode", original version, ll. 284–5).

[3] BL, II, 14–16.

(sometimes the only one) of his innermost thoughts and feelings. They constituted a private record of his sexual dreams and secret yearnings.

In utilizing these materials Mr Suther argued mainly from those bowdlerized entries which found their way into *Anima Poetae*, but the entries now coming to light, many written in cipher, afford an altogether truer picture of the forcefulness of Coleridge's erotic impulses. These entries, never intended for publication, contain the truth about Coleridge and prove that his sexual responsiveness was normally virile. He demanded a sexual rôle more positive than passive. Mere voyeurism or 'eye-gazing' did not satisfy him; such pleasures, he said, arouse the impulse of '*doing*' and, if a woman be near, they 'kindle or increase the passion of *sexual* love'.[1] He was aware, long before Freud's time, that sexual frustration is a cause of male aggressiveness.[2]

His unconscious mind was agitated as much by Freudian sexuality as by Jungian mystical or religious yearnings. The guilt complications of 1802, for example, gave rise to nightmare fantasies which were predominantly sexual:

> [In my dream] I was followed up & down by a frightful pale woman who, I thought, wanted to kiss me, & had the property of giving a shameful Disease by breathing in the face . . .[3]

Coleridge was certainly no impotent angel beating narcissistic wings in a luminous void: he has confessed that he was sexually experienced before he married. He records that as an undergraduate he was as promiscuous as any with the 'loose women' of Cambridge.[4] That this was not mere bravura the eroticism of such a passage as the following seems to confirm; for, though its full interpretation is perhaps best left to psychiatrists, it clearly reveals a knowingness about sex which cannot be ignored:

> Wednesd. Morn. 3 °clock, Dec. 13, 1803. Bad dreams / How often *of a sort* / at the university—a mixture of Xts Hospital Church / escapes there—lose myself / trust to two People, one Maim'd, one unknown / insulted by a fat sturdy Boy of about 14, like a Bacchus / who dabs a flannel in my face, (or rather soft hair brown Shawl stuff) (was this a flannel Night-cap?) he attacks me / I call to my Friends—they come & join in the Hustle against me—out rushes

[1] KC, I, 1356.   [2] ibid, I, 1552.   [3] ibid, I, 1250; and cf. HH, 152.
[4] CL, II, 734; cf. Life, 26.

a university Harlot, who insists on my going with her / offer her a shilling—seem to get away a moment / when she overtakes me again / I am not to go to another while she is *"biting"*—these were her words / —this will not satisfy her / I sit down on a broad open plain of rubbish with rails & a street beyond / & call out—whole Troops of people in sight—now [?cannot] awake.—Wind & the τα αιδοῖα πενοιλια & somewhat painful / —but what wonderful wanderings thro' the Hall, with bad Portraits of the Emperor of Russia, the Hall belonging to the E.—the wanderings thro' Streets, the noticing the Complex side of a noble Building, & saying to my Guides—"it will be long before I shall find my way here—I must endeavour to remember this" / the turning up a Lane with wall & magnificent Trees (like a quiet Park-garden wall). In the early part of the Dream, Boyer, & two young Students, & R. Allen: Legrice & I quizzing / NB arrogant sense of intellectual superiority under circumstances of depression, but no envy / —*"Obsonant"*. The Harlot in white with her open Bosom certainly was the Cambridge Girl, [Sal Hall]—One thing noticeable in an after Dream / a little weak contemptible wretch offering his Services, & I (as before afraid to refuse them) literally & distinctly remembered a former Dream, in which I had suffered most severely, this wretch leaping on me, & grasping my Scrotum.[1]

It could be argued that this reveals a Coleridge on the defensive, ashamed perhaps of sexual impotency (notwithstanding that it is commonplace in erotic dreams for the dreamer to be acted upon rather than acting). But this dream occurred in 1803, after his passion for Asra had destroyed his marriage. It symbolized probably not a fear of sexual impotency (Why should he fear this, having already fathered four children?), but rather self-disgust because his sexual life had become poisoned or, as he so accurately put it, 'gangrened in its very vitals'.[2] Once his wife became frigid in her relations with him[3] and at the same time he found his desire for Asra frustrated, sex simply turned sour on him.

There are a number of notebook entries relating to Asra which, since they were written after he composed *Dejection: an Ode*, seriously undermine the thesis that love failed before his poetry did. These leave no doubt that the 'old Adam' was still far from dormant. For example, in October 1803, we find Coleridge pondering on the effect separation from Asra would have upon him, if he persisted with his 'resolution' of surrendering her:

[1] KC, i, 1726.   [2] CL, ii, 778.   [3] See p. 269 below.

> . . . I brood over what has befallen of evil / which is the worst that could befall me? What is that Blessing which is most present & perpetual to my Fancy and Yearnings? Sara! Sara!—The Loss then of this first bodies itself out to me / —& if I have not heard from you very recently, & if the last letter had not happened to be full of explicit Love & Feeling, then I conjure up Shadows into Substances—& am miserable / Misery conjures up other Forms, & binds them into Tales & Events—activity is always Pleasure—

In this state of depression his behaviour is characteristic: he imagines himself miraculously freed from the tensions of the actual situation, released through power of fantasy to love Asra without impediment:

> —the Tale grows pleasanter—& at length you come to me / you are by my bed side, in some lonely Inn, where I lie deserted—there you have found me—there you are weeping over me!—Dear, dear Woman![1]

He breaks off abruptly, scruples of conscience preventing him from pursuing the fantasy through to the consummation of desire. A similar tension between guilt and desire exists in several of these 1803 notebook passages, but it should not be mistaken for under-sexedness. It arose because Coleridge's moral sense was outraged by the adulterous inclination of his feelings. Though he knew these desires to be improper, so potent was his need of Asra that sometimes he tried to suppress the knowledge, to pretend even that adultery might in certain circumstances actually be conducive to virtue:

> . . . I felt strongly how apart from all impurity if I were sleeping with the Beloved . . . [it] would . . . increase my active benevolence. . . . O yes, Sara! I did feel how being with you I should be so very much a better man.[2]

But he knew there was not the faintest possibility of his sleeping with Asra 'apart from all impurity'. In despair and frustration he turned deliberately to opium for compensatory or substitute gratification.[3]

On one occasion at least however—during December 1803—the wish-fulfilment fantasy escaped its moral censorship (except that it remained under cover of a precautionary cipher) and erotic imagining was given free rein. This passage has been wrongly interpreted as an account of the soporific effect induced

[1] KC, I, 1601.   [2] ibid, II, 2495.   [3] ibid.

'under the merciful influence of opium', mainly because the section from '⟨μαστοι⟩' to 'Lebens' was deleted. Miss Coburn's text repairs the omission and her notes, here appended, make the full meaning clear:

> When in a state of pleasurable & balmy Quietness I feel my Cheek and Temple on the nicely made up Pillow in Cælibe Toro meo, the fire-gleam on my dear Books, that fill up one whole side from ceiling to floor of my Tall Study—& winds, perhaps are driving the rain, or whistling in frost, at my blessed Window, whence I see Borrodale, the Lake, Newlands—wood, water, mountains, omniform Beauty—O then as I first sink on the pillow, as if Sleep had indeed a material *realm*, as if when I sank on my pillow, I was entering that region & realised Faery Land of Sleep—O then what visions have I had, what dreams—the Bark, the Sea, all the shapes & sounds & adventures made up of the Stuff of Sleep & Dreams, & yet my Reason at the Rudder / O what visions, ⟨μαστοι⟩ as if my Cheek & Temple were lying on me gale o' mast on—Seele meines Lebens!—& I sink down the waters, thro' Seas & Seas—yet warm, yet a Spirit— /
>
> ⟨οι⟩
> Pillow = mast high

KC:	Cælibe Toro meo	—	on my celibate couch
	μαστοι	—	breasts
	me gale o' mast on	—	μεγαλόμαστον = large-breasted
	Seele meines Lebens	—	soul of my life!
	Pillow = mast-high	=	mast-οι = breasts (emphasised by position of οι against mast *high*).[1]

Such a passage, despite the rhapsodizing, permits no further doubt about the virility of Coleridge's sexual impulses. It will be shown in a later chapter that, following an incident at Coleorton in December 1806, Coleridge was so consumed with sexual jealousy as to imagine he had discovered Wordsworth in bed with Asra.[2]

Coleridge then was neither passionless nor under-sexed. Mystical, sentimental, even hysterical though he often was on the subject of love, he nevertheless experienced quite normal sexual drives. His demand for a *comforter* may, it is true, have been accentuated by early emotional deprivation, as it was certainly exacerbated by that potentially neurotic imbalance which he described as 'power without strength', but it was also, in part at least, a perfectly healthy masculine craving. The realization of

[1] ibid, I, 1718; cf. II, 2938.　　[2] See p. 277 below.

his special need for Woman as both 'comforter' and 'inspirer' came to him with the force of an apocalyptic revelation.

During the 1798–9 German tour, after several months' experience of total isolation from his home and friends (he had by then parted company with the Wordsworths) the intuition came to him with almost Cartesian clarity that life without love was unendurable. The symptoms connected with this most significant experience appear also in *Lines written in the Album at Elbingerode in the Hartz Forest* and they bear a striking resemblance to those described in *Dejection: an Ode*.[1] They indicate the experiential nature of the thought-processes by which he came to convince himself that (whatever might be the case with other writers) his own creative faculties could actually be paralysed once this overpowering need for love was unsatisfied. He described the experience thus to his wife, and it is a passage which casts doubt, incidentally, on the theory that his marriage had been breaking up during his 'annus mirabilis':

March 12th [10], 1799.

My dearest Love,

It has been a frightfully long Time, since we have heard from each other. I have not written, simply because my letters could have gone no further than Cuxhaven; & would have stayed there, to the [no] small hazard of their being lost.—Even yet the Mouth of the Elbe is so much choked with Ice, that the Pacquets for England cannot set off. Why need I say, how anxious this long Interval of Silence has made me? I have thought & thought of you, & pictured you & the little ones so often & so often, that my Imagination is tired, down, flat and powerless; and I languish after Home for hours together, in vacancy; my *feelings* almost wholly unqualified by *Thoughts*. I have, at times, experienced such an extinction of *Light* in my mind, I have been so forsaken by all the *forms* and *colourings* of Existence, as if the *organs* of Life had been dried up; as if only simple BEING remained, blind and stagnant!—After I have recovered from this strange state, & reflected upon it, I have thought of a man who should lose his companion in a desart of sand where his weary Halloos drop down in the air without an Echo.—I am deeply convinced that if I were to remain a few years among objects for whom I had no affection, I should wholly lose the powers of Intellect—*Love is the vital air of my Genius* . . .[2]

[1] PW 315–16; cf. "Dejection: an Ode", stanzas 1–3.
[2] CL, I, 470–1. (The final italics are mine.)

In fact he was never wholly to recover from this malaise, however much he reflected upon it, for similar bouts of despondency assailed him repeatedly from this time onwards. The man lost in the desert hearing no friendly echoes to his weary halloos was the same Coleridge who from earliest adolescence had always pictured his life as a lonely 'voyage', and the same Coleridge who would shortly experience during his exile to Malta the living enactment of his own Ancient Mariner's story. This early bout of neurosis was almost a rehearsal of the 1802 experience which destroyed all further ambition of continuing as a poet. The scars of it remained in the rooted and ineradicable conviction, destined to rule his conduct thereafter, that without love his poetic faculty would die. The importance of his conviction that love was the 'vital air' of his genius can hardly be over-emphasized in any interpretation which seeks to find coherence in the manifold of subsequent events in Coleridge's career.

Once Coleridge persuaded himself that love was the 'vital air' of his genius, then, so a psychiatrist might say, love automatically became the vital air of his genius. It could still be that this belief was pure self-delusion. Since the announcement of this apocalyptic discovery came *after* his 'annus mirabilis', there is a primâ facie case for supposing that his marriage must have provided the 'vital air' during this peak creative period. This supposition will be considered more fully in Chapter 4. Meanwhile, it is interesting to note that the two great love-affairs of his life—with Mary Evans at Cambridge and with Asra from 1799 onwards— were both attended at their outset by a sudden access of creativity, suggesting that love did have a marked inspirational effect upon him.

It is true that only one major poem (*Dejection: an Ode*) stemmed directly from these extra-marital love-affairs, but then neither relationship was allowed to develop fully. The affair with Mary Evans collapsed under strong external pressures, while Asra appeared in Coleridge's life five years too late for their love to fructify. As a married man he could hardly acknowledge publicly the inspiration Mary and Asra gave him; nevertheless both affairs may have borne indirectly on *Kubla Khan* and *Christabel*, as well as

E

on a host of lesser poems.[1] Only after he met Asra did he become seriously discontented with his marriage, and his poetic decline thereafter coincided with his failure to find any satisfactory outlet for the sex-instinct. One cannot help wondering, then, what effect it might have had on Coleridge's work had he been free to marry either of these women, and been accepted.

Any attempt to gauge the 'marriage-potential' of personages so long dead must be at best a hazardous business, particularly when the relevant records are few and, such as they are, written almost entirely from a partisan standpoint. Inevitably, Mrs Coleridge comes out of it badly, despite the sympathy we may feel for her in her unenviable position. Her husband's friends clearly regarded her as the wrong woman for Coleridge; one who, as Dorothy Wordsworth put it, would have made a very good wife for 'another man'. It is kinder to say not that she *failed* as Coleridge's wife but that it was her misfortune to be locked in marriage with one who turned out to be so different from her not unreasonable expectations. She suffered after all quite as much as he did in her different way.

Yet, though comparisons between her and Mary Evans or Asra must finally be tentative, they may be justified when their object is to account for the breakdown of genius; particularly of a genius claiming that love was its 'vital air'. We are drawn into a consideration of what Coleridge meant by 'love', and to inquire whether one 'love' suited him better than another. As we retrace the history of these personal relationships a number of pointers do in fact emerge to suggest that either Mary or Asra might more adequately have met Coleridge's needs than did his wife, with the reservation always that no woman probably could have fulfilled them completely. Both Mary and Asra seemed more relaxed and affectionate than his wife in their relations with him, and yet were able firmly to influence his behaviour by opposing his subtle intellectualism with forthright common sense. As 'soothers' they offered the love and sympathy he needed, and at the same time they possessed notable 'Abyssinian maid' qualities. As she aged into old-maidishness Asra, it is true, became as fond of local tittle-tattle as was Mrs Coleridge, yet, like Mary Evans,

---

[1] The influence of Mary Evans may be traced, I believe, on "Kubla Khan" and "Lewti" (see Appendix II); Asra's is detectable in "Christabel" and "Love" (see Appendix IV).

she had a range of cultural and intellectual interests, and an imaginative response to the incidents of daily life, vastly superior to Sara Fricker's.

The courtship letters Coleridge wrote to his wife have not survived, but there are indications that they lacked the ease of manner which marked his correspondence with Mary and Asra. Frequently he found himself obliged to apologize to Southey for not writing often enough to Sara. He would protest that only a day or two before 'was I pouring forth the Heart to Sara Fricker', an expression scarcely redolent of genuine affection. His letters to her sisters were chill with cold formality and, as he paid his respects to his bride-to-be (very often through Southey!), the tone was nervous and dutiful, never enthusiastic. He seemed to be involved less with writing love-letters than in self-defensive litigation:

> With regard to neglect respecting —— [Sara Fricker], do you accuse me justly? I have written 5 or 4 letters since my absence—received one. I am not conscious of having injured her otherwise, than by having mistaken the ebullience of *schematism* for affection, which a moment's reflection might have told me, is not a plant of so mushroom a growth—had it ever not been counteracted by a prior attachment / but my whole Life has been a series of Blunders! God have mercy upon me—for I am a most miserable Dog—
>
> The most criminal action of my Life was the 'first letter I wrote to ——'. I had worked myself to such a pitch, that I scarcely knew I was writing like an hypocrite—
>
> However it still remains for me to be externally Just though my Heart is withered within me—and Life seems now to give me disgust rather than pain—
>
> My Love to your Mother and to Edith [Sara's sister]—and to whomever it is right or convenient.
>
> God almighty bless you / and (a forlorn wish!)
>
> S. T. Coleridge.[1]

One may infer something of the frigidity of their relationship from the ghastly jocularity of some of the letters he wrote to her after they were married:

> —If you read this Letter with half the Tenderness, with which it is written, it will do you and both of us, GOOD; & contribute it's share to the turning of a mere Cat-hole into a Dove's nest! You know Sally Pally! I must have a Joke—or it would not be me![2]

[1] CL, I, 132.   [2] ibid, II, 888.

Since he married her out of a mistaken notion of 'duty' there was little natural affection between them at the outset. In time a better relationship grew up, as was inevitable, but the affection was rarely spontaneous.

The contrast between the cold formality of this courtship and his earlier infatuation with Mary Evans could scarcely be more marked. Coleridge met Mary and her three sisters through her brother, a fellow-pupil originally at Christ's Hospital, and it was at once as though Mary provided a focal point for all those adolescent yearnings which had previously lacked a fixed objective. With Mary he began the sort of love-affair he had always pictured—roses, roses all the way:

> Oh, from sixteen to nineteen what hours of Paradise had Allen and I in escorting the Miss Evanses home on a Saturday, . . . and we used to carry thither, of a summer morning, the pillage of the flower gardens within six miles of town, with Sonnet or Love Rhyme wrapped round the nose-gay.[1]

Some of the poems which Mary may have inspired, notably *An Effusion at Evening* and *Lines on an Autumnal Evening*, were among Coleridge's happiest poems.[2] Stimulated by the novelty of reciprocated affection his feelings sought outlet in poetry and he experienced, perhaps for the first time, the joy which ever afterwards he was to associate with the harmonious integration of thought and feeling.

His letters to the Evans family (he was on affectionate terms with all of them) evinced a charming ease of manner and a teasing, playful good humour, quite different from the restrained formality which stamped his Fricker correspondence. Only very occasionally were they marred by mawkishness.[3] Signing himself 'Brother Coly' he gossiped amiably to Mary's sisters, while to Mrs Evans he observed: 'I *write* to others, but my Pen talks to you,' and he signed himself 'Your grateful and affectionate Boy'.[4] Over a lengthy period his letters to Mary were almost invariably high-spirited, as no other sequence of his letters was, after he left Cambridge. One extract may serve as illustration (there are many others equally light-hearted, containing droll anecdotes of the Cambridge don who fell into a pond of chick-weed, and of Mr De la Peuche, his violin teacher). He described with mock

[1] Life, 13.   [2] See pp. 60–1 below.   [3] See, for example, CL, I, 21–2.
[4] ibid, I, 30, 48–9.

seriousness how one Saturday night the ghost of Gray accosted him:

—I am the Ghost of Gray—there lives a young Lady (then he mentioned *your* name) of whose judgment I entertain so high an opinion, that *her* approbation of my Works would make the turf lie lighter on me: present her with this book—and transmit it to her as soon as possible—adding my Love to her. And as for you, O Young Man (*now* he addressed himself to me) write no more verses—in the first place, your poetry is vile stuff; and secondly (here he sighed almost to bursting) all Poets go to - - ll, we are so intolerably addicted to the Vice of Lying!—He vanished—and convinced me of the truth of his last dismal account by the sulphureous stink, which he left behind him.

His first mandate I have obeyed, and, I hope, you will receive *safe* your ghostly admirer's present—but so far have I been from obeying his second injunction, that I never had the scribblomania stronger on me, than for these last three or four days—nay, not content with suffering it myself, I must pester those, I love best, with the blessed effects of my disorder.[1]

The letter concluded with three of his poems, and a modest disclaimer of their lack of the 'Wit, Sense, Elegance, or Beauty' possessed by herself, delivered with the certainty that she would fall asleep perusing their dullness. The good-humoured self-effacement is quite delightful.

Some six years later he developed a similarly informal relationship with Asra, again forming affectionate links with the entire family. He met Asra in October 1799, shortly after his return from Germany, and it was a case of love at first sight. (A similar intimacy developed at the same time between Wordsworth and Asra's sister, Mary, though Coleridge was not then aware of this.) As he had done with the Evanses he again flirted with other daughters of the family, and discovered afresh the facility for writing gossip 'as gay as the Lark that sings high o'er the Lea'.[2] He began writing love-poetry again, light-hearted and playful for the most part but, since he was married, not altogether free now from constraint. Under cover of seemingly innocent fantasies, and half-apologetically, he imagined himself *marrying* into

[1] ibid, i, 27–8, 49–50.   [2] ibid, ii, 754.

the Hutchinson family, carefully directing this impulse away from the real object of his affections however. Thus, he advised Joanna, Asra's youngest sister, to seek in marriage a fellow like himself:

> Such a one now *as me* (*Nota bene, I'm married,*
> *And Coals to Newcastle must never be carried!!*)[1]

The element of wish-fulfilment here was only thinly disguised by the levity of tone and obliquity of reference.

The records of these halcyon days are disappointingly scanty, yet they suffice to indicate how closely this interlude resembled the earlier Cambridge idyll, and how different it was from Coleridge's overtures to the Frickers. The affectionate nature of his ties with the Hutchinson circle may be judged from the tone of this doggerel epistle:

> Wednesday, Aug. 19. 1801
> Respected Miss Is'bel [Isabella Addison],
> Joanna, my Dear!
> This comes to you hoping.—We're happy to hear
> By a Pigeon, that early this morn did appear
> At our window with two Billet-deux in it's Bill,
> That safe, wind and limb, you had reach'd Gallow Hill
> The Mare [all obedient to Isabel's will]
> Two such beautiful Girls in so *knowing* a Pha'ton
> (*Mem. A Board nail'd behind with a name and a date on*)
> Two such *very* sweet Girls in a Taxer so green,
> Miss Addison driving as bright as a Queen
> And Joanna so gay—by the ghost of old Jehu,
> It was well worth a shilling, my Lasses! to see you!
> Why, even the Dust fell in love, I'll be bound,
> With you both, and for Love could not rest on the ground
> And Mary, for gladness & joy did not scant any
> When she said Tom & you, with the Horse, Mare, & A[ntony.]
> But this topic [I fear] I've ex[hausted 'twere better
> With some news and advice to enliven my letter
> But e]nough is as good as a feast—and for More,
> Why, you know, it might surfeit—at least, make one snore,
> But *one thing* indeed I am *forc'd* to declare,
> You are both fair as Angels, and good as you're fair,
> And I'll purchase a glazier's diamond, my Lasses,
> To scribble your names on all windows & glasses.[2]

[1] CL, II, 754.   [2] ibid.

The resuscitated energy Asra's affection gave him produced better things than this, of course, as *On Revisiting the Sea-Shore*, *Love*, and *A Day-Dream* can testify. Under her gentle influence he felt himself a 'whole man' again:

> Dear Asra, woman beyond utterance dear!
> This Love which ever welling at my heart,
> Now in its living fount doth heave and fall,
> Now overflowing pours thro' every part
> Of all my frame, and fills and changes all.[1]

Prior to this access of fresh inspiration it had been, as he said, 'a long [time] since I have cropt a flowering weed on the sweet Hill of Poesy'.[2]

It was not only these delightfully relaxed relationships he developed with them which endeared Mary and Asra to Coleridge; his nature required something more solid than that. We may question his claim that he could have been happy with a servant girl had she only responded to his love. The chameleon-like instability of his own nature required a complementary strength, and this the robust common sense of Mary and Asra to some extent provided. Mary Evans, for example, was no Dora Spenlowe figure. The forceful tone of her letter to Coleridge entreating him to abandon the Pantisocratic nonsense, and the insight it showed into his impetuous weakness, reveal that she had a mind of her own, and was not afraid to state it:

> . . . I conjure you, Coleridge! earnestly and solemnly conjure you, to consider long and deeply, before you enter into any rash Schemes. There is an Eagerness in your Nature, which is ever hurrying you into the sad Extreme. I have heard that you mean to leave England: and on a Plan so absurd and extravagant, that were I for a moment to imagine it *true*, I should be obliged to listen with a more patient Ear to Suggestions, which I have rejected a thousand Times with scorn and anger—yes! whatever Pain I might suffer I should be forced to exclaim—"O what a noble Mind is here *o'erthrown*. Blasted with Exstacy"!—You have a Country. Does it demand nothing of You? You have doting Friends. Will you break their Hearts?[3]

---

[1] "To Asra", ll. 4–8, PW 361.   [2] CL, II, 752.

[3] ibid, I, 112–13. Though she may have written this letter at George Coleridge's request, its forceful tone and style are entirely her own.

Whereas Mrs Coleridge found her husband's intellectual subtlety beyond her, Mary was not afraid to meet it head on, as when, with customary forthrightness, she pricked the bubble of his pretended atheism:

> There is a God—Coleridge! Though I have been told (*indeed* I do not believe it) that you doubt of his Existence and disbelieve a hereafter.—No! you have too much Sensibility to be an Infidel.

She went on to outline in this letter her own attitude to religion, and the remarkable thing about this is that in its assimilation of faith to reason (Lockean rather than Kantian, admittedly) it not only tied in with the then state of Coleridge's own views but, more importantly, pointed in the direction Coleridge's whole subsequent religious development was to take. As she put it, they thought in all things alike:

> You know I never was rigid in my opinions concerning Religion —and have always thought *Faith* to be only Reason applied to a particular Subject—In short, I am the same Being, as [of whom] you used to say—We thought in all things alike.

Coleridge has confirmed that such an intellectual affinity existed between them: 'She WAS VERY lovely, Southey! We formed each other's minds— our ideas were blended—Heaven bless her!— I cannot forget her.' In the same letter, incidentally, he revealed his distaste for the Fricker family's intrusive evangelicalism, which he feared would wreck the principle of religious tolerance on which Pantisocracy was to be based:

> *That* Mrs Fricker—we shall have her teaching the Infants *Christianity*,—I mean—that mongrel whelp that goes under its name— teaching them by stealth in some ague-fit of Superstition![1]

There are plenty of indications that Coleridge and his wife did not see eye to eye on theological matters.

Mary Evans also had strong cultural affinities with Coleridge. She quoted Shakespeare with facility, and discussed with him subjects ranging from Bowles's poetry and the latest London plays to the influence of Fox on the current political situation. She appeared to have an interest similar to Asra's in the textual criticism of poetry.[2] It was not therefore mere gallantry which induced Coleridge to place her in the foremost intellectual rank of her sex:

[1] CL, I, 123.   [2] ibid, I, 32, 51; and cf. p. 65 below.

> With quick perceptions of moral Beauty it was impossible for me
> not to admire in you your sensibility regulated by Judgment, your
> Gaiety proceeding from a cheerful Heart acting on the stores of a
> strong Understanding . . .
>
> Were you not possessed of a Mind and of a Heart above the usual
> Lot of Women I should not have written you sentiments, that would
> be unintelligible to three fourths of your Sex.[1]

Intellectually, she was probably more distinguished than Asra.

What Asra may have lacked in intellectual perspicacity she
made up for in what Miss Coburn calls her 'resilient northern
practicality'.[2] Ernest de Selincourt, with a choice of phrase peculiarly significant for the present study, described Asra as 'the
family *sheet anchor*' in the Wordsworth household. The theme of
Miss Coburn's essay is that Asra excelled above all in 'vigorous
common-sense'. The fullest description we have of her person is
given in Professor de Selincourt's *Dorothy Wordsworth*, and it bears
out this impression:

> Sara Hutchinson was not imposing in appearance. Like Dorothy
> only a little over five feet in height, rather plain-featured, and with
> a plump, dumpy figure devoid of grace and dignity, she was only
> redeemed from the commonplace by a delicately fair skin and a
> profusion of light brown hair. But those who looked closer noted in
> her face a peculiarly sweet expression, and she had a real distinction
> of mind and character. More matter of fact than Dorothy, less ex-
> citable, and without her sensitive alertness of mind, she had a keener
> sense of quiet fun, and was, moreover, a woman of considerable in-
> tellectual gifts, fully worthy to be the intimate friend of two great
> poets. 'The combination', wrote Coleridge, 'of natural shrewdness
> and a disposition to innocent humour joined with perfect simplicity
> and tenderness is what distinguishes her from her sister [Mary
> Hutchinson], 'whose character is of a more solemn caste.'[3]

Her letters certainly reveal some distinction of mind and considerable intellectual gifts, which explains possibly why so many
of them have survived.[4]

Books, agriculture, and politics were her chief interests; indeed
it was partly because of her strong political views that she came
to dislike Coleridge's eldest son. As Hartley Coleridge put it:

> Had I been an out-and-outer, she could have understood it, but
> my mixture of old cavalier toryism and German liberalism . . .

[1] ibid, I, 130–1.   [2] LSH, xxxviii.   [3] ibid, xxii, xxiii.
[4] But cf. p. 64 below.

puzzled her, and she was rather shocked at my almost total disbelief in the existence of political integrity in any sect or party, to which, nevertheless, the time gives too much proof.[1]

Coleridge himself set a similar premium on political integrity, though not quite with Asra's naïveté. Though originally she was more Toryist than he, later he gravitated increasingly towards her political standpoint.

Asra was certainly no blue-stocking, but she had qualities Coleridge valued more—the Poole-like qualities of complete self-control and serene independence of moral outlook. Miss Coburn's comparison of Asra's and Mrs Coleridge's letters illustrates well this radical difference in their natures and it suggests, I think, why Mrs Coleridge's mind was totally incapable of bolstering her husband's:

> In Mrs Coleridge's letters, whether the matter is cheerful or 'vexatious', all is in disorder. Everything tumbles out, helter-skelter, dropped and picked up again, repeated, apologized for, till we do not know whether to laugh, cry, or scream. Her words come freely but out of a state of perpetual consternation . . . Asra's letters flow evenly, steadily, making for their destination, showing a ripple here and there, occasionally a rock below the surface, sometimes making an interesting change of level, but always clear, under command...[2]

Coleridge himself rarely commented in this objective way on Asra, but a remark he addressed privately to Daniel Stuart summed up what he valued in her character:

> If Sense, Sensibility, Sweetness of Temper, perfect simplicity and unpretending Nature, joined to shrewdness and entertainingness make a valuable Woman, Sara Hutchinson is so.[3]

She was far from being a dull person. 'Respectability' and 'prudence', as Mr Potter remarks, were two of Mrs Coleridge's words; Asra put respectability farther down in her list of considerations. She was, Miss Coburn says, 'incomparably the freer spirit' and somewhat iconoclastic towards Mrs Coleridge's sacred cows.[4]

Asra, like Poole, faced life squarely and confidently: like Shakespeare's Beatrice she could tell a church by daylight. Again, Miss Coburn hits the nail precisely: with Asra '. . . whatever is going on, the verb is in the affirmative mood, the active

[1] HL, 188.   [2] LSH, xxxvii–xxxviii.   [3] ibid.   [4] ibid.

voice and the present tense'. Such a positive outlook allied to her
sturdy self-reliance enabled her to exert a 'bracing' effect more
salutary to Coleridge's weakness than his wife's proneness to self-
pity, which too closely resembled his own condition to provide
the necessary support:

> Drenched by a sudden storm, [Asra] calls on friends in Patterdale
> only to find them away from home, Henry not yet arrived, and
> nothing as it ought to be. What is she to do? Does she sit down and
> write an anxious letter describing all the accidents and mishaps that
> have led up to this uncomfortable crisis, as Sara Coleridge would
> have done? No, because she is not uncomfortable and it is not a
> crisis. She stirs up the fire, sits down and dries herself off, has a cup
> of tea, and recites happily to herself some lines she has transcribed
> for William.

> > A steaming bowl, a blazing fire,
> > What greater good can man desire?
> > 'Twere worth a wise man's while to try
> > The utmost anger of the sky:
> > To *seek* for thoughts of gloomy cast,
> > If such the bright amends at last.

> It is inevitable, if very unfair, that her letters and Mrs Coleridge's
> should be compared. Asra was infinitely more favoured by events.
> And yet we cannot fail to see that 'Hutton', as the children called
> her, whatever their respective circumstances, would always have
> made a better life for herself than Mrs S.T.C., and the contrast
> considerably increases the pathos of Mrs Coleridge's position. For
> Sara Hutchinson was incomparably the freer spirit.[1]

In the firm resilience of their characters, therefore, as well as in
breadth of cultural and intellectual interests, Mary Evans and
Asra outshone Mrs Coleridge.

They excelled, too, in another respect: each seems to have
possessed the 'Abyssinian maid' qualities in which Mrs Coleridge
was deficient. The Mary Evans relationship did not have com-
parable weight in Coleridge's life with that of Asra, yet, for a
time at any rate, Coleridge probably associated Mary Evans very
closely with the creative imagination. If, as seems likely, she in-

---

[1] ibid, xxxvi. Asra's firm influence had an equally bracing effect on Coleridge's son, Derwent, apparently. In October 1804 Derwent (who was then
four years old) stayed with Asra at Park House to his great improvement:
'... he was cowardly and effeminate and indolent before he went, and is now
even daring and active' (see Whalley, 56).

spired the poem *An Effusion at Evening*, then it appears that he
represented her love as virtually synonymous with inspiration—
'IMAGINATION, Mistress of my Love', he wrote:

> Aid, lovely Sorc'ress! aid the Poet's dream.
> With faery wand O bid my Love arise,
> The dewy brilliance dancing in her Eyes;
> As erst she woke with soul-entrancing Mien
> The thrill of Joy extatic yet serene. (13–18)

This first draft was worked up some months later into *Lines on an
Autumnal Evening* which, since it was published when Coleridge
knew that he could not marry Mary Evans, was possibly redolent
with nostalgia for his past relationship with her. Chambers had
little doubt that the 'Maid' (also addressed as 'my Love'),
described in both these poems, was Mary Evans, but direct biographical evidence is lacking; indeed, in a variant text of the
second poem the 'Maid' is associated with a Miss Nesbitt. This
circumstance does not rule out a connection with Miss Evans,
since there is ample evidence—as in *Kisses*, also written in 1793,
and associated in turn with 'Mary', 'Nesbitt', and, finally, 'Sara'
—that Coleridge never hesitated to adapt a poem to suit a particular exigency. Both poems moreover assume a lengthier relationship between poet and 'Maid' than Coleridge is believed to
have had with Fanny Nesbitt. Miss Nesbitt's name first appears
in Coleridge's biography in July 1793, when he travelled with her
on the coach from Exeter to Tiverton, whereas the first draft of
the poem was written in August 1792, about seven months after
Coleridge met Mary Evans. The following extract from *Lines on
an Autumnal Evening* suggests that by 1793 Coleridge had been
looking to Mary for both inspiration and emotional fulfilment
over a considerable period of time:

> Now sheds the sinking Sun a deeper gleam,
> Aid, lovely Sorceress! aid thy Poet's dream!
> With faery wand O bid the Maid arise,
> Chaste Joyance dancing in her bright-blue eyes;
> As erst when from the Muses' calm abode
> I came, with Learning's meed not unbestowed;
> When as she twin'd a laurel round my brow,
> And met my kiss, and half-return'd my vow,
> O'er all my frame shot rapid my thrill'd heart,
> And every nerve confess'd the electric dart. (13–22)

In lines which closely resemble *Lewti*, the poem then evokes her image:

> O dear Deceit! I see the Maiden rise,
> Chaste Joyance dancing in her bright-blue eyes!
> When first the lark high-soaring swells his throat,
> Mocks the tir'd eye, and scatters the loud note,
> I trace her footsteps on the accustom'd lawn,
> I mark her glancing mid the gleam of dawn.
>
> When the bent flower beneath the night-dew weeps
> And on the lake the silver lustre sleeps,
> Amid the paly radiance soft and sad,
> She meets my lonely path in moon-beams clad.
> With her along the streamlet's bank I rove;
> With her I list the warblings of the grove;
> And seems in each low wind her voice to float
> Lone-whispering Pity in each soothing note! (23–36)

It is recorded that this poem was read by Coleridge to a party of college friends on 7 November 1793, when he was so harassed by debts and other difficulties that he was about to run away and enlist.[1] These circumstances may lend added biographical significance to the concluding movement of the poem where he repines for the trouble-free days of early childhood, before personal relationships were marred by conflicting feelings or (to use the archetypal image) before life's 'voyage' was beset by tempests:

> So tossed by storms along Life's wild'ring way,
> Mine eye reverted views that cloudless day,
> When by my native brook I wont to rove,
> While Hope with kisses nurs'd the Infant Love . . .
> Dear native brook! where first young Poesy
> Stared wildly-eager in her noontide dream!
> Where blameless pleasures dimple Quiet's cheek,
> As water-lilies ripple thy slow stream!
> Dear native haunts! Where Virtue still is gay,
> Where Friendship's fix'd star sheds a mellow'd ray,
> Where Love a crown of thornless Roses wears . . . (77–89)

The poem ended on a note of dejection, with resigned acceptance that the moonlight, associated throughout the poem with his mistress, must now give place to night, and 'Disappointment's wintry desert'.

[1] See PW 51n.

> Scenes of my Hope! the aching eye ye leave
> Like yon bright hues that paint the clouds of eve!
> Tearful and saddening with the sadden'd blaze
> Mine eye the gleam pursues with wistful gaze:
> Sees shades on shades with deeper tint impend,
> Till chill and damp the moonless night descend. (101–6)

Despite its Augustan stylization, the voice here was peculiarly Coleridge's own, especially in its imagist use of moonlight and wandering, and its close association of poetry with serenely flowing water and 'blameless' virtue.[1]

The Sigh, written partly to remind Southey of the sacrifice Coleridge had made in abandoning Mary, contained a similar theme, though this time the conclusion it reached—that true love cannot easily be put by—was identical with that in *Lewti*. Again, we find nostalgia for the happiness Mary Evans had brought him:

> When Youth his faery reign began
> Ere Sorrow had proclaim'd me man;
> While Peace the present hour beguil'd,
> And all the lovely Prospect smil'd;
> Then Mary! 'mid my lightsome glee
> I heav'd the painless Sigh for thee. (1–6)

Yet, though accepting the necessity of yielding to the 'stern decree' (by marrying Sara Fricker), the poem ends, portentously:

> Thy Image may not banish'd be—
> Still, Mary! still I sigh for thee.

And her image *did* remain with him, reappearing in *On a Discovery Made Too Late* and, more pointedly, in *Lewti*.[2]

This early love-affair may have been a more important event in Coleridge's life than is generally supposed (so much of the crucial evidence having unfortunately been destroyed). Admittedly, he dramatized its significance, focusing the spotlight on his own feelings rather than Mary's:

I am calm, dear Southey! as an Autumnal Day, when the Sky is covered with grey moveless Clouds. To *love her* [Mary] Habit has made unalterable: I had placed her in the sanctuary of my Heart, nor can she be torn from thence but with the Strings that grapple it

---

[1] This point has some bearing on my interpretation of the sacred river in "Kubla Khan"; see pp. 138–40 below.

[2] Her image may have influenced "Kubla Khan" also; see p. 153 below.

to Life. This Passion however, divested as it now is of all Shadow of Hope, seems to lose it's disquieting Power. Far distant, and never more to behold or hear of her, I shall sojourn in the Vale of Men sad and in loneliness, yet not unhappy. He cannot be long wretched who dares be actively virtuous. I am well assured, that she loves me as a favourite Brother. When she was present, she was to me only as a very dear Sister: it was in absence, that I felt those gnawings of Suspense... The Struggle has been well nigh too much for me—but praised be the All-Merciful! the feebleness of exhausted Feelings has produced a Calm, and my Heart stagnates into Peace.[1]

It was probably true that he had loved her 'almost to madness'.[2] Despite the 'stern decree' he tried, after catching a glimpse of her in Wrexham shortly afterwards, to re-establish relations. On receiving her letter advising him to forget about Pantisocracy, he spent six weeks in 'a waking Night-mair of Spirits' before writing:

Too long has my Heart been the torture house of Suspense. After infinite struggles of Irresolution I will at last dare to request of you, Mary! that you will communicate to me whether or no you are engaged to Mr —— [Fryer Todd]. I conjure you not to consider this request as presumptuous Indelicacy. Upon mine Honor, I have made it with no other Design or Expectation than that of arming my fortitude by total hopelessness... For four years I have *endeavored* to smother a very ardent attachment—in what degree I have succeeded, you must know better than I can.[3]

His final leave-taking was more dignified—'Vale, ah! formosa Maria!'[4] But even while arrangements went ahead for his marriage to Sara he told Southey privately that Mary should have been standing in Miss Fricker's place: '... my ideal Standard of female Excellence rises not above that Woman.'[5] He never ceased to regard the rupture of this love-affair as one of the major disappointments of his life.

The Evans family 'always understood' that Mary destroyed all Coleridge's correspondence to her, but in fact she preserved many of his poems and also his valedictory letter to her containing the sentence 'Far distant from you I shall journey through the vale of Men.'[6] He alluded to the Susquehanna project but,

[1] CL, I, 145.
[2] 'I loved her, Southey, almost to madness. Her Image was never absent from me for three Years—for *more* than three Years' (ibid, I, 113).
[3] ibid, I, 129–30.   [4] "Ave, Atque Vale!", PW 56.   [5] CL, I, 145.
[6] ibid, I, 144n.

if she turned this letter up any time after 1802, did she recognize, one wonders, its prognostic accuracy. Or did she notice the lines he added to the 1796 version of the second *Chatterton Monody*? If so, she could hardly fail to have realized that he believed her loss had 'blacken'd the fair promise of my spring'.[1] Her own marriage to Fryer Todd turned out badly,[2] yet she had embodied practically all the qualities Coleridge desired in a wife: deep affection, moral strength, affinity of cultural and intellectual tastes, and, above all, a capacity for inspirational regeneration. If in 1816 she read *Kubla Khan* did she suspect it might be herself that lurked behind the vision 'once I saw' of a damsel whose influence, could he but revive it, would enable him to re-erect the paradisal dome, and earn the ritual dread of one possessing true poetic afflatus? It is impossible to say for, having once parted from Coleridge, she prudently kept him at a distance: 'Farewell —Coleridge! I shall always feel that I have been your *Sister*.'[3]

There is no need to demonstrate how many of Coleridge's attempts to resuscitate the creative energy were associated with Asra; her influence on his work is well established.[4] For ten years his love for her was the focus of his emotional life and it overflowed in countless directions right up to *The Friend* venture, which she largely inspired. The sad thing is that we know so little about *his* effect on her for, so far as is known, only three letters which she wrote during the crucial period 1799–1805 have survived, none of which concerns Coleridge. She, who was right at the centre of the nexus of relationships formed around Wordsworth and Coleridge, the recipient of Coleridge's passionate yet hopeless poems and letters, has left no record of her feelings upon receiving *Dejection: an Ode*, nor have we any insight into what her feelings were when Coleridge set out for Malta in 1804 to try to forget his love for her. By 1818 she had withdrawn herself from all involvement and went out of her way to avoid him. Unlike Mary Evans she remained a spinster, and her comment on mar-

---

[1] PW 130. This significant line appeared in stanzas which Coleridge added to the poem after parting from Mary Evans (see p. 82 below).

[2] Life, 211; CL, III, 85–6, 91.   [3] CL, I, 113; and cf. p. 277 below.

[4] See George Whalley, *Coleridge and Sara Hutchinson and the Asra Poems* (London, 1955).

riage might be interpreted as expressing relief that she had never been linked in that way with Coleridge:

> . . . Old Maid as I am don't think that, though I firmly believe the balance of *comfort* is on our side, I am a favorer of a single life—comfort is but a meagre thing after all—but I have seen such misery in the marriage life as would *appal* you if you had seen it. Such millstones about the necks of worthy men! that I would have you be *wary*— . . . Of course you will not suppose that I think all the fault belongs to the women.[1]

These were, however, the sentiments of mature experience, not of the years of infatuation.

Leaving aside the question of whether she ever seriously entertained the notion of marrying a divorcee, or whether she would have preferred marrying John Wordsworth to incurring the animosity of Coleridge's children,[2] we may nevertheless speculate on the sort of partner Asra might have made for Coleridge, particularly as he himself frequently imagined what it would be like to be married to her. As we have seen, she was well fitted in temperament and intellectual qualities to be Coleridge's wife. The many poems addressed to her confirm that she possessed also the vital inspirational attributes. She had too what might be called 'secondary Abyssinian maid' qualities, which Coleridge would certainly have valued in his wife, and which Wordsworth actually did exploit in her. Coleridge complained that there was no dear heart that loved his verses for, though his wife occasionally helped in the final phase of transcribing his work for the press, her influence was generally cramping rather than liberating. Asra, on the other hand, not only cheerfully spent whole days in the drudgery of an amanuensis, but obviously enjoyed hearing Wordsworth and Coleridge recite their verses. She was, furthermore, capable of suggesting textual improvements. Wordsworth, as Miss Darbishire has shown, encouraged Asra to criticize his poems and often made use of her criticism. Her objections to *The Leech-gatherer* caused him to rewrite a key stanza which is now the imaginative core of the poem.[3] It made Coleridge's lot

[1] LSH, xxxv.

[2] Family tradition has it, supported by an entry in one of Coleridge's notebooks, that John Wordsworth wished, or the family wished him, to marry Asra (see LSH, xxvi; Whalley, 54; Life, 164–6).

[3] See Helen Darbishire, *Wordsworth, Poems in Two Volumes*, 1807 (Oxford, 1952), Appendix III.

F

all the more bitter therefore that Wordsworth had so many willing petticoats to serve him—'three wives', as Crabb Robinson put it—while he had none.[1]

The general incompatibility between Coleridge's temperament and his wife's will emerge in the ensuing chapters. After the brief honeymoon rapture Sara showed little capacity for promoting her husband's work. Because this is an oft-told and familiar tale, it may be more interesting, instead of following the usual track of S. T. Coleridge's and Dorothy Wordsworth's strictures on Sara, to consider the testimonies of the Coleridge children, who owed allegiance to both parents.

Young Sara Coleridge was, if anything, biased in her mother's favour and constantly refused to disparage her intellectual qualities. Nevertheless, she could not conceal her mother's radical deficiencies as a poet's wife:

> The sort of wife to have lived harmoniously with my father [she informed her own husband] need not have possessed high intellect or a perfect temper—but greater enthusiasm of temperament than my mother possessed. She never admires anything she doesn't understand. Some women, like Mrs Wilson and Mrs Wordsworth, see the skirts of a golden cloud—they have unmeasured faith in a sun of glory and [a] sublime region stretching out far beyond their ken, and proud and happy to think that it belongs to them are ready to give all they have to give in return. This faith, this docility, is quite alien to the Fricker temperament. . . They are too literal and do not believe as I do that matters of imagination . . . can work as many practical effects as what we see with our eyes and touch with our hands, and then my mother's very honesty stood in her way. . . . She has no power over her mind to keep the thought of petty cares and passing interests (the importance of which is often mere matter of fancy) in abeyance. She never compares on a wide scale the real importance of the thing with the degree of energy and time and vital spirit that she spends upon it; and though her talents are above mediocrity and her understanding clear and good—on its own range—she has no taste whatever for abstractions. . . But to say broadly or to imply unreservedly that she is harsh-tempered or narrow-minded . . . or more unintellectual than many women who have pleased my father is to misrepresent the subject. My father has a good opinion of her understanding and a very high one of her personal attractions.[2]

[1] Whalley, 150.   [2] CF, 105–6.

For all its filial loyalty, this analysis pin-points three important deficiencies in Mrs Coleridge's character, namely: an incapacity to enthuse over ideas, an almost total lack of imaginative response to life, and an impatience with anything that could be classed under 'abstractions'. Bored by the intellectual pursuits that engrossed her husband she had, as Stephen Potter put it, '. . . no world of her own, only a suburb, received at fourth hand from the standards of Bristol respectability'.[1] Tension manifested itself in a number of small ways, as in her irritableness when he stayed up reading or composing, instead of coming to bed.[2] It also embarrassed her that she found herself, when questioned, quite incapable of saying what her husband's political sentiments were, and forced to seek enlightenment from his friends: 'It is very unpleasant to me to be often asked if Coleridge has changed his political sentiments, for I know not properly how to reply. Pray furnish me.'[3] Such was their lack of contact after three years of living together.

She was mentally no less isolated from her eldest son, whose interests—literary, philosophical, political—were, like his father's, almost wholly intellectual. These interests opened up a world for father and son in which she had no part. She sent Hartley once a copy of Young Sara's *Pretty Lessons for Good Children* and her son's active mind at once began surmising whether the fables of Aesop, Phaedrus, Pilpay, and Avienus were not in fact allegories suggested by the 'Zoographic Hieroglyphics of Aegypt', whereas Spenser's *Mother Hubbard's Tale* and the children's books of an earlier age might more properly be considered burlesque satires. He started to develop these thoughts then, recollecting that it was to his mother he wrote, broke off abruptly:

> But I dare say all this is very uninteresting to you, who were never fond of critical discussion, or discussion of any sort at any time, and least of all when you are anxious for information of a more household interest. I am afraid that we small fry of the press are about the worst letter-writers in the world. We always smell of the shop so confoundedly, and will be scribbling about literature or politics, or mayhap metaphysics, to people who would rather hear news of their friends or economics of the wardrobe.[4]

Hartley's letters to his mother were full of this sort of thing: re-

[1] S. Potter, *Coleridge and S. T. C.* (London, 1935), 56.
[2] See Sandford, I, 239; II, 291.   [3] ibid, I, 300–1.   [4] HL, 173–4.

peatedly he broke off a discussion of Wordsworth's poetry or of his father's failure to finish *Christabel* to allay her anxiety about the state of his socks or shirts.[1] E. L. Griggs is right in saying that we should pity rather than condemn Mrs Coleridge, wife and mother to so eccentric a pair:

> . . . a good, honest, practical, and intelligent woman, she might have lived contentedly with a successful family; as it happened, she had the misfortune to marry a man of rare genius and to be the mother of 'the oddest of all God's creatures . . . [who] becomes quainter and quainter every day'.[2]

None the less, she certainly wounded both father and son where their susceptibilities were most tender. Hartley's literary work during 1832–3, when he published his *Poems* and *Biographia Borealis, or Lives of Distinguished Northerns*, both of which were favourably received by the critics, suggests that with more encouragement he might have made a moderately successful career as a writer. But his mother, distrustful of bread and cheese by literary means, gave him no encouragement and did her best to dissuade him from going to Leeds where all his best work was achieved. After the Leeds period his life tended increasingly to become as aimless and unproductive as his father's had been during its middle years.

Sara proved anything but encouraging to the literary activities of her family; indeed she seemed to take perverse delight from the poor reception which, initially, the *Lyrical Ballads* enjoyed. 'The Lyrical Ballads', she wrote to a friend, 'are laughed at and disliked by all with very few excepted.'[3] When the managers of Drury Lane returned the script of *Zapolya* for alteration, this again evoked her carping dissatisfaction with her husband who, she complained:

> . . . instead of instantly setting about [it] . . . got in a fit of despondency and was confined 3 weeks to his bed . . . he will alter his play for next season.
>
> You will also be sorry for another thing respecting him—Oh! when will he ever give his friends anything but pain? he has been so unwise as to publish his fragments of *Christabel* and *Koula-Khan*

---

[1] HL, 220; cf. 211, 176. Like his father, Hartley reached a point where he could scarcely endure reading Mrs Coleridge's letters (see HL, 127).
[2] CF, 229.   [3] ibid, 3.

[sic]. Murray is the publisher, and the price is 4s 6d—we were all sadly vexed when we read the advertizement of these things.[1]

Sara then is scarcely to be identified with the Abyssinian maid in 'Koula Khan'; she was perhaps more akin to the wailing woman!

She could have put up with her husband's eccentricities had he been 'successful' in the commercial sense. As one of five daughters (Mary, Edith, Sara, Martha, and Eliza) of the widow of a Gloucestershire manufacturer of sugar-pans who had been ruined by the stoppage of trade with America, she was brought up to appreciate the harsh realities of life. She understood as well as any Jane Austen character the sheer economic problem of providing for five unmarried daughters. Indeed, the elder Fricker girls were obliged to support themselves by their needles.[2] Hartley perceived how strongly such considerations weighed with his mother:

> You, I know, are always disposed to look with an eye of apprehension, if not of censure, on all matrimonial engagements, where ought is left to be provided for by the bounties of Tomorrow . . .[3]

Had Coleridge's books sold consistently, it may be doubted whether Sara would have cared much what they contained, so long as she could have held her head high in Bristol. As it was, the ideas he pursued were not only exasperatingly incomprehensible to her, but they did little to alleviate their financial difficulties. She doubtless felt that his books did not sell *because* of their strange ideas. He had actually married her in pursuance of an abstract and fanciful idea and, when that fell through, she became virtually an anachronism in his life, a person whom at any other period of his life he would have recognized as the least suitable of wives for himself. In her domestic routine his irregular mode of life, bookish and detached, was out of place and unpopular; it was a house more adapted to confinements than poetry or art.[4]

On almost every count, therefore, Mrs Coleridge fell short of

---

[1] ibid, 41.

[2] Life, 27; see Potter, op. cit., 52. Eliza and Martha Fricker, both of whom were unmarried, eked out a slender livelihood and never became dependent upon their relatives, Martha leaving an estate of £500. Mary Fricker, early left a widow on her husband's (Robert Lovell's) death, made every effort to be self-supporting (see CF, 230).

[3] HL, 98.   [4] S. Potter, op. cit., 56–7.

the ideal standard of excellence her husband sought in a wife. She rarely established a relaxed intimacy with him and in the end became sexually frigid, while in him the sexual urge remained strong. Whereas his own weak will required 'strength' as its complement, her 'Frickerish nerves', as Hartley called them, made her as prone to querulous self-pity as he was himself. Lacking in imagination and sensibility, 'the lightest weakest silliest woman' as Dorothy Wordsworth called her,[1] she was incapable either of enthusing over his work or of remotely sharing his cultural interests. Except in the brief period when she gave him sexual satisfaction she wholly failed to inspire him to creativity, and tended indeed to regard whatever he did achieve with discouraging or malicious cynicism. When they finally separated it must have been a relief to both of them. How different was this separation from the wrench he felt at parting from Mary Evans and Asra.

The frustration of Coleridge's feelings for Asra produced pain and suffering much worse than anything he experienced in regard to Mary Evans. The tragic unfolding of this story is the theme of the later chapters of this book. When communicating the news of Coleridge's death, Asra's comment was simply: 'Poor dear Coleridge is gone! He died a most calm and happy death— tho' he had suffered great pain for some time previous. He was opened—the disease was at his heart.'[2] The disease was indeed at his heart, and well she knew it. For ten years he had loved her as few women can have been loved, not like some disembodied angel, but passionately.

Either Mary or Asra, therefore, might have fulfilled the dual rôle of 'soother' and 'inspirer', whereas Sara Fricker succeeded in neither. Why *did* Coleridge marry her and so deprive his genius of its 'vital air', when, as he said, their temperaments were 'exact antitheses'? 'Never, I suppose, did the stern Match-maker bring together two minds so utterly contrariant in their primary and organical constitution.'[3] They could agree neither on choice of friends nor residence,[4] and his whole way of life exasperated her. How could this 'Meek daughter in the family of Christ' link her

[1] *Early Letters*, 303.
[2] LSH, xxxii. Coleridge died on 25 July 1834. He saw little of Asra following their quarrel in 1810 (see Chapter 10).
[3] CL, II, 832.   [4] Sandford, II, 2.

name moreover with that of a confessed 'infidel'?[1] Why should they have married at a time when he was patently in love with someone else, while she herself, it appears, was receiving attentions from two other men, one 'of large Fortune'?[2]

The customary explanation—that, like Burnet, he needed a wife in a hurry to meet the requirements of Pantisocracy—hardly goes deep enough. Why, for example, should he put that scheme before Mary Evans? His decision was, I think, influenced by certain other factors in a way entirely in accordance with what we know of his character and habitual motivation. The pressure exerted on him to marry Miss Fricker—'so much remonstrance that I am deranged'—was such that he had no effective counter to it. It is within the context of his wider personal relationships that his decision to do his 'duty' should be judged. The line he eventually followed was that best calculated to please his elder brother and Southey (and possibly Cottle), 'sheet-anchors' on whom he was exceptionally dependent at that time. Perplexed and miserable, afraid to act on his own initiative for fear of being wrong, he found it the line of least resistance to submit. To stick out against the pressure was to risk alienation and even the isolation which he dreaded, whereas marriage meant keeping in with the Bristol circle upon which he depended (much as he later depended on the Dove Cottage circle). He succumbed, and they married on 4 October 1795, Coleridge being just twenty-three.

One can sympathize with Coleridge in being the prisoner of his temperament and yet be shocked by his self-centredness and total want of consideration for Sara's feelings. With histrionic purposefulness he followed the path of abstract 'duty', regardless of the consequences and seemingly oblivious to the suffering such folly must entail:

> To lose her [Mary Evans]! I can rise above that selfish Pang. But to marry another. O Southey! bear with my weakness. Love makes all things pure and heavenly like itself:—but to marry a woman whom I do *not* love, to degrade her whom I call my Wife by making her the Instrument of low Desire, and on the removal of a desultory Appetite, to be perhaps not displeased with her Absence! Enough! These Refinements are the wildering Fires that lead me into Vice. Mark you, Southey! *I will do my Duty.*[3]

---

[1] See pp. 94–5 below for further discussion of this point.　　[2] CL, I, 151.
[3] ibid, I, 145.

Paradoxically, therefore, in doing his 'duty' he did Sara and his own moral nature the greatest affront conceivable, and in the long run he paid dearly for it. That great leading theme of his poetry—the tension between duty and desire—is thus seen to have its counterpart in his own marriage. It was not a promising beginning.

3

Thought and Feeling

'Resolved—but wretched' then, Coleridge made plans to marry a woman whom he did not love, 'but whom by every tie of Reason and Honour [he] *ought* to love'! Stoically he repressed his feelings for Mary Evans and, for a time at least, turned a blind eye to Sara's obvious shortcomings. Yet the strain told upon him: life's 'voyage' suddenly became both 'tempest-tossed in thought' and troubled by cross-currents of emotion, as many of the 1794–5 poems show.[1]

Though the complexity of Coleridge's intellectual development precludes any proper examination of it in a study of this kind, the briefest outline may suffice to indicate the formidable disparity between Sara's mind and his. Already his erudition was prodigious and fast becoming legendary: anything and everything was grist to the mill of what he wryly called his 'omni-pregnant nihili-parturient' genius. Yet for all its singular power and energy his mind, intellectually no less than emotionally, was still in an immature, formative stage of development. It was, like some highly precocious undergraduate's, tangential, inconsequential, divergent rather than convergent, and essentially unstable. Sir Humphry Davy's description of the 'brilliant images of greatness which floated upon it' and Wordsworth's account of it in *The Prelude* both bear out this impression.[2]

[1] See PW 58, 84–5 particularly.
[2] cf. Life, 169. Wordsworth wrote:
> . . . I have thought
> Of thee, thy learning, gorgeous eloquence,
> And all the strength and plumage of thy youth,
> Thy subtle speculations, toils abstruse
> Among the schoolmen, and Platonic forms
> Of wild ideal pageantry, shaped out
> From things well-matched or ill, and words for things,
> The self-created sustenance of a mind

Apart from the extraordinary diversity of his interests, his intellectual and moral life at this time was characterized chiefly by extreme earnestness and equally extreme uncertainty. The motto he prefixed to *Religious Musings* and the laboured didacticism of many of his early poetic pieces indicated the serious level of his interests.[1] Yet in politics, philosophy, and religion his convictions were quite unsettled and his thinking, though pyrotechnically brilliant sometimes, was in the last resort fluid and eclectic. Good-humouredly he recognized as much himself when later he looked back upon this period:

> It was the pride & passion of my Youth
> T'impersonate & colour moral Truth
> Rare allegories in those Days I spun,
> That oft had mystic senses oft'ner none.[2]

Not surprisingly, readers found his poetry 'too metaphysical', for he burdened it with a cognitive weight it could scarcely carry. As he himself admitted: 'I *think* too much for a Poet.'[3] Not until 1797–8 did he succeed in blending thought and feeling satisfactorily, but by then the tensions of 1794–6 had relaxed considerably.

In the grave earnestness of Coleridge's juvenilia one detects the embryonic strugglings of a moral intelligence which was to mature (in John Stuart Mill's phrase) into one of the two great seminal minds of the age.[4] Already the high ethical quality which is the hall-mark of his later prose writings was plainly in evidence —that same spirit which informed his proposals for the abolition of the slave-trade, for the improvement of working conditions for

---

> Debarred from Nature's living images,
> Compelled to be a life unto herself,
> And unrelentingly possessed by thirst
> Of greatness, love, and beauty.
> ("The Prelude", vi, 294–305)

---

[1]   What tho' first,
> In years unseason'd, I attun'd the lay
> To idle Passion and unreal Woe?
> Yet serious Truth her empire o'er my song
> Hath now asserted . . .

This motto, adapted from Akenside's *Pleasures of the Imagination*, was prefixed to "Religious Musings" in the early editions of the poem (PW 108n).

[2] See Whalley, 17–18.   [3] CL, I, 294 (137).

[4] cf. *Mill on Bentham and Coleridge*, ed. R. F. Leavis (London, 1950), 40.

factory children, for the universal provision of moral and religious education, for the equality of women, together with his
reverence for law and concern for the preservation of the cultural
heritage. From the outset Coleridge was always more interested
in formulating a philosophy of society at large and with the search
for ethical principles by which 'the amelioration of the Human
race in its present state' could be effected, than in narrow party
advocacy.[1] It is absurd, therefore, to represent him as 'a speculative genius rather than a moral intelligence', as a man detached
from practical life and bored and perplexed by the laws and
duties prescribed by society.[2]

Yet, as compared with the sober reflective quality of his mature
work, his 1794–5 theorizing was aggressively polemical and vehe-
ment. Indeed, the imprudence with which he helped to prosecute
the Whig campaign against Pitt amounted almost to recklessness.
It was, nevertheless, a crusade informed throughout by an insistence on the priority of principle, based largely upon the Godwin-
ian proposition that 'upon the morality of Britain depends the
safety of Britain'.[3] Thus, he denounced the war against France
as unnecessary, unreasonable, and contrary to human nature.
He condemned the extra security measures imposed after an
attempted assassination upon the King as repressive both of the
subject's liberty and of free speech. As an anonymous Bristol
'Observer' commented, this ardent young firebrand was a moral
force to be reckoned with (very different from the 'poor Col' we
have been taught to patronize):

> This Cantab. is well versed in Greek and in Latin, indeed is a
> superior scholar to most of his years; that love of his species, that
> detestation of human butchery and legalised murder called War,
> are worthy traits in his character. He has delivered many Lectures
> here, one of which (on the slave trade), is a proof of the detestation
> in which he holds that infamous traffic. . . Undaunted by the forms
> of popular prejudice, unswayed by magisterial influence, he spoke
> in public what none had the courage in this City to do before—he
> told men they have Rights—.[4]

[1] ibid, 130.
[2] See J. Charpentier, *Coleridge the Sublime Somnambulist* (trans. M. V. Nugent,
London, 1929), 131.
[3] IH, 278–9.
[4] ibid, 63. It required unusual courage to speak against the slave-trade in
Bristol at that particular time.

Though shadowed by government agents and menaced by riotous mobs he was not afraid to translate principle into action.[1] Yet his recklessness in 1795 must have alarmed his wife. 'Unawed I sang, amid a slavish band,' he boasted (not without justification), but one suspects that her own loyalties were divided between this 'band' and her husband.[2] It was not likely, when her father had been ruined by the war with America, that she could readily approve his dangerous conduct or share in his radical sentiments—especially when he was himself so uncertain about them.

For, despite his fervour, Coleridge was still far from settled in his political convictions and indeed he later abandoned most of them. He maintained, nevertheless, that all along his thinking exemplified an inner moral consistency: 'My speculative Principles were wild as Dreams—they were "Dreams linked to purposes of Reason"; but they were perfectly harmless—a compound of Philosophy and Christianity!' Moral insight, however erratic, is the prerogative of Youth, he claimed—Youth knows 'what is right in the abstract, by a living feeling, by an intuition of the uncorrupted Heart'.[3] Like many another angry young man, however, he discovered that the Establishment either ignores such claims or contemptuously dismisses their advocate with the nearest tag to hand—in Coleridge's case 'Democrat' or 'Jacobin'. Though he indignantly rejected such facile labels, he could not conceal the fact of his own political immaturity: 'How often and how unkindlily are the ebullitions of youthful disputatiousness mistaken for the result of fixed Principles!'[4]

His philosophical and religious principles were equally fluid, pursued with similar earnestness, and, in the last resort, equally beyond Sara's comprehension. Trying to pin down any fixed standpoint here is a task bristling with a complexity that almost defies analysis. The shifting eddies of thought indicated a restless, turbulent mind, at odds with itself, seeking always something ever beyond its present horizons of knowledge and experience. In fact, as his daughter later pointed out, it is practically impossible to separate his philosophical from his religious principles, for they were inextricably intermingled.[5] In 1795, for instance,

---

[1] IH, 62.   [2] See "France: an Ode", stanza 2, PW 245.
[3] CL, II, 999–1000.   [4] ibid, I, 125.
[5] Edith Coleridge, *Memoir and Letters of Sara Coleridge* (London, 1875), 267.

he contrived to be not only a necessitarian, a materialist, and a Berkleyan, but a Unitarian as well. The record of his borrowings from the Bristol library in 1795 (only *one* source of his intellectual nourishment) and the testimonies of Hazlitt and others give some indication of the formidable range of his eclecticism.[1] It is because of this breadth and essential fluidity of interest that it has proved possible to establish a whole spectrum of different philosophical 'influences' upon his work—Platonist, Plotinian, Kantian, Cabbalistic, and even Cambridge Platonist.[2]

A rough synopsis of Coleridge's philosophical development might begin with the 'inspired charity-boy' deep in Plato and the Neo-Platonists, followed by his introduction at Cambridge to the works of Voltaire, Boehme, and the Christian mystics. At the time of his marriage he was under the spell of Priestley and Hartley, but in 1796 he called himself a Berkleyan. Shortly after that he became 'sunk in' Spinoza and Leibniz. In Germany he encountered Transcendentalism with the result that, in March 1801, he finally rejected materialism and necessitarianism. Yet so bald an account scarcely touches on the true nature of his inner development, or begins to explain the odd blend of materialism, pantheism, and quasi-Christian elements in such a poem as *Religious Musings*. Certainly, Coleridge's contemporaries found it impossible to pin-point his standpoint with accuracy; some, like Southey, found his eclecticism merely irritating: 'The truth is that he plays with systems, and any nonsense will serve him for a text from which he can deduce something new and surprising.'[3] Yet there *was* a common denominator amid this flux and, as with his political opinions, it was to be found in a sort of constant moral vitalism. Despite the logical switches and processes of the intellect

[1] See P. Kaufman, "The Reading of Southey and Coleridge: The Record of their Borrowings from the Bristol Library, 1793-8", in *Modern Philology* (Chicago), Vol. XXI, 317-20.

[2] J. H. Muirhead, *Coleridge as Philosopher* (1939), examined the 'Platonist influence'; Margaret Sherwood, in *Coleridge's Imaginative Concept of the Imagination* (Mass., 1937), the 'Plotinian'; René Wellek (among many others), in *Immanuel Kant in England 1793-1838* (Princeton, 1931), the 'Kantian'; J. Beer, in *Coleridge the Visionary* (London, 1959), the 'Cabbalistic'; and Claud Howard, in *Coleridge's Idealism* (Boston, 1924), the 'influence' of the Cambridge Platonists on Coleridge. J. V. Baker in *The Sacred River* (Louisiana, 1957) adduces additional 'influences'.

[3] See J. D. Campbell, *Samuel Taylor Coleridge* (London, 1894), 165.

he somehow held on to 'faith' and, once his initial agnosticism broke down, the mystics enabled him 'to keep alive the heart in the head'.[1] His whole development can be expressed as a swing away from mechanism and mental passivity, through pantheism to the acceptance of vitalistic principles of activity and love.

His religious development ran a similar gamut: sceptic, infidel, Unitarian, anti-ritualist, deist, ritualist, Anglican—he was each and every one of these at some phase in his life.[2] Influenced perhaps by his own retrospective statements of later years (notoriously untrustworthy), critics have been tempted too easily into dismissing his 1794–6 standpoint as one of 'happy godlessness'.[3] Though theoretically he called himself an 'infidel', his correspondence with the atheist Thelwall during this period was in fact animated by deep Christian fervour. Not all of his 1795 Bristol lectures were incendiary; he spoke, too, on an imposing array of theological issues. In January 1796, he began conducting Unitarian services.[4] A month or two later he claimed that he had converted Lovell from atheism to Christianity (admittedly on the latter's death-bed[5]). Mary Evans had been right, therefore, in dismissing his atheistical pose as nonsense, and possibly she understood him as well as anyone did.

It will be evident from even so cursory an outline of the range of his intellectual concerns that, given the fact of Sara's known narrowness of outlook, Coleridge's decision to marry her must have been accompanied by misgivings. In the twelve-month interval between his relinquishing Mary Evans and marrying Sara, though he did not voice these apprehensions openly, they betrayed their presence occasionally in his work. Thus, in *To a Young Lady*, written in September 1794, he announced his readiness to abandon political activity in favour of genteel pursuits more acceptable to female taste:

> Red from the Tyrant's wound I shook the lance,
> And strode in joy the reeking plains of France!

---

[1] See Shawcross, BL, I, xv–xvi.

[2] See James D. Boulger, *Coleridge as Religious Thinker* (Yale, 1961).

[3] cf. S. Potter, *Coleridge and S. T. C.* (London, 1935), 232.

[4] CL, I, 176. Boulger errs, I think, in ascribing the commencement of Coleridge's Unitarian sentiments to 1797 (op. cit., 175n.).

[5] ibid, I, 208.

Fallen is the Oppressor, friendless, ghastly, low,
And my heart aches, though Mercy struck the blow.
With wearied thought once more I seek the shade,
Where peaceful Virtue weaves the Myrtle braid.
And O! if Eyes whose holy glances roll,
Swift messengers, and eloquent of soul;
If Smiles more winning, and a gentler Mien
Than the love-wilder'd Maniac's brain hath seen
Shaping celestial forms in vacant air,
If these demand the empassion'd Poet's care—
If Mirth and soften'd Sense and Wit refined,
The blameless features of a lovely mind;
Then haply shall my trembling hand assign
No fading wreath to Beauty's saintly shrine.
Nor, Sara! thou these early flowers refuse—
Ne'er lurk'd the snake beneath their simple hues;
No purple bloom the Child of Nature brings
From Flattery's night-shade: as he feels he sings. (25–44)

Actually, this poem was addressed originally to Elizabeth Brunton, an actress who had recently performed in Cambridge, and not until the 1796 edition was Sara's name tactfully substituted in line 41 for 'BRYNTON'. It may be surmised, none the less, that the above sentiments related principally to the woman Coleridge was about to marry. The poem first appeared in a letter dated 21 October 1794, in which Coleridge revealed that his attachment to Miss Brunton was developed as a deliberate means of erasing the memory of Mary Evans and to allay his misgivings in regard to his impending marriage:

> . . . I endeavoured to be perpetually with Miss Brunton—I even hoped, that her Exquisite Beauty and uncommon Accomplishments might have cured one Passion by another. The latter I could easily have dissipated in her absence—and so have restored my affections to her, whom I do not love—but whom by every tie of Reason and Honor I ought to love.[1]

The desire expressed in the poem to seek a place 'Where peaceful Virtue weaves the Myrtle braid' is related, surely, to the sentimental description in this letter of the life of simple virtue which Sara and he would lead in Pantisocracy. The 'Myrtle' (as *The Eolian Harp* and *Reflections* demonstrate) was a stock emblem for Coleridge's marital relationship with Sara. The proposition put

[1] ibid, I, 113–18.

forward in the letter, that 'The leading Idea of Pantisocracy is to make men *necessarily* virtuous by removing all Motives to Evil —all possible Temptations,' acquires additional significance possibly in the light of this disclosure concerning Miss Brunton.

From what is known of Sara's background and provincial aspirations it seems likely that she would have heartily endorsed the undertakings upon which Coleridge now proposed to employ his talents. But, in reference to the concluding stanza of the poem, did Coleridge *really* feel as he sang? Was there no lurking snake beneath these 'early flowers' to threaten Sara's Eden? In fact, in the poems which ensued there gradually appeared a deep contempt for the drawing-room skills of 'soften'd Sense and Wit refined' and, increasingly, a preference for the unconventional. Coleridge's apparent repudiation of political commitment in *To a Young Lady* parallels his recantation of philosophical inquiry in *The Eolian Harp* (which, again, was made in deference to Sara's wishes) and like that volte-face it proved insincere and equally short-lived.[1] Coleridge had no real intention of forsaking public life in 1794-5, and in the year that followed he was indeed politically at his most militant.

Where can 'Domestic Peace' be found, he inquired in a sonnet of that title written a year before his wedding-day? 'In a cottag'd vale She dwells / Listening to the Sabbath bells,' came the reply. But somehow he could never believe in Sara's 'cottag'd vale', though precisely why he felt he would not find contentment in it eluded definition.

> O'er the ocean swell
> Sublime of Hope, I seek the cottag'd dell
> Where Virtue calm with careless step may stray,
> And dancing to the moonlight roundelay,
> The wizard Passions weave an holy spell.

Had Coleridge himself any clear idea what these final lines meant? It is doubtful. They belong to the same period as *To a Young Lady* and were first included in a letter to Southey, dated 18 September 1794, in which Coleridge admitted that he felt 'almost ashamed' of their inferiority.[2] They resemble the deli-

---

[1] See pp. 93-6 below.

[2] "Pantisocracy", ll. 4-8, PW 68-9. Southey erroneously attributed this poem to S. Favell, but Coleridge's letter of 18 September 1794 confirms that it was Coleridge's authorship (CL, I, 104).

cious 'witchery of sound' ascribed to twilight elfins in *The Eolian Harp*, or the holy ritual accorded to the *Phaedrus*-like figure in *Kubla Khan* ('Weave a circle round him thrice / And close your eyes with holy dread'). Equivocally they adumbrated the sort of bardic frenzy which Coleridge admired in Chatterton or Schiller, but they hardly belonged with the 'cottag'd vale' and its Sabbath bells. Two years later Coleridge re-employed the identical lines in the *Chatterton Monody*, this time with a strong suggestion that actually they signified erratic inclinations of which Sara disapproved.

The *Monody on the Death of Chatterton* is crucial to the understanding of Coleridge's poetical development. Until he met Wordsworth, Chatterton as a 'poète maudit' figure had a special interest for him and, perhaps because of his presentiments that he would eventually waste his own talents, there was considerable self-identification mixed with his admiration. Coleridge's interest in this subject may be gauged from the numerous revisions he made to the Monody right up to 1829. The earliest version (1790) terminated with an invocation that he might one day resemble Chatterton: 'Grant me, like thee . . . with fire divine to glow', though he hoped to ride out life's stormy 'voyage' more successfully. The phrase 'with fire divine to glow' epitomized those qualities of poetic ardour and mystic insight he was anxious to cultivate in himself. Chatterton was for him a model of romantic feeling ('In tides of power his life-blood seems to flow'). He possessed also, Coleridge thought, the inspired insight of the bardic seer or vates of tradition: 'His eyes have glorious meanings, that declare / More than the light of outward day shines there.'

In 1794, before he was engaged to Sara, Coleridge added a further stanza, which he considered the best part of the poem because 'truly romantic' in spirit. It anticipated *Shurton Bars* and *Dejection: an Ode* in associating the impetus to create with wild storm-winds rather than sheltered domesticity.[1] Coleridge's Monody was an early example of the Chatterton cult popular among romantic writers like Vigny, Gautier, Shelley, Blake, Keats, and Byron.[2] Its hero was the 'poète maudit' figure, isolated from his fellows, who suffers in order to bring the word which is salvation. Thus, in Coleridge's 1794 stanza, Chatterton

[1] See pp. 87–90, 261–4 below.   [2] See Warren, 258.

G

walked alone amid the trackless wastes best suited to his turbulent spirit:

> Here, far from men, amid this pathless grove,
> In solemn thought the Minstrel wont to rove,
> Like star-beam on the slow sequester'd tide
> Lone-glittering, through the high tree branching wide.
> And here, in Inspiration's eager hour,
> When most the big soul feels the mastering power,
> These wilds, these caverns roaming o'er,
> Round which the screaming sea-gulls soar,
> With wild unequal steps he pass'd along,
> Oft pouring on the winds a broken song:
> Anon, upon some rough rock's fearful brow
> Would pause abrupt—and gaze upon the waves below.
>   (118–29)

Though this contains some of the stock-in-trade of Gothic sublimity, it represented also Coleridge's youthful ideal of the poet—
scarcely one which would appeal to Sara.

This then was the context into which, after he had been married a year, he inserted four further stanzas including again the
obscure lines from the sonnet *Pantisocracy* which are so difficult
to elucidate. Self-identification with Chatterton's fate was again
unmistakable, though Coleridge attributed his own misfortunes
to the loss of Mary Evans which, he said, had 'blacken'd the fair
promise of my spring'. Nevertheless, he resolved to make the best
of the 'cottag'd dell':

> Where Virtue calm with careless step may stray;
> And, dancing to the moonlight roundelay,
> The wizard Passions weave an holy spell! (145–7)

In such a context the uneasy alliance between domesticity and
wizard spells appeared both fragile and precarious, especially as
the 'poète maudit' genius was shown to be averse to domesticity.
It seemed only too likely that the 'dirgeful wind' associated with
the bardic furore might sooner or later render the 'cottag'd dell'
untenable, while the forces unleashed when, Chatterton-like, he
'spread the canvas to the gale' might wreck domestic peace entirely. On the other hand the reference to Mary Evans suggests
that she, with her empathic affinity to his moods, might even
have helped to hoist the canvas.

This curious image-cluster of *dancing/moonlight/wizard passions/*

holy spells belongs finally to a peculiarly Coleridgean category of imagination. It is not strictly in the *Phaedrus* tradition of 'the poet's eye in a fine frenzy rolling', nor is it quite what Mr Beer defines as the 'Typhonic' element in the 'daemonic sublime'.[1] If anything it is nearest to what Addison, following Dryden's lead, called the 'faery way of writing'.[2] The famous *Midsummer Night's Dream* speech on the imagination of lunatics, lovers, and poets is, we may recall, associated specifically with 'antique fables' and 'fairy toys'.[3] Coleridge's image-cluster may have had its roots therefore in the fecund loam of English folk-lore. The importance of the 'faery way' lay, however, not in the introduction of fairies, witches, magicians, and demons, but in the poet's right to *invent* such creatures. The poetic imagination, Addison said, 'has not only the whole circle of nature for its province, but makes new worlds of its own, shows us persons who are not to be found in being', and so forth. It was an attempt to unshackle the creative imagination from the fetters neo-classicism had placed upon it.

Coleridge, who 'dearly, dearly loved the works of his own countrymen' and delighted in 'converse deep . . . with all the famous sons of old',[4] was certainly familiar with the tradition. Through the efforts of Akenside, Young, and Hurd (three writers he admired) it persisted indeed right through the eighteenth century. Thus Akenside, describing in *Pleasures of the Imagination* (1744) the plastic potency of the poet's imagination, seemed almost to unite the traditional 'rolling eye' with Coleridgean wizardry:

> . . . with loveliest frenzy caught,
> From earth to heaven he rolls his daring eye,
> From heaven to earth. Anon ten thousand shapes,
> Like spectres trooping to the wizard's call,
> Flit swift before him. (Bk III, 383–7)

Young's attempt to liberate imagination (1759) contained an almost perfect defence of the poetry of Coleridge, Blake, and Shelley yet to come—of such poems particularly as *Christabel*, *The Ancient Mariner*, and *Kubla Khan*:

---

[1] Beer, Ch. IV.

[2] J. Addison, *Spectator*, No. 419; cf. J. Dryden, *Epistle Dedicatory to King Arthur* (1691).

[3] *M.N.D.*, V, i, 2–8.   [4] CL, II, 811; PW 32.

Moreover, so boundless are the bold excursions of the human mind, that, in the vast void beyond real existence, it [i.e. poetry] can call forth shadowy beings, and unknown worlds, as numerous, as bright, and, perhaps, as lasting, as the stars; such quite-original beauties we may call paradisaical.[1]

It was Richard Hurd, in *Letters on Chivalry and Romance* (1762), who offered perhaps the boldest justification for the romantic imagination to be found in literary theory prior to 1798. Invoking the by now conventional image of the 'rolling eye' Hurd asserted that truth to the laws of imagination matters more than truth to sense-experience, a claim very dear to Coleridge's heart:

> So little account does this wicked poetry make of philosophical or historical truth: all she allows us to look for, is poetical truth; a very slender thing indeed, and which the poet's eye, when rolling in its finest frenzy, can but just lay hold of. (No. x)

This is perhaps not very different from what Coleridge meant when he said that wisdom may be gathered from the maddest flights of imagination.

The 'faery way' appeared in Coleridge's *The Eolian Harp*, in *Religious Musings*, and, earlier, in *Songs of the Pixies*. In this last poem the *dancing/moonlight/wizard passions/holy spells* cluster was again linked to the theme of his own poetic aspirations. The hero of this poem, by virtue of his intellectual pretensions, was Coleridge now, not Chatterton: 'A youthful Bard, "unknown to Fame," / Wooes the Queen of Solemn Thought'. The 'thought', however, was of a sort which might offend more prosaic susceptibilities. It belonged peculiarly with elfin-haunted groves, with twilight and pagan ritual:

> O'er his hush'd soul our soothing witcheries shed
> And twine the future garland round his head ... (45–6)

> Or through the mystic ringlets of the vale
> We flash our faery feet in gamesome prank;
> Or, silent-sandal'd, pay our defter court,
> Circling the Spirit of the Western Gale ... (61–4)

If, by chance, Sara shrugged off as unintelligible her husband's quaint determination to locate their home where 'dancing to the moonlight roundelay / The wizard Passions weave an holy spell',

[1] Edward Young, *Conjectures on Original Composition in a Letter to the Author of "Sir Charles Grandison"* (1759).

she did so without suspecting probably that here lurked the threat to her security. It is hardly surprising if she failed to detect it amid such innocent-seeming verbiage. None the less, out of such amorphous origins were to swell the 'dim unhallow'd' bubbles [from] 'Philosophy's aye-babbling spring' which, in *The Eolian Harp*, she immediately recognized as dangerous and promptly rejected.

Coleridge, likewise, ignored these warning signals and seemed bent on compromise. He encouraged Sara to develop creative interests herself, like writing poetry or singing to the flute ('the Poet's kindred strain'), but she did both in a fashion peculiarly her own, producing *The Silver Thimble* by the first and notes '*correctly* wild' by the second.[1] During this lull his own work too became curiously muted in tone and manner, as though accommodated to the acoustics of the front parlour rather than the echoing sea-caverns beloved of Chatterton. It is interesting to compare, for example, his 1795 and 1798 versions of *The Nightingale*. Already in 1795 the nightingale was for him a key poetic symbol, closely associated with moonlight and therefore with the 'wildly-working dreams' and mystic insights of true romantic poetry. 'O! I have listen'd, till my working soul / Waked by those strains to thousand phantasies, / Absorb'd hath ceas'd to listen!' The nightingale was much more for him than the conventional conceit of inferior rhymsters: 'How many wretched Bards address *thy* name . . . But I *do* hear thee.' Yet, in 1795 he relapsed into exactly this sort of conceit himself, utilizing the nightingale merely to fashion an elaborate compliment to his wife:

> Oft will I tell thee, Minstrel of the Moon!
> 'Most musical, most melancholy' Bird!
> That all thy soft diversities of tone . . .
> Are not so sweet as is the voice of her,
> My Sara—best beloved of human kind!
> When breathing the pure soul of tenderness,
> She thrills me with the Husband's promis'd name!
>
> (16–18, 23–6)

[1] PW 92, 104. Actually, Mrs Coleridge told her daughter (*Biog. Lit.*, 1847, ii, 411) that she wrote very little of "The Silver Thimble" and that Coleridge wrote most of it himself. Even so, the poetic treatment was developed at a peculiarly Sara-like level and, on Lamb's advice, "The Thimble" was dropped from the 1803 edition of Coleridge's poems.

To renounce a favourite emblem of romantic inspiration for the more decorous pleasure of becoming Sara's husband was mere gallantry perhaps, not to be taken too seriously; nevertheless, it was of a piece with the faltering loss of purposiveness evident in his work about this time.

Certainly, there was no retracting of the symbol in the 1798 version of the poem, for he had in the meantime met Wordsworth and had confidently reinstated the nightingale as emblematic of true poetic energy and joyful rapport with the One Life. Here, the earlier conceit is contemptuously brushed aside in favour of a better 'lore':

> My Friend, and thou, our Sister! we have learnt
> A different lore: we may not thus profane
> Nature's sweet voices, always full of love
> And joyance! 'Tis the merry Nightingale
> That crowds, and hurries, and precipitates
> With fast thick warble his delicious notes . . . (40–5)

It may be significant that in 1798 Coleridge imagined nightingales flourishing in the very spot where domesticity has been overrun by nature, where 'trim walks are broken up' and the garden-plot runs wild and tangled. Here, the poem suggests, reside the ideal conditions for creative originality for, with the moon's symbolic rising, the bird-chorus bursts forth, 'As if some sudden gale had swept at once / A hundred airy harps!' The density of symbolization in the image-cluster of *nightingale, moon, gale, harp* leads to the poem's rapturous climax, which delineates the ecstasy of 'Joy':

> . . . And she hath watched
> Many a nightingale perch giddily
> On blossomy twig still swinging from the breeze,
> And to that motion tune his wanton song
> Like tipsy Joy that reels with tossing head. (82–6)

This Keatsian sense of exuberant, tipsy abandonment to the delight of spontaneous physical movement (so different from the self-imposed constraint of 1795) indicates strikingly how by 1798 the earlier tension in Coleridge's poetry had departed. One has only to compare it with the staider ending of the earlier version (quoted above) to *feel* the difference. When originally he elected for Sara's 'voice' rather than the nightingale's he may have been, half-consciously, rejecting Mary Evans, whose love he had always associated with moonlight and inspiration.[1] The 1798 *Nightingale* poem may have provided (in the Freudian sense) symbolic outlet for long-repressed feelings and desires. We know, after all, that Coleridge was still in love with Mary Evans long after his wedding-day.[2]

The tension between thought and feeling emerged again in a group of poems Coleridge wrote in the two months spanning his wedding-day. It was apparent in certain conflicting sets of imagery. Thus, descriptions of domestic privacy—'cottag'd dell', 'cottag'd vale', 'holy ground', 'Valley of Seclusion', 'quiet Dell', etc.—were constantly placed in opposition to something wider: 'ocean swell', 'mountain surges bellowing deep', 'distant sea', or 'stony Mount and shoreless Ocean'. Sometimes, it is difficult to determine which attracted him more—the myrtle, jasmine, and rose-leaf beds associated with the 'Cot', or the strange, insistent call of his old enemy, the sea. A similar antithesis occurs between the hushed silence of his home and the sounds produced by the Eolian harp and stormy winds. Ironically, he now seemed afraid that the domestic refuge, at last achieved, might in the end prove claustrophobic.

In a poem addressed to Cottle, *To the Author of Poems*, he distinguished between two sorts of poetry.[3] One is the poetry appropriate to gentility: sober, respectable, and totally undistinguished. It is engendered in 'musing Quiet' and 'sweet undersong 'mid jasmine bowers', and its characteristic epithets are 'smooth', 'charm'd', 'undazzled', 'soften'd', 'pleasant', and 'modest'. It is a 'gentler song' as befits the 'Bard polite' (Cottle), inspirer of a poem like *The Silver Thimble*. The second is romantic poetry, which 'demands th' *impassion'd* theme'. Cottle gets no farther than the 'meadows' at the foothills of the poetic mount, whereas the true poet seeks the heights and scales the 'cloud-climb'd rock, sublime and vast', where 'the Pine-grove to the midnight blast / Makes solemn music!'

In *Shurton Bars* Coleridge could not conceal his own hankering after Chattertonian ecstasies. He used the poem partly to score a point off Southey, comforting Sara because her brother-in-law's 'Chill'd Friendship' had led to differences of feeling between her sister Edith and herself (ll. 7–18).[4] Yet there was much else in

[1] See pp. 59–60 above.   [2] See Appendix II.   [3] PW 102–4.
[4] ibid, 97; cf. CL, I, 167 and p. 308 below.

this poem which should have disturbed her. After the customary quiet opening a low wind begins to moan harp-like through the ruins of a house near by—signifying the awakening of imaginative activity. It recalls Chatterton and it is significant that Coleridge recollects with pleasure the sweetness of poetic self-abandonment:

> Even there—beneath that light-house tower—
> In the tumultuous evil hour
>   Ere Peace with Sara came,
> Time was, I should have thought it sweet
> To count the echoings of my feet,
>   And watch the storm-vex'd flame.
>
> And there in black soul-jaundic'd fit
> A sad gloom-pamper'd Man to sit,
>   And listen to the roar:
> When mountain surges bellowing deep
> With an uncouth monster-leap
>   Plung'd foaming on the shore. (43–54)

The 'hour / Ere peace with Sara came' refers to the tumultuous ending of the Mary Evans affair and there is a suggestion therefore that the sort of inspiration Mary had provided was well suited to the 'poète maudit's' melancholy. Though such feelings are now rejected as 'jaundiced' and 'gloom-pampered' we may doubt whether Coleridge genuinely wished for no return of them.

A stark contrast follows between domesticity and the furious storm-wind which howls its disapproval of the poet's taking refuge from it. Sara, who sees the wind as a threat to her happiness, shields her husband from it, as though to smother his awakening discontent:

> When stormy Midnight howling round
> Beats on our roof with clattering sound,
>   To me your arms you'll stretch:
> Great God! you'll say—To us so kind,
> O shelter from this loud bleak wind
>   The houseless, friendless wretch! (73–8)

Thus, a tension exists at the centre of the poem as Coleridge is pulled this way and that by his desire for sexual union with Sara (ll. 85–96), and his fear that marriage means renouncing the

bardic frenzy still so dear to him. The problem is further complicated by the fact that the lines used to describe the anticipatory
delights of sexual union with Sara are almost a copy of lines used
previously in connection with Mary Evans.[1]

Many of Coleridge's poems indicate that the storm-wind was
used metaphorically to represent the ferment of creative activity.
Two of them may be referred to here as illuminating the difference between Sara's attitude (in *Shurton Bars*) to the creative
storm from that of what might be termed a true 'Abyssinian
maid'. In the first, *The Old Man of the Alps* (1798), there appears
a young lady about to get married whose outlook bears some
comparison with Sara's. She is incapable of responding imagi-
natively to the totality of life, but lives only for the return of her
lover from the wars so that they can get married. She neither
knows nor cares why he is fighting nor what he is fighting for,
but is concerned solely with establishing a home with him when
he returns. She has no interest in other people, and refuses to
consider their misfortunes. Within her 'sunny dell' she seeks to
make herself immune from storms and tempests:

> And if I spoke of hearts by pain oppress'd . . .
> Impatient of the thought, with lively cheer
> She broke half-closed the tasteless tale severe.
> *She* play'd with fancies of a gayer hue,
> Enamour'd of the scenes her *wishes* drew;
> And oft she prattled with an eager tongue
> Of promised joys that would not loiter long,
> Till with her tearless eyes so bright and fair,
> She seem'd to see them realis'd in air!

[1] "Shurton Bars" ends:

> 'Tis said, in Summer's evening hour
> Flashes the golden-colour'd flower
>   A fair electric flame:
> And so shall flash my love-charg'd eye
> When all the heart's big ecstasy
>   Shoots rapid through the frame! (91-6)

In "Lines on an Autumnal Evening" (see p. 60 above) Coleridge had
written:

> When as she twin'd a laurel round my brow,
> And met my kiss, and half return'd my vow,
> O'er all my frame shot rapid my thrill'd heart,
> And every nerve confess'd the electric dart. (19-22)

> In fancy oft, within some sunny dell,
> Where never wolf should howl or tempest yell,
> She built a little home of joy and rest,
> And fill'd it with the friends whom she lov'd best:
> She named the inmates of her fancied cot,
> And gave to each his own peculiar lot . . . (18–38)

Nothing her father does can modify her self-centredness and, when news arrives that her lover has been killed, her mind, without other resources to sustain it, gives way. She dies finally in a storm upon the mountain tops, so that the storm-wind, as often with Coleridge, assumes the force of a moral avenger. Like Sara, whose compassion for the 'houseless, friendless wretch outside' seemed largely sentimental, she guarded her 'cot' too jealously from the life outside the 'dell'. Like Kubla Khan's hers was a paradise with walls and towers girdled round.

The second poem, *Lines Composed in a Concert Room* (1799), creates in contrast a picture of the ideal 'Abyssinian maid'. When in her case the storm arises and gusts pelt down upon the roof, she welcomes it whole-heartedly and attunes her song to the tone 'the things of Nature utter'. Instead of imposing a check upon Coleridge's political crusading, she loves him the more because of the exhilaration this gives him:

> But O, dear Anne! when midnight wind careers,
> And the gust pelting on the out-house shed
>   Makes the cock shrilly in the rainstorm crow,
>   To hear thee sing some ballad full of woe,
> Ballad of ship-wreck'd sailor floating dead,
>   Whom his own true-love buried in the sands!
> Thee, gentle woman, for thy voice remeasures
> Whatever tones and melancholy pleasures
>   The things of Nature utter; birds or trees,
> Or moan of ocean-gale in weedy caves,
> Or where the stiff grass mid the heath-plant waves,
>   Murmur and music thin of sudden breeze.
>
> Dear Maid! whose form in solitude I seek,
>   Such songs in such a mood to hear thee sing,
>   It were a deep delight!—But thou shalt fling
> Thy white arm round my neck, and kiss my cheek,
>   And love the brightness of my gladder eye
>   The while I tell thee what a holier joy

It were in proud and stately step to go,
 With trump and timbrel clang, and popular shout,
 To celebrate the shame and absolute rout
Unhealable of Freedom's latest foe,
 Whose tower'd might shall to its centre nod. (29–51)

We do not know the date of composition of this poem. If, as J. D. Campbell suggested, it was a recast of some earlier verses written in 1793, then the 'dear Anne' of line 29 may have referred to Mary Evans's sister. The last two stanzas quoted above suggest that the Lewti-like 'Maid, whose form in solitude I seek', instead of requiring Coleridge to disavow his political and philosophical interests, would actively have encouraged them. If, as seems possible, this 'dear Maid' was in any way related to Mary Evans, this might explain why Coleridge deleted these last two stanzas from the poem after he met and fell in love with Asra.[1]

The Eolian Harp, written just prior to Coleridge's wedding, established the pattern of curving emotion and circular progression of thought characteristic of all his conversational poems;[2] such tension as exists between thought and feeling (whatever its biographical significance) except at the end is aesthetically not unpleasing. He had written nothing previously to compare with the power of detailed observation, the natural ease and firm blank-verse rhythm which this new personal style of writing immediately produced. In the poem's quiet opening movement 'thought' seems dormant as Coleridge and Sara are discovered together, responsive only to feeling, situation, and atmosphere. He seems, for once, wholly to surrender himself to the delights of Sara's 'Cot' as, with lyrical sensuousness, he evokes a world of flowers and clouds, of exquisite scents and silence. There is no dissonance, no sense of self-constraint; the bower of bliss is virtually idyllic.

But a desultory breeze awakens an Eolian harp left on the

---

[1] 'Dear Anne' could refer to Coleridge's sister, which would make it a still earlier poem however, since Anne Coleridge had died in March 1791. Or was 'dear Anne' a cover for Mary Evans herself? It may be recalled that Coleridge later paid his addresses to Asra through her sister, Joanna, and Anne was the name of Mary Evans's sister (see p. 54 above). 'Anne' could even refer to Anna Buclé, afterwards Mrs Cruikshank.

[2] See Schulz, 82.

nearby casement and Coleridge's imagination begins to stir. They were about to be married and it is not surprising that the developing melody is first described in wholly sexual terms. It builds up to a sort of rhythmic orgasm, as though tempting, blandishing, and finally seducing Sara into accepting what normally her understanding would reject:

> And that simplest Lute,
> Placed length-ways in the clasping casement, hark!
> How by the desultory breeze caress'd,
> Like some coy maid half-yielding to her lover,
> It pours such sweet upbraiding, as must needs
> Tempt to repeat the wrong! (12–17)

Sensing perhaps a rare attunement between them while the beauties of sight, scent, and music beguile their senses, with mounting confidence he seeks to carry her with him into most unSara-like territory. Almost surreptitiously the 'faery way' is introduced and so potent is the incantatory magic that disbelief is temporarily suspended:

> And now, its strings
> Boldlier swept, the long sequacious notes
> Over delicious surges sink and rise,
> Such a soft floating witchery of sound
> As twilight Elfins make, when they at eve
> Voyage on gentle gales from Fairy-Land,
> Where Melodies round honey-dropping flowers,
> Footless and wild, like birds of Paradise,
> Nor pause, nor perch, hovering on untam'd wing!
> (17–25)

Analysing such lines is like trying to unweave the texture of a rainbow. (Lines 21–5 were indeed omitted from the 1803 edition, then restored to the text, suggesting that Coleridge himself was not entirely happy with them.) At the 'faery' level the passage is a tribute surely to the range and beauty of the creative imagination, vindicating its independence of the ordinary understanding and its legitimate preoccupation with moonlight and magic. On the personal level it may be regarded as a persuasive attempt to wean Sara from literal matter-of-factness to a more imaginative response to life. One senses underlying tension in the fundamental resistance he has to overcome ('half-yielding ... upbraiding ... tempt to repeat the wrong'), but his confidence develops as he meets only tacit opposition and, consequently, the strings are 'boldlier swept' and the assault continues. Now temptation is laid on thicker and the soul-ravishing music rises and falls in 'delicious surges' with 'soft floating witchery' of sound. The subtle verse-rhythms enchant and the long-drawn cadences brook no interruption, so that only afterwards have we time to reflect on the bizarre irregularity of it all. There is nothing *'correctly* wild' about these paradisaical melodies: they are 'footless', 'wild', and 'untam'd'. At the same time, so *Religious Musings* would imply,[1] they are in their strange way closely connected with the highest morality.

Lines 26–33 (O! the one Life within us and abroad . . .') then develop the preceding thought more clearly, exploiting the mood of receptivity carefully built up in the reader by crystallizing the metaphysical ideas towards which the poem is working into a firm statement of the joyful sense of integration and harmony which a true rapport with nature entails. This passage, however, did not appear in the original text (being first inserted in 1817) and for the moment we may defer consideration of it.

To return to the original version then, the way is now open for Coleridge, having lulled Sara into a state of acquiescence by his ravishing witcheries, to administer the metaphysical pill which he has been carefully sugaring. 'Thought' suddenly springs to life and the mood alters as, with a bold change of tactics, he switches the setting from the hush of evening to the blazing light of noon. The restful star of evening, *'serenely* brilliant', is replaced by dancing diamond sunbeams, like flashing points of thought. His torpid intellect, until now 'indolent' and 'passive', wakes to life, roused by the 'untam'd' melodies of the harp, and his mind is agitated by 'phantasies . . . As wild and various as the random gales / That swell and flutter on this subject Lute!' The tone with which he addresses Sara is disarmingly placatory—'And thus, my Love!'—and yet constraint is evident in the profuse apologetics. His off-handedness in dismissing his thoughts as 'uncall'd', 'undetained', mere 'idle, flitting' phantasies rings false, for they are precisely what the poem has been leading up to. There is a total lack of the self-assured conviction with which the 1817 'one Life' passage was introduced (or the similar passage in *The Destiny of Nations* (ll. 36–46), 1797 draft). The metaphysic is here prof-

[1] See pp. 101–2 below.

fered tentatively, diffidently, with a hypothetical 'And *what if* all of animated nature / Be but . . .':

> And what if all of animated nature
> Be but organic Harps diversely fram'd,
> That tremble into thought, as o'er them sweeps
> Plastic and vast, one intellectual breeze,
> At once the Soul of each, and God of all? (44–8)

Twelve months later, in *The Destiny of Nations*, the harp was used quite uninhibitedly to represent a symbol of free-ranging thought, of the poet's obligation to interpret the spiritual world as he thinks fit, whether intelligible or not to more limited understandings.[1]

Regarding lines 44–8 (just quoted) Mr House objected that there seemed no reason why such vague Neo-Platonic theological speculating should offend what he called Sara's 'extremely narrow and governessy' Christian orthodoxy, since it is 'not wholly incompatible with the scheme of Christian redemption'.[2] Two comments may be made on this. First, though to a sophisticated intelligence Coleridge's Neo-Platonism is reconcilable with the Christian standpoint, Sara plainly lacked such sophistication. The 'trembling' thought and 'intellectual breezes' of Plotinianism were distasteful to her, because incomprehensible. They were of a piece with that over-subtle casuistry of her husband's which irritated not only Sara but the Rev. George Coleridge and Southey, too. Coleridge's Christianity was always more an 'intellectual passion' than a matter of simple faith. Indeed, because he had no faith in the accepted sense, his mind was most at home in a deistic *'religious Twilight'*, where he could 'play off [his] intellect *ad libitum*', bewildering everyone including himself with sheer 'dazzle of Wit' and 'subtlety of Argument'.[3] Perplexed and not a little disturbed by it all, Sara found it vaguely unrespectable.

Secondly, Mr House (like Mr Burke) may have accepted too readily that Sara was a 'narrowly orthodox Christian', doubtless because she was so represented in the poem. In fact we know very little about her religious background, but enough to be fairly certain that she was the last person to be troubled by niceties of doctrinal distinction. To save breaking the thread of this argu-

---

[1] cf. "The Destiny of Nations", ll. 7–26, PW 132.   [2] HH, 77.
[3] See CL, I, 78 and cf. pp. 168–9 below.

ment, I have relegated further discussion of this point to an appendix.[1]

It is in the light of this intellectual dyspathy that Sara's 'mild reproof' should be regarded. For despite all the earlier blandishments she promptly rejects his 'thoughts' the moment their intrusion disrupts the delicate attunement of feeling which has hitherto promoted acquiescence. Empathy between them ceases immediately his intellect asserts itself, for it is his 'thoughts' and the 'shapings of [his] unregenerate mind' which introduce a note of dissonance. Because on this eve-of-wedding occasion he is anxious to preserve their new-found attunement, he no sooner realizes his error of judgement than he retracts his metaphysical hypothesis.

The real opposition in the final movement of the poem is between 'thought' and the faith that inly *'feels'*. It is conveniently expressed as an opposition between Sara, as 'Meek Daughter' of Christ, and himself with his 'unregenerate mind'. I suspect that this was (partly at least) a device for dramatizing the conflict within himself, between his own intellectual pride and his genuine desire for the faith that *feels*. Be that as it may, 'thought' is now repudiated as obscure, 'unhallow'd', ephemeral, and, all too often, 'vain'. The Plotinian philosophy is ruled out as too intellectual, too barren of feeling to afford true insight into the mysteries of animated nature. Ratiocinative metaphysics amounts finally to no more than 'babbling', for ultimate reality remains for ever 'Incomprehensible' to the unaided intellect. True spiritual awareness requires humility and a 'Faith that inly *feels*', which is in fact the lesson of *The Ancient Mariner*. It is a mistake, therefore, to regard this as a wholly disappointing ending, in the sense that Coleridge abandoned a rare vision of truth in favour of something much more conventional. The poem does give that impression certainly, but, in a sense, Sara's resistance to the light-that-never-was approach was valuable in pegging him back to earth, forcing him to recognize that 'intellectual passion' was no substitute for natural feeling.

> But thy more serious eye a mild reproof
> Darts, O belovéd Woman! nor such thoughts
> Dim and unhallow'd dost thou not reject,
> And biddest me walk humbly with my God.

[1] See Appendix I; also K. Burke, *The Philosophy of Literary Form* (Louisiana, 1941), 71–2, 93 ff.

> Meek Daughter in the family of Christ!
> Well hast thou said and holily disprais'd
> These shapings of the unregenerate mind;
> Bubbles that glitter as they rise and break
> On vain Philosophy's aye-babbling spring.
> For never guiltless may I speak of him,
> The Incomprehensible! save when with awe
> I praise him, and with Faith that inly *feels*;
> Who with his saving mercies healéd me,
> A sinful and most miserable man,
> Wilder'd and dark, and gave me to possess
> Peace, and this Cot, and thee, heart-honour'd Maid!
>
> (49–64)

The final lines bring him back to the anticipatory pleasure of possessing the 'Cot' and Sara. Rather than dwell longer on their temperamental incompatibilities he prefers to let the matter drop. Yet he was aware now of the curb which Sara's narrowness imposed upon his intellectual freedom, and even more aware perhaps of the conflict within himself.

Mr House's contention that the late grafting-on of lines 26–33 virtually makes nonsense of the original ending of the poem is valid, though not primarily because this had the effect of reducing Sara to 'governessy orthodoxy'. The 1817 passage describes a *true* rapport with the 'one Life', true in the sense that it postulates not a wholly intellectual relationship, but a joyous and emotional one that is built upon *love*, and embraces the world of perception and feelings:

> O! the one Life within us and abroad,
> Which meets all motion and becomes its soul,
> A light in sound, a sound-like power in light,
> Rhythm in all thought, and joyance every where—
> Methinks, it should have been impossible
> Not to love all things in a world so fill'd;
> Where the breeze warbles, and the mute still air
> Is Music slumbering on her instrument. (26–33)

In 1817, Coleridge vastly improved the over-all philosophical meaning by thus adding a statement of his fundamental belief in the attunement of man's whole spirit to nature.[1] This clarified the amorphousness of the preceding lines, defining that joy which

[1] N.B. ll. 26–9 were first included in the *Errata* to *Sybilline Leaves* (1817); ll. 30–3 appeared originally in 1803.

the paradisaical melodies only signified. But it wrecked the original structure completely, since for Coleridge to reject *these* thoughts as 'unhallow'd' and 'unregenerate' was mere nonsense.

Reflections on Having Left a Place of Retirement (composed just *after* his wedding) exposes the deficiencies of Sara's 'Cot'. The chief difference between its opening description and that of *The Eolian Harp* is that the viewpoint here is taken from *within* the cottage, with a corresponding reinforcement of the feeling of being enclosed. The chamber-window allows only a narrow glimpse of the 'little landscape round'. Rather like the miniature landscape in *Kubla Khan*, it is a 'Valley of Seclusion'. While the honeymoon ecstasies lasted, however, the sense of confinement was not oppressive; it was especially gratifying to Coleridge, for instance, that a passer-by should look with envy at their cottage: '. . . it was a Blesséd Place. / And we *were* bless'd.'

In the second stanza the lens widens, enlarging from the 'dell' until it encompasses the panoramic view from the nearby mountain-top. The 'But' with which this stanza commences marks an antithesis between microcosm and macrocosm, and forms a hinge on which the thought-movement of the poem swings (in much the same way that it does between stanzas 1 and 2 of *Kubla Khan*). In both poems there is a movement outwards from what is narrow, circumscribed, and private to what is spacious, open, and free, and in either landscape a great river winds bright and full.[1] As Coleridge describes his difficult ascent of the 'stony Mount' which walls in the 'dell', one is half-prepared for 'Chattertonian' euphoria but, instead, we are given a carefully ordered description of the panorama outspread before him. Though he walks apart from men, his thoughts remain with them, so that instead of seeking the windy heights he pauses to identify places of human interest—the 'seats, and lawns, the Abbey and the wood, / And cots, and hamlets, and faint city-spire' (34–5). This renewed concern with human habitations suggests a re-awakening of moral and political interests.

When the One Life vision comes (ll. 38–42) it awakens self-reproach, forcing him to abandon honeymoon delights and to

[1] This stanza in some ways resembles Dyer's "Grongar Hill".

H

recollect his former moral aspirations. On sudden impulse he resolves to quit the 'dell':

> Ah! quiet Dell! dear Cot, and Mount sublime!
> I was constrain'd to quit you. Was it right,
> While my unnumber'd brethren toil'd and bled,
> That I should dream away the entrusted hours
> On rose-leaf beds, pampering the coward heart
> With feelings all too delicate for use? (43–8)

The phrase 'entrusted hours' suggests Coleridge's sense of high vocation, a recollection of the poet's sacred moral rôle. Sated for a time with sensual pleasures, he can no longer ignore the larger life beyond the 'dell'. 'Cold beneficence' and the 'dainty sympathies' of the sentimentalist are not enough; he seeks a more positive moral commitment:

> I therefore go, and join head, heart, and hand,
> Active and firm, to fight the bloodless fight
> Of Science, Freedom, and the Truth in Christ. (60–2)

The motto '*sermoni propriora*', which Coleridge later prefixed to the poem, is fair comment on the sententious quality of lines 44–62. The object of the 'crusade' described above is obscured in rhetoric. At the same time, this resolution reaffirms the importance of political commitment.[1] indicating that the poet's true vocation cannot be worked out on sheltered rose-leaf beds. Paradise must be earned, for between morality and pleasure there exists a constant dialectic.

In the final stanza, therefore, the marriage is placed upon a different footing. Coleridge claims the right to divide his time in future between the 'dell' and his public concerns, so establishing the pattern of life which was in fact to endure so long as Sara and he lived together:

> Yet oft when after honourable toil
> Rests the tir'd mind, and waking loves to dream,
> My spirit shall revisit thee, dear Cot!
> Thy Jasmin and thy window-peeping Rose,
> And Myrtles fearless of the mild sea-air.
> And I shall sigh fond wishes—sweet Abode!
> Ah!—had none greater! And that all had such!
> It might be so—but the time is not yet.
> Speed it, O Father! Let thy Kingdom come! (63–71)

---

[1] See pp. 78–80 above.

Shortly after writing this poem Coleridge began lecturing again
and energetically collecting subscribers for the *Watchman*.[1] But in
this he may have been motivated not wholly by public-spirited-
ness; the Gutch memorandum-book suggests that it was also a
means of sublimating his continuing passion for Mary Evans.[2]

Once the group of 'wedding-poems' was finished Coleridge
wrote little poetry for some months, except for spasmodic wrest-
lings with *Religious Musings* and *The Destiny of Nations*. Pulled this
way and that by political, Unitarian, and journalistic commitments, and struggling to earn 'bread and cheese', he neglected
poetry: 'My poor crazy ark has been tossed to and fro on an
ocean of business, and I long for the Mount Ararat on which it
is to rest.'[3] Even his *Watchman* readers wrote in to demand more
poetry, but he found it too difficult and when *The Destiny of
Nations* met with adverse criticism from Lamb he disconsolately
abandoned the poem.[4]

Yet one or two notable poems were produced in 1796 and early
1797, and in these it is interesting to find Coleridge defending the
romantic genius, despite his wife's and eldest brother's disapproval. He informed the latter, in the poem addressed to him,
that a change was taking place in his work: 'My song hath
sounded deeper notes . . . such as, tuned to these tumultuous
times, / Cope with the tempest's swell' (64–68). In *Ode to the
Departing Year* (1796) he laid claim to the prophet's mantle, fear-
lessly standing out against his countrymen's opinions and warn-

---

[1] Late in 1795 Coleridge determined to publish a periodical, to be known
as the *Watchman*, and early in January 1796 he set off on a five-week tour of
the industrial midlands and north in search of subscribers. Ten numbers were
issued between 1 March and 13 May 1796, which contained news items,
accounts of parliamentary debates, and some original matter in prose and
verse, the bulk of which Coleridge wrote himself. In the last number, as the
enterprise was about to collapse, Coleridge wrote: 'O Watchman! thou hast
watched in vain!' (For fuller details, see *Life*, 49–54.)

[2] On the first page of the Gutch notebook Coleridge wrote:

> I mix in life, and labour to seem free,
> > With common persons pleas'd and common things,
> While every thought and action tends to thee,
> > And every impulse from thy influence springs.

Chambers called this Coleridge's 'farewell to Mary Evans' (*Life*, 38).

[3] *CL*, I, 176.   [4] ibid, I, 195, 309n.

ing them, on the authority of a 'vision' vouchsafed to him, of the
evils in store for England. He spoke like some inspired Tiresias,
or one of Kubla's ancestral voices prophesying war. Whatever
Sara's and George's opinion of such visions he claimed that 'no
unholy madness' inspired them. They were 'Wild phantasies, yet
wise'.[1]

The same exalted claims are found in *Religious Musings* (1794–
6), a poem in which orthodox Christian sentiments jostle uneasily
with elements of Neo-Platonism, and with the 'faery way' and
tributes to the materialists. This poem exemplifies perfectly the
confused and eclectic nature of Coleridge's intellectual development during these formative years. Intended to 'describe the
Character and Doctrines of Jesus Christ',[2] its opening paragraph
begins by blurring Christian and Plotinian ideologies. The
'thought-benighted Sceptic' of the second paragraph sounds very
much like Coleridge himself. Tribute is paid to those who adore
God with 'trembling . . . unpresuming gaze', yet no sooner does
Coleridge write this than his heart 'lifts and swells' and 'Behold
a Vision gathers' in his soul (ll. 66–8, 1803 edition). The spiritual core of the poem (ll. 105–18) is a mixture of Christian and
Neo-Platonic doctrines, though with a shade too much intellectual self-assurance to please conventional Christians:

> From himself he flies,
> Stands in the sun, and with no partial gaze
> Views all creation; and he loves it all,
> And blesses it, and calls it very good! (110–13)

A meek daughter in the family of Christ might detect some
hubris in the superb magnanimity of this gesture of approval.
('This is *indeed* to dwell with the Most High!'; cherubim and
seraphim can press no nearer.) There seems also to be a deliberate vindication of the noon-tide 'phantasies' of *The Eolian Harp*
(which Sara had indignantly rejected) as he continues:

> 'Tis the sublime of man,
> Our noontide Majesty, to know ourselves
> Parts and proportions of one wondrous whole! (126–8)

He adds, however, that man requires 'sacred sympathy' to make
'the whole one Self'.

In a notable passage one would like to have had Sara's views

---

[1] See PW 161, 135.   [2] CL, I, 147.

upon, Coleridge suggests that it should be given to 'Philosophers and Bards' to reconcile the social inequalities that have grown up from the development of private rights of property. I am concerned here less with his 'democratic' sentiments than with his elevation of the poet to the rôle of moral arbiter, or bridler of chaos:

> These, hush'd awhile with patient eye serene,
> Shall watch the mad careering of the storm;
> Then o'er the wild and wavy chaos rush
> And tame the outrageous mass, with plastic might
> Moulding Confusion to such perfect forms,
> As erst were wont,—bright visions of the day!—
> To float before them, when, the summer noon,
> Beneath some arched romantic rock reclined
> They felt the sea-breeze lift their youthful locks . . .
>
> (243–51)

Highly rhetorical though this is, it is a further justification of bright noon-tide visions, a fresh assertion that phantasies, though wild, may yet be wise. It requires the poets to take over, Coleridge says, because the bulk of humanity, clinging to their narrow 'Cots', lack the knowledge or intellect to take a longer perspective on the myopic narrowness of their lives (ll. 260–6). Turgid as these passages are, they may have provided outlet for ideas that Sara's restrictive influence cramped.

Farther on in the poem, he predicts the coming of the Millennium when capitalism shall fall (through the purifying moral agency of a *storm*) and 'Pure Faith' and 'meek Piety' return. But their imagined return is in a form very different from Sara's understanding of these terms; for they are accompanied by the 'unearthly melodies' of Paradise, firmly and defiantly associated now with moral goodness:

>   Such delights
> As float to earth, permitted visitants!
> When in some hour of solemn jubilee
> The massy gates of Paradise are thrown
> Wide open, and forth come in fragments wild
> Sweet echoes of unearthly melodies,
> And odours snatched from beds of Amaranth,
> And they, that from the crystal river of life
> Spring up on freshened wing, ambrosial gales!
> The favoured good man in his lonely walk

> Perceives them, and his silent spirit drinks
> Strange bliss which he shall recognise in heaven.
> And such delights, such strange beatitudes
> Seize on my young anticipating heart
> When that blest future rushes on my view! (343–57)

Such 'strange beatitudes' belong to him who walks apart from men, who cherishes his separateness and isolation, and patiently awaits his visionary hour. By implication, therefore, the sheltered 'dell' again comes under fire.

Towards the end of the poem Coleridge exhorts *himself*, as though to reinforce his determination: 'Believe thou, O my soul, / Life *is* a vision shadowy of Truth' (395–6). There are to be no more recantations, therefore, no more vacillating. The final stanza expresses his resolve to unfetter his faculties and fulfil the obligations of his high vocation (regardless of Sara's disapproval):

> Contemplant Spirits! ye that hover o'er
> With untired gaze the immeasurable fount
> Ebullient with creative Deity!
> And ye of plastic power, that interfused
> Roll through the grosser and material mass
> In organizing surge! Holies of God!
> (And what if Monads of the infinite mind?)
> I haply journeying my immortal course
> Shall sometime join your mystic choir! (402–10)

Religious Musings is an unsatisfactory poem because of its obscurity of thought, and the fact that the various metaphysical elements are insufficiently assimilated for purposes of organic unity. There is no real union of thought and feeling. He himself remarked of it at one stage, 'Thus far my scanty Brain hath built the rhyme / Elaborate and swelling: but the Heart / Not owns it.'[1] Considered alongside the group of 'wedding-poems', however, it again demonstrates something of the strain and tension Coleridge was under in 1794–6 and, in the last resort, his immaturity.

Coleridge's failure to achieve a satisfactory blend of thought and feeling in his poetry prior to 1797 was basically psychological. As this and the preceding chapters have shown, his character during his early twenties was remarkably immature, whether

---

[1] CL, I, 147.

looked at in its emotional, intellectual, or moral aspects. It is a psychological commonplace nowadays to stress the importance in early life of a proper love-relationship with a mother-figure as a prerequisite to the development of a stable character. 'To be deprived of this', Mr Peters has stated, 'is likely to lead to distractability, unreliability and lack of self-inhibition, which are almost definitions of having *no* character . . . in the sense of autonomous self-direction.'[1] These traits match Coleridge's case fairly obviously. It is also commonplace that persons of high intelligence who are emotionally deprived will seek attention and sympathy through displays of cleverness. This also, I believe, fits Coleridge's case. One thing capable of radically altering these conditions is the rôle demanded by parenthood, in the opportunities it affords for new and deeper emotions. This occurred, too, in Coleridge's case.

His first child, David Hartley Coleridge, was born on 20 September 1796, some few months before the 'annus mirabilis' commenced. This event, more than anything else, I think, accelerated the maturation of Coleridge's character; it brought husband and wife much closer together, and consequently made for a reduction in the strain and tension which had been growing between them. It may also have exorcised the memory of Mary Evans somewhat (though she did appear again in *Lewti*). Significantly, the immediate effect of Hartley's birth was to upset a number of Coleridge's intellectual notions, producing 'confuséd thought and shapeless feelings' such as 'perplex the soul self-questioned in her sleep'.[2] During Sara's pregnancy he suddenly lost interest in politics and, after the birth, he announced (with a pertinent image) that he had snapped his 'squeaking *baby*-trumpet of sedition'.[3] Precisely at this time (November 1796) he began also to discover something like a real faith: 'I am daily more and more a religionist' and (again in the imagery of the nursery) he threw over metaphysics for a considerable period: 'My philosophical refinements, & metaphysical Theories lay by me in the hour of anguish, as toys by the bedside of a Child

[1] R. S. Peters, "Freud's Theory of Moral Development in Relation to that of Piaget's", *British Journal of Educational Psychology*, xxx, 111, 256.
[2] See Coleridge's sonnet, "On Receiving a Letter Informing Me of the Birth of a Son", PW 153; and cf. CL, I, 192.
[3] CL, I, 240.

deadly-sick.'[1] Faced with the realities of life, in other words, he began to dismiss his more recondite intellectual subtleties as childish toys and to shed many of his callow undergraduate pretensions.

The child gave an entirely new focus to Coleridge's emotional life, providing a fresh outlet for love and novel sensations of parental pride and responsibility. His first glimpse of the babe at Sara's breast electrified him: '. . . then I was thrilled & melted, & gave it the Kiss of a FATHER.'[2] He discovered during Sara's pregnancy that his sexual libido was being channelled increasingly into affection; while, after the birth, affection for his wife mounted almost to veneration: '*Wife* is a solemn name to me because of its influence on the more solemn duties of *Mother*.'[3] Intellectual incompatibilities were forgotten in these new emotional experiences and the effect was cathartic: 'Our David Hartley is a very Seraph in Clouts—and laughs, till he makes us cry for very overflowing joy and tenderness.'[4] Through these experiences Coleridge's mind was deepened and stabilized, while Sara, with so much more to occupy her, found less time to bother about his other activities.

Hartley's birth more than anything else brought the cognitive and emotional elements in Coleridge's make-up into something closer to a 'whole man' harmony. Whereas in 1794 he had said: 'I *think* too much for a Poet', by December 1796 he was praying as a means of subverting his intellect:

> May God continue his visitations to my soul, bowing it down, till the pride & Laodicean self-confidence of human Reason be utterly done away; and I cry with deeper & yet deeper feelings, O my Soul! thou art wretched, and miserable, & poor, and blind, and naked![5]

On 12 December he informed Poole that his habits and feelings had suffered 'a total alteration' and that he needed no other company now than 'My Sara, my Babe, my own shaping and disquisitive mind, my Books, my beloved Friend, Thomas Poole, & lastly, Nature'.[6] He was soon to enjoy all six, and also the company of the Wordsworths, for the 'annus mirabilis' was at hand.

---

[1] CL, I, 253, 267.   [2] ibid, I, 236.   [3] ibid, I, 306; and cf. 351.
[4] ibid, I, 317.   [5] ibid, I, 267.
[6] ibid, I, 271. He added: 'If I were capable of being tired with all these, I should then detect a Vice in my Nature, and would fly to habitual Solitude to eradicate it'—words which proved remarkably prophetic.

On New Year's Eve 1796 he exhaled the last of his political furore
and promised:

> Now I recentre my immortal mind
> In the deep Sabbath of meek self-content.[1]

But this was not a return to the uxorious timidity of *The Eolian
Harp*. This self-content was born of a sudden access of maturity.

[1] "Ode to the Departing Year", ll. 158–9, PW 168.

Annus Mirabilis

There was an interval extending roughly from July 1797 to April 1798 (his 'annus mirabilis') when in poem after poem Coleridge wrote with a spontaneity of feeling and a self-assurance unparalleled in anything he composed prior to this period or afterwards. Between February and May 1798 he completed, or was working on, *Frost at Midnight, The Old Man of the Alps, France: an Ode, The Ancient Mariner, Kubla Khan,*[1] *Christabel, Lewti, Fears in Solitude, The Dark Ladie,* and *The Nightingale*—a vintage crop paralleled only perhaps by Keats's 1819 harvest. Not only were these poems written in a more natural style than hitherto, but they explored a range of feelings and were permeated by a warmth (a sociability, almost) quite new to Coleridge's work. After this brief access of emotional and moral strength, his poetry tended to become guilt-ridden and pessimistic, argumentative rather than persuasive. This remarkable energy of achievement in 1797–8 coincided with a period in Coleridge's life when his personal circumstances favoured the flowering of his strange and temperamental genius. Secure in his family-life and friends, he was relatively free from the moral misgivings and emotional stresses which subsequently beset him.

This was probably the happiest period of Coleridge's married life. He grumbled a good deal about the difficulties of providing for a family by authorship, but there is little to suggest that his marriage was 'failing by 1797', or that by 1798 it was 'virtually finished'.[2] Against any statements which Coleridge made in after

[1] See p. 136, note 2, concerning the date of "Kubla Khan".

[2] Marshall Suther states that Coleridge's marriage was 'certainly failing' by 1797. In his concern to show that Coleridge '*used*' love to satisfy obscure religious longings, he may have minimized Coleridge's deep-felt need for affection and the strength of his attachment to Hartley. Mr Suther's case rests not on the 'annus mirabilis' poems, but mainly on items written many years afterwards (Suther, ch. 2).

years about his domestic life at this time—statements notoriously unreliable—should be set the evidence of poems like *Frost at Midnight*, *Fears in Solitude*, *The Nightingale*, or the verses addressed *To the Rev. George Coleridge*. Dorothy Wordsworth's *Alfoxden Journal* and *The Prelude*, which speaks of Coleridge's 'happy heart' that summer, bear out the impression of Coleridge's contentedness at this time.[1] Richard Reynell's eye-witness report on the Coleridges' life at Stowey concluded: 'I have seen domestic life in all its beauty and simplicity, affection founded on a much stronger basis than wealth—on esteem.'[2] It is true that Sara could not rouse the feelings in Coleridge that Asra, subsequently, did, and that her narrowness of outlook aften irritated him, but because she was the mother of his child he could overlook most of her shortcomings.[3] Only after Coleridge met Sara Hutchinson, in October 1799, did his marriage start to 'fail'.

During this 'annus mirabilis', as at no other period in his life, Coleridge enjoyed to the full the intimacy and protection of his major 'sheet-anchor' friendships. Having established his home next-door to Poole, only three miles away from Alfoxden where the Wordsworths were living, he could draw at will upon the strength and stimulus which these favourite 'sheet-anchors' provided. There is no doubt that Coleridge himself regarded these circumstances as highly conducive to creativity:

> . . . beside one Friend,
> Beneath the impervious covert of one oak,
> I've rais'd a lowly shed, and know the names
> Of Husband and of Father; not unhearing
> Of that divine and nightly-whispering Voice,
> Which from my childhood to maturer years
> Spake to me of predestinated wreaths,
> Bright with no fading colours![4]

Other friends, like Lamb, Cottle, Lloyd, and Thelwall, sought

---

Mr Beer dismisses the 'propitious circumstances' explanation for Coleridge's achievements in 1797–8 somewhat cursorily, arguing that 'one can only fully explain' Coleridge's happiness at this time in terms of a 'myth' which he had recently seized upon as a means of reconciling his artistic and intellectual interests. 'This is', as Mr Beer himself acknowledges, 'a large claim to make for any myth' (Beer, 42).

[1] See Life, 90; "Prelude", xiv, 392–413.   [2] Life, 84.
[3] See pp. 103–4.
[4] "To the Rev. George Coleridge", ll. 32–9, PW 174.

his company readily, and he had even to dissuade Thelwall from setting up home alongside him.[1] He was even reconciled with Southey, and also with his relatives at Ottery.[2] Above all, he had Wordsworth at hand to inspire him—'The Giant Wordsworth', whom he reckoned 'the greatest Man' he had ever encountered.[3] In 1797–8, therefore, Coleridge experienced a rich sense of emotional well-being such as never before or subsequently; if love *was* the 'vital air' of his genius, his life now overbrimmed with it.

An immediate effect of Wordsworth's example was to cause Coleridge radically to change his poetic manner, thereby stimulating a dramatic advance from what Mr Schulz calls the 'farrago voice'[4] to the low-keyed naturalness of his conversational poems. As late as December 1796, Coleridge had observed that his own poetry seldom exhibited 'unmixed & simple tenderness or passion', despite his efforts during 1794–6 to reconcile thought with feeling.[5] He was thus seeking a more natural style even before he met Wordsworth, but was uncertain how to set about it. Wordsworth's poetry provided the model he needed: 'There was here no mark of strained thought, or forced diction, no crowd or turbulence of imagery.'[6] He saw that it was not enough to be activated by strong feelings; these feelings must issue naturally:

A young man by strong feelings is impelled to write on a particular subject—and this is all his feelings do for him. They set him upon the business & then they leave him.—He has such a high idea of what Poetry ought to be, that he cannot conceive that such things as his natural emotions may be allowed to find a place in it—his

---

[1] cf. Life, 83. Charles Lloyd (1775–1839), the poet, met Coleridge in 1796, and later lived with the Coleridges as a paying-guest and pupil (see CL, I, 235–6n). Coleridge's poem *To A Young Friend On his Proposing to Domesticate with the Author* commemorates the event (PW 155).

John Thelwall (1764–1834) was imprisoned in the Tower in May 1794 and tried for treason, but was later acquitted. A minor poet, he is remembered best perhaps as the Jacobin 'spy' reported to the Government by the county gentlemen around Nether Stowey in 1797 (see Life, 79–83).

[2] See CL, I, 336; Life, 60. Unfortunately, the rapport which existed between Coleridge and Southey in July 1797 was ruptured by Coleridge's publication of his Nehemiah Higginbottom sonnets in the *Monthly Magazine*, November 1797. Both Southey and Lamb were offended by these sonnets, and their relationships with Coleridge were cool for some time afterwards (see PW 209–10; CL, I, 358–9).

[3] CL, I, 325, 391.   [4] Schulz, chs II, v.   [5] CL, I, 278–9.
[6] BL, I, 58.

learning therefore, his fancy, or rather conceit, and all his powers of buckram are put on the stretch.[1]

He now disowned the overpitched feelings of the *Chatterton Monody* and, significantly, he chose *Reflections* as the 'best', and *The Eolian Harp* as the 'favourite' of his earlier poems, both of them experiments in the conversational style.[2] The obscurity of the dancing roundelay and the wizard trappings of the 'faery' style were discarded, and his aim became the attainment of 'innocent nakedness'—to 'masquerade' no more in 'flesh-coloured Silk'.[3]

In Wordsworth's example Coleridge discovered too a moral purposiveness quite the obverse of his own unstable ebullience. Whereas his own didacticism tended to lapse into sermonizing or benevolent, but essentially generalized, crusading, Wordsworth's (he saw) was infused with absolute conviction and a feeling for men as individuals. In *Biographia Literaria* Coleridge has recorded the sudden effect produced on his mind in 1795–6 on hearing Wordsworth recite his own verses: 'It was the union of deep feeling with profound thought', etc.[4]—the very synthesis, in other words, towards which he himself was struggling. On analysing Wordsworth's poetry Coleridge found that, while it had strong moral affinities with his own, it had a sharper relevance, a closer connection between the vision and its practical applications. The following passage from *The Ruined Cottage* characterized for him these essential attributes of Wordsworth's strength:

> Not useless do I deem
> These shadowy Sympathies with things that hold
> An inarticulate Language: for the Man
> Once taught to love such objects, as excite
> No morbid passions, no disquietude,
> No vengeance & no hatred, needs must feel
> The Joy of that pure principle of Love
> So deeply, that, unsatisfied with aught
> Less pure & exquisite, he cannot chuse
> But seek for objects of a kindred Love
> In fellow-natures, & a kindred Joy.
> Accordingly, he by degrees perceives
> His feelings of aversion softened down,
> A holy tenderness pervade his frame!

[1] CL, I, 333.   [2] ibid, I, 295.   [3] ibid, I, 379.   [4] BL, I, 59.

His sanity of reason not impair'd,
Say rather that his thoughts now flowing clear
From a clear fountain flowing, he looks round—
He seeks for Good & finds the Good he seeks.[1]

The opening statement here concerning 'shadowy' communion with things that hold 'an inarticulate Language' might have come straight from Coleridge's own *Religious Musings,* but there the resemblance ends. Where Coleridge might have expanded this (in Mr House's phrase) into a 'Theistic Metaphysic of Nature' Wordsworth was more interested in the precise effects upon the concrete, particular 'Man' who enjoys the experience, and the application of the visionary experience to actual moral life. In Wordsworth's poem, thought, language, and moral intention are perspicuous and persuasive. Coleridge decided there and then to model his didactic style on Wordsworth's (without considering sufficiently perhaps whether this was suited to his own most natural 'voice'):

. . . I devote myself to such works as encroach not on the anti-social passions—in poetry, to elevate the imagination & set the affections in right tune by the beauty of the inanimate impregnated, as with a living soul, by the presence of Life. . . I love fields & woods & mounta[ins] with almost a visionary fondness—and because I have found benevolence & quietness growing within me as that fondness [has] increased, therefore I should wish to be the means of implanting it in others . . .[2]

He did not succeed immediately in pruning his style of 'sermoni propriora' qualities—which re-appeared in *Fears in Solitude* ('Like mere abstractions, empty sounds to which / We join no feeling and attach no form!')—but, despite such lapses, a tautness and precision appeared in his work which had hitherto been lacking.

Because of the emotional security he experienced during 1797–8, a fresh field of poetic subject-matter was opened up for Coleridge. The romantic isolate who dwells 'apart from men' still appeared from time to time, but other poems were written treating of a whole new range of family and personal relationships. Thus, auditors appeared as recipients for the conversational pieces, dialogues were needed and narrators to tell their stories

[1] CL, I, 397–8. These lines originally formed part of the conclusion to "The Ruined Cottage".
[2] ibid.

within the framework of the main narrative (as in *The Ancient Mariner*, *The Old Man of the Alps*, and *The Three Graves*). In *To a Young Friend*, for example, though the treatment is somewhat sugary and over-sentimentalized, the poet (no longer alone) walks arm in arm with his friend (Lloyd) and *together* they 'unlock the treasur'd heart', while down in the dell, 'smiling with blue eye', Sara waits to greet them.[1] The era of 'chasing chance-started friendships' was over, Coleridge felt, and such was his sense of confident self-assurance that, in the first of the great 'annus mirabilis' poems, it was not he who stood in need of sympathy, but Lamb. This sense of emotional well-being was reflected in several of the autobiographical poems of 1797–8.

This Lime-tree Bower my Prison (July 1797) opens with an imprisonment image and a situation of loneliness in which one might expect from Coleridge some indulgence in self-pity, especially as a painful foot injury has prevented him from accompanying Lamb and the Wordsworths in a walk over the neighbouring Quantocks:

> Well, they are gone, and here must I remain,
> This lime-tree bower my prison! I have lost
> Beauties and feelings, such as would have been
> Most sweet to my remembrance even when age
> Had dimm'd mine eyes to blindness! They, meanwhile,
> Friends, whom I never more may meet again,
> On springy heath, along the hill-top edge,
> Wander in gladness ... (1–8)

In fact the mood is one of resignation, not self-pity, for repining soon turns outwards—to benevolent gladness that Lamb, released from London, is free to enjoy the countryside. Already, one detects a mature assurance quite new to Coleridge's poetry as, self-forgetful for once, he projects a wish that Lamb may enjoy the ecstatic communion from which he himself is temporarily debarred. Without the vision, in fact, Coleridge achieves a philosophic acceptance of his situation and (by proxy, as it were)

---

[1] PW 156. "To a Young Friend" belongs actually to 1796, when the poet Charles Lloyd was negotiating to become Coleridge's paying-guest and pupil (see CL, I, 235–6). It represents an early expression therefore of the sense of emotional well-being which was to characterize the 'annus mirabilis' poems.

something of Lamb's own joy: 'A delight / Comes sudden on my
heart, and I am glad / As I myself were there!' Poetically, at any
rate, this leads to something more satisfying than his former metaphysical rhapsodies; instead of the incomprehensible sublime we
are invited rather to regard the transmogrification of the concrete
and the particular as effected by the attuned poetic imagination:

> . . . Nor in this bower,
> This little lime-tree bower, have I not mark'd
> Much that has sooth'd me. Pale beneath the blaze
> Hung the transparent foliage; and I watch'd
> Some broad and sunny leaf, and lov'd to see
> The shadow of the leaf and stem above
> Dappling its sunshine! And that walnut-tree
> Was richly ting'd, and a deep radiance lay
> Full on the ancient ivy, which usurps
> Those fronting elms, and now, with blackest mass
> Makes their dark branches gleam a lighter hue
> Through the late twilight . . . (47–56)

This, I think, presents a clearer picture of what rapport with
nature means than do the majority of his formal Theistic passages. He writes now with his eye upon the object rather than the
clouds, and with natural feeling. Where, earlier, he had seemed
too much upon the stretch, as though trying to compel acceptance, he writes now with relaxed and easy confidence.

The improved poetic technique carries him with confident
assurance through the beautifully controlled rhythms leading up
to the conclusion of the poem, while the tone of this passage
evinces clearly the strength that this experience has given him:

> . . . Henceforth I shall know
> That Nature ne'er deserts the wise and pure;
> No plot so narrow, be but Nature there,
> No waste so vacant, but may well employ
> Each faculty of sense, and keep the heart
> Awake to Love and Beauty! and sometimes
> 'Tis well to be bereft of promis'd good,
> That we may lift the soul, and contemplate
> With lively joy the joys we cannot share.
> My gentle-hearted Charles! when the last rook
> Beat its straight path along the dusky air
> Homewards, I blest it! deeming its black wing
> (Now a dim speck, now vanishing in light)

> Had cross'd the mighty Orb's dilated glory.
> While thou stood'st gazing; or, when all was still,
> Flew creeking o'er thy head, and had a charm
> For thee, my gentle-hearted Charles, to whom
> No sound is dissonant which tells of Life. (59–76)

The qualification 'be but Nature there' is important as indicating one of the factors which makes this 'prison' tolerable—a point Coleridge amplifies in *The Dungeon, Kubla Khan,* and *The Foster-Mother's Tale.* It is only in the merest physical sense a prison since, as the ease with which the thought moves outward from the steady centre of his own mind exemplifies, it has none of that cramping mental inhibition which he reacted against in *Reflections.* More pertinently, it was not a prison because, though his friends were gone, they would return. It was this sense of emotional security probably, much more than any vicarious intuition of the Absolute, which produced Coleridge's new-found equanimity.

An important letter which he wrote to Thelwall about this time suggests (as later did the lines written in the Harz Forest and *Dejection: an Ode*) that Coleridge could not achieve communion with the 'One Life' except in a state of emotional well-being. After quoting in this letter the metaphysical portion of *This Lime-tree Bower*: 'Struck with the deepest calm of Joy' I stand—

> Silent, with swimming sense; and gazing round
> On the wide Landscape gaze till all doth seem
> Less gross than bodily, a living Thing
> Which acts upon the mind, & with such Hues
> As cloath th'Almighty Spirit, when he makes
> Spirits perceive his presence (38–43)—

he went on to admit: 'It is but seldom that I raise and spiritualize my intellect to this height.' More commonly, he said, the universe seemed to him a 'heap of *little* things', and he was tempted to flee from it into escapist 'voyage' fantasies or utter mental passivity. Only one thing, he told Thelwall, could 'beat away this deep contempt for all things': 'I need the sympathy of human faces.'[1] Evidently, he possessed this sympathy at the time he wrote *This Lime-tree Bower my Prison,* which may partly explain why his poetic imagination could irradiate everyday particulars in the way it

[1] CL, I, 349–50.

I

did.[1] But the Thelwall letter indicates how precariously his equilibrium was poised between susceptibility to 'Joy' and his proneness to fanciful escapism. The least emotional upset might send his mind voyaging again through strange seas of thought, feeding chameleon-like on the 'universal air' of Vishnuism instead of on the 'vital air' of ordinary affection.

In *Frost at Midnight* (February 1798), though thought and feeling blend less exquisitely, the strength and richness of the feeling are quite unprecedented. This time, the emotion focuses mainly upon his infant child (Hartley). At first Coleridge's mind is 'vexed' and restless but, as the strong currents of feeling get under way, tension relaxes and the concluding lines of the poem are among the most beautiful and satisfactory he ever wrote. In the middle section, once intellectual speculation gives way to mellower associative thought-processes, he explores with a sense of novel pleasure a whole range of ordinary human feelings.

The poet is virtually alone when the poem commences, the inmates of his cottage being all at rest and his baby cradled peaceably beside him. His mind is only half-attuned to the influxes of nature, and dissonance is detectable in the details of the *frosty* silence and the reproving owlet's cry. (In *Osorio* it is suggested, incidentally, that the wakeful scritch-owl can maintain One-Life attunement when a poet's mind has lost the wavelength.[2]) Certainly the beauty of the frost-tracery is lost upon *him* and he finds the solitude oppressive. In this dead silence 'abstruser musings' occupy his attention and, while the 'subtilizing' intellect is in command, feeling lies dormant.

His speculative intellect, making an idle 'toy of Thought', originally intruded quite disproportionately into the poem at this point, as Mr House has demonstrated.[3] Finding some companionship between itself and the film which fluttered on the grate, it commenced a metaphysical disquisition on whether life

[1] The poem was written in Poole's arbour, while Lamb and the Wordsworths were Coleridge's guests, and these happy circumstances have some bearing on the unaccustomed self-assurance it reveals (see CL, I, 334–6). The poem exists in its own right, of course, apart from biographical considerations.

[2] See CL, I, 350.

[3] HH, 81–2. I am indebted here, as in many other instances, to Mr House's valuable reading of the poems.

could be transfused into the inanimate by force of mental voli-
tion. In all the earlier variant readings of the lines now numbered
19–25 this cognitive weight quite upset the balance of thought
and feeling, and not until 1828 did Coleridge find the tauter
rendering he needed, which does in fact prepare the reader for
the flow of associative ideas and images that follows. In other
words, unwelcome intrusions of the meddling intellect still persisted even when he had the powerful incentive Hartley's presence afforded to write in the simple, natural way he wanted.
Only by a long and difficult apprenticeship did Coleridge sub-
jugate this egocentric self-centredness which, in *The Nightingale*
(ll. 14–34), he condemned as undesirable in poetry.

He is vexed and impatient then with the hushed stillness, much
as he is at the commencement of *Shurton Bars* and *Dejection: an
Ode*. This time, however, it needs no storm to change his mood,
for suddenly he becomes aware of the presence of life in the
breathing of the child beside him. It recalls his own childhood
and, prompted by the fluttering 'stranger' on the grate (which,
according to legend, portended the arrival of some absent friend),
he remembers the loneliness of his own schooldays, his homesick-
ness and exhilaration at the prospect of a visitor from home. The
sequence of thought is now determined wholly by the recollected
emotions of childhood—credulous belief, nostalgia, fear, hope,
and joy—while all of these are overlaid by his immediate awareness of the child beside him, whose gentle breathings fill up 'the
interspersèd vacancies / And momentary pauses of the *thought*!'
The reverie ends in a flood of tender parental emotion: 'My babe
so beautiful! it thrills my heart / With tender gladness, thus to
look at thee'. Once the verse becomes charged with feeling it runs
on with confident and sweeping energy, and Coleridge never
needed to torture these lines with corrections as he had done lines
19–25. When thought and feeling coalesced thus readily, he
found his most mature poetic expression.

Ranging far and wide from its anchorage in the present his
mind turns from his own past to Hartley's future, and tender
feeling for his child now comes through strongly. He vows that
his son shall have a happier childhood than his own, and one less
inhibited:

> For I was reared
> In the great city, pent 'mid cloisters dim,
> And saw nought lovely but the sky and stars.

> But *thou*, my babe! shalt wander like a breeze
> By lakes and sandy shores, beneath the crags
> Of ancient mountain, and beneath the clouds,
> Which image in their bulk both lakes and shores
> And mountain crags. (51–8)

In structure and feeling this passage resembles closely Coleridge's altruistic gesture to Lamb in *This Lime-tree Bower*, though the emotion here is more intense. It builds up in similar fashion to the spiritualization of the intellect described in the letter to Thelwall—'so shalt thou see and hear / The lovely shapes and sounds intelligible' etc. (59–64). Here, the metaphysic arises naturally out of the preceding lines though, finally, it obtrudes perhaps too openly (like the moral apothegm in *The Ancient Mariner*). In comparison with what has gone before it seems cerebral and abstract, as though thought out previously. In *The Nightingale*, where the metaphysic is played down (ll. 27–9, 76–82), it is greatly to the improvement of the poem, and there the mature conversational tone duplicates almost perfectly the shifting flow of natural speech and feelings.

The exquisite final stanza is altogether more satisfying (and convincing) as Coleridge's thoughts return to the present and the sleeping child. In the interest of following the Christ's Hospital anecdote and the description of Hartley's future one has scarcely noticed how this current of feeling has changed the poet's own mental attitude since his earlier vexedness. His sense of isolation has gone and with it the irritable searching after fact and reason: his mind is now filled with tender emotion and deep love of nature, frosty or otherwise. This stanza, instead of rhapsodizing with hands upraised, virtually *enacts* for us the 'One Life' attunement, *shows* us rather than tells us, and makes us *feel* something of its Joy for ourselves:

> Therefore all seasons shall be sweet to thee,
> Whether the summer clothe the general earth
> With greenness, or the redbreast sit and sing
> Betwixt the tufts of snow on the bare branch
> Of mossy apple-tree, while the nigh thatch
> Smokes in the sun-thaw; whether the eave-drops fall
> Heard only in the trances of the blast,
> Or if the secret ministry of frost
> Shall hang them up in silent icicles,
> Quietly shining to the quiet Moon. (65–74)

Originally six additional lines were appended to this stanza, which were later deleted. They contained a graphic picture of the child playing in its mother's arms and, while the poem may be better without them, they were nevertheless a pointer to the deep emotional source of this most successful poem—the pleasure this baby had brought to Coleridge's married life.[1]

Fears in Solitude (April 1798), though disproportionate in qualities of thought and feeling (and one of the less successful therefore of the major 'annus mirabilis' poems), exemplifies the problems Coleridge had to wrestle with in assimilating didacticism to the requirements of poetic organization. It was written only a month after he had declared his intention of cultivating Wordsworthian benevolence and the techniques for 'implanting' similar feelings in his readers. This first attempt was not entirely successful; nevertheless, it contained a number of felicitous passages, as well as having interesting things to say about his relations with his family and his own moral standpoint.

Again, the circular structure of the poem is determined by a curving pattern of thought which begins and ends with the 'green and silent' dell at Stowey. In the opening stanza Coleridge expresses unmistakable delight and satisfaction with the haven of peace his home affords in a country which is menaced by threat of armed invasion—'Oh! 'tis a quiet spirit-healing nook!' The silence and stillness of the Stowey 'dell' parallels almost exactly the details of the 'Valley of Seclusion', described earlier in *Reflections*:

> A green and silent spot, amid the hills,
> A small and silent dell! O'er stiller place
> No singing sky-lark ever poised himself. (1–3)

[1] Originally the poem ended as follows:
> Or whether the secret ministry of cold
> Shall hang them up in silent icicles,
> Quietly shining to the quiet moon,
> Like those, my babe! which ere tomorrow's warmth
> Have capp'd their sharp keen points with pendulous drops,
> Will catch thine eye, and with their novelty
> Suspend thy little soul; then make thee shout,
> And stretch and flutter from thy mother's arms
> As thou wouldst fly for very eagerness. (See HH, 82)

The benign, contented tone is that of one who, after a long and troubled search, has found at last his refuge and with it peace of mind. He responds with genial warmth to the natural beauties of his situation, describing these with rare and tender lyricism:

> . . . but the dell,
> Bathed by the mist, is fresh and delicate
> As vernal corn-field, or the unripe flax,
> When, through its half-transparent stalks, at eve,
> The level sunshine glimmers with green light. (7–11)

There is here a quality of particularization and, still more, an imaginative transformation of the commonplace into something novel and exciting which exemplifies perfectly the aim expressed in the Preface to *Lyrical Ballads*.[1]

Coleridge's former apprehensions about life in the 'dell' appear to have vanished for, in appreciating its profuse natural attractions, feelings of thankfulness are aroused which lead him to acknowledge what a contented married-life has done for him. *Any* man, he says (recalling possibly the envious passer-by in *Reflections*), would treasure such a home, but especially one whose earlier life had been as wayward as his own:

> Oh! 'tis a quiet spirit-healing nook!
> Which all, methinks, would love; but chiefly he,
> The humble man, who, in his youthful years,
> Knew just so much of folly, as had made
> His early manhood more securely wise! (12–16)

The tension which in *The Eolian Harp* had earned him Sara's 'mild reproof' seems now to have disappeared for, without misgivings or self-consciousness, he confidently develops here a conception of 'animated nature [as] organic Harps diversely fram'd' not dissimilar from the Plotinian speculations which previously his wife had found offensive:

> And from the sun, and from the breezy air,
> Sweet influences trembled o'er his frame;
> And he, with many feelings, many thoughts,
> Made up a meditative joy, and found
> Religious meanings in the forms of Nature! (20–4)

Though this is not radically different from the 'trembling thought' and 'intellectual breezes' of the earlier metaphysic, yet it is de-

[1] See Schulz, 97.

livered now without fear of acrimonious contradiction. Possibly Sara no longer cared about these subtleties but, whatever the reason, her indulgent dispensation goes some way towards explaining Coleridge's present satisfaction with the 'dell'. Granted this freedom to pursue his speculations uninhibitedly, Coleridge could endorse the conclusion arrived at in *This Lime-tree Bower my Prison*: 'No plot so narrow, be but Nature there,' will keep the heart 'awake to Love and Beauty'. If the 'dell' was a prison, it was at least an 'open' prison, since in it he could

> . . . to the influxes
> Of shapes and sounds and shifting elements
> [Surrender] his whole spirit.[1]

There was, however, a still more important reason now for his satisfaction with it.

In this poem, as in *Reflections*, he again experiences the moral compulsion to 'feel / For all his human brethren'. In the earlier poem this had decided him to *quit* the 'rose-leaf beds', though he had promised to return after his crusade, when the time was ripe for it. Since then, Coleridge's circumstances had changed and, consequently, the moral impulse is here significantly different, both in motivation and in the effects it leads to. Where, in *Reflections*, he appeared guilt-stricken that he had neglected his moral obligations as a poet in favour of sensual indulgence ('pampering the coward heart / With feelings all too delicate for use'), now the Cassandra-like warning he delivers to his countrymen springs from the much deeper emotional source of fear for his family's safety in the event of a French invasion (over-pitched though this is):

> Spare us yet awhile,
> Father and God! O! spare us yet awhile!
> Oh! let not English women drag their flight
> Fainting beneath the burthen of their babes,
> Of the sweet infants, that but yesterday
> Laughed at the breast! (129–34)

As his wife's and child's protector he no longer thinks of 'quitting' the dell, but, instead, after delivering his sermon, returns to it with grateful affection.

When, however, he turns from the feelings associated with his home to develop the moral argument, the poem suffers from over-

[1] cf. "The Nightingale", ll. 27–9, PW 265.

cerebration. The same amorphous rhetoric which marred *Reflections* now disfigures *Fears in Solitude* for, once 'thought' obtrudes, the quality of the verse deteriorates—as Coleridge himself admitted: 'N.B. The above is perhaps not Poetry,—but rather a sort of middle thing between Poetry and Oratory—sermoni propriora.'[1] As in *Reflections* the fault may have sprung from the lack of any specific auditor, so that the address became a harangue or diatribe, tempting him to lapse into the lecturing manner of a preacher. There is thus an incongruous mixture of styles in the poem,[2] of which the more lyrical and emotional passages are incomparably the best. Coleridge evidently experienced difficulty in sustaining natural feeling throughout the length of a poem; he had still to learn that high moral purpose may best be effected not by forceful implantation nor with buckram on the stretch, but when, as in *Frost at Midnight*, it takes the reader almost unawares.

An interesting feature of this sermonizing, however, is its unabashed self-confidence, its almost complacent sense of superior moral integrity. Though modestly he includes himself in the general indictment—'We have offended, Oh! my countrymen!' —in fact he stands apart from it, assuming unhesitantly the authoritativeness of an elder Cato or (in lines 70–80 especially) the mantle of a latter-day Lear. Confident in his own integrity, he holds himself aloof from his countrymen while loftily exhorting them—'make yourselves pure!' After he contracted his clandestine relationship with Asra, Coleridge was never again capable of pontificating in this assertive, pugnacious manner.

The diatribe ends on the organ-like note of a patriotic hymn and inflation suspires to make way once more for ordinary feeling. The mood softens to the temper of the opening movement and the structure comes full circle with a beautiful description of the sunset which now irradiates the 'soft and silent spot'. The throes of mind are finished and Coleridge hastens 'homeward' to rejoin the family circle. He seems glad to have got the 'poète maudit' business over with, and eager for renewed society:

> And now, belovéd Stowey! I behold
> Thy church-tower, and, methinks, the four huge elms
> Clustering, which mark the mansion of my friend;
> And close behind them, hidden from my view,

[1] See PW 257n.   [2] See Schulz, 98.

Is my own lowly cottage, where my babe
And my babe's mother dwell in peace! With light
And quickened footsteps thitherward I tend,
Remembering thee, O green and silent dell!
And grateful, that by nature's quietness
And solitary musings, all my heart
Is softened, and made worthy to indulge
Love, and the thoughts that yearn for human kind.

(221–32)

One may discern in such a passage his appreciation of the three major sources of emotional contentment which in 1798 had given stability to his life—his home, and his two chief 'sheet-anchors', Poole and Wordsworth.

Many of Coleridge's 'annus mirabilis' poems were inspired then by affection for his friends and delight in family life. Yet, in the latter case, the emphasis was on the home and the child rather than on Sara, for it is always the 'spirit-healing nook' and the 'babe', not she, that provide the focus of emotion. Sara remains a shadowy figure, referred to once as 'my babe's mother' and otherwise included in such formal groupings as 'the inmates of my cottage' or the 'English women' menaced by invasion. How different is this from the specific directness with which Mary Evans or Asra were brought into the very foreground of poems like *Ave Atque Vale*, *The Sigh*, *To Asra*, and *A Day-Dream*. The fact was that following Hartley's birth late in 1796 Coleridge and Sara evolved a modus vivendi which provided the best possible compromise in the light of their temperamental incompatibilities. They could co-habit amicably and be thankful for possessing at last a home of their own, something which had always ranked very high in their respective priorities. Without being passionately in love, they could yet live together and have children, and sensibly they made the best of what they had. It was quite feasible, therefore, for an outside observer like Reynell to consider theirs a life of domestic contentment, for only in Coleridge's poetry were its essential deficiencies exposed. Here he could enthuse about his home and child with genuine spontaneity, but never about his wife.

With the child it was quite different. In lines *To the Rev. George Coleridge*, *Fears in Solitude*, *Frost at Midnight*, *Christabel* (Part II, Conclusion), and *The Nightingale*, Coleridge's 'beloved babe' provided a major focus of interest, and a deep source of feeling which governed the flow of ideas. Whenever the child is mentioned, it becomes apparent that it is the feelings associated with him that give life and meaning to the 'dell' existence. Nowhere is this more clearly shown than in *The Nightingale* where, writing under impulse of uninhibited, outgoing feeling, Coleridge achieved his most mature and natural expression of the conversational style, in lines which follow exactly, in their parentheses and the delightfully off-handed 'Well!—It is a father's tale', the speech-rhythms of ordinary conversation:

> And now for our dear homes.—That strain again!
> Full fain it would delay me! My dear babe,
> Who, capable of no articulate sound,
> Mars all things with his imitative lisp,
> How he would place his hand beside his ear,
> His little hand, the small forefinger up,
> And bid us listen! And I deem it wise
> To make him Nature's play-mate. He knows well
> The evening-star; and once, when he awoke
> In most distressful mood (some inward pain
> Had made up that strange thing, an infant's dream—)
> I hurried with him to our orchard-plot,
> And he beheld the moon, and, hushed at once,
> Suspends his sobs, and laughs most silently,
> While his fair eyes, that swam with undropped tears,
> Did glitter in the yellow moon-beam! Well!—
> It is a father's tale: But if that Heaven
> Should give me life, his childhood shall grow up
> Familiar with these songs, that with the night
> He may associate joy.— (90–109)

Coleridge delighted in young children and through spontaneous and uncomplicated interchange of affection with Hartley he developed feelings which had hitherto lain dormant. The disproportion of treatment and tone as between child and mother indicates that it was the child's presence which more than anything else reconciled Coleridge to his home. At the same time, it is significant that in both *Frost at Midnight* and *The Nightingale* he promises his son a dimension of liberty greater than he had himself enjoyed.

It is remarkable with what frequency images associated with imprisonment or confinement recur in the sequence of 'annus mirabilis' poems, beginning with the '*prison*' of the lime-tree bower. Kubla Khan's paradise is 'with walls and towers girdled round' while Christabel's misfortunes befall her within the moat, behind 'the gate that was ironed within and without'. An extract from *Osorio* was published in *Lyrical Ballads* under the actual title of *The Dungeon*, and dungeon-effects appear prominently in *The Foster-Mother's Tale* and *The Ancient Mariner*. The recurrence of this image-cluster looks very much like the projection of some unconscious fear or inhibition, particularly as Coleridge had always feared that Sara's type of domesticity might stifle his poetic genius. Each time he used the image it was invariably set up against some contrasting concept of freedom which thus became its foil or obverse. The details varied but, usually, the 'free' dimension included some cognizance of the undivided life or (as in *France: an Ode*—a pæan to '*Liberty*') a regression to Chatterton-ian 'outsiderism', where liberty is discovered on the 'sea-cliff's verge' amid the waves and '*homeless* winds'. Coleridge, it seemed, was anxious to secure for Hartley from the outset the conditions which he conceived as prerequisite to the full development of the romantic imagination, and an upbringing more like Words-worth's than that which he and Lamb had had: 'But *thou*, my babe! shalt wander like a breeze / By lakes and sandy shores'. Coleridge may have revealed in these compensatory fantasies of Hartley's future his own frustrated hankerings after something different from the 'dell'. He could not realize that he would never enjoy a more congenial life than this, or that these very tensions had contributed to the fine balance of thought and feeling in his recent poetry.

In *The Dungeon* all the worst aspects of the 'dell' appear writ large, for this poem deals not simply with the paraphernalia of the Gothic but with a theme close to the subliminal sources of Coleridge's associative powers. If freedom consists, as he had said, in 'the *unfettered* use / Of all the powers which God for use had given',[1] then physical incarceration represents the very obverse of such freedom:

> ... Merciful God!
> Each pore and natural outlet shrivell'd up
> By Ignorance and parching Poverty,
> His energies roll back upon his heart,

[1] cf. "The Destiny of Nations", ll. 13–14, PW 132.

> And stagnate and corrupt; till chang'd to poison,
> They break out on him, like a loathsome plague-spot . . .
>
> (5–10)

Coleridge's handling of this subject is interesting. He was no 'Monk' Lewis and was chiefly concerned with the moral implications (for jailers as well as prisoner) of total imprisonment, and especially with the moral deterioration which results when a human being is deprived of affection or contact with nature.

The prisoner's predicament represents for Coleridge the ultimate horror, a claustrophobic confinement in which, unnourished, the mental faculties decay, while devoid of female sympathy or 'sheet-anchor' support ('uncomforted' and 'friendless') the wretch is left in utter solitude to face existence amid 'savage faces'. Of the whole range of feelings he explored in poetry none was more personally poignant to him than this. In *The Ancient Mariner*, of course, the exploration was carried a good deal farther. After he wrote *The Dungeon* and *The Ancient Mariner* there was for Coleridge no more courting of romantic solitude after the fashion of the Chatterton cult, nor anything like the awesome self-sufficiency with which Wordsworth welcomed inviolate retirement. Isolation Coleridge now dreaded as a state of helplessness and vulnerability, and repeatedly in *Osorio* he emphasized that it requires the counterbalance of human sympathy. Without such sympathy Coleridge found that his own imagination lost the power of spiritual insight, so that nature disintegrated into a 'mass of *little* things' or mere 'outward forms'. Similarly, without 'sheet-anchor' support or female sympathy, the moral fibre of the prisoner in the dungeon collapses:

> So he lies
> Circled with evil, till his very soul
> Unmoulds its essence, hopelessly deform'd
> By sights of ever more deformity! (16–19)

In the second stanza Coleridge, following the stereotype romantic convention of 'Nature the healer', suggests that criminal tendencies might be better cured by exposure to nature's influence rather than by physical incarceration, much as in *This Limetree Bower my Prison* Lamb's troubled spirit was supposed to have been soothed by the Quantock landscape:

> With other ministrations thou, O Nature!
> Healest thy wandering and distemper'd child:

Thou pourest on him thy soft influences,
Thy sunny hues, fair forms, and breathing sweets,
Thy melodies of woods, and winds, and waters,
Till he relent, and can no more endure
To be a jarring and a dissonant thing,
Amid this general dance and minstrelsy;
But, bursting into tears, wins back his way,
His angry spirit heal'd and harmoniz'd
By the benignant touch of Love and Beauty. (20–30)

The Foster-Mother's Tale narrates the story of another prisoner who in fact escapes from his dungeon and flees to nature's bosom —'And all alone, set sail by silent moonlight / Up a great river'.[1] One suspects, however, that Coleridge was influenced here more by romantic convention than by his deepest instincts. Subsequent experience was to teach him that, in his own case (as in the Ancient Mariner's), the sympathy of human faces mattered more to mental health than any natural ministrations. Indeed, nature became for him 'a tough old witch' in the end with whom his mind grappled in vain.[2] The development of this realization may be traced through the great tetralogy of *Kubla Khan, The Ancient Mariner, Christabel*, and *Dejection: an Ode* which, in the following chapters, it is proposed to examine in detail.

[1] PW 184.   [2] See pp. 288–9 below.

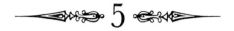

Kubla Khan

In Xanadu did Kubla Khan
A stately pleasure-dome decree:
Where Alph, the sacred river, ran
Through caverns measureless to man
    Down to a sunless sea   5
So twice five miles of fertile ground
With walls and towers were girdled round:
And there were gardens bright with sinuous rills,
Where blossomed many an incense-bearing tree;
And here were forests ancient as the hills,   10
Enfolding sunny spots of greenery.

But oh! that deep romantic chasm which slanted
Down the green hill athwart a cedarn cover!
A savage place! as holy and enchanted
As e'er beneath a waning moon was haunted   15
By woman wailing for her demon-lover!
And from this chasm, with ceaseless turmoil seething,
As if this earth in fast thick pants were breathing,
A mighty fountain momently was forced:
Amid whose swift half-intermitted burst   20
Huge fragments vaulted like rebounding hail,
Or chaffy grain beneath the thresher's flail:
And 'mid these dancing rocks at once and ever
It flung up momently the sacred river.
Five miles meandering with a mazy motion   25
Through wood and dale the sacred river ran,
Then reached the caverns measureless to man,
And sank in tumult to a lifeless ocean:
And 'mid this tumult Kubla heard from far
Ancestral voices prophesying war!   30
    The shadow of the dome of pleasure
    Floated midway on the waves;
    Where was heard the mingled measure
    From the fountain and the caves.

It was a miracle of rare device,   35
A sunny pleasure-dome with caves of ice!

A damsel with a dulcimer
In a vision once I saw:
It was an Abyssinian maid,
And on her dulcimer she played,   40
Singing of Mount Abora.[1]
Could I revive within me
Her symphony and song,
To such a deep delight 'twould win me,
That with music loud and long,   45
I would build that dome in air,
That sunny dome! those caves of ice!
And all who heard should see them there,
And all should cry, Beware! Beware!
His flashing eyes, his floating hair!   50
Weave a circle round him thrice,
And close your eyes with holy dread,
For he on honey-dew hath fed,
And drunk the milk of Paradise.

There is a peculiar ambivalence in *Kubla Khan*, allowing the widest divergencies of critical interpretation, which, according to Mr Eliot, arises from the fact that the imagery in the poem has not been '*used*', because the 'organization' needed to complement the 'inspiration' is lacking.[2] Certainly, the enigmatic personages who appear in the poem (the wailing woman, the ancestral voices, the Abyssinian maid, the youth with flashing eyes) and the vaguely incantatory proper names (Xanadu, Kubla Khan, Alph, Mount Abora) appear to adumbrate rather than crystallize the poet's intention. Yet, though generally speaking intentions in poetry are nothing save as 'realized', we are unable to ignore the poem, despite Mr Eliot's strictures on its 'exaggerated repute'. We may question without end *what* it means, but few of us question if the poem is worth the trouble, or whether the meaning is worth the having. While the feeling persists that there is something there which is profoundly important, the challenge to elucidate it proves irresistible.

The ambiguities inherent in the poem pose a special problem

[1] 'Abora' appears as 'Amara' in the autograph MS of the poem (see photograph reproduction on the jacket of this book).
[2] T. S. Eliot, *The Use of Poetry and The Use of Criticism* (1933), p. 146.

of critical approach. If we restrict ourselves to what is 'given', appealing to the poem as a 'whole', we shall fail probably to resolve its various cruxes.[1] Hence, there is a temptation to look for 'external' influences—to consider *Kubla Khan* in relation to Coleridge's general reading, to relate it to his later critical theory, or to regard the whole thing as the product of an opium experience.[2] The trouble with all these approaches is that they tend finally to lead *away* from the poem itself. Alternatively, we can examine Coleridge's handling of his acknowledged source-material (Purchas), rather as we might evaluate Shakespeare's modifications of Holinshed or North, a technique which has the virtue at least of grappling with the actual raw material. Or, again, we can consider *Kubla Khan* in relation to the rest of Coleridge's poetry, especially in the imagery it employs, which may be a less dangerous form of influence-tracing than pursuing him through the byways of his reading, since we start from the firmer basis of the author's professed or, at any rate, customary standpoint. This approach moreover is validated by Coleridge's own *Preface* to the poem, in which he recorded the remarkable extent to which the composition arose from a free association of ideas:

> The Author continued for about three hours in a profound sleep, at least of the external senses, during which time he has the most vivid confidence, that he could not have composed less than from two to three hundred lines; if that indeed can be called composition in which all the images rose up before him as *things*, with a parallel production of the correspondent expressions, without any sensation or consciousness of effort.[3]

Doubtless he wrote this *Preface* partly in self-defence, anticipating the charge of obscurity which the poem's acknowledged imperfection of organization would produce, but it provides nevertheless a useful clue to the elucidation of *Kubla Khan.*

[1] Thus, Mr House's appeal 'to the poem as a whole', to 'its total effect as a poem of fulfilment', fails to account adequately for the 'wailing woman' and the 'Abyssinian maid'.

[2] See J. L. Lowes, *The Road to Xanadu* (1930); J. B. Beer, *Coleridge the Visionary* (1959); R. C. Bald, "Coleridge and The Ancient Mariner", in *Nineteenth Century Studies*, ed. H. Davis (New York, 1940); and E. Schneider, *Coleridge, Opium and Kubla Khan* (Chicago, 1953).

[3] The Preface appeared in 1816, though the poem was written in either October 1797 or May 1798 (see Life, 100–3, and CL, I, 348–9n). See p. 136, note 2.

'*Acceptance* of the Paradise, *in sympathy*, is the normal response,' claimed Mr House, arguing that the opening stanza represents a 'conjunction of pleasure and sacredness' emblematic of the ideal, balanced life.[1] Since, however, this stanza has also been taken to represent a 'fallen paradise' or the pleasures of a 'utilitarian materialist' it is evident that interpretation pivots on the construction we choose to place upon it.[2] We may inquire what in fact there is in stanza 1 which engages sympathy and promotes spontaneous acceptance. Is it a paradise at all? Apart from the 'sacred river' there is an oriental Prince about whom we are told very little,[3] also a stately pleasure-dome and a barricaded garden which is described in remarkably general terms ('there were gardens', 'many a tree', 'here were forests', 'sunny spots of greenery', etc.). At first glance it seems that the sacred river might as validly stand in antithesis as in reinforcement of the other details, implying a *disjunction* of pleasure and sacredness.

The rhythmical development of the stanza, too, though technically brilliant, evokes admiration rather than delight. The unusually heavy stresses and abrupt masculine rhymes impose a slow and sonorous weightiness upon the movement of the iambic octosyllabics which is quite in contrast, say, to the light fast metre of the final stanza where speed of movement matches buoyancy of tone. Except for lines 3–5, where beautiful cadences suggest the fall of the sacred river through the caverns, the insistent beat of the rhythm carries a hammer-like quality (especially in lines 1–2, 6–7) suggesting perhaps the forcefulness with which the oriental despot's decree is imposed upon its living materials. Mr House remarked of stanza 3, 'If this were a poem of frustration and failure, the movement would be slow and heavy,' overlooking apparently that his description fitted exactly the deliberately ponderous movement of the opening stanza.

The Khan himself is peculiarly situated. Cut off from normal personal relationships he inhabits a solitude almost like that of *The Dungeon* prisoner or the Ancient Mariner. He hears only the

[1] HH, 120.

[2] See Beer, 212; Carl R. Woodring, "Coleridge and the Khan", *Essays in Criticism*, Vol. IX, October 1959, No. 4.

[3] 'Cublai Chan began to reign, 1256 the greatest Prince in Peoples, Cities and Kingdoms that ever was in the World.' Coleridge copied this sentence from *Purchas his Pilgrimes* (1625), Bk I, Ch. IV, §5, into a personal notebook. See KC, I, 1840.

ghostly voices of his menacing ancestors and (possibly) that of the wailing woman. His relationship with the slave-force which, presumably, enacts his decree for him is utterly impersonal—to judge from the syntactical use of the passive voice ('So twice five miles . . . were girdled round' and 'there were gardens'). Self-sufficient, seemingly, he feels no need of that female inspiration which the poet himself (denoted in stanza 3 by the use of the first person) requires before he can build *his* dome.

As for the stately pleasure-dome, Kubla's first creation, it should be observed that 'dome' was Coleridge's word, not Purchas's. Purchas mentioned a 'house of pleasure' which became transmogrified through the 'palace' of Coleridge's *Preface* to the final poetic concretization of 'pleasure-dome'. Considered simply as artefacts, 'house', 'palace', 'dome' may be said to form a scale of diminishing functional utility or, conversely, of increasingly contrived refinement. (The same might be said of Coleridge's substitution of 'rills' for the 'springs' found in Purchas, and possibly of 'gardens' for 'meddowes'.) It is not a point to be pressed since 'dome' possessed euphonious qualities poetically preferable for Coleridge's immediate purpose to either 'house' or 'palace'. Nevertheless, to regard a dome as the quintessential refinement of artifice, and as therefore farthest divorced from integral relationship with nature, might be closely in accordance with the poetic intention here.

Since twice in the poem 'dome' is linked with 'pleasure', interpretation of the paradise depends on what this '*pleasure*' signifies. Purchas quite obviously equated pleasure with 'sensuality'. In *Purchas his Pilgrimage* we read that Cublai Can built a stately palace with a garden encompassing 'a sumptuous house of pleasure', where 'sumptuous' implies 'luxurious'. Furthermore, as Lowes demonstrated, Coleridge drew also upon Purchas's account of Aloadine's Paradise in framing *Kubla Khan*.[1] The paradise described in this second account was quite emphatically sensual: 'Mahomet had promised such a *sensuall* Paradise to his devout followers.' Its delights were carnal and synthetic and, since access to them was open only to 'Assasines', it was decidedly an unethical and inferior paradise: '—the Fooles thought themselves in Paradise indeed.' Since Coleridge certainly borrowed many of the physical details from this description for his *Kubla*

[1] See Lowes, 360–4.

Khan, it is only a question of whether he adopted their original sensual colouring too. Inferential evidence suggests he did.

'Pleasure' was, in fact, a concept closely bound up with moral considerations for Coleridge:[1] ideally, duty and pleasure should be synonymous but, in practice, this is seldom the case.[2] Pleasure was not for him the same as 'joy'—'there is joy above the name of pleasure'—and joy demands the prior experience of God.[3] Thus, pleasure pursued for its own sake, and devoid of moral or spiritual considerations, is a transitory thing, 'unholy, frail and feverish'.[4] In poetry he generally represented pleasure in harsh pejorative terms: 'A hideous hag th' Enchantress Pleasure seems / And all her joys appear but feverous dreams'.[5]

The 'dome'-image, moreover, when employed elsewhere in Coleridge's poetry, was evaluated strictly according to the moral context in which it appeared. Thus, as associated with the religious feeling of 'deep, heartfelt inward *joy*' the 'dome' was wholly admirable: 'So will I build my altar in the fields, / And the blue sky my fretted dome shall be'.[6] But, as the synechdochic representation of material values it was quite unacceptable:

> Is not true Love of higher price
>   Than outward Form, though fair to see,
> Wealth's glittering fairy-*dome* of ice,
>   Or echo of proud ancestry?[7]

He used 'dome'-images to suggest also moral laxity[8] or, within a context of decadent luxury ('the soft couch, and many-coloured robe, / The timbrel, and arched dome and costly feast') to denote gross sensual excesses.[9] In much the same way dome-like images of 'bubbles' and 'hives' were employed to signify the purposeless-

[1] cf. PL, 153.

[2] There is a long notebook entry, dated April 1805, concerning this distinction, which concludes: 'For when Duty & Pleasure are absolutely co-incident, the very nature of our Organization necessitates that Duty will be contemplated as the Symbol of Pleasure, instead of Pleasure being (as in a future Life we have faith it will be) the Symbol of Duty' (KC, II, 2556, f 74).

[3] See "The Night-Scene", ll. 50–1, and "A Hymn", PW 422, 423–4.

[4] See PW 55 and 76; also KC, I, 272.

[5] See "Honour", ll. 49–60; also "Happiness", ll. 42–55, PW 25, 31.

[6] "To Nature", PW 429.   [7] "Separation", PW 398.

[8] "On a Late Connubial Rupture in High Life", PW 152.

[9] "Religious Musings", ll. 206–7, PW 117.

ness of an existence in which sensuality overrides spiritual in-sight.[1] The bald ambivalence of 'did Kubla Khan / A stately pleasure-dome decree' scarcely permits of a positive conclusion one way or the other about the desirability of the dome, but we have both Purchas's authority and the evidence of Coleridge's parallel usages to suggest that the hyphenating of 'pleasure-dome' may have implied strong moral disapproval.

Turning next to the pleasure-garden we may be struck by the elaborate fortifications with which its privacy is guarded:

> So twice five miles of fertile ground
> With walls and towers were girdled round.

These lines are placed in close and obvious antithesis to the caverns '*measureless* to man' through which the sacred river runs. This juxtaposing of infinite and finite is deliberate, intended as ironic comment surely upon the precise and mathematical de-tails of Kubla's fussy little paradise. The 'measureless' caverns of sacredness suggest mysterious eternities which the oriental despot, intent upon the mechanical trigonometry of his palisades, scarcely guesses at. One recalls Coleridge's own dislike of mathe-matics:

> ... though Reason is feasted, Imagination is starved; whilst Reason is luxuriating in its proper Paradise, Imagination is wearily travel-ling on a dreary desert.[2]

Kubla's paradise, one may feel, was a paradise for reason to luxuriate in.[3] By adding 'towers' to these walls moreover (an-other detail superimposed upon Purchas), Coleridge seemed in-tent on emphasizing the garden's exclusive differentiation from the larger, spiritual life of the universe.

From a poet's point of view such wilful self-incarceration was

[1] cf. 'The charm is vanish'd and the *bubble's* broke,— / A slave to *pleasure* is a slave to smoke!', PW 26; also 'O Man! thou vessel purposeless, unmeant, / Yet *drone-hive* strange of phantom purposes!', PW 425.

[2] CL, I, 7; cf. "A Mathematical Problem", PW 21.

[3] Carl Woodring suggests that 'The true contraries in *Kubla Khan*, far from being the supernatural against the natural, are the organic and the mechani-cal, the natural and the artificial, the Romantic and the rationalistic' (op. cit.). See also Richard Harter Fogle, "The Romantic Unity of 'Kubla Khan'", in *College English*, XXII (1960), 115; and Edward E. Bostetter, *The Romantic Ventriloquists* (Seattle, 1963), 87–8.

depressing.[1] These worlds within worlds, implying exclusiveness and separation, militated against that unitary wholeness, that fusing, blending reconciliation of the One in the Many, which formed the seminal principle of all Coleridge's thinking. Such self-imposed imprisonment, beyond the reach of natural influxes, led finally to claustrophobia and spiritual acedia:

> No such sweet sights doth Limbo den immure,
> Wall'd round, and made a spirit-jail secure,
> By the mere horror of blank Naught-at-all.[2]

Kubla Khan stands in fact at the opposite pole from the sick-minded lover described in *The Picture*.[3] This lover, too, sought sequestration in a place 'as safe and sacred from the step of man / As an invisible world' but, in his case, with the object of communicating *directly* with what he called 'the spirit of unconscious life'. It amounts to much the same in the end for, whereas Kubla excludes nature, this lover seeks to by-pass her in order to enjoy direct, immediate communion with the Absolute. Either approach is wrong since, in Coleridge's view, true spiritual insight is attainable only through the prior intermediary experience of 'wedding' nature.[4] Certainly, Kubla's was no *poet's* paradise, since 'a poet's heart and intellect should be *combined, intimately* combined and *unified* with the great appearances of nature'.[5] By opting for the artificial in preference to the natural the Khan ran the risk of alienation from nature, as *This Lime-tree Bower my Prison* reminds us.[6] His microcosm exemplified, perhaps, many of the least attractive aspects of the Coleridgean 'dell' and, considered in that light, its limitations at once become apparent. One may recall *The Dungeon* affirmation that provided man remains susceptible to nature's 'healing ministrations' then jarring dissonance can be held at bay; but that, walled-off from these,

---

[1] cf. "The Triumph of Loyalty", PW 560:

Earl Henry . . . The gloom which overcast me, was occasioned by causes of less public import.

Sandoval. Connected, I presume, with that Mansion, the spacious *pleasure grounds* of which we noticed as we were descending from the mountain. Lawn and Grove, River and Hillock—it looked within these high walls, like a World of itself.

[2] "Limbo", ll. 31–3, PW 430.   [3] PW 369.

[4] See p. 149 below; and cf. Tennyson's "The Palace of Art".

[5] CL, ii, 864.   [6] See pp. 112–13 above.

the soul 'unmoulds its essence' and the spiritual energies stagnate and are corrupted.

This opening stanza has been admired for its 'precision and clarity', for its 'unmistakable air of concreteness' (whatever *that* phrase means[1]). Yet one looks in vain for anything like the detailed particularization and rare felicities of, say, the lyrical descriptions in *Frost at Midnight* or *Fears in Solitude* amid the general terms of this description:

> And *there* [?] were *gardens* bright with sinuous rills,
> Where blossomed *many an incense-bearing tree*;
> And *here* [?] were forests ancient as the hills,
> Enfolding sunny *spots of greenery*.[2]

Such precision and concreteness as the stanza contains consist rather in the geometric ordering of the massive walls than in the details of the landscape. Add to this the heaviness of rhythmic stress and the metallic quality of 'gardens bright with sinuous rills' and our response to the passage is rather one of awe than actual delight.

Coleridge seems deliberately to have modified the attractiveness implicit in Purchas's original description. Some diminution of its attractiveness appeared even in the *Preface* where it was stated that the following sentence, 'or words of the same substance', provided the poem's source:

> Here the Khan Kubla commanded a palace to be built, and a stately garden therunto. And thus ten miles of fertile ground were inclosed with a wall.

The sentence alluded to should in fact read:

> In Xamdu did Cublai Can build a stately Palace, encompassing sixteene miles of plaine ground with a wall, wherein are fertile Meddowes, pleasant Springs, delightfull Streames, and all sorts of beasts of chase and game, & in the middest thereof *a sumptuous house of pleasure*, which may be removed from place to place.

---

[1] 'Precision and clarity' is Mr House's phrase; 'poetic air of concreteness' is Mr Woodring's.

[2] Professor J. T. Boulton points out to me that vagueness may be an important contributory factor to the over-all effect of mystery here. This mystery is increased by some reference to generic nouns which are given a *relative* precision with reference to their vague surroundings. Thus, 'forests' is as precise a reference as one need expect when set against the 'hills' that are important only for their antiquity.

In the poem the live creatures have disappeared and only the colourless epithet 'fertile' has been retained from 'fertile Meddowes, pleasant Springs, delightfull Streames', the rest being transformed into the considerably less inviting 'gardens bright with sinuous rills'. The remaining details (the incense-bearing trees, the forests and spots of greenery) were Coleridge's own invention and they may all have carried special overtones for him.

The substitution of 'bright/sinuous' for 'pleasant/delightful' produces sinister, almost reptilian, associations, recalling perhaps *The Ancient Mariner* or this description of the 'thing unblest' from *Christabel*, where snake joins 'bright' and 'green' (the only colour details found in Kubla's garden) in a cluster of positive malignancy:

> When lo! I saw a *bright green snake*
> *Coiled* around its wings and neck
> *Green* as the herbs on which it couched.

'Bright' is used repeatedly in both poems in reference to the abnormal, especially to describe the wildly glittering eyes of the Mariner or Geraldine. Furthermore, both 'bright' and 'stately' (cf. 'stately' pleasure-dome) were epithets Coleridge employed to sharpen that distinction between 'art' and 'nature' which, as has been hinted, is integral to the theme of *Kubla Khan*. Thus, Georgiana, the Duchess of Devonshire, was complimented by Coleridge on having quitted a microcosm which with '*stately*' ornament and 'many a *bright* obtrusive form of *art* / Detained [her] eye *from Nature*'.[1] By rejecting artifice in favour of becoming 'free Nature's uncorrupted child' she acted in a manner ethically superior, presumably, to that of the self-indulgent Khan.

The 'ancient' forests, one imagines, are encompassed by, but not assimilated into, the general artificiality of Kubla's creation. They belong with the 'rude forests' and 'inclemencies' of nature which Coleridge associated with the 'Gothic' genius (a point I shall return to) and are left untouched by Kubla's artifice. The other details of the pleasure-garden, by contrast, may be associated with sensuality. 'Incense', for instance, suggests a manufactured perfume rather than delicate, natural fragrance. Blossom images, furthermore, were frequently employed by Coleridge to develop an antithesis between the ethical and the sensual

[1] PW 336.

life—better to die young, he said, than degenerate into 'full blown joys and *Pleasure's gaudy bloom*'.[1] Such parallels should not, however, be pressed too far. The 'sunny spots of greenery', for example, must on any unprejudiced reading of the poem form an attractive feature of the garden even though, at the time the poem was written, it seemed like a deliberate echo of Coleridge's description of the gratification opium affords ('a spot of inchantment, a green spot of fountains, & flowers & trees').[2]

If the sacred river is left aside, the description of the garden is not particularly attractive or engaging. Had it been intended for 'acceptance' it would surely have resembled more what Coleridge considered a true paradise to be like.[3] An obvious parallel is his *Garden of Boccaccio*, itself an earthly paradise containing a Palladian palace, fountains, gardens, rills, and works of art. Yet the differences between Kubla's paradise and Boccaccio's are striking. The latter was ethically unimpeachable, an '*Eden*' which recalled the innocence of youthful poetic aspiration. Here, 'art' was organically integrated with 'nature' and, whereas Kubla's could arouse in the poet no more than the wishful desire to outdo the pleasure-dome with something better, Boccaccio's possessed a regenerative power which rescued the poet from the 'numbing . . . dull continuous ache' of dejection with which he first encountered it.[4]

The romantic distinction between 'art' and 'nature' was not

[1] "To a Primrose", PW 150.

[2] The quotation is taken from a letter written on or near 10 March 1798 (CL, I, 394). It is difficult to determine the date of *Kubla Khan* since Coleridge himself referred it, variously, to both 'the summer' and the 'fall of the year 1797'. E. H. Coleridge and J. D. Campbell assigned it to May 1798; E. K. Chambers and E. L. Griggs think October 1797 a likelier date (see Life, 102, and CL, I, 348–9n).

[3] There are several clues as to Coleridge's notion of a true paradise: cf. "Religious Musings", ll. 343–54; "Fears in Solitude", ll. 176–93; also KC, I, 191.

The thesis that the sacred river is inserted to modify the sensual nature of the pleasure-dome is supported by an article which appeared while this book was going to press (see John Shelton, "The Autograph Manuscript of 'Kubla Khan' and an Interpretation", in *A Review of English Literature*, Vol. VII, No. 1, January 1966). Mr Shelton does not however regard the landscaped garden as artificial, preferring to interpret it as 'the embodiment of the divine power that inspires art of all ages'.

[4] PW 478; ll. 1–10, 60, 28–56, 87.

confined to Coleridge's work however, and we might infer from Cowper's *Task*[1] or Wordsworth's *Prelude* how these two poets would have interpreted Kubla's paradise. Wordsworth stated categorically that nature was a 'tract more fair' than any artificial paradise 'for delight / Of the Tartarian dynasty composed'. After giving his own description of such a paradise—a 'sumptuous' dream of '*domes of pleasure*' and landscaped gardens—he concluded: 'But lovelier far than this, the paradise / Where I was reared.' Only a child, he concluded, would prefer an artificial paradise.[2] Coleridge's own poem *To Nature* consolidates the point:

> So will I build my altar in the fields,
> And the blue sky my fretted dome shall be,
> And the sweet fragrance that the *wild* flower yields
> Shall be the incense *I* will yield to thee.[3]

By placing emphasis on 'wild' and the second 'I' in this passage, the acceptability of Kubla's paradise may be further invalidated.

The poet himself intrudes finally into *Kubla Khan* desiring to build a dome *in air*, aligning it as closely as possible in other words to the divine dome imaged in 'the blue sky [that] bends over all'.[4] Before he steps in, however, the artificiality of the oriental paradise is thrown into sharp relief by descriptions of the 'romantic' chasm and the sacred river. Though, geographically, chasm and river are encompassed by the girdling walls, and contiguous therefore to the site of the pleasure-palace, presumably they remain impervious to its general colouring. The rugged 'romanticness' of the one and the 'sacredness' of the other seem like a deliberate foil or counter-balance to artifice and sensuality.[5] The

---

[1] In "The Task", Bk v, Cowper commented on the incapacity of 'Art' to rival 'Nature'. His disapproving remarks on the ingenious Russian palace of ice are illuminating:

> 'Twas transient in its nature, as in show
> 'Twas durable; as worthless as it seemed
> Intrinsically precious; to the foot
> Treacherous and false; it smiled, and it was cold.

[2] "The Prelude", vIII, ll. 75–127. Compare Mr House on "Kubla Khan": 'Acceptance of the Paradise, in sympathy, is the normal response, from childhood and unsophistication to criticism.'

[3] PW 429.   [4] cf. "Christabel", l. 331; also KC, II, 2346.

[5] In the details of the poem itself there are, I agree, favourable and sinister features on both sides of the 'antithesis'. My reason for assuming a *disjunction*

Prince never grasps the significance of this river. He may succeed in conduiting artful 'rills' from it, he may decree pleasure-domes, walls, and incense-bearing trees along its banks, but its irrational, mazy motion finally remains impervious to his will, and its tangential, divergent sacredness eludes his understanding.

Because the sacred river does not appear in Purchas there has been endless disputation as to its precise identity. Lowes equated it (a little uneasily) with the Nile: 'The sacred river is and is not the Nile', whereas Mr Beer held out for the legendary Alpheus which, after flowing underground, sprang forth again in the fountain Arethusa.[1] The latter hypothesis, though plausible, can finally be no more conclusive than have been the attempts to identify Mount Abora or the Abyssinian maid. If it *were* proved, one would still have the problem (as Mr Beer acknowledges) of transporting to Tartary a Greek river and an Abyssinian maid. More probably, Coleridge coined the name 'Alph' as a deliberately vague word serving as a centre for cumulative emotion.[2] This seems the more likely if we consider its euphonic merits; it fits exactly the pattern of chiming assonance set up in the opening lines. Thus line 1, which is virtually a vowel palindrome hinged by its caesura into antithetical halves, requires (after the slow movement of the beautiful long vowel sounds of line 2) another balanced line (l. 3) to pick up again and echo the two ă sounds in line 1. This, the happy choice of 'Ălph' effectively accomplishes:

> In Xănadu ‖ did Kubla Khăn
> A stately pleasure dome decree:
> Where Ălph, the sacred river, răn . . .

Whatever the mythological or geographical advantages of 'Alph', euphonically Coleridge could not have chosen a better name. The best test of its effectiveness is to try replacing it; it is quite irreplaceable.

It is in any case less important to establish mythological antecedents for 'Alph' than to determine its function and significance

---

between romanticness and art, sacredness and pleasure, is that, at the time the poem was written, this seems broadly to have been Coleridge's own view, judging by the parallels in other poems.

[1] Lowes, 372; Beer, 207, 218. It could, of course, derive from 'Alpha', the beginning—the sacred source of all things.

[2] See Maud Bodkin, *Archetypal Patterns in Poetry* (1934), 104.

within the poem. One obvious function it serves is the structural one of linking stanzas 1 and 2. Its other functions will depend on our estimate of its significance, which, it seems, is twofold. It may represent symbolically both the poet's life itself and the actual processes of creativity. As an emblem of life the river symbol is almost archetypal among poets. Thus, Shelley in *Alastor* wrote: 'O stream! . . . Thou imagest my life,' and Wordsworth, in the poem which revealed the growth of his own poetic mind, concluded:

> . . . we have traced the stream
> From the blind cavern whence is faintly heard
> Its natal murmur; followed it to light
> And open day.[1]

Leigh Hunt, Tennyson, and Arnold each employed river-images to similar effect.[2] Coleridge, as we have seen, frequently represented life as either a voyage or a 'crystal river':

> Life's current then ran sparkling to the noon,
> Or silvery stole beneath the pensive Moon:
> Ah! now it works rude brakes and thorns among
> Or o'er the rough rock bursts and foams along.[3]

When the poet Southey compromised his moral integrity, Coleridge told him that his 'Stream' had run foul, though it could yet 'filtrate and become pure in its subterranean Passage to the Ocean of Universal Redemption'.[4] (Was the sacred river similarly 'purified' in the subterranean 'ocean' after its desecration in Kubla's empire?) The river-image, it should be noticed, was employed by Coleridge to differentiate sharply between the poet's life and life generally, as this notebook entry indicates: 'The current in the river like another river =Genius amongst his fellow-men'.[5]

We have seen already how Coleridge would assess creative originality in terms of flowing water. Cottle's modest verses he described as a 'nameless Rivulet' whereas Chatterton's, inspired by a 'holier triumph and a sterner aim', were characterized by tidal energy:

---

[1] "Alastor", ll. 494–514; "The Prelude", XIV, ll. 194–7.
[2] cf. Leigh Hunt, "The Nile"; Tennyson, "The Brook"; Matthew Arnold, "The Future".
[3] PW 59, 122.   [4] CL, I, 168; and cf. p. 21 above.   [5] KC, I, 1143.

> And while the numbers flowing strong
> In eddies whirl, in surges throng,
> Exulting in the spirits' genial throe
> In tides of power his life-blood seems to flow.[1]

In *Songs of the Pixies, The Reproof and Reply*, and his Preface to *Christabel* Coleridge employed similar water-images to represent the act of poetic creativity.[2] When used to describe the highest form of such activity—the work of a poetic genius—these images generally involved the further notion of the sacredness of the poetic vocation, as in this light-hearted sally on Charles Lamb's imagined baptism:

> Dear Charles! whilst yet thou wert a babe, I ween
> That Genius plung'd thee in that wizard fount
> Hight Castalie: and (sureties of thy faith)
> That Pity and Simplicity stood by.
> And promis'd for thee, that thou shouldst renounce
> The world's low cares and lying vanities,
> Steadfast and rooted in the heavenly Muse,
> And wash'd and sanctified to Poesy.[3]

Because 'sacred', poetry is therefore immortal and, whereas the pleasure-paradise will decay (may in fact have done so, since—as Mr Woodring points out—it is uniformly described in the past tense), poetry's 'sacred Balm' affords perpetual delight.[4] Thus, *The Prelude*, a 'sacred Roll', would ensure Wordsworth a 'permanent' place among the 'choir of ever-enduring men'.[5] A year before writing *Kubla Khan*, Coleridge had expressed his own determination to join this choir:

> Contemplant Spirits! ye that hover o'er
> With untired gaze the immeasurable fount
> Ebullient with creative Deity! . . .
> I haply journeying my immortal course
> Shall sometime join your mystic choir! Till then
> I discipline my young and novice thought
> In ministeries of heart-stirring song.[6]

The '*immeasurable fount* / Ebullient with creative Deity' is identical surely with the fountain-head of the sacred river in *Kubla Khan*, and is totally unlike the hedonistic impulse which motivated the building of Kubla's pleasure-dome.

[1] See p. 87 above.   [2] PW 43, 442, 214.   [3] ibid, 158.
[4] ibid, 36 (see p. 142, note 4).   [5] ibid, 406; cf. KC, I, 1129.
[6] "Religious Musings", ll. 402–12, PW 124.

The movement of the poem hinges upon the emphatic 'But' with which the second stanza commences. This is so stressed by word-order and metrical transposition that it can only signify a contradiction of what has gone before, or something wholly anti-thetical. The interjectory 'But oh!' introduces a fresh level of statement, suggesting that the accomplishments of Kubla Khan are now subjected to the scrutiny of the 'I' of the poem, in other words of the poet himself.[1] The description of primeval unviolated nature which follows represents, in fact, the mysterious, fecund birthplace of the Gothic or romantic genius:

> This was the other part of the Gothic mind—the inward, the striking, the romantic character, in short the genius, but genius marked according to its birthplace; for it grew in rude forests amid the inclemencies of outward nature where man saw nothing around him but what must owe its charms mainly to the imaginary powers with which it was surveyed. There nothing outward marked the hands of man. Woods, rocks and streams, huge morasses, nothing wore externally the face of human intellect. . .[2]

This romantic genius poses ultimately a threat to decadent artistic talent, which misuses nature and is emasculated by over-intellectualism. The more virile Gothic genius will endure when Kubla's dome and towers lie in ruins:

> Nor shall not Fortune with a vengeful smile
> Survey the sanguinary Despot's might,
> And haply hurl the Pageant from his height
> Unwept to wander in some savage isle.[3]

When 'the Great, the Rich, the Mighty Men' are cast to earth, their place will be taken by 'the Purifiers . . . the true Protoplasts, Gods of Love who tame the Chaos'.[4]

The wailing woman clearly belongs with this Gothic landscape which, indeed, she haunts:

> But oh! that deep romantic chasm which slanted
> Down the green hill athwart a cedarn cover!
> A savage place! as holy and enchanted
> As e'er beneath a waning moon was haunted
> By woman wailing for her demon-lover!

Since she wails beneath a *waning* moon (a Coleridgean emblem for declining powers of imagination), and takes her stand beside

---

[1] cf. Schulz, 117.   [2] PL, 291.   [3] PW 90, 423.
[4] ibid, 121; and KC, II, 2355.

the *romantic* chasm and the *sacred* fount of creativity, her lamenta-
tions may be associated with the struggle which the creative
imagination experiences in operating amid these inimical conditions. Her 'wailing' (anticipating the seething 'turmoil' of the
(fountain stands in direct contrast to the delightful harmony of
'symphony and song' associated (in stanza 3) with the inspiration
given by the Abyssinian maid.[1]

Though the fountain's inexhaustible energy signifies the act of
creativity, it is important to observe the *struggle* which it has
before issuing forth as the sacred river. Its whole course thereafter is, moreover, towards anti-climax, a theme skilfully reinforced by the subtly changing verse-rhythms. After rising with
difficulty it wanders 'mazily' through the pleasure-garden, then
sinks into a lifeless ocean. It appears to seek at first to challenge
and disrupt the ordered artificiality of the paradise, scattering
fragments of rock like hail or chaffy grain. But amid such inimical
conditions nothing comes of the creative energy; there is no
fusion of the One and the Many, only fissiparous differentiation
and a mass of things which counterfeit infinity.[2]

This sense of the fountain's struggling into life is quite explicit
in the text:

> And from this chasm, with *ceaseless turmoil seething*,
> As if this earth in *fast thick pants* were breathing,
> A mighty fountain momently *was forced*.

This is different from the run of Coleridge's fountain descriptions, which were generally associated with harmony or delight,
with 'the gladness of Joy, when the fountain overflows ebullient'.[3]
Usually, fountains represented for him a source of spiritual re-
freshment, where the soul 'Hangs o'er the fall of Harmony /
And drinks the *sacred* Balm'.[4] Another striking feature of this
fountain is the totally unexpected simile 'As if this earth in fast
thick pants were breathing'. Yet 'thick' was a favourite Cole-

[1] Mr Beer develops an interesting theory about the 'daemon lover', his
suggestion that Coleridge's fountain represents daemonic energies being quite
at variance with my own view (Beer, 237).

[2] See Coleridge's letter to Thelwall, referred to on p. 169 below.

[3] KC, II, 2279.

[4] E. H. Coleridge hesitated to assign the Ode in which these lines appear
to Coleridge. The internal imagery of life-as-journey, of flowing water and of
'breezy influence' points fairly clearly, however, to Coleridge's authorship
(see PW 36n, 382).

ridgean word for denoting either the macabre or the 'poète maudit' agony. Thus, in *The Ancient Mariner*, Life-in-Death 'thicks man's blood with cold' and at the nightmarish moments of the crew's death and their ghastly reincarnation the night and the threatening clouds are 'thick' and sinister, the pathetic fallacy being used to emphasize the Mariner's lack of spiritual attunement. 'Thick and struggling' also described the 'poète maudit' agony of trying to fuse an ethical ideal with intractable reality (a theme with obvious bearing on *Kubla Khan*):

> Cold sweat-drops gather on my limbs;
> My ears throb hot; my eye-balls start;
> My brain with horrid *tumult* swims;
> Wild is the tempest of my heart;
> And my *thick and struggling* breath
> Imitates the toil of death.[1]

The river issues at last only to meander with purposeless 'mazy' motion, and 'mazy', likewise, was a characteristic Coleridgean term for describing moral and spiritual uncertainty. *Mahomet* (1799), a poem with remarkable verbal and thematic affinities to *Kubla Khan*, thus describes the spiritual bewilderment produced in men's minds when false religions struggle for dominion:

Utter the song, O my soul! the flight and return of Mohammed,
Prophet and priest, who scatter'd abroad both evil and blessing,
Huge wasteful empires founded and hallow'd slow persecution,
Soul-withering, but crush'd the blasphemous rites of the Pagan
And idolatrous Christians.—For veiling the Gospel of Jesus,
They, the best corrupting, had made it worse than the vilest.
Wherefore Heaven *decreed* th' enthusiast warrior of Mecca,
Choosing good from iniquity rather than evil from goodness.
Loud the tumult in Mecca surrounding the fane of the idol;—
Naked and prostrate the priesthood were laid—the people with
    mad shouts
Thundering now, and now with *saddest ululation*
Flew, as *over the channel of rock-stone the ruinous river*
Shatters its waters abreast, and in *mazy uproar* bewilder'd
Rushes dividuous all—all rushing impetuous onward.[2]

Here 'tumult' and 'mazy' bewilderment prevail because true sacredness belongs neither to the iniquitous Mohammedans nor to the corrupt and idolatrous Christians. By 1807, feeling himself

[1] "Ode to the Departing Year", ll. 107–12, PW 166.
[2] PW 329–30, my italics.

similarly bewildered and despondent—as though hope lived in a 'charnel house'—Coleridge described his own life as having become 'rugged and mazy' in its course.[1]

After running its obstacle race then the sacred river finally sinks in tumult to a lifeless ocean, amid which tumult Kubla hears from far, 'Ancestral voices prophesying war'. The identity and immediate relevance of these voices is puzzling.[2] As literal ancestors they could simply be warning the Khan of dangers from outside, which may be a natural function for ancestral spirits (as the explanation given by Horatio and Bernardo for the apparition of King Hamlet might suggest). The objection to this interpretation is that it makes the 'war' extrinsic to the theme of the poem (unless war is seen as the penalty of neglecting duty for the sake of pleasure). Perhaps they are to be regarded as ostensible rather than actual ancestors (the poem does not say *whose* ancestors they are) —having affiliations not so much with former inhabitants of Xanadu as with the conservers of tradition and the moral arbiters whom Coleridge called the 'Clerisy'.[3] As the 'Purifiers' who seek to bridle the Prince's activity, they represent perhaps Coleridge's deep sense of the general influence of the past upon the present.[4] It is within the 'sacred' context of creativity that past and present actually meet; it is here that tradition and originality are seen as part of a continual process of regeneration. The highest art is not of an age but for all time and the influence of the 'truly great' (like Chatterton's or Wordsworth's) is perpetually pervasive. This passage from Coleridge's later tribute to Wordsworth indicates as clearly as anything perhaps the tradition to which these ancestral voices may belong:

> O great Bard!
> Ere yet that last strain dying awed the air,
> With stedfast eye I viewed thee in the choir

---

[1] KC, II, 3075.

[2] Elisabeth Schneider, for example, has stated that these 'ancestral voices' serve no proper function and even detract from the poem's claim to greatness. See E. Schneider, *Coleridge, Opium and Kubla Khan* (Chicago, 1953).

[3] See S. T. Coleridge, *On the Constitution of the Church and State* (1850), Ch. v.

[4]
> For lovely appear the Departed
> When they visit the dreams of my rest!
> But disturb'd by the tempest's commotion
> Fleet the shadowy forms of delight.
> ("The Complaint of Ninathoma", PW 39–40)

Of ever-enduring men. The truly great
Have all one age, and from one visible space
Shed influence! They, both in power and act,
Are permanent, and Time is not with them,
Save as it worketh for them, they in it.
Nor less a sacred Roll, than those of old,
And to be placed, as they, with gradual fame
Among the archives of mankind, thy work
Makes audible a linkéd lay of Truth . . .[1]

Consciousness of being part of this tradition impelled Coleridge himself to adopt the 'poète maudit' rôle, condemning his countrymen's over-concern with materialistic considerations by appealing to traditional values. Thus he had with 'thick and struggling' breath 'wailed' his country with 'loud Lament', and had even prophesied war. It was not his fault if 'the Birds of warning' sang in vain.[2]

When in the first edition of *Kubla Khan* Coleridge made a division in the poem at this point so that stanza 2 ended with the ancestral threats, the totality of meaning was clearer possibly than in the present arrangement of the lines.[3] By the earlier arrangement almost everything in stanza 2—the 'romantic' landscape, the struggling river, the wailing woman, and the ancestral voices—joined together in cumulatively opposing the unattractive features of the pleasure-paradise. Lines 31–6 concerning the shadow-dome being thus detached could more easily be seen as marking a further advance in the 'argument', as representing a miracle *'midway'* between pleasure and sacredness.

Quite clearly this second dome is held up for admiration: as a 'miracle' of rare device it is superior to the earlier pleasure-dome. Since it actually floats upon the sacred river, it is in some way related to the source of genuine creativity. In contrast to Kubla's fabricated 'art', which is detached from the prior experience of nature, this 'miracle' affords a fleeting glimpse, before the river disappears, of what a true organic synthesis is like. As Coleridge's *Preface* indicated, the entire poem was an attempt to recover a 'vision' or 'phantom', and the description of the shadow-

---

[1] PW 406; cf. also "Monody on the Death of Chatterton", ll. 33–5.

[2] See "Ode to the Departing Year", stanza 9; also "France: an Ode", "Fears in Solitude", and CL, I, 267.

[3] But see Mr Shelton's article on the manuscript of "Kubla Khan", published since this chapter went to press (John Shelton, op. cit.).

L

dome approximates perhaps to the vision he was attempting to recapture.

By separating this description from stanza 2 we associate the second dome not with 'tumult' (which would be absurd) but more positively with harmony. The 'mingled measure' then echoes ironically the earlier juxtaposition of 'measureless' and trigonometry, introducing a superior 'measure' in which the noisy energy of the fountain is mingled with the echoing roar of the river as it drops through the vast caverns. The intricate, delightful rhythms of lines 31–6, light and fluid compared with the falling cadences of the lines immediately preceding, themselves constitute a 'mingled measure' appropriate to the miracle. The reconciliation of energy and sublimity suggests at last the perfect interfusion of creative imagination with the mysterious life of the universe, which the true artist always seeks.

In this miracle of sunny dome with caves of ice a synthesis is achieved between seemingly discordant opposites—heat and cold, life and death (fountain and departing river), convex and concave (dome and caverns). But sun, ice, and music can only thus be interfused under the impetus of sacred inspiration:

> . . . aye on Meditation's heaven-ward wing
> Soaring aloft I breathe the empyreal air
> Of Love, omnific, omnipresent Love,
> Whose day-spring rises glorious in my soul
> As the great Sun, when he his influence
> Sheds on the frost-bound waters—The glad stream
> Flows to the ray and warbles as it flows.[1]

The miracle occurs again in *Hymn Before Sunrise* when, to the accompaniment of sacred song, the sun melts the mountain-ice and the living waters are called forth in torrents from their 'dark and icy caverns'.[2] To the sensualist who lacked the sacred inspiration, the caves of ice would always *be* ice, as 'glittering, cold and transitory' perhaps as the Russian palace of ice associated with Catherine, that most sensual of despots.[3]

As an emblem of the sacred relationship between art and nature, occurring directly after the intercession of the ancestral voices, the shadow-dome has the quality of a 'poète maudit' vision. Thus, these voices both condemn the sensualist's paradise

---

[1] "Religious Musings", ll. 413–19.   [2] PW 378–9.
[3] See BL, I, 12; also Woodring (op. cit.).

and point to where a higher synthesis lies. What they cannot provide however is the inspiration necessary to develop this vision beyond weak adumbration and, consequently, it remains a vision merely 'shadowy of truth'. Before the poet can build *his* 'dome', the 'vital air' of love is needed. A woman's entry into the poem is virtually inevitable at this point, and is indeed anticipated by the 'mingled measure', it being Coleridge's 'faith' that 'there's a natural bond / Between the female mind and measured sounds'.[1]

Harbingered thus, the Abyssinian maid now appears, in terms so impersonal as to discourage precise identification. It is less important that she is Abyssinian than that she is *a* maid, a generic symbol for woman the inspirer. Her remoteness from particular reference is deliberate: she is simply 'a damsel with a dulcimer' whom the poet 'once' saw in a 'vision'. Thus she achieves a universality aloof from the poet's private feelings and, though she may be traceable from information outside the poem, within it she functions adequately without the need for such identification. She epitomizes the 'vital air' of inspiration, which other poets have discovered in a 'Beatrice' or a 'Stella'. (Nor is it necessary to localize 'Mount Abora', the subject of her song: like 'Alph' it is vaguely emotive and, *as* a mountain, emblemizes the Gothic or 'romantic' landscape.)

The 'Could I revive within me', the line on which Mr House's whole interpretation of the poem hinges, cannot, as he claimed it could, be construed into 'I can and I shall' except by a feat of implausible linguistics. The qualifying 'Could I' means rather '*If only* I could', and what follows is therefore no more than wish-fulfilment.[2] The poem is really stating, though obliquely, that the 'deep delight' of Joy is as much beyond the poet's own reach at this moment as (for different reasons) it is beyond the Prince's. No clue is given as to why this is, beyond the hint that the maid's influence exists now only as a recollected 'vision' which, though it helps, does not quite go far enough. It enables him to describe

[1] "To Matilda Betham from a Stranger", ll. 21-2, PW 375; and cf. KC, II, 3092.

[2] The 'Could I' is roughly equivalent perhaps to the 'If' of this notebook entry: 'If a man could pass through Paradise in a dream, and have a flower presented to him as a pledge that his soul had really been there, and if he found that flower in his hand when he awoke—Aye! and what then?' (AP, 282).

what he '*would*' achieve, given her full inspiration directly, and how others 'should' in that case respond to his achievement, but not finally to attain an ecstasy beyond that of *imagined* fulfilment.[1] Certainly there is rapture in the final lines, but there is, too, an ominous emphasis on the inner, psychological aspect of poetic inspiration, which anticipates *Dejection: an Ode*. 'Could I revive *within me* . . . To such a deep delight 'twould *win* me' resembles, both lexically and thematically, the *Dejection* couplet:

> I may not hope from outward forms to *win*
> The passion and the life, whose *fountains* are *within*.

It is not a gratuitous analogy; without such meaning the phrase 'within me' is redundant ('Could I revive [within me] Her symphony and song'). We are left to speculate why, at the height of his poetic powers, Coleridge should entertain such misgivings.

The inference is that something more than a visionary recollection of the female inspirer is needed before the ultimate in creative originality (the 'dome in air') can be achieved. As a notebook entry puts it: 'Tho' Genius, like the fire on the Altar, can only be kindled from Heaven, yet it will perish unless supplied with appropriate fuel to feed it.'[2] An inner psychological harmony matching the harmony of her song is requisite before he can reconcile inner and outer and produce the final masterpiece. Given this harmony, however, he would experience not pleasure but joy:

> Could I revive within me
> Her symphony and song,
> To such a deep delight 'twould win me,
> That with music loud and long,
> I would build that dome in air.

It is difficult to determine whether this is wish-fulfilment, self-delusion, or simply an excuse for not delivering the goods. It looks like an attempt to transfer responsibility for his failure to accomplish real fulfilment (by actually *building* the dome before our eyes) from himself to external circumstances which, being antecedent to the poem, are extrinsic to it. *If only* her symphony could be revived—by which he seems to mean: if only his past relationship with the maid could be re-established—*then* the full potentialities of his creative imagination could be realized. This is neither satis-

[1] See Bodkin, op. cit., 95.   [2] KC, II, 3136.

factory nor wholly convincing. It argues self-defensively that, in different circumstances (not adequately disclosed), more would have been possible in the poem than was actually achieved.

But what more *was* there to achieve? A fine description per-haps of the actual building of the 'dome in air'? At most, one feels, this would have led merely to another subject/object merger, a further Theistic metaphysic of the sort which Coleridge could write to order. Or it might have resulted in 'music loud and long', like the pæan to 'Joy' which he sounded later in *Dejection: an Ode*:

> O pure of heart! thou need'st not ask of me
> What this strong music in the soul may be!
> What, and wherein it doth exist,
> This light, this glory, this fair luminous mist,
> This beautiful and beauty-making power.
> Joy, virtuous Lady! Joy that ne'er was given,
> Save to the pure, and in their purest hour,
> Life, and Life's effluence, cloud at once and shower,
> Joy, Lady! is the spirit and the power,
> Which wedding Nature to us gives in dower
> A new Earth and new Heaven,
> Undreamt of by the sensual and the proud—
> Joy is the sweet voice, Joy the luminous cloud—
> We in ourselves rejoice!
> And thence flows all that charms or ear or sight,
> All melodies the echoes of that voice,
> All colours a suffusion from that light. (59–75)

Some such revelation of 'Joy', because 'undreamt of by the sen-sual and the proud', would neatly have rounded off the theme by demonstrating the sort of sacred delight which Kubla's pleasure-paradise could not provide. Why then did not Cole-ridge build the dome? The excuse of uncongenial circumstances is hardly convincing when in *Dejection*, though lamenting the *failure* of his 'genial spirits', he yet went on to give a description of 'Joy' which could scarcely have been bettered.

In fact, it is the intrinsic development *within* the poem that matters, not some alleged goal beyond its reach. Such extrinsic goals are in any case to be distrusted. Wisely, Coleridge resisted the temptation to treat us to another Theistic metaphysic, which would needlessly have underlined what already was sufficiently explicit, and he chose instead to describe superbly the ecstasy of *imagined* poetic fulfilment. This, rather than another 'dome', was what the poem demanded. By leaving the dome 'in air', where it could not disappoint the expectations raised by the excitement generated in the final verse, he avoided the risk of displaying a gimcrack thing which might have stained the radiance of the poem's ending.[1] It was more valuable, having shown the futility of hedonistic artifice, then to allow the poem itself by cumulative effect to lead sympathy away from the pleasure-palace to a revelation of the potentialities of the sacred imagination. The whole movement of the poem is therefore outwards, away from a microcosm of *little* things towards a triumphant final suggestion (it is no more) of what lies potentially within the poet's power. Coleridge's judgment has proved sound; his poem exists as an intrinsic whole without the 'dome in air', and it has since been placed by popular consent where he always hoped his work would live —with the 'sacred Rolls . . . among the archives of mankind'.[2]

Though Coleridge's 1816 *Preface* to the poem invited us to regard it as an exotic 'psychological curiosity', *Kubla Khan* in fact grew naturally out of a consistent poetical development. Far from being unique it bore obvious relevance to recurrent Coleridgean themes (such as male isolate, dell/microcosm, shadowy vision, unattainable female, bardic tradition) while its predominant imagery (of prison, blossom, sun, moon, ice, and flowing water)

---

[1] It could be argued that the poet's assertion 'I would build *that* dome in air' means that he would, given the right inspiration, 'build, but in air, *that* dome which Kubla had built in stone'; or that he would build what Kubla in fact built, 'a dome in air' (assuming that the dome was not squat, but was itself raised high in air). My whole argument is intended to rule out such an interpretation. 'That dome' must refer to the 'shadow of the dome of pleasure', admired earlier as a 'miracle of rare device', since the poet's dome would likewise be a union of opposites (reconciling 'sunny dome' with 'caves of ice'). I have indicated already why this shadow-dome which the poet would emulate is much more than a mere reflection of the pleasure-dome. In this instance, however, 'dome' signifies not a building at all, surely, but a genuine work of art (such as Kubla's failed to be)—that is to say, a *poem* ('. . . *with music* loud and long, I would build . . . And *all who heard* should . . .'). The youth with flashing eyes is not an architect or mason, but a poet. The emphasis rests finally not upon 'that dome', but on what '*I* would' do, '*Could* I' recover the damsel's inspiration. (Cf. also J. Shelton, op. cit., 42.)

[2] See PW 406.

was entirely characteristic. Similarly, though the imagery was borrowed in part from Purchas, the use Coleridge made of it was determined largely by long-standing psychological factors. It is evident from the unmistakably sexual character of this imagery (dome of pleasure, caverns, fountain, milk) that Purchas's description of a house of pleasure tapped a reservoir of private feelings and associations, notwithstanding Coleridge's success in universalizing them.

Thus, despite its oriental trappings, Kubla's paradise contains many basic features of the Coleridgean 'dell': it is claustrophobic, sensual, and more congenial to 'art' than to nature. All the more unpleasant aspects of the 'dell' seem peculiarly magnified in *Kubla Khan*. Here, massive walls and towers reinforce the privacy of the 'Valley of Seclusion', and the musky incense of the blossoming trees is even more oppressive than the profuse luxuriance of blossom which always threatened to over-run the Coleridgean 'Cot'.[1] The elaborate artifice of the stately pleasure-dome and landscaped garden belong rather to the world of 'softened Sense and Wit refined' than to the romantic sublime.[2] Unconsciously, therefore, the description of the pleasure-paradise may have been a further projection of Coleridge's apprehensiveness lest the Sara type of domesticity should stifle his creative powers.

Considered in this light, *Kubla Khan* bears thematic affinities with *Reflections On Having Left a Place of Retirement*, which Coleridge had written immediately after his honeymoon. This autobiographical poem described how he personally had indulged in a life of sensual pleasure and then repudiated it in favour of a re-alignment with the sacred and the immeasurable. 'Was it right', he demanded:

---

[1] In *The Eolian Harp* we find the 'Cot *o'er grown* / With white-flower'd Jasmin, and the broad-leav'd Myrtle' (3–4). *Reflections* contains another such description of the Clevedon cottage:

> ... our tallest Rose
> *Peep'd* at the chamber-window ...
> ... In the open air
> Our Myrtles *blossom'd*; and *across the porch*
> *Thick Jasmins twined*. (1–6)

Similarly, the 'green and silent spot' at Nether Stowey (cf. the 'sunny spots of greenery' in "Kubla Khan") was surrounded by '*never-bloomless* furze / Which *now blooms most profusely*'; see "Fears in Solitude", ll. 1–7.

[2] See pp. 78–80 above.

That I should dream away the entrusted hours
On rose-leaf beds, pampering the coward heart
With feelings all too delicate for use?

Because the honeymoon bed was pleasurable it had required a
considerable *struggle* to scale the girdling walls and towers ('steep
up the stony Mount / I climb'd with perilous toil'). But the effort
was worth it, since he had been rewarded by a vision which exposed for him the limitations of the dell. Beyond the microcosm
he had seen 'the whole World . . . imag'd in its vast circumfer-
ence'.

Kubla's 'decreeing' of the pleasure-paradise was in some ways
analogous to Coleridge's own decision to obey the 'stern *decree*'
and live in Sara's dell[1]—the pleasure-dome (as an inverted breast-
image) signifying perhaps her former sexual attractiveness for
him.[2] He had chosen to fix his 'empire' on 'spotless Sara's breast',
though recognizing that Sara could never be more to him than
an 'instrument of low desire'. With nothing else to sustain it,
however, appetite had cloyed, subsiding gradually into aversion
and then, on Sara's part, frigidity ('Mrs C. is to me all *strange*,
& the Terra incognita always lies near to or under the frozen
Poles' . . . [We dress together in silence] as 'deep Frost'[3]). Unconsciously, therefore, the sacred river in *Kubla Khan*, frustrated at
its fountain-head and terminating in a lifeless sea, may have
signified a sexual life turned sour. Since, moreover, the 'stern
decree' had necessitated his abandonment of Mary Evans, the
'waning moon' and the 'woman wailing for her demon-lover'
constituted reproachful reminders perhaps of the price of self-
indulgence—namely, a loss of inspiration.

If stanza 1 of *Kubla Khan* is partly an indictment of the 'dell',
then, equally, stanzas 2 and 3 are a vindication of the larger life
outside the microcosm. The rugged details of the 'romantic
chasm' and the bizarre ritual of the bardic tradition are quite
alien to the 'correctly wild' preferred by Sara. This 'holy and

[1] cf. 'I yielded to the stern decree, / Yet heav'd a languid Sigh for thee
[Mary]', PW 63.
[2] Mr Beer has suggested, incidentally, that "Kubla Khan" may have been
influenced by the Song of Solomon. He points out the "Kubla-Khan"-like
terms with which Solomon's bride practises enticement: 'Let my beloved
come into his garden [her body], and eat his pleasant fruits . . . I am a wall,
and my breasts like towers' (see Beer, 269–71).
[3] KC, 1, 1816, 979; and see p. 269 below.

enchanted' chasm provides indeed a local habitation and a name for the spot where 'dancing to the moonlight roundelay / The wizard passions weave an holy spell' (lines which previously we found so enigmatical). The 'dancing roundelay' and 'holy spell' anticipate the ritual dread accorded to the inspired poet who has seen beyond the light of outward day:

> Weave a circle round him thrice,
> And close your eyes with holy dread,
> For he on honey-dew hath fed,
> And drunk the milk of Paradise.

Though Sara would reject such a conception of holiness as 'dim and unhallow'd', in *Kubla Khan* Coleridge triumphantly declared his conviction that the 'faery way' (linked firmly now with the *Phaedrus* tradition), far from being 'unholy madness', represented a mode of inspiration sanctified by long tradition.

Finally, there is the Abyssinian maid herself who, though to some extent an amalgam of all the qualities Coleridge sought in Woman, was a cover perhaps for Mary Evans who, even after three years of marriage, was still the centre for his sexual fantasies. The evidence for supposing a connection between Mary Evans and the Abyssinian maid may be found in Appendix II. She had always exercised an Abyssinian maid-like influence on Coleridge:

> Aid, lovely Sorceress! aid thy Poet's dream!
> With faery wand O bid the maid arise.[1]

Mary may well have been the damsel 'in a vision once I saw'[2] and perhaps in *Kubla Khan* her image arose again obedient to the faery wand.

In *Kubla Khan* it is suggested that only a renewal of female inspiration could restore for Coleridge the possibility of absolute fulfilment which conditions in the 'dell' denied. Yet, just as he wrote *Dejection: an Ode* in the knowledge that Asra (the second of his 'Abyssinian maids') was forever unattainable, so the fact that Mary Evans *was* out of reach may have done more to ensure the success of *Kubla Khan* than her actual presence could have

[1] See PW 51.
[2] The Mary Evans poem, "Written at the King's Arms, Ross", indicated that Mary would always be a comforting vision to him, a '*dream* of Goodness ... never felt'. See PW 58; also CL, 144n.

done. From the tranquil distance of recollected emotion Mary could more readily be idealized, and, after all, universalization of his private feelings was Coleridge's real intention in *Kubla Khan*.[1]

---

[1] cf. 'Must not the maid I love like thee inspire / *Pure* joy and *calm* Delight?' ("To the Evening Star", PW 17).

My interpretation of the Abyssinian maid may be contrasted, incidentally, with that of Mr Bostetter, who identifies the maid with Sara Fricker (op. cit., 88–9).

6

The Ancient Mariner

It is no accident that the 'framework' for *The Ancient Mariner* is provided by a wedding, the symbolic union of two individuals; the presence of the Wedding-Guest is a constant reminder of this basic symbol. Yet ultimately the marriage of two individuals proves to be an unsatisfactory expression of the higher, universal power of love with which the poem is concerned. It is significant too that in 1817 (while revising *The Ancient Mariner* for *Sybilline Leaves*) Coleridge amended also *The Eolian Harp*, the earlier poem about individual and universal love which he had written on the eve of his wedding. Because in 1795 Sara had objected to his tentative 'undivided life' hypothesis, Coleridge had retracted it—leaving an impression nevertheless of some narrowness in Sara's outlook. In 1817 he added a new passage to *The Eolian Harp*, re-asserting the principle of universal love in terms which bear closely on the theme of *The Ancient Mariner*:

> O! the one Life within us and abroad,
> Which meets all motion and becomes its soul,
> A light in sound, a sound-like power in light,
> Rhythm in all thought, and joyance every where—
> Methinks, it should have been impossible
> Not to love all things in a world so fill'd;
> Where the breeze warbles, and the mute still air
> Is Music slumbering on her instrument. (26–33)[1]

The Ancient Mariner is both a love-poem, in the profoundest sense of Love, and a vindication of the mystery (and the richness of the mystery) of a universe beyond the reach of narrow understanding. Though the poem can be interpreted in fairly orthodox Christian terms, no *one* theological system embraces all the elements of Catholicism, daemonology, and Neo-Platonism which it contains.

[1] See pp. 96–7 above.

155

The poem begins and ends in the world of ordinary values (Sara's world), a world of cheering and merriment and noisy din. But once the ship reaches the strange land of ice, where familiar bearings are lost ('Nor shapes of men nor beasts we ken'), these values prove unsatisfactory. The sailors are relieved when the Albatross appears, hailing it 'in God's name' and receiving it with 'great joy and hospitality'—'As if it had been a Christian soul'. The implication (particularly in view of what follows) is of a soul redeemed by Christ's sacrifice of love. Consequently, the killing of the bird is a crime against love and against the hospitality that goes with love.[1]

The significance of this action is a major source of disputation. We may regard it as a re-enactment of 'the Fall', as an act of wantonness, or—following clues given in *The Statesman's Manual*, Appendix C (1816)—as the 'remorseless despotism' of a human will which, because abstracted from reason and religion, finds 'in itself alone the one absolute motive of action'.[2] It should be emphasized, however, that the bald matter-of-factness of the original statement—'With my cross-bow / I shot the ALBATROSS' —seemed designed to discourage speculations as to motive. Even the marginal gloss (added in 1817) said no more than that the Mariner acted 'inhospitably'. The nearest Coleridge came to specific comment on the Mariner's action was in a notebook observation made during his sea-trip to Malta:

> Hawk with ruffled Feathers resting on the Bowsprit—Now shot at & yet did not move—how fatigued—a third time it made a gyre, a short circuit, & returned again / 5 times it was thus shot at / left the Vessel / flew to another / & I heard firing, now here, now there / & nobody shot it / but probably it perished from fatigue, & the attempt to rest upon the wave!—Poor Hawk! O Strange Lust of Murder in Man!—It is not cruelty / it is mere non-feeling from non-thinking.[3]

If the analogy holds, this last sentence would suggest that the Mariner had no feelings for the Albatross because it had simply never *occurred* to him that all living creatures are 'parts and proportions of one wondrous whole'. It is 'the sublime of man' to

---

[1] cf. "Christabel", p. 177 below.
[2] See Warren, 222–30; HH, 95 ff. The Mariner's action is discussed more fully in Appendix III.
[3] KC, II, 2090.

transcend his 'small particular orbit', to view 'all creation', and love it all (so *Religious Musings* claimed); but such sublime awareness had not yet been vouchsafed to the Mariner. The following passage from *Religious Musings* (1794–6) would suggest that the Mariner's Cain-like destructiveness was the product of narrow 'unfeelingness':

> There is one Mind, one omnipresent Mind,
> Omnific. His most holy name is Love,
> Truth of subliming import! with the which
> Who feeds and saturates his constant soul,
> He from his small particular orbit flies
> With blest outstarting! From himself he flies,
> Stands in the sun, and with no partial gaze
> Views all creation; and he loves it all,
> And blesses it, and calls it very good!
> This is indeed to dwell with the Most High!
> Cherubs and rapture-trembling Seraphim
> Can press no nearer to the Almighty's throne.
> But that we roam unconscious, or with hearts
> Unfeeling of our universal Sire,
> And that in His vast family no Cain
> Injures uninjured (in her best-aimed blow
> Victorious Murder a blind Suicide)
> Haply for this some younger Angel now
> Looks down on Human Nature: and, behold!
> A sea of blood bestrewed with wrecks, where mad
> Embattling Interests on each other rush
> With unhelmed rage!
>   'Tis the sublime of man,
> Our noontide Majesty, to know ourselves
> Parts and proportions of one wondrous whole!
> This fraternises man, this constitutes
> Our charities and bearings. But 'tis God
> Diffused through all, that doth make all one whole . . .
>   (105–31)

Without this insight, the passage continues, man's moral life has no cohesion or 'common centre'. If, impervious to the harmony of the universal life, he relies on his individual self-sufficiency, then he is fated ultimately to experience such alienation as befell the Ancient Mariner, and to discover too late that self-sufficiency is merely an illusion:

> . . . A sordid solitary thing,
> Mid countless brethren with a lonely heart
> Through courts and cities the smooth savage roams
> Feeling himself, his own low self the whole;
> When he by sacred sympathy might make
> The whole one Self! . . . (149–54)

At the beginning of the poem the Mariner's 'charities and bearings' are uninformed by higher insight and it requires a revelation through means of grace to rescue him from the limitations of his finite understanding.

The crew are likewise devoid of true spiritual insight, for they value the Albatross not as a fellow creature but as an emblem of 'good luck'. Though they describe the killing of the Albatross as a 'hellish thing', their condemnation has little to do with morality; there is no awareness that it has violated the sanctity of the One Life, their reasoning being based primarily on a narrow, self-centred notion of expediency:

> And I had done a hellish thing,
> And it would work 'em woe:
> For all averred, I had killed the bird
> That made the breeze to blow.
> Ah wretch! said they, the bird to slay,
> That made the breeze to blow!

When the fog clears they reverse their arguments and (in the words of the prose gloss to the poem) 'justify' the killing, thus making themselves 'accomplices to the crime'. Again, their rationalization of the crime rests upon self-interest and operates only at the shallow level of sense-inference. Their ' 'Twas right' is a selfish, not a moral, judgment, the true conception of 'right' and 'hospitality' transcending the level of their understanding:

> Nor dim nor red, like God's own head,
> The glorious Sun uprist:
> Then all averred, I had killed the bird
> That brought the fog and mist,
> 'Twas right, said they, such birds to slay
> That bring the fog and mist.

In the phrase 'such birds' all sense of the individuality of the Albatross, which like an intimate friend had come to their call and shared their food, is submerged in a phrase of unfeeling

generalization. Their minds are incapable of discriminating between the individual and the species.[1] Only 'in *dreams*' do they
acquire any real insight into the nature of their plight—'And
some in dreams assuréd were / Of the Spirit that plagued us so'.
This spirit ('one of the invisible inhabitants of this planet, neither
departed souls nor angels') is the first manifestation in the poem
of the mysterious entities that lie beyond the range of ordinary
cognition.

Again and again the narrow understanding proves incapable
of accounting for the mysterious events that befall the ship. The
categories of space, time, and causality, on which it depends,
have no validity in the areas the poem is exploring. No rational
explanation is possible for the mysterious locomotive powers
which drive the Mariner's ship or the spectre-bark, nor for the
abrupt transitions of time and place. It is futile to look for principles of ordinary mechanics here:

> FIRST VOICE
> 'But why drives on that ship so fast,
> Without or wave or wind?'
>
> SECOND VOICE
> 'The air is cut away before,
> And closes from behind . . .'

Though there *are* aids to navigation, like the 'kirk', the 'line' (or
equator), and the varying positions of the sun, these provide only
a general spatial dimension for the geography of the voyage—'the
land of mist and snow' and the 'silent sea' being really archetypal
and symbolic. The hour-long span of chronological time provided by the framework of the wedding ceremony is (rather as
in *Frost at Midnight*) less important than the months of psychic
time it encloses, within which all the more interesting experiences
occur. Coleridge's commendation of 'the marvellous independence and true imaginative absence of all particular space or
time in the *Faery Queene*' might be taken as a vindication of his
own method here.[2] Like the *Faerie Queene* Coleridge's poem obeys

[1] cf. HH, 98.

[2] 'You will take especial note of the marvellous independence and true
imaginative absence of all particular space or time in the *Faery Queene*. It is
in the domains neither of history or geography; it is ignorant of all artificial
boundary, all material obstacles; it is truly in land of Faery, that is, of *mental
space*. The poet has placed you in a dream, a charmed sleep, and you neither

only the logic of a dream and (as he said) we do not question a dream's intelligibility, but accept each shape or incident quite unconscious of the absurdity of the transitions and the absence of all logical copulae.[1]

Mr Warren's illuminating essay on *The Ancient Mariner* starts from the premise that as 'rational creatures' we must try to understand the poem by analysing it; that the only *test* of what is 'latent' in the poem is the 'test of coherence'. His search for a rational schematization of the different spiritual agencies in the poem led him, however, into perplexities and inconsistencies not unlike those which troubled the personages in the poem who attempted 'explanations'.[2] 'Can it be a ship that comes onward without wind or tide?' the puzzled intellect inquires. 'Why, this is strange, I trow,' says the Pilot, having never seen 'aught like' to the ship that now confronts his sight: 'Dear Lord! it hath a fiendish look.' In these critical points of interaction between the supernatural and the world of ordinary values the theme of the poem is vividly dramatized. In the final stanza it is driven home with conclusive force, in the description of the shattering effect the Mariner's story has had upon the consciousness of the Wedding-Guest:

> He went like one that hath been stunned,
> And is of *sense forlorn*:
> A sadder and a wiser man,
> He rose the morrow morn.

All the Mariner's clearest insights into the true significance of the experiences befalling him occur in moments when his consciousness is suspended and the intuitive power (associated with words like 'swound', 'dream', 'trance', and 'spell') takes over.[3] Whenever he fails to make 'a *proper use* of his senses', his insight immediately weakens:

---

wish, nor have the power, to inquire where you are, or how you got there' (MC, 36).

[1] IS, 204.

[2] Warren, 281–2. See HH, 105–13, where some of the inconsistencies in Mr Warren's analysis of the poem are discussed. Mr Warren's essay has permanently enriched our understanding of the poem but, as House observed, it tends to make the poem 'seem more technical and diagrammatic . . . than Coleridge could ever have admitted it to be'.

[3] In "Christabel", likewise, it is Bard Bracy's dream which comes closest to the truth of the mystery enshrouding Geraldine.

And now this spell was snapt: once more
I viewed the ocean green,
And looked far forth, yet little saw
Of what had else been seen—.[1]

A main object of the poem was to recover the sense of 'the Vast'
which is denied to those who place too much reliance on 'the
constant testimony of their senses'.[2] It was intended deliberately
to blur the boundary between the world of dreams and the world
of things, and to stress that imaginative insight, rather than
rationality, provides the best clue to the spiritual mysteries which
are part of the totality of life's meaning.[3]

Part II closes with a further reference to the Mariner's crime
against love which amplifies and confirms what has been said
already concerning its Christian implications:

Instead of the cross, the Albatross
About my neck was hung.

Thus, the Mariner, having killed the symbol of Christian redemption (so rejecting the values represented by the crucifix
around his neck), has to wear the emblem of his crime against
self-sacrificing love. And within twenty lines he has to sacrifice
his own blood to enable him to hail the skeleton-ship which
makes its sudden appearance. Faced by this horrifying spectacle,
which defies the laws of nature, he echoes the *Ave Maria*, 'Mary
full of grace' ('Heaven's Mother send us grace!'), thereby introducing the key word 'grace' (a very Coleridgean kind of grace)
which provides an important clue to the poem's meaning.
Though spared actual death, he is claimed by Life-in-Death
in the game of dice that follows, and is overcome with mortal
fear:

[1] The Prefatory Note to "The Wanderings of Cain" informs us that Cain
was to have suffered in this poem 'because he neglected to make a proper use
of his senses'. It will be recalled that "The Ancient Mariner" was written
only after Coleridge's attempted collaboration with Wordsworth in a poem
about Cain had failed. See PW 285–7.

[2] See pp. 169–70 below.

[3] De Quincey recorded that 'Before meeting a fable in which to embody
his ideas, he [Coleridge] had meditated a poem on delirium, confounding its
own dream-scenery with external things, and connected with the imagery of
high latitudes.' The Burnet motto, prefixed to the poem in 1817, drew attten-
tion to 'a greater and better world' which exists beyond the petty thoughts
connected with daily trivialities.

M

> Fear at my heart, as at a cup,
> My life-blood seemed to sip!

It is not however the blood of Christ (with all its implications of redemption from sin and sacrifice for the love of mankind) which fills a chalice for fear to drink, but the blood of a man who has repudiated grace. Part III ends with the forcible reminder that responsibility for the death of his fellows, as well as for that of the Albatross, rests primarily on him:

> And every soul, it passed me by,
> Like the whizz of my cross-bow.

His position is thus the obverse of Christ's, his action having led to the deaths of his fellow-men.

The 'penance' which, according to the gloss, now begins takes (predictably) the form of utter loneliness:

> Alone, alone, all, all alone,
> Alone on a wide wide sea!
> And never a saint took pity on
> My soul in agony.

As we might expect, the penalty is exacted in what is virtually a 'prison', a fact we were to some extent prepared for on the appearance of the spectre-bark:

> And straight the Sun was flecked with bars
> (Heaven's Mother send us grace!)
> As if through a dungeon-grate he peered
> With broad and burning face.

This is the most terrible of all Coleridge's 'prisons', a charnel-house which floats upon a rotting sea amid a thousand, thousand slimy things. Tortured by thirst, fettered by the Albatross about his neck, the Mariner endures an extreme of solitary confinement, surrounded by bodies 'for a charnel-dungeon fitter'. Each night, the distant beauty of the moon and stars is held before him as a visible paradigm of the 'hospitality' he has abused, while by day the bloody sun, which transfixes the vessel to the ocean, tortures his flesh unremittingly. Until the spell begins to break there are no sensual compensations in this prison to relieve its harshness or the blank horror of unending desolation. Self-exiled from society and spiritual comfort the Mariner must face his universe of death alone, this being the price he pays for having offended against society, religion, and the harmony of the undivided life.

At the end of the poem his recollection of this 'prison' impels the Mariner to seek human society, to join in prayer for 'man and bird and beast', but at this stage he is motivated merely by self-pity ('And never a saint took pity on / My soul in agony') and by envy that the sea-creatures, whom he 'despiseth', should have life while 'the many men, so beautiful' lie dead. He sees these creatures as a mass of 'slimy things' and, because his heart is 'dry as dust', he cannot pray. He is unable to recognize the wholeness of living creation—to see man and animal nature as integral parts of one whole. It is important however to notice the means by which his personal re-integration is now made possible—a combination of 'grace' and the revitalizing of his imagination. Whereas poems like *This Lime-tree Bower* and *Frost at Midnight* had revealed how natural objects like a walnut-tree or snow-covered thatch can be irradiated by imaginative insight, this poem goes further by *enacting*, in moving dramatic terms, how the *same* object (namely sea-serpents) appears first to the dis-attuned mind and then to this mind after it has been redeemed by spiritual beneficence.

The Mariner's attempts to pray during the 'seven days, seven nights' his acedia lasts bring no relief. Only under the kindly light of the moon is awareness of the beauty and of the living quality of the things around him created. The beautiful prose-gloss at this point of the poem suggests that the heavens are a paradigm of the harmony and the hospitable love which the Mariner has sinned against:

> In his loneliness and fixedness he yearneth towards the journey-ing Moon, and the stars that still sojourn, yet still move onward; and everywhere the blue sky belongs to them, and is their appointed rest, and their native country and their own natural homes, which they enter unannounced, as lords that are certainly expected and yet there is a silent joy at their arrival.

'By the light of the Moon' the Mariner is made aware of the *beauty* of 'God's creatures':

> Within the shadow of the ship
> I watched their rich attire:
> Blue, glossy green, and velvet black,
> They coiled and swam; and every track
> Was a flash of golden fire.

and then of their *joy*, which is the first revelation to him of his participation in the general life:

> O happy living things!

Immediately, his own re-integration commences:

> A spring of love gushed from my heart,
> And I blessed them unaware:
> Sure my kind saint took pity on me,
> And I blessed them unaware.

Here, love is seen both as a redemptive, liberating power and as evidence of a feeling of being at one with nature and God. The recognition of such an integration is simultaneous with the beginning of a personal re-integration within the Mariner himself. Immediately, the symbol of his sin against love—the dead Albatross—falls from his neck, suggesting (in view of what has been said) the working of grace. But it is important to notice that the 'kind saint' intervenes 'By the light of the Moon'—in the most propitious circumstances, in other words, for rekindling the Mariner's imagination.

The opening of Part v confirms this supposition of the action of grace, the Mariner attributing to 'Mary Queen' the sleep which has been 'sent' to him 'from Heaven'. It is through her intervention, implored in Part iii when he was confronted by the ship of Death, that spiritual ease now comes. As the gloss puts it: 'By grace of the holy Mother the ancient Mariner is refreshed with rain.' The 'strange sights and commotions' which follow are not 'meaningless marvels', as as has sometimes been objected, but an attempt to describe the cosmic energy and beauty of the universe as they *really* exist beyond the veil of ordinary sense-perception. The Mariner 'heareth' and 'seeth' these miracles as a mystic might 'see' them; sights are possible in this light, blessed state (ll. 305–8) that 'had been strange, even in a dream' (l. 333):

> The upper air burst into life!
> And a hundred fire-flags sheen,
> To and fro they were hurried about!
> And to and fro, and in and out,
> The wan stars danced between.
>
> And the coming wind did roar more loud,
> And the sails did sigh like sedge;
> And the rain poured down from one black cloud;
> The Moon was at its edge.

> The thick black cloud was cleft, and still
> The Moon was at its side:
> Like waters shot from some high crag,
> The lightning fell with never a jag,
> A river steep and wide.

At last the Mariner begins to perceive the integratedness of the universe around him, as natural elements, the moon, the world of spirits, and the world of man (represented by the Mariner himself) combine to urge onwards the ship that had been becalmed. The stress here on music is purposeful: the 'sweet' sounds emitted by the spirits, the 'sweet jargoning' of birds, the music 'like all instruments', the 'angel's song', and the 'pleasant noise' made by the sails, all underline the harmonious working of angels, spirits, external nature, and man. It recalls the 'mingled measure' of *Kubla Khan* and the exquisite 'one Life' music of *The Eolian Harp* (quoted at the beginning of this chapter).

The sin has not yet been expiated, however; the gloss reminds us that the Polar Spirit 'still requireth vengeance'. His 'fellow-daemons' now take up his case, recalling the seriousness of the Mariner's sin, which is again noted as a sin against love—the universal love symbolized by Christ's sacrifice which united all things:

> How long in that same fit I lay,
> I have not to declare;
> But ere my living life returned,
> I heard and in my soul discerned
> Two voices in the air.
>
> 'Is it he?' quoth one, 'Is this the man?
> By him who died on cross,
> With his cruel blow he laid full low
> The harmless Albatross.
>
> The spirit who bideth by himself
> In the land of mist and snow
> He loved the bird that loved the man
> Who shot him with his bow.'
>
> The other was a softer voice,
> As soft as honey-dew:
> Quoth he, 'The man hath penance done,
> And penance more will do.'

As usual, it is in a semi-conscious state that the Mariner learns the truth about himself. When his 'trance' is abated and the curse of the dead men's eyes removed, he experiences an interval of spiritual calm and—'Oh! dream of joy!'—sees at last his native country. But his mind is now so disturbed that he is no longer sure if he is awake or asleep, so effectively has the boundary between the world of dreams and the world of things been blurred:

> O let me be awake, my God
> Or let me sleep alway.

Through dreams he has learnt that love can unite spirits, nature, and man, and that his sin has disrupted this unity; but before full personal integration can be achieved he must *consciously* acknowledge his sin—as he himself realizes:

> I saw a third—I heard his voice:
> It is the Hermit good! . . .
> He'll shrieve my soul, he'll wash away
> The Albatross's blood.

Yet even though (as we assume) he is given absolution, a life-long penance still awaits him. Elevated (by virtue of unique experience) to something like 'poète maudit' status, he must suffer 'ever and anon throughout his future life' in order to bring to others the word which is salvation:

> Since then, at an uncertain hour,
> That agony returns:
> And till my ghastly tale is told,
> This heart within me burns.

> I pass, like night, from land to land;
> I have strange power of speech;
> That moment that his face I see,
> I know the man that must hear me:
> To him my tale I teach.

Finally the Mariner's tale is brought to a close by the 'loud uproar' from the marriage-feast, and by the ringing of the 'vesper bell', a direct link with the Albatross which had perched on the ship's mast for 'vespers nine'. Both the communal happiness and the call to prayer remind him of the hell of loneliness he had experienced:

> So lonely 'twas that God himself
> Scarce seeméd there to be.

His present reaction is understandable: he desires above all to

pray together with a 'goodly company'. The union of two individuals and the communal happiness accompanying it are now
seen to be inadequate as a symbol of the love which experience
has revealed to the Mariner. They are less significant than the
communal act of prayer, and participation in the undivided life
which embraces 'man and bird and beast'.

The trials the Mariner undergoes, Charles Lamb remarked,
'overwhelm and bury all individuality or memory of what he
was'. Agreed: but the peculiarly Coleridgean aspects of these
trials forcibly remind us of what their originator was for, though
the poem attempted (successfully) to transcend the personal, its
treatment of the archetypal situation of utter loneliness bore
everywhere the stamp of Coleridge's individual touch. In *The
Ancient Mariner* the life-as-voyage image, engraved upon Coleridge's mind since childhood, at last became central to the theme
and structure of a major poem. Because the Mariner's imagined
feelings lay so close to the subliminal sources of the poet's own
imagination, he was able to express them with startling vivacity.
The more remarkable stanzas of the poem distilled succinctly,
and with uniquely Coleridgean poignancy, the anguish of a host
of letters and notebook entries:

> Alone, alone, all, all alone,
> Alone on a wide wide sea!
> And never a saint took pity on
> My soul in agony.

Similes like that of the fearful traveller upon a lonesome road
bore a 'poetic signature' unmistakably Coleridge's:

> Like one, that on a lonesome road
> Doth walk in fear and dread,
> And having once turned round walks on,
> And turns no more his head;
> Because he knows, a frightful fiend
> Doth close behind him tread.

The wise decision to relate the Mariner's story in the first person
greatly enhanced its authenticity by enabling Coleridge to call
more readily upon these private feelings. His remarkable success
in universalizing a theme so close to his personal experience
should be a warning however against pressing too far the poem's

autobiographical significance. Mr Burke overstepped the mark, one feels, in equating the killing of the Albatross with the 'murder' of Coleridge's wife and in regarding this symbolic act as a fanciful resolution of the poet's 'marriage problem'. Doubtless there are 'things that the act is doing for the poet and no one else', but precise identifications of the sort Mr Burke attempted are unjustifiable.[1]

There are nevertheless aspects of the Mariner's act in killing the Albatross which do bear strongly on the poet's own case. In its implicit rejection of religion (the repudiation of 'a Christian soul') and the Mariner's subsequent inability to pray, it closely paralleled Coleridge's own recent experiences. 1797–8 was a period of earnest soul-searching for Coleridge and of self-reproach for his past neglect of religious observances:

> I have been too neglectful of practical religion—I mean, actual & stated prayer . . . for want of habit my mind wanders, and I cannot *pray* as often [as] I ought. Thanksgiving is pleasant in the performance; but prayer & distinct confession I find most serviceable to my spiritual health when I can do it. But tho' all my doubts are done away, tho' Christianity is my *Passion*, it is too much my *intellectual* Passion: and therefore will do me but little good in the hour of temptation & calamity.[2]

The following description of the acedia the Mariner experiences in consequence of denying his spiritual nature—

> I looked to heaven, and tried to pray;
> But or ever a prayer had gusht,
> A wicked whisper came, and made
> My heart as dry as dust.
>
> I closed my lids, and kept them close,
> And the balls like pulses beat;
> For the sky and the sea, and the sea and the sky
> Lay like a load on my weary eye,
> And the dead were at my feet.

—echoes closely part of a letter Coleridge had written to Benjamin Flower at the time he vowed to 'recentre' his mind in the Sabbath of 'meek self-content':

> I have known affliction, yea, my friend! I have been myself sorely afflicted, and have rolled my dreary eye from earth to Heaven, and

[1] See K. Burke, *The Philosophy of Literary Form* (Louisiana State University Press, 1941), 71–3.   [2] CL, I, 407.

found no comfort, till it pleased the Unimaginable High & Lofty
One to make my Heart more tender in regard of religious feelings.[1]

The implication of this—that only by grace and the liberating
power of love can the unfeeling heart be redeemed—indicates
considerable identification between Coleridge and the Mariner.

The further theme of the poem—that intuitive empathy counts
for more than rational understanding—coincided with a re-
orientation in Coleridge's thinking which developed during his
correspondence with John Thelwall in 1797:

> I can *at times* feel strongly the beauties, you describe, in them-
> selves, & for themselves—but more frequently *all things* appear little
> —all the knowledge, that can be acquired, child's play—the uni-
> verse itself—what but an immense heap of *little* things?—I can con-
> template nothing but parts, & parts are all *little*—!—My mind
> feels as if it ached to behold & know something *great*—something
> *one & indivisible*—and it is only in the faith of this that rocks or water-
> falls, mountains or caverns give me the sense of sublimity or majesty!
> —But in this faith *all things* counterfeit infinity![2]

He wrote this less than a month before he began *The Ancient
Mariner* and its bearing on the Mariner's experience is unmistakable. Two days later, in his fourth autobiographical letter to
Poole, Coleridge developed a major attack upon the Empiricists
in which he claimed that, because since childhood his own mind
had been 'habituated *to the Vast*—I never regarded *my* senses in
any way as the criteria of my belief'. Education, he maintained,
should aim primarily at liberating the imagination; too often, it
provides merely an intellectual strait-jacket:

> Should children be permitted to read Romances, & Relations of
> Giants & Magicians & Genii?—I know all that has been said
> against it; but I have formed my faith in the affirmative.—I know
> no other way of giving the mind a love of 'the Great', & 'the Whole'.
> —Those who have been led to the same truths step by step thro' the
> constant testimony of their senses, seem to me to want a sense which
> I possess—They contemplate nothing but *parts*—and all *parts* are
> necessarily little—and the Universe to them is but a mass of *little
> things*.—It is true, that the mind *may* become credulous & prone to
> superstition by the former method—but are not the Experimental-
> ists credulous even to madness in believing any absurdity, rather
> than believe the grandest truths, if they have not the testimony of
> their own senses in their favour?—I have known some who have

[1] ibid, 1, 267.   [2] ibid, 1, 349.

been *rationally* educated, as it is styled. They were marked by a microscopic acuteness; but when they looked at great things, all became a blank and they saw nothing—and denied (very illogically) that any thing could be seen; and uniformly put the negation of a power for the possession of a power—& called the want of imagination Judgment, & the never being moved to Rapture Philosophy![1]

Collaboration with Wordsworth also had a considerable influence upon Coleridge's thinking at this time; indeed Wordsworth's recitation, in June 1797, of his *Lines Left upon a Seat in a Yew-tree* may have had a direct bearing upon the shaping of *The Ancient Mariner*.[2]

The slaying of the Albatross signified a violation of the Mariner's family ties, the full consequences of which emerged only after the crew had died:

> The body of my brother's son
> Stood by me, knee to knee:
> The body and I pulled at one rope,
> But he said nought to me.

This incommunication between blood-relations represented an extreme of punishment for Coleridge, since he made it the most painful aspect of Christabel's 'martyrdom' also. It followed automatically (on Coleridgean premises) that once the Mariner was cut off from the sympathy of human faces his universe would degenerate into a 'mass of *things*'.[3] As the bodies lie about him on the deck, each cursing him with its stony eye, he is never allowed to forget the consequences of his crime. As Mr House observed, these graphic descriptions bring home to the Mariner

[1] CL, I, 354–5.

[2] Coleridge may have identified himself partly with the character in this poem, a person of uncommon genius who over-indulged the 'visionary' fancy and 'the food of pride'. The didactic message of Wordsworth's poem has obvious bearing upon "The Ancient Mariner":

> If Thou be one whose heart the holy forms
> Of young imagination have kept pure,
> Stranger! henceforth be warned; and know that pride,
> Howe'er disguised in its own majesty,
> Is littleness; that he who feels contempt
> For any living thing, hath faculties
> Which he has never used; and thought with him
> Is in its infancy. (48–55)

[3] See p. 113 above.

the full extent of his crime by dramatizing it to his consciousness, and this is their purpose in the poem. On a more personal level they may at the same time, in their representation of an outcast isolated from the herd, have been a projection of Coleridge's own sense of insecurity. They represent perhaps, among the further 'things that the act is doing for the poet and no one else', the bitter memory of his broken relationships with his own family and his rejection by his brothers. Only one with Coleridge's unique 'case-history' could have expressed so feelingly the 'ache of solitariness' implied in these descriptions.

There is one further respect in which, for all its objectivity, the poem was doing something for the poet and no one else. I refer to the typically Coleridgean antithesis it contains between the domestic aura of the wedding-ceremony and the turbulent rest-lessness of the 'poète maudit' spirit. The merriment, festivity, and singing belong in the main to Sara's world, with the values of ordinary domesticity which continue in their humdrum way un-troubled by considerations of deeper import. In this world the Mariner (now promoted to something like 'poète maudit' status by dint of the 'strange power of speech' invested in him) is a divisive influence, who scorns the marriage-feast and induces the Wedding-Guest finally to turn *from* the bridegroom's door. His attitude to this world is strangely ambivalent, for he appears both to despise and to envy it. He seeks the company of people solely for purposes of communal worship, not for a renewal of such in-timate personal relationships as the wedding symbolizes.

The Mariner's affinity with traditional figures like Cain and the Wandering Jew has long been apparent; to Mr Warren (and Mr Beer) we owe his further identification with the 'poète maudit'. He is 'constrained' to pass like night from land to land and to suffer, intermittently, the burning agony involved in re-lating his story to those it is decreed shall hear his message. He is akin to the Cassandra-like warning voices which appeared in *Ode to the Departing Year*, in *France: an Ode*, and in *Fears in Solitude*. In the first and last of these poems Coleridge, having himself dis-charged the 'poète maudit's' obligation, returned thankfully to the security of the 'dell'. *France: an Ode* and *The Ancient Mariner* seemed to indicate, however, that the consequence of possessing 'poète maudit' insight was that ultimately it could never be ac-commodated within the 'dell' existence. In *Dejection: an Ode*, written four years later, the same antithesis between the tragic genius and domestic contentment re-appeared, the 'dell' this time being brutally repudiated.[1] Coleridge's many explorations of this antithesis suggest that, in the last analysis, it contained the paradox posed by possession of so bizarre a genius within such a temperament as his own. He needed the sympathy of human faces as few men have done, but the peculiar cast of his genius and temperament constantly denied it to him.

Finally it is interesting to find that when, in 1804, Coleridge took ship for Malta in the hope of resolving his personal problems, he consciously identified himself with the Mariner. As he stepped aboard the *Speedwell* he felt he was returning '*Home*', recommencing the 'voyage' of life which had been the constant theme of his adolescent poetry.[2] The first letter he wrote at sea began with an allusion to *The Ancient Mariner* and five days out from land his notebook recorded:

> . . . Saw, a nice black faced bright black-eyed white-toothed Boy running up to the Main Top with a large Leg of Mutton swung, Albatross-fashion about his neck . . .[3]

When the *Speedwell* narrowly avoided collision with another vessel he observed: 'What a Death for an old hardy skilful Mariner, to be run down while at anchor by a set of Lubbers!'[4] Clearly, this real-life voyage had become a living allegory of the ancient Mariner's experiences. As the *Speedwell* lay becalmed it seemed to emblematize the purposelessness of Coleridge's own life since the time of the 'annus mirabilis':

> Tuesday Afternoon, one o'clock, May Day—We are very nearly on the spot, where on Friday last about this same Hour we caught the Turtles—And what are 5 days' toiling to Windward just not to lose ground, to almost *5 years*? Alas! alas! what have I been doing on the Great Voyage of Life since my Return from Germany but fretting upon the front of the Wind—well for me if I have indeed kept my ground even![5]

Coleridge was quick to notice parallels between events that occurred on this voyage and incidents in *The Ancient Mariner*; these confirmed his tendency to identify himself with the hero of his poem. The shooting of the hawk which came to rest upon the bowsprit seemed a vivid portent. When, off Carthagena, fog and

[1] cf. p. 264 below.   [2] CL, II, 1123; cf. pp. 2–3 above.
[3] KC, II, 1997.   [4] ibid, II, 2051.   [5] ibid, II, 2063.

mist caused the favourable breeze to drop, Coleridge was fasci-
nated by the reaction of the sailors: the Captain of the *Speedwell*
(like the Mariner's 'accomplices') at once began to 'look around
for the Jonas in the fleet', some scapegoat on which to pin blame
for this misfortune. Coleridge commented:

> . . . Vexation, which in a Sailor's mind is always linked on to
> Reproach and Anger, makes the Superstitious seek out an Object
> of his Superstition, that can feel his anger—Else the Star, that
> dogged the Crescent or my 'Cursed by the last Look of the waning
> moon' were the better—What an extensive subject would not super-
> stition form taken in its philos. and most comprehen. sense for that
> mood of Thought & Feeling which arises out of the having placed
> our summum bonum (what we think so, I mean) in an absolute
> Dependence on Powers & Events, over which we have no Controll.[1]

Twice on the voyage, he noticed that the water at the side of the
ship seemed 'brilliant with Life':

> . . . [moonlit water] thickly swarming with insect life, *all* busy-
> swarming in the path their swarming makes—but within the
> Shadow of the Ship it was—scattered at distances—scattered O s,
> rapidly uncoiling into serpent spirals . . . always Spirals, coiling,
> uncoiling, *being* . . .[2]

He noted that their vessel tacked and veered (like the spectre-
bark); that seasickness resembled Life-in-Death; that on landing
in Malta, he felt 'light as a blessed Ghost'.[3]

When he had written the poem originally it had not been intended probably as a conscious allegory of life, for there is no
hint of such a purpose at the outset of the Mariner's voyage.[4]
Not until we encounter the figure of Life-in-Death in Part III do
we first suspect a possible allegorical significance. It was not until
after Coleridge's return from Malta however that this figure was
deliberately allegorized; in all the earlier editions of the poem
she appeared more like a creature of Gothic romance.[5] Similarly

[1] ibid, II, 2060; and cf. II, 2048.
[2] ibid, II, 2070, 2015.   [3] ibid, II, 2071, 2078, 2100.   [4] See HH, 93–6.
[5] In the 1798 *Lyrical Ballads* version she was described thus:

> Her lips are red, her looks are free,
>   Her locks are yellow as gold:
> Her skin is as white as leprosy,
> And she is far liker Death than he;
>   Her flesh made the still air cold.

This description was not significantly altered in the 1800, 1802, and 1805
editions.

with the important stanza I referred to earlier:

> We listened and looked sideways up!
> Fear at my heart, as at a cup,
> My life-blood seemed to sip!
> The stars were dim, and thick the night,
> The steersman's face by his lamp gleamed white;
> From the sails the dew did drip—

None of this appeared in the 1798, 1800, 1802, and 1805 editions of the poem; it originated probably in this notebook entry of April 1804, in which Coleridge imagines M. [Mary Wordsworth] dead, W. ÷ Sā [William married to Asra], and *Hydrocarb*. [himself, probably] dead also:

> SICKLY Thoughts about M. mort. & W. ÷ Sā—*Hydrocarb.* / died looking at the stars above the top mast; & when found dead, these Stars were sinking in the Horizon / —a large Star? a road of dim Light?—Light of the Compass & rudderman's Lamp reflected with forms on the Main Sail.[1]

This personal anguish, wholly transcended in the superb objectivity of the finished stanza, adds a fresh dimension to the lines 'Fear at my heart, as at a cup, / My life-blood seemed to sip!' One other entry which he made on the voyage, combining suggestions for both *The Ancient Mariner* and *Constancy to an Ideal Object*, indicates, in conjunction with the passage just quoted, that it was his hopeless passion for Asra which had driven Coleridge to embark on this Mariner-like voyage to Malta. As the latter poem puts it:

> —'Ah! loveliest friend [Asra]!
> That this the meed of all my toils might be,
> To have a home, an English home, and thee!'
> Vain repetition! Home and Thou are one.
> The peacefull'st cot, the moon shall shine upon,
> Lulled by the thrush and wakened by the lark,
> Without thee were but a becalméd bark,
> Whose Helmsman on an ocean waste and wide
> Sits mute and pale his mouldering helm beside.[2]

---

[1] KC, II, 2001.

[2] PW 456. There is no evidence as to the date of composition of "Constancy to an Ideal Object". J. D. Campbell believed that it 'was written at Malta', as seems highly probable in view of the evidence furnished by the notebook entry (KC, II, 2052 n).

It is significant that on his return to England Coleridge at once began revising *The Ancient Mariner*. He wrote a new stanza, combining the details of the chalice of fear and the helmsman's white face, which suggests that during the sea-trip to Malta the life-as-voyage image, engraved on Coleridge's mind since childhood, had indeed become a nightmare reality.[1]

[1] KC, ii, 2880.

7

Christabel

Though much admired for its qualities of atmosphere, its technical mastery, and certain individual felicities, *Christabel* has not in the main attracted the critical attention which *Kubla Khan* and *The Ancient Mariner* have excited. Except perhaps to Mr Nethercot the road to Tryermaine has somehow proved less enticing than that to Xanadu.[1] The fact that only two of the poem's intended five parts were written—two parts so different 'that they scarcely seem to belong to the same poem'[2]—while three conflicting accounts survive of how the story was to end, are circumstances which have disposed us to treat this poem less seriously than some of Coleridge's other work. His intermittent struggles to finish *Christabel*, extending over twenty years, suggest that it developed difficulties for him he knew no way of overcoming. Three years elapsed between the composition of Parts I and II, and during this interval critical events occurred which may have given a fresh direction to his original intention, leading him finally to weight the poem with a personal significance which proved too much for it.

The poem was begun in 1797, more or less as a Gothic romance within the tale-of-terror convention:

> 'Tis the middle of night by the castle clock,
> And the owls have awakened the crowing cock . . .

The exquisite description of the setting, the atmosphere of moonlight and mystery are handled with a skill and sensitivity however which immediately place the poem above the general level

[1] See A. H. Nethercot, *The Road to Tryermaine* (Chicago, 1939). Notable studies of the poem have been made by Humphry House and John Beer, by Charles Tomlinson in *Interpretations*, ed. John Wain (London, 1955), and by Edward E. Bostetter in *The Romantic Ventriloquists* (Seattle, 1963).

[2] cf. HH, 122. Coleridge told Byron that the poem would have '5 books' when finished (CL, IV, 601).

of this genre. Into its dream-like landscape the 'lovely lady' Christabel is introduced, almost a stock figure initially of the defenceless, vulnerable woman typical of the tale of terror.[1]

This heroine is about as different a person from the Mariner as one could well imagine. Where he becomes 'a jarring and a dissonant thing', self-alienated from the undivided life, she is a 'child of nature' (to use Mr Beer's phrase) possessing obvious affinities with that other 'gentle Maid' whose rare attunement to the One Life is described so glowingly in *The Nightingale*, a poem Coleridge was working on at the same time as *Christabel*:

> A most gentle Maid,
> Who dwelleth in her hospitable home
> Hard by the castle, and at latest eve
> (Even like a Lady vowed and dedicate
> To something more than Nature in the grove)
> Glides through the pathways; she knows all their notes,
> That gentle Maid! and oft, a moment's space,
> What time the moon was lost behind a cloud,
> Hath heard a pause of silence; till the moon
> Emerging, hath awakened earth and sky
> With one sensation, and those wakeful birds
> Have all burst forth in choral minstrelsy,
> As if some sudden gale had swept at once
> A hundred airy harps! And she hath watched
> Many a nightingale perch giddily
> On blossomy twig still swinging from the breeze,
> And to that motion tune his wanton song
> Like tipsy Joy that reels with tossing head. (69–86)

Christabel, similarly, epitomizes hospitality, even offering to share her bed with her unexpected guest, in contrast to the Mariner, who 'inhospitably' kills the Albatross he had earlier welcomed. By this action, as we have seen, the Mariner destroys his family ties, but Christabel's life seems securely anchored in affection: her father loves her 'well', her mother's spirit protects her, and she is betrothed to a knightly lover. She has, too, a deep-seated religious faith, being constantly found in prayerful 'her-mitress' attitudes, whereas when the Mariner tries to pray his heart is 'dry as dust'. Ordinary beings like the Wedding-Guest and Pilot's boy are appalled and frightened by the Mariner's

---

[1] I am following Mr Tomlinson's argument here (cf. Tomlinson, op. cit., 108).

N

appearance; but the ingenuous Christabel wins our (no less than the Narrator's) immediate sympathy—'Jesu, Maria, shield her well'. Yet for all her child-of-nature qualities, her possession of (to Coleridge) enviable emotional and spiritual resources, Christabel is brought finally to a condition of 'pathological isolation' as serious as the Mariner's,[1] suffering herself the bitter effects of alienation and imprisonment. Once she re-enters the castle with Geraldine, crossing the moat and passing by way of iron gates and corridors 'still as death' to her own dim-lit chamber, shades of the 'prison-house' close about her until finally the embrace of evil encircles her completely:

> A star hath set, a star hath risen,
> O Geraldine! since arms of thine
> Have been the lovely lady's *prison*. (302–4)

Like the Mariner (who must suck his own blood before he can speak) she too endures the torture of total incommunication, her feelings pent up inside her by a spell which is 'lord' of her utterance. There seems some paradox here, some inconsistency with the Coleridgean sequence of poems about imprisonment and the principle laid down in the first of them that 'Nature ne'er deserts the wise and pure'. Christabel has neither Kubla Khan's sensuality nor the Mariner's spiritual blindness, but seems possessed of every attribute requisite for 'Joy'. Why should this innocent suffer as she does?

The explanation is to be found in the particular religious doctrine which underlies the story. The account in Gillman's biography of how the poem was conceived provides the clearest exposition:

> The story of Christabel is partly founded on the notion, that the virtuous of this world save the wicked. The pious and good Christabel suffers and prays for
> > 'The weal of her lover that is far away,'
> exposed to various temptations in a foreign land; and she thus defeats the power of evil represented in the person of Geraldine. This is one main object of the tale.[2]

Derwent Coleridge's alternative account of how *Christabel* was to have finished also invoked the 'vicarious' theory:

---

[1] Tomlinson, op. cit., 105.

[2] cf. James Gillman, *The Life of Samuel Taylor Coleridge* (London, 1838), Vol. I, 283.

The sufferings of Christabel were to have been represented as vicarious, endured for her 'lover far away'; and Geraldine no witch or goblin, or malignant being of any kind, but a spirit, executing her appointed task with the best good will, as she herself says:—

> All they, who live in the upper sky
> Do love you, holy Christabel, &c. (ll. 227–32).

In form this is, of course, accommodated to 'a fond superstition', in keeping with the general tenour of the piece; but that the holy and the innocent do often suffer for the faults of those they love, and are thus made the instruments to bring them back to the ways of peace, is a matter of fact, and in Coleridge's hands might have been worked up into a tale of deep and delicate pathos.[1]

Christabel's sufferings then were contracted voluntarily since, for the 'weal' of her absent lover, she chose deliberately to undergo a martyrdom. In *Table Talk* Coleridge has recorded that Crashaw's poem on the martyrdom of St Teresa directly influenced the writing of the second part of *Christabel*, if indeed it did not 'suggest the first thought of the whole poem'. Crashaw's heroine, it may be observed, experienced an alienation from home and family similar to Christabel's, except that she was *prepared* for it, whereas it was the form of suffering Coleridge's heroine least expected. Crashaw described Teresa's alienation thus:

> Since 'tis not to be had at home,
> She'l travel to a martyrdome.
> No home for her confesses she,
> But where she may a martyr be. . . .
> Farewell then, all the world—adieu,
> Teresa is no more for you:
> Farewell all pleasures, sports, and joys,
> Never till now esteemed toys—
> Farewell whatever dear'st may be,
> Mother's arms or father's knee;
> Farewell house, and farewell home,
> She's for the Moores and martyrdome.[2]

Such cheerful fortitude and deliberate self-exile was as much beyond Christabel's capacity perhaps as Coleridge's, and characteristically Coleridge rendered the rupture of Christabel's family ties as the most painful aspect of her martyrdom. Nevertheless,

[1] cf. HH, 126–7n, where the authority for this quotation is discussed; and see Beer, 176–7.

[2] cf. Beer, 177–8.

she *chose* to suffer by an act of positive altruism, whereas the
Mariner's sufferings were partly the consequence of unpremedi-
tation. Their respective reactions under torture are therefore
opposite: he is self-pitying and afraid ('never a saint took pity
on / My soul in agony') but Christabel—at least until the morning after her ordeal—is ecstatic:

> And see! the lady Christabel
> Gathers herself from out her trance;
> Her limbs relax, her countenance
> Grows sad and soft; the smooth thin lids
> Close o'er her eyes; and tears she sheds—
> Large tears that leave the lashes bright!
> And oft the while she seems to smile
> As infants at a sudden light! (311–18)

She never doubts but that the saints above are on her side, 'For
the blue sky bends over all'.

With these clues to guide us Part 1 of *Christabel* would be
straightforwardly intelligible were it not for the mystery surrounding Geraldine. The ambivalence of her function and significance appears not only in the poem itself but in both the
accounts we have considered on how the poem should end. Thus,
in Gillman's account Geraldine was said to represent 'the power
of evil', whereas according to Derwent Coleridge's she was 'no
witch or goblin, or malignant being of any kind, but a spirit'.
In yet a third account (the longer Gillman explanation) she was
again represented as unequivocally evil, a being possessed of 'wily
arts' akin to those of the witches in *Macbeth*.[1] It is virtually impossible to determine finally whether the Geraldine of Part 1 represents a power of evil or is an unwilling instrument of Christabel's martyrdom, obliged to perform her mission in the name of
those 'who live in the upper sky'. The points for and against
either conclusion balance about equally.[2] On the one hand there
are the sinister implications of her inability to cross the threshold
unaided, her refusal to pray, the reactions to her presence of the
mastiff, the fire-embers and Christabel's guardian spirit, and on

---

[1] This third account, too long to quote here, may be found in HH, 127–8.
The reference to *Macbeth* has some significance for my ensuing argument
(p. 195, note 5).

[2] Mr Beer regards this very 'ambivalence' of Geraldine's as a pointer to her
'daemonic nature' (op. cit., 189).

the other her foreknowledge of the purposes of those 'who live in the upper sky', whose agent she purports to be. Nevertheless, apart from the fact that in two of the three conjectural accounts of how the poem should end Geraldine is represented as unequivocally evil, as the story develops in Part II her evil qualities undoubtedly predominate.[1]

In the three-year interval between the writing of Parts I and II of the poem Coleridge may himself have become uncertain what Geraldine and Christabel actually represented. Already, it seemed, their relationship had become as much a psychological matter as the dramatization of a moral encounter between evil and innocence. He must have realized, long before critics drew attention to it, that there was something perversely sexual about the consummation of the heroine's martyrdom, whatever original significance it might have had. He seemed as nervous of publishing *Christabel* as *Kubla Khan*, both being held back until 1816 when they appeared behind defensive Prefaces. The critics (Hazlitt particularly) pilloried these poems, especially *Christabel*, whose sexual features induced one pamphleteer to describe it as 'the most obscene Poem in the English Language'.[2] *The Examiner*, of 2 June 1816, objected:

> There is something disgusting at the bottom of his subject, which is but ill glossed over by a veil of Della Cruscan sentiment and fine writing—like moon-beams playing on a charnel-house, or flowers strewed on a dead body.

Hazlitt, the author, probably, of this review, even spread the rumour apparently that Geraldine was actually a man in disguise.[3] In reacting against the poem's 'obscenity' these reviewers proved remarkably blind to its other merits, but their recognition of its sexual implications showed that Coleridge's apprehensions

---

[1] Ernest Hartley Coleridge argued strongly for Geraldine's being 'at the mercy of some malign influence not herself'. The passage on which his argument mainly rested (ll. 256–62; see pp. 200–1 below) was not added to the poem however until 1828. Gillman, on the other hand, seemed in no doubt about Geraldine's malignity, calling her 'an evil being, not of this world' (op. cit., 284; and cf. HH, 125).

[2] The anonymous pamphlet *Hypocrisy unveiled, and Calumny Detected: in a Review of Blackwood's Magazine*, 1818, referred to Byron's "Parisina" and Coleridge's "Christabel" as 'poems which sin as heinously against purity and decency as it is well possible to imagine' (see CL, IV, 918).

[3] CL, IV, 918.

had been justified. His letter to Byron, who was instrumental in bringing about the publication of *Christabel*, betrayed his sensitivity to this sort of accusation.[1]

One may doubt whether Coleridge would have continued with Part II at all but for the considerable pressure Wordsworth exerted upon him to finish the poem. On returning from Germany in May 1799, Wordsworth had become preoccupied with the sale of *Lyrical Ballads*, and in April 1800 he determined to reissue the *Lyrical Ballads* of 1798 as volume I, to prepare a second volume made up of new poems, and to publish the work in his own name. Coleridge, though faced with pressing obligations of his own, unhesitatingly allowed Wordsworth to utilize the four poems he had contributed to the 1798 volume, and agreed that *Christabel* should conclude the second volume. He made a tremendous effort between 29 June and early October, and by 4 October 1800 succeeded in composing Part II of *Christabel*. Wordsworth at first seemed pleased with the poem, but then changed his mind abruptly. On 6 October Dorothy Wordsworth's *Journal* remarks laconically: 'Determined not to print *Christabel* with the L.B.'[2] An unpublished letter of Wordsworth's to Longman suggests that he rejected the poem because its style was too 'discordant' from his own to be printed with any 'propriety'.[3] One wonders, however, if the Wordsworths had not also become sensitive to the poem's unusual sexual features.

A letter Coleridge wrote to Josiah Wedgwood on 1 November 1800 gave a graphic account of the difficulties he had experienced in writing Part II of *Christabel*:

> . . . immediately on my arrival in this country [from Germany] I undertook to finish a poem which I had begun, entitled *Christabel*, for a second volume of the Lyrical Ballads. I tried to perform my promise; but the deep unutterable Disgust, which I had suffered in the translation of that accursed Wallenstein, seemed to have stricken me with barrenness—for I tried & tried, & nothing would come of it. I desisted with a deeper dejection than I am willing to

[1] In his Preface to "Christabel" (1816) Coleridge blamed his failure to finish the poem on 'indolence', but a letter to Byron, of 22 October 1815, indicates that 'disgusts . . . most certainly not originating in my own opinion or decision' were also to blame; see B. R. McElderry, Jr, "Coleridge's 'Preface' to Christabel", in *Wordsworth and Coleridge*, ed. E. L. Griggs (New York, 1962), p. 168.

[2] See CL, I, 631n, 592n.   [3] ibid, I, 643n.

remember. The wind from Skiddaw & Borrodale was often as loud as wind need be—& many a walk in the clouds on the mountains did I take; but all would not do—till one day I dined out at the house of a neighbouring clergyman, & some how or other drank so much wine, that I found some effort & dexterity requisite to balance myself on the hither Edge of Sobriety. The next day, my verse making faculties returned to me, and I proceeded successfully— till my poem grew so long & in Wordsworth's opinion so impressive, that he rejected it from his volume as disproportionate both in size & merit, & as discordant in it's character.[1]

The reason given here for Wordsworth's rejection of the poem differs significantly from that given by Wordsworth himself. Coleridge deceived Wedgwood in claiming that the 'size & merit' of his poem debarred it from inclusion in the 1800 edition of *Lyrical Ballads*. He may have been equally deceitful in implying that the Wallenstein translation was the sole cause of the 'deep unutterable Disgust' which had stricken him with barrenness.[2] The summer and autumn of 1800 was a bad period of depression for Coleridge: he was short of money, feverishly rheumatic, becoming seriously addicted to opium, on the verge of quarrelling with Lloyd and Wordsworth, and experiencing increasing domestic discord.[3] A striking feature of the above letter is Coleridge's confession that the mountain wind—a sure stimulus usually for his creative energy—would no longer function for him. Ultimately, alcohol did the trick; one suspects because it blunted the outraged moral susceptibilities which (as I hope to show) were possibly the real impediment to finishing *Christabel*.

In Part II of the poem the heroine undergoes a transformation: her former self-assurance and confidence in the 'saints' above are undermined. As Tomlinson observes, the 'blue sky' she trusts in *never* operates in the poem, and the sinister manner in which it is 'covered but not hidden' adds to our appreciation of Christabel's growing feelings of helplessness and isolation.[4] The first

---

[1] ibid, 1, 643.

[2] In response to Longman's proposal in 1799 for a translation of Schiller's plays on Wallenstein Coleridge produced *The Death of Wallenstein*, though not *Wallenstein's Camp* or an essay on the genius of Schiller, as promised. The translation was not a financial success. In 1823 Coleridge tried to adapt the play for Edmund Kean to appear in on the stage (Life, 124–5, 289).

[3] cf. KC, 1, 834 n. [4] op. cit., 107.

words Christabel speaks in Part II are fraught with perplexed anxiety:

> 'Sure I have sinn'd!' said Christabel,
> 'Now heaven be praised if all be well!'
> And in low faltering tones, yet sweet,
> Did she the lofty lady greet
> With such perplexity of mind
> As dreams too lively leave behind. (381–6)

Her past innocence is clouded (like the sky) by 'sins unknown' and, though she still professes confidence in the outcome of events, the tone of her apprehensive 'All will yet be well!' belies this. Her scope of action is circumscribed by the spell which Geraldine has placed upon her utterance; she can only stand by now while others decide her fate for her. This is an aspect of her martyrdom she had not bargained for (though alienation from family relationships had been the feature of Teresa's fate which Coleridge had found most poignant in Crashaw). This alienation was moreover to have been the theme of Part III of the poem, had Coleridge ever written it: 'Were I free to do so, I feel as if I could compose the third part of *Christabel*, or *the song of her desolation*.'[1] In some respects, Christabel seems much more a child now than in the earlier part of the story. Significantly, her absent lover is never once mentioned in Part II, a circumstance which further isolates her and increases the pathos of her helpless vulnerability. Like a tongue-tied child she stands helpless while adults wrangle over her, resembling somewhat the little lost child described later in *Dejection: an Ode*:

> Not far from home, but she hath lost her way:
> And now moans low in bitter grief and fear,
> And now screams loud, and hopes to make her mother hear.
>
> (123–5)

As Christabel's stature diminishes, the other characters are allowed to develop and come more into the foreground.

Geraldine, for example, reveals new traits of character in Part II, traits decidedly more sensual and lamia-like than angelic. Her beauty (constantly alluded to) resembles that of the practised courtesan as deliberately she sets out to captivate the Baron, drawing her 'girded vests . . . tight beneath her heaving breasts' and arraying herself for him almost like a bride:

[1] See K. Coburn, *University of Toronto Quarterly*, 1956, xxv, 127.

> . . . rises lightly from the bed;
> Puts on her silken vestments white,
> And tricks her hair in lovely plight. (363–5)

Sir Leoline welcomes her as the daughter of his former friend, but she meets his embrace like a lover's, 'prolonging it with joyous look'. Soon the Baron's attitude to her seems less avuncular than infatuated—'His eyes made up of wonder and love'. Like some young gallant almost, he addresses her 'in courtly accents fine' and, receptive to the change of attitude, she reciprocates accordingly, *feigning* a modesty she does not genuinely possess:

> . . . in maiden wise
> Casting down her large bright eyes,
> With blushing cheek and courtesy fine. (573–5)

Increasingly, Geraldine becomes the *femme fatale*, the destroyer of family relationships.

It is Christabel's father however who in Part II of the poem provides the richest source of fresh dramatic interest. The sickly valetudinarian of Part I, sleeping fitfully in a room 'as still as death', now becomes a much more virile figure. Since his wife died in giving birth to Christabel he has deliberately withdrawn from life, stolidly incarcerating himself both physically (behind massive gates 'ironed within and without') and mentally. Whereas the youthful Christabel's hopes are centred on the future, his mind is *imprisoned* in the past, in memories of old quarrels and a love that lies buried:

> Each matin bell, the Baron saith,
> Knells us back to a world of death.
> These words Sir Leoline first said,
> When he rose and found his lady dead:
> These words Sir Leoline will say
> Many a morn to his dying day! (332–7)

Each day since his wife died the protracted funeral obsequies, imposed by his decree upon the castle and the living neighbourhood outside, have re-enacted the ghastly ritual of death. They symptomatize his mental sickness, and it is apparent already that his neurotic obsession with death implies an incapacity for vital, living relationships.[1]

---

[1] It is wholly in character that a toothless mastiff bitch is his chief companion.

Beneath his carapace however strong passions still lie dormant, for his emotional nature before he retreated into this semi-catatonic state had always been tempestuous and unpredictable, as can be gauged from the manner of his quarrel with Lord Roland, 'his heart's best brother':

> Alas! they had been friends in youth;
> But whispering tongues can poison truth;
> And constancy lives in realms above;
> And life is thorny; and youth is vain;
> And to be wroth with one we love
> Doth work like madness in the brain.
> And thus it chanced, as I divine,
> With Roland and Sir Leoline.
> Each spake words of high disdain
> And insult to his heart's best brother:
> They parted—ne'er to meet again!
> But never either found another
> To free the hollow heart from paining—
> They stood aloof, the scars remaining,
> Like cliffs which had been rent asunder;
> A dreary sea now flows between;—
> But neither heat, nor frost, nor thunder,
> Shall wholly do away, I ween,
> The marks of that which once hath been.[1]

It is one of the ironies of the poem that no sooner does Geraldine's arrival resurrect living feeling in Sir Leoline than immediately and impetuously he perpetrates his former mistake again, becoming 'wroth' this time with his only child and his faithful retainer, banishing both from his presence with Lear-like unreasonableness. The lines just quoted—which Coleridge considered 'the best and sweetest' he ever wrote[2]—referred possibly to his own breach with Southey and obviously had deep personal significance for him, as his many later references to them showed. The feelings associated in them with loss of friendship and the characteristic images ('life is thorny' and 'a dreary sea now flows between') suggest also that Coleridge may have felt some self-identification with Sir Leoline.

The Baron's response to Geraldine's story is activated at first by chivalrous compassion as his 'noble' anger swells, but this soon

---

[1] ll. 408–26. The situation is reminiscent of the first Act of *The Winter's Tale*.
[2] CL, III, 435.

degenerates into self-indulgent emotional abandonment. In the novel thrill of his rejuvenated feelings, age and infirmity are forgotten. He sees this unexpected situation entirely as a means of making his private peace with the friend he had wronged, but he is so wrapped up in self-centredness and the feelings Geraldine's nearness excites in him, that he rides roughshod over his daughter's feelings, never bothering to seek the cause of her odd behaviour nor of the perturbation manifested by his old retainer. He luxuriates in oscillating from violent anger to tearful sentimentality.

At this point in the poem Sir Leoline appears more the creature of his senses than Kubla Khan, more impulsive and intellectually limited than the Mariner, and more deficient in imaginative insight than either of them. Bard Bracy's dream provides a symbolical interpretation of the situation in which they are all now locked, intended as a corrective to Sir Leoline's misunderstanding of it, but the Baron scarcely has patience to listen to the poet. Through the device of Bracy's dream Coleridge juxtaposes again the antithetical levels of intuitive insight and ordinary understanding much as he had done in *The Ancient Mariner*, the dream providing a symbolical 'explanation' of the mysterious events befalling them, which the Baron's shallow understanding is unable to grasp. Bard Bracy in fact represents the bardic tradition here, having a keen sense of both the sacredness of his vocation and his responsibility for interpreting the visions vouchsafed to him. His privileged insight informs him that evil is still operative in their midst, something 'unholy' and 'unblest' which it is his task to exorcise 'with music strong and saintly song'. Unable as yet to interpret fully the symbolism of his dream, he nevertheless knows that the 'dove' of his vision represents Christabel:

> For in my sleep I saw that dove,
> That gentle bird, whom thou dost love,
> And call'st by thy own daughter's name—
> Sir Leoline! I saw the same
> Fluttering, and uttering fearful moan,
> Among the green herbs in the forest alone. (531–6)

Intuitively Bard Bracy realizes that the dream-symbolism is hinting at the presence of mysterious forces which pose a threat to Christabel and, though he lacks the reader's knowledge of what has in fact already happened, his inspired guess is not far out:

> I stooped, methought, the dove to take,
> When lo! I saw a bright green snake
> Coiled around its wings and neck.
> Green as the herbs on which it couched,
> Close by the dove's its head it crouched;
> And with the dove it heaves and stirs,
> Swelling its neck as she swelled hers! (548–54)

This symbolism tends to heighten and underline, if anything, the sexual connotations of Christabel's 'martyrdom'.

Earlier it had seemed that Sir Leoline recognized the special sacredness of Bracy's calling, or was at any rate prepared to exploit it for the diplomatic purposes of effecting a reconciliation with Lord Roland de Vaux. He had ordered Bracy to ride up to Lord Roland's hall and with 'your music so sweet' to prepare the way for a reunion. But in the last resort he trusts more to force of arms than sacred song, resorting (Mariner-like) to crude violence as the simplest way of dealing with problems he cannot understand:

> 'Sweet maid, Lord Roland's beauteous dove,
> With arms more strong than harp or song,
> Thy sire and I will crush the snake!' (569–71)

In these curt words he not only rejects the bardic insight but, by equating the dove with Geraldine rather than Christabel, reveals that the dream's significance has been totally lost upon him. Like the Mariner he 'little saw of what had else been seen'.[1] In fact, he had been only 'half-listening' to Bracy's account of it, with a derisive 'smile' upon his lips.

Once his obtuse mind is made up nothing can move it, not even Christabel's overwrought appeal to the long-cherished memory of his wife. Great pressures are put upon him to change his mind, Christabel being momentarily freed from the spell which binds her utterance and the Narrator himself interceding for her— 'Wouldst thou wrong thy only child?' His mind is however as closed to rational argument or family feeling as to imaginative insight, and he gives way instead to the violence of private feelings. For the second time in his life 'madness in the brain' causes him to be 'wroth' with one he loves:

---

[1] cf. pp. 160–1 above.

> Within the Baron's heart and brain
> If thoughts, like these, had any share,
> They only swelled his rage and pain,
> And did but work confusion there.
> His heart was cleft with pain and rage,
> His cheeks they quivered, his eyes were wild. (636–41)

This wilful refusal to profit from past experience is important as indicating his own responsibility for his actions. To regard Sir Leoline simply as a puppet which Geraldine manipulates is to ignore the depth of characterization here.[1]

The Baron justifies his conduct by vague appeals to misconceived notions of 'hospitality' and 'honour' (oblivious to the fact that Christabel is the very paradigm of both). His concept of 'hospitality' is as shallow as that of the Mariner's 'accomplices' for, if theirs was based ultimately on expediency, his is based on narrow pride:

> Dishonoured thus in his old age;
> Dishonoured by his only child,
> And all his hospitality
> To the wronged daughter of his friend
> By more than woman's jealousy
> Brought thus to a disgraceful end. (642–7)

Thus, in dismissing Christabel in favour of Geraldine, he deliberately chooses evil in preference to virtue, at the same time effectively destroying the only personal relationship that still survives to him.[2] It is an unlooked-for development in the poem, shifting the centre of interest from the heroine to her father, and introducing psychological complexities which place it in a different genre altogether from the conventional tale of terror. Dramatically, the characters have become something more than the stock

---

[1] Mr Schulz, for instance, says that 'Just as [Coleridge] had resorted in "The Ancient Mariner" to supernatural machinery to return the ship to home port, so in the second part of "Christabel", he turns to Lamia witchcraft to motivate the actions of Geraldine, Christabel and Sir Leoline' (Schulz, 65).

[2] cf. "Psyche" (1808):

> For in this earthly frame
> Ours is the reptile's lot, much toil, much blame,
> Manifold motions making little speed,
> And to deform and kill the things whereon we feed. (4–7)

figures of 'the unambiguous Morality statement',[1] thus realizing the *Lyrical Ballads* aim of transferring

> . . . from our inward nature a human interest and a semblance of truth sufficient to procure for these shadows of imagination that willing suspension of disbelief for the moment, which constitutes poetic faith.[2]

For the fullest explanation of the factors which may have influenced this shift of emphasis in the poem we must turn however to biographical sources more immediate than *Biographia Literaria*.

The second half of *Christabel* was written some two to three years after the 'annus mirabilis' had ended, and in the remainder of this chapter we shall be concerned with the events of 1800 which had a bearing upon the poem's development. An obvious difference between the two halves of *Christabel* is the sudden abandonment in Part II of romantic strangeness in favour of more concrete particularization. The 1797 section was characterized by a rich concatenation of mystery and a deliberate absence of verisimilitude entirely in keeping with a primary aim of the *Lyrical Ballads*.[3] The 1800 landscape, in contrast, is set specifically in Cumberland, amid the realistic landmarks of Bratha Head, 'Wyndermere', and Borrowdale. Coleridge had in the interval between writing these sections transferred his home and family from Nether Stowey in Somerset, to Keswick, and he saw no incongruity apparently in allowing this change of circumstances to be reflected in the poem. This may be a first indication of how the poem was acquiring deeper personal significance for him.

He moved to Keswick partly to be nearer Sara Hutchinson, with whom some months before he had begun a secret love-affair.[4] Had there been only his wife to consider at this time Coleridge might have sought a separation there and then, but paren-

---

[1] J. F. Danby, *Shakespeare's Doctrine of Nature*; see Tomlinson, op. cit., 111–12.

[2] BL, II, 5–6.   [3] ibid.

[4] Sara Hutchinson was then living on a farm at Sockburn on the banks of the Tees, with her brothers, Thomas and George, and her sisters, Mary and Joanna. Mary Hutchinson (later Wordsworth's wife) had been a close friend of Dorothy Wordsworth in her youth at Penrith.

tal responsibilities obliged him to take his family with him. He suffered from the inner conflict these divisive loyalties produced, particularly since he felt that Asra could sustain his creative energies in a way his wife did not. His affection for Hartley was the chief impediment, probably, to his pursuit of Asra. Then, to make matters worse, Sara became pregnant again, giving birth to another child (Derwent Coleridge) in September 1800—at the very time when Coleridge was working on Part II of *Christabel*. The arrival of this child, an added responsibility to turn his 'Error' (in marrying Sara) to 'Necessity',[1] marked the first phase probably in the development of the grave emotional crisis which occurred soon afterwards. Hearing this baby's sickly cries his mind harked back to the memory of their second child, Berkeley, who had died in infancy while Coleridge was in Germany.[2] An involuntary wish for Derwent's death—only partially suppressed —appears to have been reflected in the poem he was writing.

Coleridge's failure to finish *Christabel*, despite many attempts to do so, may have arisen primarily from the fact that in 1800 he discovered unexpected analogies between the story in the poem and his real-life situation, causing him to load it with a weight of personal significance from which he was unable afterwards to rescue it. It was not just a case of the original intention miscarrying (*The Eolian Harp*, *Religious Musings*, and *The Ancient Mariner* are proof that Coleridge could at any time recast 'original intentions') but rather that a degree of self-identification obtruded into the plot of *Christabel* which finally destroyed it. Instead of following the original plan therefore, he may have begun utilizing this poetic representation of a father's repudiation of his child as a vehicle (a safety-valve almost) for the imaginative exploration of his own altered feelings towards his offspring.

This hypothesis enables us to make sense at least of that otherwise enigmatical Conclusion to Part II of the poem (so unrelated seemingly to the rest of the narrative) which critical comment tends sometimes to ignore. Part II ends with Sir Leoline dismissing Bracy on his errand to Lord Roland and turning *from* his child to lead forth the lady Geraldine. Then comes this 'Conclusion':

---

[1] cf. the original draft of "Dejection: an Ode", ll. 272–85.
[2] Berkeley died of consumption on 10 February 1799.

A little child, a limber elf,
Singing, dancing to itself,
A fairy thing with red round cheeks,
That always finds, and never seeks,
Makes such a vision to the sight
As fills a father's eyes with light;
And pleasures flow in so thick and fast
Upon his heart, that he at last
Must needs express his love's excess
With words of unmeant bitterness.
Perhaps 'tis pretty to force together
Thoughts so all unlike each other;
To mutter and mock a broken charm,
To dally with wrong that does no harm.
Perhaps 'tis tender too and pretty
At each wild word to feel within
A sweet recoil of love and pity.
And what, if in a world of sin
(O sorrow and shame should this be true!)
Such giddiness of heart and brain
Comes seldom save from rage and pain,
So talks as it's most used to do. (656–77)

This is intended surely to parallel Sir Leoline's anger with Christabel (especially in the 'giddiness of heart and brain' that produces 'wild' words of 'unmeant bitterness'), but at the same time
it raises the curious love–hate relationship between father and
child from the particular dramatic situation to a level of universality where it can be analysed more objectively. What occurred
between Sir Leoline and Christabel, it implies, could happen in
any father–child relationship. An interesting feature of this analysis is that, apart from some natural sympathy with the child,
the burden of sympathy lies mainly with the father, whose unintentional cruelty is the product rather of too much than of
too little affection. Coleridge wrote these lines after finishing
Part II of the poem and his concern to re-appraise the father's
feelings points to his dissatisfaction with some psychological im-
plausibility in Sir Leoline's treatment of Christabel. A notebook
entry, written two years later, suggests that Coleridge was still
unhappy about this scene and anxious to exculpate Sir Leoline
further:

A kindhearted man obliged to give a refusal, or the like, that will give great pain, finds relief in doing it roughly & fiercely—explain this, & use it in Christabel /.[1]

Such a modification, by engaging greater sympathy for the father, might at a deeper level have been assuaging also to the poet's own self-esteem.

Despite their seeming universality the 'limber elf' lines were in fact a description not of any child but of Coleridge's own son, Hartley—a circumstance which at once throws fresh significance on Sir Leoline's anger with Christabel. The fictional quarrel may have been a reflection partly of Coleridge's divided attitude towards his son and, since in 1800 Hartley was only four, we may remind ourselves again how Coleridge seems deliberately to have diminished Christabel's stature in this scene, making her much more child-like than originally. We know that the 'limber elf' lines referred to Hartley, because they first appeared in a letter to Southey of 1801, coupled with this rather revealing comment:

> Dear Hartley! we are at times alarmed by the state of his Health —but at present he is well—if I were to lose him, I am afraid, it would exceedingly deaden my affection for any other children I may have—
>
> A little child, a limber Elf. . . .[2]

Since they were first employed therefore within the context of a letter in which Coleridge was contemplating what the '*loss*' of Hartley would signify for him, there was clearly some connection in Coleridge's mind between Sir Leoline's abandonment of Christabel and his own relationship with Hartley.

Yet, as the passage just quoted implies, it was Derwent's arrival which was the immediate cause of Coleridge's re-examining his feelings towards his children. Derwent arrived at the wrong time in Coleridge's life—appearing as a further harassment to 'bind and pluck out the Wing-feathers' of his mind, when he badly wanted to be free from such impediments.[3] It was doubtful at first if the baby would survive, and Coleridge seems to have expected (and secretly half-wished) that it would die before he became attached to it. The recently published private notebooks reveal that, during the fortnight in which the infants' life hung in the balance, Coleridge's mind was obsessed with child mortality and they suggest that he deliberately withheld affection from the child.

[1] KC, I, 1392.　　[2] CL, II, 728.　　[3] cf. p. 270 below.

O

One is struck for instance by the joyless brevity with which he 'registered' the birth, a response totally different from his delightful excitement in 1796 on the occasion of Hartley's appearance:

Sunday Night ½ past 10, Septemb. 14, 1800—a boy born / Bracy?[1]

The indication given here that he first thought of '*Bracy*' as a possible name for the child is a circumstance lending extra significance perhaps to the *Christabel* lines, 'Why, Bracy! does thou loiter here? I bade thee hence!' Part II of *Christabel* was completed at latest by 4 October 1800; hence the 'abrupt, austere' dismissal of Bard Bracy it contains must have been written almost simultaneously with the birth of the infant 'Bracy', and may conceivably have represented therefore a figurative rejection of the child. This impression of dissociation is reinforced if we turn to succeeding entries in this curious notebook sequence.

Immediately under the registration of Derwent's birth appears what is in fact a transcript of an item published in *The London Star* concerning the death of a child in St James's Park:

Star of Wed. 10 Sept.—1800
On Saturday Morning, a spectacle &c the body an infant &c—from the length of time the body had remained in the water the legs had assumed a greenish hue, *probably from the weeds*, and the flesh was more yielding to the touch than is either necessary or agreeable to describe.[2]

What impelled Coleridge to preserve this macabre item next to the announcement of his son's birth, rather than in another of the several notebooks he was using at that time? It seems odd that he was not himself struck by the incongruity of such a juxtaposition. The absence of any explanatory comment might indicate that there was a *deliberate* collocation here, the full significance of which he dared not acknowledge even to himself. As we trace this 'Notebook No. 5½' sequence further, the possibility of this being a purely accidental juxtaposition recedes. Two entries after the newspaper transcript we find Coleridge recollecting the feelings he had experienced when Berkeley died:

The most melancholy time after the death of a Friend, or Child is when you first awake after your first Sleep / when the dizziness,

---

[1] KC, I, 806; and cf. p. 104 above.
[2] ibid, I, 809. The italics are Coleridge's and the '&c's' represent local references which he deleted.

heat, & drunkenness of Grief is gone / and the pang of hollowness is first felt.[1]

Having already lost one baby it was natural perhaps that these old memories should be revived in Coleridge's mind, especially as the new arrival was already displaying disturbing symptoms:

> Sept. 27. 1800—The child being very ill was baptized by the name of Derwent / The Child hour after hour made a noise exactly like the Creeking of a door which is being shut very slowly to prevent its creeking.[2]

A most striking feature of these entries however is their quite unusual emotional detachment, the very last reaction one would normally have expected in such circumstances from Coleridge. One recalls his hysteria at the time of Berkeley's death and the remark he had made while reproaching himself for being absent from home on that occasion: 'I have a strange sort of sensation, as if while I was present, none could die whom I intensely loved.'[3] Those words were written before Asra had appeared in Coleridge's life however, and before he had learnt to think of his children as *obstacles* to his happiness.

In the entry immediately following, the focus of interest shifts back (rather as in the 'Conclusion' to the poem) to the effect upon a parent of parting with its child:

> 'To part with a little Babe one has had 9 months in one's arms— and to be glad to part with him too!'[4]

This refers apparently to a conversation Coleridge had recently overheard. It is difficult to determine the true source of Coleridge's interest here—whether in the parent, whose unnatural indifference towards its offspring paralleled possibly his own antipathy towards Derwent, or in the sharp astonishment of the speaker, whose horrified reaction to such alienation of normal human instincts may have driven Coleridge to conceal still deeper any guilty feelings he himself was harbouring.[5]

---

[1] ibid, i, 812.   [2] ibid, i, 813.   [3] CL, i, 490.   [4] KC, i, 814.

[5] Another enigmatical notebook entry appeared soon afterwards:
> Butcher, Chickens will you kill 'em?—Neay—I don't much like it— I had far fainer kill an Ox.—Novem. 24, 1800. (KC, i, 839.)

We know that "Christabel" was closely linked in Coleridge's mind with *Macbeth* (see p. 180, note 1; also E. L. Griggs, *Wordsworth and Coleridge* [New York, 1962], 174). Did this scrap of overheard conversation recall to Coleridge's

Because in each of the above passages Coleridge's personal feelings are closely masked it can only be supposition, of course, that they indicate a suppressed desire for Derwent's death. But their cumulative effect is to suggest something other than a merely accidental or strangely innocent recording of the quirks of human personality. Their obliquity was possibly deliberate, in the sense that in 1800 Coleridge could not face squarely the full implications of his altered feelings towards his children. By 1802 this reticence had vanished, neurosis and the habits of his 'coarse domestic life' having blunted somewhat his former delicate susceptibilities. In 1802 he admitted openly that, because his children came between him and his love for Asra, 'I have half-wish'd they never had been born'.[1] Discovering in 1802 that his wife was pregnant again, his antipathy this time was frank and unconcealed:

> Mrs Coleridge is indisposed, & I have too much reason to suspect that she is breeding again / an event, which was to have been deprecated.[2]

In the light of subsequent events, therefore, it seems that Coleridge's repression of his natural instincts in 1800 may have marked the first phase in a dissociation from his children which was to culminate in his abandoning them entirely.[3] But, while

---

mind Macduff's outburst on hearing of the slaughter of his children by Macbeth, the 'butcher'? (see *Macbeth*, IV, 3, 204–19; V, 8, 69).

[1] cf. "Dejection: an Ode" (original version), l. 282.

[2] CL, II, 799. Coleridge's daughter, 'Young Sara', was born on 23 December 1802; see pp. 211–12 below.

[3] Coleridge's subsequent relationship with his children is discussed in Chapters 8 and 9 below. When he left for Malta in 1804, relinquishing his children to the care of their mother and uncle (Robert Southey), he seems to have made up his mind then that he would never return to Greta Hall (cf. pp. 212, 235 below). He came back from Malta intent on a separation from his wife, which she agreed to in 1807 and, thereafter, his contacts with his children diminished. There is no evidence however that they felt rejected by their father; indeed, both Derwent and Young Sara took pains in later life to vindicate his reputation (see p. 280, note 1; and cf. CF, 113, 144–9).

'Antipathy' is perhaps too strong a word to describe Coleridge's attitude towards Derwent in the days immediately following the child's arrival. The letters Coleridge wrote about this time suggest that he was greatly agitated by Sara's distress: 'My wife has given me another Son,—but alas! I fear, he will not live. She is now sobbing & crying by the side of me' (CL, I, 626). Whatever his feelings for Asra, Coleridge was not impervious to Sara's suffering. Yet it was the very pathos of Sara's situation which made his own prehe found it relatively to easy detach himself from Derwent and Young Sara, with Hartley, his favourite child, the situation was different. His eldest child was linked too closely with happier times at Nether Stowey and with the years of rich achievement for Coleridge not to be aware of the injury he did his son by this affair he was carrying on with Asra.

The fact that Coleridge connected Christabel's plight with Hartley's lends added poignancy to the scene in which Coleridge, as Narrator, himself intrudes into the poem to take the side of the stricken child. His speech might be interpreted almost as a dialogue between the poet and his conscience in which, under cover of a fiction, he confronted himself with the consequences involved in giving way to selfish desire. When Christabel pleads with her father:

> 'By my mother's soul do I entreat
> That thou this woman send away!' (616–17)

the language, atmosphere, and drama in the poem almost recall those of divorce proceedings, Geraldine being the 'other woman' in an age-old situation. We need not look for exact parallels here to perceive a basic similarity between the fictional and the real-life situation. The Narrator's protest, charged with emotion, again shows great concern to understand the father's feelings, using the pathos surrounding the child mainly as a means of heightening the antithesis between Sir Leoline's feelings and the demands of ordinary conscience:

> Why is thy cheek so wan and wild,
> Sir Leoline? Thy only child
> Lies at thy feet, thy joy, thy pride,
> So fair, so innocent, so mild;
> The same, for whom thy lady died!
> . . . wouldst thou wrong thy only child
> Her child and thine? (621–35)

---

dicament unbearable. He could not abandon Sara now, still less this helpless infant, yet he knew that their marriage was finished. A letter Coleridge wrote three days after Derwent's birth indicates the divided state of his affections at this time: '—The delay in Copy has been owing in part to me, as the writer of *Christabel*—Every line has been produced by me with labor-pangs' (CL, I, 623). In the months that followed, in spite of everything, Coleridge became increasingly attached to his 'fat pretty child' (CL, I, 650). For a further link between "Christabel" and Derwent see Coleridge's letter to Southey in February 1808 (CL, III, 72).

In the poem 'conscience' loses however as, 'turning *from* his own sweet maid', Sir Leoline leads 'forth the lady Geraldine', dismissing 'Bracy' at the same time.

It is as though, having brought the issue to the surface through the Narrator's intercession, Coleridge then retired into the background again, allowing his creatures to play out the situation for him. The solution they came to might almost be regarded as wish-fulfilment, on the supposition that the Sir Leoline/Geraldine attachment was a projection somehow of Coleridge's own relationship with Asra. But what connection *could* there be between Geraldine and Asra, when so many of the basic features of Geraldine's characterization had been established in 1797, before Coleridge and Asra had even met? No one less resembled the fatal woman of romantic literature, which Geraldine typifies, than the physically undistinguished, real-life Asra. Though there are striking parallels between Geraldine and 'Genevieve' (the heroine of the poem *Love*, which Coleridge wrote six months before he began Part II of *Christabel*)—and Genevieve, as Appendix IV shows, is unmistakably Asra—yet genealogical links like these fail to demonstrate any obvious similarity between the monster-like Geraldine and the woman Coleridge loved. At most there was only some analogy of general *situation*, in the sense that both the fictional and the real-life woman were the cause of a domestic upheaval injurious to innocent children and provoking opposition from a 'mother' resentful at the usurpation of her place. If we assume however that in *Christabel* Coleridge was concerned with precisely such domestic repercussions (whereas in *Love* he sought rather to vindicate romantic love), then it was the 'other woman's' general *function* rather than her individual qualities which mattered. Geraldine may not have resembled Asra physically, but her disruptive effect on family relationships was very similar. As the poem developed Geraldine came to represent not Asra herself perhaps so much as the guilty feelings Coleridge associated with Asra.

Stripped of the 'guileless' modesty and charming tenderness which make Genevieve endearing, Geraldine is (apart from some modification to her character made in 1828, which I shall return to shortly) a lifeless and improbable creature. From the first description we are given of her she is devoid of individualizing traits, simply resembling Coleridge's stock-in-trade ideal of woman—mysterious, unapproachable, and totally unreal:

> . . . a damsel bright
> Drest in a silken robe of white,
> That shadowy in the moonlight shone:
> The neck that made that white robe wan,
> Her stately neck, and arms were bare;
> Her blue-veined feet unsandal'd were,
> And wildly glittered here and there
> The gems entangled in her hair. (58–65)

Here lies the clue possibly to the real nature of her puzzling ambivalence. It is not she and Christabel that are aspects of the *same* person (representing respectively love sacred and profane, or a conflict between the super-ego and the id), but Geraldine herself who embodies two aspects of one person.[1] Her twofold nature is entirely consistent with the basic dualism in Coleridge's whole attitude to the other sex. He could both venerate woman as a symbol of divinity or 'the God within' him, and yet lust lasciviously after harlots like Sal Hall.[2] Both aspects of this dualism are detectable in the fountain image which expressed his ideal of sexual love:

> O best reward of Virtue! to feel pleasure made more pleasurable, in legs, knees, chests, arms, cheeks—all in deep quiet, a fountain with unwrinkled surface yet still the living *motion* at the bottom that 'with soft and even pulse' keeps it full . . .[3]

Thus, Geraldine is both 'a thing divine' and a combination of vulpine and reptilian characteristics which (as the original text indicates) belongs with the sexual nausea of nightmare:

> . . . and full in view,
> Behold! her bosom and half her side—
> It was dark and rough as the Sea-Wolf's hide
> A sight to dream of, not to tell![4]

[1] R. H. Fogle, *The Idea of Coleridge's Criticism* (Berkeley and Los Angeles, 1962), suggests that a psychologist might regard Christabel and Geraldine as aspects of one person, representing the ego or super-ego and the id, or love sacred and profane (p. 130). C. Tomlinson, discussing the significance of Bard Bracy's dream, says—'we are on the brink of the suggestion that the identity of Christabel is coveted by Geraldine and that Christabel has unconsciously assumed something of the evil identity of the other' (op. cit., 110).

[2] See pp. 37, 44–5 above.   [3] Quoted Beer, 238–9.

[4] See Coleridge, *Poems*, 1828, II, 54 (MS. amendment by Coleridge to copy now in Fitzwilliam Museum, Cambridge). Mr Beer has drawn attention to this amendment (op. cit., 191).

Adapting Mr Fogle's terminology it might be said that Geraldine is a creature of the id, while the Narrator's intercession on Christabel's behalf (written after Coleridge had become involved with Asra) is the protest of his super-ego at the consequences entailed by an abandonment to sexual gratification. Geraldine's courtesan-like qualities, her repellent snake and vampire attributes (magnified after 1800) were an extension of these aspects of sex-nausea. Shelley seems to have recognized them as something of the sort immediately, for it is related that on hearing the poem read aloud he rushed from the room, declaring afterwards that he had seen eyes in the breasts of Mary Godwin.[1]

Unlike the Abyssinian maid in *Kubla Khan*, whose objective function within the poem overrode whatever private significance she may have had for Coleridge, Geraldine's function was never objectified with anything like the same success. In Part I she remained intransigently ambivalent, and accreted further irreconcilable attributes in Part II which have resulted in the most improbable amalgam. Apart from the uncertainty as to her actual function in the poem, the true nature of her relationships with Christabel and Sir Leoline is never finally made clear. An alteration Coleridge made to the poem in 1828, intended to deepen her characterization by introducing greater psychological complexities, had the effect ultimately only of causing further confusion. Possibly this interpolation was made in response to the criticisms which the 1816 reviewers had levelled against the poem but, while it certainly made Geraldine less monster-like, it also produced a shift of emphasis in the relationship with Christabel quite different, one suspects, from that originally intended. Like the modification Coleridge proposed for Sir Leoline's character (once he had become conscious of the poem's autobiographical significance) it had the effect of diverting sympathy from the child to the sufferings of the tormented adult, in this case those of the 'other' woman. Geraldine was thus made much more conscious of her own repugnance to the child whose mother's place she was usurping:

> Ah! what a stricken look was hers!
> Deep from within she seems half-way
> To lift some weight with sick assay,
> And eyes the maid and seeks delay;

[1] See Beer, 189.

> Then suddenly, as one defied,
> Collects herself in scorn and pride,
> And lay down by the Maiden's side! (256–62)

Coleridge may have inserted these lines to protect himself from criticism, but they gave a quite new significance to the original lines in which Geraldine is seen to be 'accepted' by the child:

> And lo! the worker of these harms,
> That holds the maiden in her arms,
> Seems to slumber still and mild,
> As a mother with her child. (298–301)

Taken in conjunction these passages convey almost literally what Asra's feelings must have been in regard to Coleridge's children. After his return from Malta Coleridge planned to take his children away from Sara, and to set up home with them and Asra under Wordsworth's roof. His chief anxiety—that Asra would not be 'acceptable' to Hartley—was dispelled on Christmas Day 1806, at Coleorton, when he discovered them together on terms of affectionate intimacy:

> All here love him [Hartley] most dearly: and your name sake [Asra] takes upon her all the duties of his Mother & darling Friend, with all the Mother's love & fondness. He is very fond of *her*.[1]

It is not suggested that Coleridge deliberately modified the poem in 1828 thus to point a personal allegory; indeed, most of the personal significances we have elicited are oblique or purely speculative. Nevertheless, the fact remains that all the personal issues we have been discussing came to the surface openly less than two years afterwards in the naked self-exposure of *Dejection : an Ode*. In 1800, as my next chapter will show, Coleridge stood on the brink of a great emotional crisis which almost wrecked his health; it is highly probable that the factors which produced his breakdown were precisely those which underlay his failure to finish *Christabel*. Mr Whalley's suggestion that Coleridge could not finish the poem because 'it had so little personal significance for him' seems highly questionable; *Christabel* may have been left unfinished because it had too *much* personal significance.[2] Indeed,

---

[1] CL, ii, 1205.
[2] See George Whalley, "The Mariner and the Albatross", in *University of Toronto Quarterly*, 1947, xvi, 391n. Mr Whalley says: 'Christabel was far more "a work of pure imagination" than *The Ancient Mariner*: it had so little per-

what Mr Tomlinson has remarked of the plot contained in the poem might as aptly perhaps be applied to the writing of it: it ends 'as a tragedy in which *neurosis*, not death, strikes the final blow'.[1] This neurosis forms the theme of the following chapter.

---

sonal significance for [Coleridge] that he was unable to overcome the practical difficulties of completing it.'

[1] Tomlinson, op. cit., 105. Mr Bostetter regards the failure to finish "Christabel" as marking the collapse of Coleridge as a significant poet. His view is not dissimilar from mine: 'The poem sticks at the point at which Coleridge himself is stuck. Until he solved the problem of evil in his own life, it was hardly likely that he could finish it. To attempt to continue with the poem would have been only to torture and exacerbate his feelings by confronting the hopelessness of finding any solution to Christabel's situation or his own' (op. cit., pp. 118, 226).

8

The Emotional Equation

The German visit (September 1798–July 1799) marked a water-shed in Coleridge's life, terminating a period of splendid creative achievement and relative domestic happiness, and anticipating, in the poetry he wrote at Ratzeburg and Elbingerode, the bitter loneliness and dejection which lay in store for him.[1] After his return to England, his vital 'sheet-anchor' relationships deteriorated and his marriage broke down. Years of restlessness, illness, and financial difficulties ensued, while his moral and emotional equilibrium—always precarious—suddenly collapsed. During the critical period 1801–3 Coleridge discovered the impossibility of living up to the articles of his faith—that the true Poet must be a *good* man, whose happiness is built upon a foundation of *virtue* and truth[2]—and consequently he lost his self-confidence and abandoned poetic ambition to his rivals. What provoked his disgust with his work and manner of living was partly envy of Wordsworth and Southey but chiefly his love for Asra, which led him not only to alter his earlier views on the indissolubility of marriage but, more shattering to his conscience, to find himself wishing his wife and children dead. The guilt complex which resulted developed into an acute psychoneurosis and *this*, rather than illness or his addiction to opium and metaphysics, brought about his breakdown as a poet. For that there was a 'breakdown', despite Dr Richard's recent denial of it, seems inescapable: after 1802 his poetical output dropped both qualitatively and quantitatively, while he said, repeatedly, that as a poet he was 'finished'. In the course of this chapter, as a preliminary to the analysis of *Dejection: an Ode*, the causes of his neurosis will be examined, and it will be argued that rather than the Philosopher, or opium, or

[1] cf. "Hexameters", and "Lines Written in the Album at Elbingerode in the Hartz Forest", PW 304–5, 315–16.

[2] cf. KC, I, 1057, 1375.

ill-health 'killing' the Poet, these were ancillary and symptomatic aspects of a much deeper problem. The theories that the over-all problem was 'religious' or due to 'flight from reality' tendencies err likewise in mistaking symptoms for causes.[1]

Though, as we have seen, tensions were inherent in Coleridge's marriage from the start, not until he met Asra did they result in serious discord. Certainly, Sara was distressed by his refusal to return from Göttingen when she lost her child (Berkeley), and he was hurt by her spiteful remarks about the reception given to *Lyrical Ballads*, and by her tactless praise of Lamb, Lloyd, and Southey with whom he had recently quarrelled.[2] But he had learnt to accept their incompatibility, and seemed genuinely anxious to preserve the considerable basis of affection that still existed between them.[3] Eleven days before his first meeting with Asra he wrote: 'The Wife of a man of Genius who sympathises effectively with her Husband in his habits and feelings is a rara avis with me,'[4] but there was no thought in his mind then of parting from Sara. On his return from Germany they resumed their curiously amicable modus vivendi in which, while she was engrossed with household chores, he, 'sunk in Spinoza, remain[ed] as undisturbed as a Toad in a Rock'.[5] There is no saying how long this state of affairs might have continued had he not met Asra but, in July 1800, he took Sara away from Stowey and the proximity of the Fricker circle at Bristol, installing her at Greta Hall, Keswick, where he could be near the Wordsworths and Asra. This move was a turning-point in Coleridge's life.

From the outset his affair with Asra was shrouded in secrecy and furtiveness. He had left his wife in October 1799 for Bristol, hinting that he might go on to London, but instead had gone off with Cottle to Sockburn, where the Wordsworths were staying with the Hutchinsons. Sara believed for some time afterwards that he was still in Bristol, and not till December did he write to her.[6] Meanwhile he was enjoying an 'affectionate reception' from his new female acquaintances, and recording in his diary 'The

---

[1] Marshall Suther reviews various theories as to the cause of Coleridge's 'breakdown' in an Introduction to his own study of this question; he rejects Mr Richards's thesis and follows Winkelmann and Nettesheim in regarding 'religion' as the real key to the problem. See Suther, 2–10.

[2] cf. CL, I, 489n.   [3] ibid, I, 417, 483.   [4] ibid, I, 540.

[5] ibid, I, 534.   [6] ibid, I, 542n.

long Entrancement of a True-Love's Kiss'.[1] Because Asra appeared too late in Coleridge's life he was forced, as a married man and a father, to conceal his feelings for her from others, thus initiating a long and corrosive process of guilt which eventually destroyed his health. Consequently, those high-minded principles on which he had been so fond of expatiating were now at variance with his own behaviour. He who in Germany had condemned the waltz as a 'lascivious' and disgusting incitement to sexual intrigue and adultery,[2] now found himself condoning 'concupiscence' and clandestine relations. Poole wrote to him about the scandalous affair of a Stowey youth who had seduced a girl and secretly married her, and Coleridge replied: 'I see no moral wrong in the clandestineness whatever.' He insisted that his notions of a 'Father's' and 'Husband's' moral responsibilities had in no way altered; but they had.[3]

Sara probably became aware of her husband's infatuation during the winter of 1800–1, but it was Coleridge's month-long visit with the Hutchinsons in the summer of 1801 which precipitated the crisis. After this visit he began to fill his letters with complaints about his wife and to talk about a separation—'for what is Life, gangrened, as it is with me, in it's very vitals—domestic Tranquillity?'[4] Having parted from Poole by coming north, he had no one to confide in now but Southey, 'who did not and could not sympathize with ... the nature of my domestic feelings',[5] and thus he found outlet for frustrated feelings only in querulous letters and notebook entries. Weakness overflowed in self-pity:

> If any woman wanted an exact & copious Recipe, 'How to make a Husband compleatly miserable', I could furnish her with one—with a Probatum est, tacked to it.—Ill tempered Speeches sent after me when I went out of the House, ill-tempered Speeches on my return, my friends received with freezing looks, the least opposition or contradiction occasioning screams of passion, & the sentiments, which I held most base, ostentatiously avowed—all this added to the utter negation of all, which a Husband expects from a Wife—especially, living in retirement—& the consciousness, that I was myself growing a worse man / O dear Sir! no one can tell what I have suffered. I can say with strict truth, that the happiest half-

[1] KC, I, 578, 493 (1587).   [2] CL, I, 458.   [3] ibid, II, 772–3.
[4] ibid, II, 778, 762n.   [5] ibid, II, 767.

hours, I have had, were when all of a sudden, as I have been sitting alone in my Study, I have burst into Tears.—[1]

The list of complaints was interminable: 'Our virtues & our vices are exact antitheses. . . Never, I suppose, did the stern Match-maker bring together two minds so utterly contrariant in their primary and organical constitution.'[2] But Sara had changed only because *he* had changed, and because of the situation in which he had placed her—cut off from her own circle of friends and close to the hated Wordsworth–Hutchinson circle. She had sym-pathetic supporters in Cottle and Poole and her comments on her husband were more charitable than his on her:

> My husband is a good man—his prejudices—and his preposses-sions sometimes give me pain, but we have all a somewhat to en-counter in this life—I should be a very, very happy Woman if it were not for a few things—and my husband's ill health stands at the head of these evils![3]

More reticent than he, it was probably true, as Dorothy Words-worth alleged, that her main objection to a separation was 'that this person, and that person, and everyone will talk'.[4] Such sub-urban notions of respectability irritated Coleridge: 'You . . . exist almost wholly in the world *without* you / . . . you depend upon the eyes & ears of others for a great part of your pleasures.'[5] *He* cared nothing for public opinion, he objected, but no amount of such scolding could break down her resistance.

He could not shrug off so easily however the consciousness of his own guilt, for it was his awareness 'that I was myself growing a worse man' probably, which made his comments on Sara so vituperative. At first, his affair with Asra was light-hearted and its effect resuscitative,[6] genuine exuberance being evident in the energy of his achievement in the summer of 1800, when he re-wrote his poem *Love* and made far-reaching revisions of *The Ancient Mariner*, as well as writing Part II of *Christabel*. But creati-vity subsided with the birth of Derwent, and as awareness deep-ened of the personal issues implicit in the *Christabel* theme:

> He knew not what to do—something, he felt, must be done—he rose, drew his writing-desk suddenly before him—sate down, took the pen—& found that he knew not what to do. Octob. 30. 1800.[7]

[1] CL, II, 876.   [2] ibid, II, 832.   [3] ibid, II, 975n.
[4] See Stephen Potter, *Minnow Among Tritons* (London, 1934), xxiv–xxv.
[5] CL, II, 882; KC, I, 979.   [6] See pp. 54–5 above.   [7] KC, I, 834.

Though his nature, he said, was 'made for Joy' he could no longer yield to it—'I am a genuine *Tantalus*'.[1] He was beset instead by the torture of repressed desires: 'Month after month, year after year, the deepest Feeling of my Heart hid and wrapped up in the depth & darkness—solitary chaos'.[2] Thus, as neurosis gripped him, he became imprisoned in the circle of his own thoughts, a prison more terrible than any he had previously invented—'A Prison without ransome, anguish without patience, a sick bed in the house of contempt'.[3]

In fact, Coleridge was more susceptible to gossip than Sara realized, being really very angry and embarrassed about the stories that were circulating ('He [Coleridge] has left his native country, commenced citizen of the world, left his poor children fatherless and his wife destitute'[4]). It distressed him that his love-affair would, if made public knowledge, be a target for ribaldry and vulgar derision. This partly explains why he idealized Asra so, insisting that '*true*' love, far from being adulterous, was ethereal and divine:

> Love—and the grandeur of loving the Supreme in her—the real & symbolical united / —and the more because I love her as being capable of being glorified by me & as the means & instrument of my own glorification / In loving her thus I love two Souls as one, as compleat, ⟨by anticipation, & yet in consequence of anticipation⟩ as the *ever-improving* Symbol of Deity to us, still growing with the growth of our intellectual Faculties:—⟨and so uniting the moving impulse & the *stationary* desire.⟩ O that I may have heart & soul to develope this Truth so important and so deeply felt. Well, tomorrow I will take courage & write my *confession* [Never traced, unfortunately]—& try to lighten my chest, my Brain / the something that weighs *upon* & *against* my Eyebrows! [O Asra!] Miserere mei, Domine![5]

This passage revealed the hopelessness of rationalization, as reasoning collapsed finally in an upsurge of guilt—a stifling weight of guilt like the psychic state described in *Dejection: an Ode*.

There are many passages of a similar sort in Coleridge's notebooks, some of which have been wrongly interpreted as evidence that he '*used*' love to satisfy obscure religious longings.[6] What they

---

[1] ibid, I, 1609.   [2] ibid, I, 1670.   [3] ibid, I, 878.
[4] See CL, I, 552n, 549n; and cf. Potter, op. cit., xxx–xxxi.
[5] KC, II, 2530.   [6] See Suther, Chap. II.

really show is his attempt to justify an illicit attachment by reference to some sanction higher than social convention. This was
the only way he could get round his earlier avowal of the indissolubility of marriage. He sought to make his a special case: that
of an 'unfortunate' individual who had married rashly and afterwards fallen in love not with an adultress or *femme fatale* but
with a virtuous woman. If domestic discord degraded a man's
'moral character' and incapacitated him for any 'worthy' exertion of his faculties, then, Coleridge argued, extra-marital love
was ethically permissible.[1] Such love, because 'true', might even
be regenerative, developing that health and wholeness of the
fully integrated personality prerequisite to spiritual harmony.
Hence, the '*truly* Beloved' might become the spiritualizing influence the wife had failed to be:

> The best, the truly lovely, in each & all is God. Therefore the
> truly Beloved is the symbol of God to whomever it is truly beloved
> by!—but it may become perfect & maintained lovely by the func-
> tion of the two / The Lover worships in his Beloved that final con-
> summation ⟨of itself which is⟩ produced in his own soul by the
> action of the Soul of the Beloved upon it, and that final perfection
> of the Soul of the Beloved, ⟨which is in part⟩ the consequence of
> the reaction of his (so ammeliorated & regenerated) Soul upon the
> Soul of his Beloved / till each contemplates the Soul of the other as
> involving his own, both in its givings and its receivings, and thus
> still keeping alive its *outness*, its *self-oblivion* united with *Self-warmth*,
> & still approximates to God! . . .[2]

The self-persuasive force of the reiterated 'truly' in this passage
indicates again that this was basically a rationalization of feelings
which his conscience persistently rejected. Such tortuous arguments proved too tenuous even for him: Asra never produced
this 'wholeness' for him, but only a sense of guilt and failure.

The feats of moral gymnastics Coleridge now attempted are
scarcely credible. He sought to persuade his wife that he had a
'duty' to himself to safeguard his own happiness and genius by
claiming the right to 'move, live & love, in perfect Freedom'. He
begged her to be more liberal-minded and permissive: 'Have
confidence in my honor & virtue—& suffer me to love & to be
beloved without jealousy or pain.'[3] She might have responded
more readily to these appeals had he not boasted shortly before

---

[1] CL, II, 875.   [2] KC, II, 2540.   [3] CL, II, 908.

that while absent from her in London he had won the reputation of being 'the very *tonish* Poet & Jemmy Jessamy fine Talker in Town'—

> If you were only to see the tender Smiles that I occasionally re-ceive from the honorable Mrs. Damer—you would scratch her eyes out, for Jealousy / And then there's the *sweet* (N.B. musky) Lady Charlotte—nay, but I won't tell you her name / you might perhaps take into your head to write an Anonymous Letter to her, & disturb our little innocent amour.[1]

The heavy jocularity was strained and tasteless in the circum-stances, as was the moral superiority he assumed when he lec-tured Sara on her provincial narrowness. It is a miserable mis-take, he said, to suppose 'we can love but one person':

> My bodily Feelings are linked in so peculiar a way with my Ideas, that you cannot *enter into* a state of Health so utterly different from your own natural Constitution—you can only see & know, that so it is. Now, what we know only by the outward fact, & not by sym-pathy & inward experience of the same, we are ALL of us too apt to forget; & incur the necessity of being *reminded* of it by others. And this is one among the many causes, which render the marriage of unequal & unlike Understandings & Dispositions so exceedingly miserable. Heaven bear me witness, [I often say inly—in the words of Christ—Father forgive her! she knows not what she does]—Be assured, my dear Love! that I shall never write otherwise than *most* kindly to you, except after great *Aggressions* on your part: & not then, unless my reason convinces me, that some good end will be answered by my Reprehensions.—My dear Love! let me in the spirit of love say two things / 1. I owe duties, & solemn ones, to you, as my wife; but I owe equally solemn ones to Myself, to my Child-ren, to my Friends, and to Society. Where Duties are at variance, dreadful as the case may be, there must be a Choice. I can neither retain my Happiness nor my Faculties, unless I move, live, & love, in perfect Freedom, limited only by my own purity & self-respect, & by my incapability of loving any person, man or woman, unless I at the same time honor & esteem them. My Love is made up 9/10ths of fervent wishes for the permament *Peace* of mind of those, whom I love, be it man or woman; & for their Progression in purity, goodness, & true Knowledge. Such being the nature of my Love, no human Being can have a right to be jealous. My nature is quick to love, & retentive. Of those, who are within the immediate sphere of my daily agency, & bound to me by bonds of Nature or Neigh-

[1] ibid, II, 789.

P

bourhood, I shall love each, as they appear to me to deserve my Love, & to be capable of returning it. More is not in my power. If I would do it, I could not. That we can love but one person, is a miserable mistake, & the cause of abundant unhappiness. I can & do love many people, dearly—so dearly, that I really scarcely know, which I love the best. Is it not so with every good mother who has a large number of Children—& with many, many Brothers & Sisters in large and affectionate Families?—Why should it be otherwise with Friends? Would any good & wise man, any warm & wide hearted man marry at all, if it were part of the Contract—Henceforth this Woman is your only friend, your sole beloved! all the rest of mankind, however amiable & akin to you, must be only your *acquaintance*!—? It were well, if every woman wrote down before her marriage all, she thought, she had a *right* to, from her Husband —& to examine each in this form—By what *Law* of God, of Man, or of general reason, do I claim *this* Right?—I suspect, that this Process would make a ludicrous Quantity of Blots and Erasures in most of the first rude Draughts of these Rights of Wives—infinitely however to their own Advantage, & to the security of their true & genuine Rights. 2.—Permit me, my dear Sara! without offence to you, as Heaven knows! it is without any feeling of Pride in myself, to say—that in sex, acquirements, and in the quantity and quality of natural endowments whether of Feeling or of Intellect, you are the Inferior. Therefore it would be preposterous to expect that I should see with your eyes, & dismiss my Friends from *my* heart, only because you have not chosen to give them any Share of *your* Heart; but it is not preposterous, in me, on the contrary I have a *right* to expect & demand that you should to a certain degree love, & act kindly to, those whom I deem worthy of my Love.—[1]

A week later he regaled his wife with a glowing description of the agreeable time he was having with the Allen girls and Sally Wedgwood—'What sweeter & more tranquillizing pleasure is there, than to feel one's self completely innocent among compleatly innocent young Women—!'[2] Were he not so naïvely tactless he must have seemed a monster of callousness to his wife who, practically deserted now, was in the last month of her fourth pregnancy.

When one gambit failed he tried others yet more extraordinary as when, instead of idealizing or justifying it, he pretended that his love-affair was nothing more than a 'brotherly friendship':

A lively picture of a man, disappointed in marriage, & endeav-

[1] CL, II, 887–8.   [2] ibid, II, 890.

ouring to make a compensation to himself by virtuous & tender & brotherly friendship with an amiable Woman—the obstacles—the jealousies—the impossibility of it.—Best advice that he should as much as possible withdraw himself from pursuits of morals &c— & devote himself to abstract sciences.[1]

He wrote this in a private notebook, indicating the astonishing capacity he sometimes showed for self-deception. But the most remarkable ploy of all, executed with a tactlessness which is quite spectacular, was to try to persuade his wife to invite Asra to tend her during her confinement, while he gallivanted about South Wales with his fellow drug-addict and hypochondriac, Tom Wedgwood—like a 'Comet tied to a Comet's Tail'.[2] 'Both she and Mary Wordsworth are good Nurses', he assured her, as he had reason to know.[3] Sara had never fully recovered from the shock of losing Berkeley, her second child, and her anxieties as this confinement approached may be imagined. Short of money, cut off from her own family, jealous of Asra, and with little idea where her husband had spent his time the last three months, what must her feelings have been when a few days before she gave birth she received this suggestion from him:

—I will give you notice, as soon as I know myself, where a Letter from you will meet me.—I hope, that Sara Hutchinson is well enough to have come in—it would be a great comfort, that one or the other of the three Women at Grasmere should be with you— & Sara rather than the other two because you will hardly have another opportunity of having her by yourself & to yourself, & of learning to know her, such as she really is. How much this lies at my Heart with respect to the Wordsworths, & Sara, and how much of our common Love & Happiness depends on your loving those whom I love,—why should I repeat it?—I am confident, my dear Love! that I have no occasion to repeat it.[4]

What were her feelings also when the Wordsworths and Asra arrived for the birth, Dorothy all the while eying distastefully her 'miserably cold and ill-built house' and wondering how soon she could communicate the news to 'poor Coleridge'?[5] Coleridge arrived a day too late, but brought Wedgwood with him as compensation. It was Christmas Eve.

[1] KC, I, 1065. [2] CL, II, 918–19. [3] ibid, II, 892. [4] ibid, II, 894.
[5] E. de Selincourt, *The Early Letters of William and Dorothy Wordsworth, 1787–1805* (Oxford, 1935), 314.

By the New Year he was away again and on 5 January 1803 he wrote a puzzling letter to Sara, much of which has been cut away by Coleridge's executors, and which we cannot therefore wholly elucidate. In this letter he informed his wife that he was going next to Grasmere, but that he would 'strive' to return from there to Keswick bringing Asra with him—'whom I have *some few reasons* for wishing to be with you immediately, which I will inform you of'. There has been much speculation about what Coleridge was going to tell his wife, Chambers suggesting that it was the rumour that Asra was going to marry John Wordsworth. This possibility cannot be ruled out, but there is also a hint in Coleridge's letter that Asra was under severe emotional and nervous strain herself prior to this visit. She had toothache, which Coleridge suspected 'to be in part nervous—& the cause, which I more than suspect, has called this nervousness into action, I will tell you when I am alone with you'.[1] Asra came to Keswick on 7 January 1803 for a few days, but there is no record of what was said at her meeting with Sara. What is certain is that soon after this visit Coleridge began to make arrangements for Southey to take over at Keswick, to make insurance provisions for Mrs Coleridge, and to express the hope that if he died she would marry again, this time happily.[2] It is possible therefore that Coleridge confronted his wife with Asra so that they could talk over the situation together, and that when Sara proved adamant in her opposition to a separation Coleridge began deliberately to make plans to leave home and go abroad.

Though in retrospect Coleridge's tortuous manœuvres seem so incredible as to be almost comic, yet he suffered more from them probably than did Sara. Only occasionally did she reveal rancour or bitterness even after Coleridge abandoned her finally. She struggled on amiably, more contented probably in Southey's ménage than keeping house for a never-present husband. The emotional turbulence of 1802 quite upset Coleridge's mental balance however and destroyed his confidence in himself. It was at this period particularly that the haunting sense of being like a hollow tree, of having 'power' without 'strength', overwhelmed him. He felt now that he could never be the 'good' Poet/'good' man Wordsworth was (overlooking perhaps that inner conflict may be a source of poetic strength). His poem *Love's Sanctuary*

[1] Life, 164–6; and cf. CL, II, 909n.   [2] CL, II, 926, 941, 943.

illustrates well the faltering loss of confidence that guilt had imposed upon him:

> This yearning heart (Love! witness what I say)
> Enshrines thy form *as purely as it may,*
> Round which, as to some spirit uttering bliss,
> My thoughts all stand ministrant night and day
> Like saintly Priests, *that dare not think amiss.*[1]

The *Pains of Sleep* describes vividly the 'unfathomable hell' of neurotic guilt, where 'desire' is 'with loathing strangely mixed':

> But yester-night I prayed aloud
> In anguish and in agony,
> Up-starting from the fiendish crowd
> Of shapes and thoughts that tortured me:
> A lurid light, a trampling throng,
> Sense of intolerable wrong,
> And whom I scorned, those only strong!
> Thirst of revenge, the powerless will
> Still baffled, and yet burning still!
> Desire with loathing strangely mixed
> On wild or hateful objects fixed.
> Fantastic passions! maddening brawl!
> And shame and terror over all!
> Deeds to be hid which were not hid,
> Which all confused I could not know
> Whether I suffered, or I did:
> For all seemed guilt, remorse or woe,
> My own or others still the same
> Life-stifling fear, soul-stifling shame. (14–32)

Coleridge sent a first draft of these lines to Southey in September 1803, apologizing that he had scribbled them out when 'my heart was aching, my head all confused', but adding that they represented 'a true portrait of my nights'.[2] The notebook-records about this period of recurrent nightmare dreams and frightful female pursuers corroborate his statement.[3] In the same letter he said that 'this beginning to write makes a beginning of living feeling within me' and the poem revealed his inability now to detach his work from his private feelings. The nightmares he suffered, the poem went on, were fitting punishment for persons 'deepliest stained with sin':

[1] PW 362—my italics.   [2] CL, II, 984.   [3] KC, I, 848, 1619, 1726.

> But wherefore, wherefore fall on me?
> To be beloved is all I need,
> And whom I love, I love indeed. (50–2)

This was, however, the querulousness of a mind incapable for the moment of that honest self-analysis which is the strength of *Dejection: an Ode*. His own 'nature' was deeply stained with 'sin', with sensual inclinations destructive of his family life.

Coleridge's sexual desire for Asra was a corrosive force undermining the moral structure of his personality and it led to a violation of his own personal relationships such as he had imagined in *The Ancient Mariner* and *Christabel*. The following notebook entry, in which the wished-for death of his wife was only partly suppressed, indicates the extent to which infatuation for Asra was destroying his moral balance:

> . . . There is one thing wholly out of my Power. I cannot look forward even with the faintest pleasure of Hope, to the Death of any Human Being, tho' it were, as it seems to be, the only condition of the greatest imaginable Happiness to me, and the emancipation of all my noblest faculties that must remain fettered during that Being's life.—I dare not, for I can not: I cannot, for I dare not. The very effort to look forward to it with a stedfast wish would be a suicide, far beyond what the dagger or pistol could realise—absolutely suicide, coelicide, not mere viticide.—
>
> But if I could secure you [Asra] full Independence, if I could give too all my original Self healed & renovated from all infirm Habits; & if by all the forms in my power I could bind myself more effectively even in relation to Law, than the Form out of my power would effect—then, *then*, would you be the remover of my Loneliness, my perpetual Companion?[1]

His two chief articles of faith abandoned,[2] he had reached the point now of identifying his own happiness with the destruction of his wife's and children's, with the egocentric desire to live and love as he pleased.

His children by this time had become as much an embarrassment to him as was Sara for, despite his very real affection for them, they were the chief obstacle between him and his desires. The slow curdling of his feelings towards his children had been in process since 1800. Where, ironically, Hartley's birth in 1796 had 'saved' his marriage, and Berkeley's death in 1799 had been a fresh reason for sinking 'deep the foundations of a lasting Love',[3]

[1] KC, I, 1421.   [2] See p. 203 above.   [3] CL, I, 483.

Derwent's birth in 1800 and Young Sara's in 1802 were unwanted fetters binding him to an anachronistic marriage. This love–hate relationship with his own children, the precipitating factor probably in Coleridge's neurosis—though thinly disguised in *Christabel*—in *Dejection: an Ode* became quite explicit.[1] It produced the guilt and divisive tensions which caused the dissociation of his personality. As he was about to leave for Malta, he confided to Southey that he could face the situation no longer; only when he escaped his problems and set foot aboard ship would he become his own 'Master' again:

> ... I am heartily glad that the affair is settled / I could not have much longer endured the state of anxiety & suspense—at day I can do well enough; but at night my children, & other things & thoughts, lie hard & heavy upon me / & when they chance to combine with rain & damp, affect me wildly. Only last night I had a long hysterical weeping in my Sleep—long it must have been, from the wetness of the Pillow & my Shirt Collar.—What my Dream was, is not to tell; but when I awoke, the rain was beating against the Casement.—It is not *Cold* that hurts me—I am never better than in dry Frost—It is *Damp* without & anxiety, or Agitation, within that cause my Disease ... and I am resolved to be tranquil.[2]

But this voyage solved nothing, and it came in fact to resemble the Mariner's nightmarish experiences. There was no obvious way of escaping his guilt, the manifestations of which may now be considered.

The last sentence in the passage above suggests that by 1804 Coleridge himself had realized that his 'Disease'—the interminable bouts of rheumatism, bowel disorders, 'atonic gout', 'scrofula', skin eruptions, and so forth—was mainly psychosomatic. Not that his illness was pretended—the symptoms were real enough—but, like Elizabeth Barrett Browning perhaps, he did to some extent *develop* illness as a means of obtaining sympathy and affection.[3] He was by nature a hypochondriac who delighted in

---

[1] See p. 270 below.

[2] CL, II, 1084–5. The words, 'What my Dream was, is not to tell', echo the "Christabel" lines, 'A sight to dream of, not to tell! / O shield her! shield sweet Christabel!' (253–4). One cannot be certain whether the allusion was deliberate or unconscious.

[3] See Leslie D. Weatherhead, *Psychology, Religion and Healing* (London, 1951), 354–8.

recounting his symptoms and in being '*deliciously* unwell' so that he could command attention.[1] The profusion of sick-room images in his poetry and letters shows how much he relished the privileges accorded to a valetudinarian, and the fastidious pleasure he took in ordering his sick-room arrangements:

> I take the chalybeated Aquafortis, with benefit—& find considerable benefit from eating nothing at breakfast, & taking only a single cup of strong Coffee—then at eleven o'clock I take a couple of eggs, kept in boiling water one minute, folded up in a napkin for a minute & a half, & then put into the boiling water, which is now to be removed from the fire, & kept there with the saucepan covered from 4 to 6 minutes, according to the size of the eggs, & quantity of water in the saucepan.—The superiority of eggs thus boiled to those boiled in the common way proves to me the old proverb—there is reason in roasting of Eggs.—I empty the eggs out into a glass or tea cup, & eat them with a little salt & cayenne peper—but no bread.—What a pretty Book one might write, entitled 'Le petite Soulagement [sic], or Little Comforts, by a Valetudinarian[']—comprizing cookery, sleeping, travelling, conversation, self-discipline—poetry, morals, metaphysics—all the alleviations, that reason & well-regulated self-indulgence, can give to a good sick man.[2]

He was barely thirty when he wrote this. Poole, at least, was not deceived by Coleridge's symptoms, guessing that they were psychosomatic:

> If your disease be really *bodily*, and not the consequence of an irritated mind, and if that bodily disease will be lessened or healed by a warmer climate, to a warmer climate you must go; but I never yet heard that complaints like yours were particularly alleviated by a warmer climate.[3]

Coleridge *used* his illness sometimes to alarm his friends, convincing Wordsworth and Southey that he really was about to die. It was also one of his subtlest devices for bringing his wife to heel:

> ... about two months ago after a violent quarrel I was taken suddenly ill with spasms in my stomach—I expected to die—Mrs. C. was, of course, shocked & frightened beyond measure—& two days after, I being still very weak & pale as death, she threw herself upon me, & made a solemn promise of amendment.[4]

[1] CL, II, 888.   [2] ibid, II, 910–11.   [3] Sandford, II, 46.
[4] CL, II, 875.

Poole was not taken in by such theatricality, and ridiculed Coleridge's morbid presentiments: 'Of your death! What a curious thing to talk of to a man under thirty!'[1]

Actually, Coleridge's was an unusually tough and resilient constitution. In the summer of 1802, for example, he rose from a 'sick-bed' and in eight days walked 263 miles over rough lakeland country, scaling mountains and wading through bogs and streams until his shoes fell apart.[2] Clearly, he revelled in the demands which the physical dangers and gruelling distances made upon his courage, stamina, and vitality. Tom Wedgwood asked 'Why in God's name' he had not turned back when he saw the state of the weather, to which Coleridge replied: 'The true reason is simple, tho' it may be somewhat strange—the thought never once entered my head.'[3] It is evident that damp weather affected him little once he had left the problems associated with the 'dell' behind him. In the athleticism of mountain-scrambling he found a form of escapism which induced a state of healthful euphoria:

> I never find myself alone within the embracement of rocks & hills, a traveller up an alpine road, but my spirit courses, drives, and eddies, like a Leaf in Autumn: a wild activity, of thoughts, imaginations, feelings, and impulses of motion, rises up from within me —a sort of *bottom-wind*, that blows to no point of the compass, & comes from I know not whence, but agitates the whole of me; my whole Being is filled with waves, as it were, that roll & stumble, one this way, & one that way, like things that have no common master. . . The farther I ascend from animated Nature, from men, and cattle, & the common birds of the woods, & fields, the greater becomes in me the Intensity of the feeling of Life; Life seems to me then a universal spirit, that neither has, nor can have, an opposite. God is every where. . . I do not think it possible, that any bodily pains could eat out the love & joy, that is so substantially part of me, towards hills, & rocks, & steep waters! And I have had some Trial.[4]

Only when he returned to the 'dell' and its problems did his anxieties recommence, and the sense of well-being and 'wholeness' depart:

> —I have walked 263 miles in eight Days—so I must have strength

---

[1] Sandford, II, 45.   [2] CL, II, 834–46; and cf. 979–82.
[3] ibid, II, 916.   [4] ibid.

somewhere / but my spirits are dreadful, owing entirely to the Horrors of every night.[1]

In fact there was little physically wrong with Coleridge, as Poole was the first to realize; only his mind was full of scorpions. But, because he gave way to sickness, his work suffered, provoking further anxiety and disquietude. 'I am a crazy, crazy machine', he complained: 'Body & soul are going—Soul is going into Body, and Body is going into Dung & Crepitus.'[2]

It was primarily to relieve these psychosomatic sufferings that Coleridge turned originally to opium and metaphysics, using these deliberately as anodynes. A good deal of nonsense has been talked about Coleridge's addiction to opium, which Mr Griggs's recent re-examination of the whole subject should go some way towards correcting.[3] Griggs finds that Coleridge's addiction began during the recurrent illnesses of 1801, as the direct result of the *nervous and emotional stress* arising out of his unhappy domestic situation. It was the 'perpetual Struggle' with Mrs Coleridge and the 'endless heart-wasting' over Asra which mainly engendered it:

> I was struggling with sore calamities, with bodily pain, & langour —with pecuniary Difficulties—& worse than all, with domestic Discord, & the heart-withering Conviction—that I could not be happy without my children, & could not but be miserable with the mother of them.[4]

Griggs's conclusion is fully borne out by the following letter, which shows how opium was used principally to relieve emotional disturbances associated with Sara:

> On my arrival at St. Clear's I received your Letter, & had scarcely read it, before a fluttering of the Heart came on, which ended (as usual) in a sudden and violent Diarrhoea—I could scarcely touch my Dinner, & was obliged at last to take 20 drops of Laudanum— which now that I have for 10 days left off stimulus of all kinds, excepting $\frac{1}{3}$ of a grain of opium, at night, acted upon me more powerfully than 80 or 100 drops would have done at Keswick. I slept sound what I did sleep; but I am not *quite* well this morning. . .

---

[1] CL, II, 982.   [2] ibid, II, 771, 742.

[3] See CL, III, Introduction, xxx ff.; also II, 731n. 'Young Sara' always insisted that her father used opium mainly to relieve nervous disorders arising from emotional stress; see E. L. Griggs, *Coleridge Fille* (Oxford, 1940), 153.

[4] CL, II, 783–4.

> You must see by this, what absolute necessity I am under of *dieting*
> myself—& if possible, the still greater Importance of *Tranquillity*
> to me.[1]

It was a vicious circle: guilt producing incapacitating illnesses,
which interfered with his work and so produced further anxieties
and guilt. It is doubtful which pained him more—the agony of
trying to break the addiction and its painful withdrawal symptoms,[2] or the degradation which destroyed his self-respect and
undermined his health:

> . . . all the realities about me lose their natural *healing* powers . . .
> Who that thus lives with a continually divided Being can remain
> healthy! ⟨And who can long remain body-crazed, & not at times
> use unworthy means of making his Body the fit instrument of his
> mind? Pain is easily subdued compared with continual uncomfort-
> ableness—& the sense of stifled Power! . . .⟩[3]

Because no physical palliatives can heal a neurosis, opium merely
touched the symptoms of his trouble, producing in the end only
further shame and self-disgust:

> —The Disgust, the Loathing, that followed these Fits [of illness]
> & no doubt in part too the use of the Brandy & Laudanum which
> they rendered necessary.[4]

Opium proved therefore just as ineffective an anodyne for emotional stress as did his addiction to metaphysics in 1801; and
ultimately it almost ruined his health.

The three months' period of 'intellectual exsiccation' which
Coleridge imposed upon himself in 1801 was also an attempt,
initially, to provide relief for physical suffering—'In my long Illness I had compelled into hours of Delight many a sleepless, painful hour of Darkness by chasing down metaphysical Game.'[5] As
time went on, however, he used metaphysics less to relieve physical sufferings than to escape '*some other and worse afflictions*' and as
an asylum from 'that sphere of acute feelings' which was now
associated in his mind with the writing of poetry.[6] It is as naïve
to suppose that the 'Philosopher killed the Poet' in Coleridge as
to say that opium did, for both addictions were by-products really
of a much deeper problem. We are bound to accept Coleridge's

[1] ibid, II, 888–9.
[2] See E. Schneider, *Coleridge, Opium and Kubla Khan* (Chicago, 1953).
[3] KC, II, 2557.   [4] CL, II, 731; and cf. KC, II, 2368.
[5] CL, II, 713–14.   [6] ibid, II, 814 (my italics).

word for it that he used metaphysical speculation as a refuge from life and art because, as Miss Snyder remarked, 'the evidence is only too patent'.[1]

The Idealist, anti-Mechanical/Materialist functions of Coleridge's metaphysicizing have been rather over-emphasized; consequently the psychological motivation which determined the direction of his intellectual development has been somewhat overlooked. To ignore this motivation, however, is to mistake the character of his philosophy. It is specially important, for example, that it was as the poet of 'thought and *feeling*' that he commended Wordsworth as a Philosopher—a point I shall return to.[2] His rejection of the Associationist psychology, though it grew out of an intensive preliminary study of Locke and Descartes, narrowed down rapidly to a close examination of the psychological area in which thoughts and feelings interact. The revealing title of a work Coleridge planned in 1804 is a pointer to the stimulus which lay behind it: *Consolations and Comforts from the exercise and right application of the Reason, the Imagination, and the moral Feelings, addressed especially to those in Sickness, Adversity, or Distress of Mind, from speculative Gloom.*[3] His approach throughout was marked by an insistence on the healthful activity (rather than passivity) and the wholeness of mind which, as *Dejection: an Ode* reveals, he could himself in fact no longer achieve. This Ode describes vividly the dissociation of personality which results from isolating thought from feeling—'For not to think of what I needs must feel', etc.

Coleridge's notebooks reveal that his theory of the close affinity between thought and feeling arose directly out of introspective analysis, out of the 1801–3 experiences particularly of trying to reconcile his love of Asra with his obligations to his family. He came to reject the Associationist theory—that ideas are linked by purely mechanical laws, of cause and effect, identity, contiguity, and so forth[4]—insisting that ideas are also united by recurrent states of feeling, because this was what happened in his own ex-

[1] Alice D. Snyder, "The Critical Principle of the Reconciliation of Opposites as Employed by Coleridge", in *Contributions to Rhetorical Theory*, ed. F. N. Scott (Ann Arbor, 1918), Vol. IX, 12.

[2] cf. p. 236 below.   [3] CL, II, 1036.

[4] J. V. Baker suggests, by the way, that David Hartley was much more aware of the emotional aspects of association than Coleridge gave him credit for. See Baker, 13–14, 31.

perience. The sheer impossibility of pushing out of his mind ideas and images associated with Mary Evans or Asra proved to him that trains of ideas may be governed entirely by powerful states of feeling:

I entered into a curious and tho fanciful yet strictly true and actual, exemplification. Many of my Instances recalled to my mind my little poem on *Lewti*, the Circassian / and as by this same force joined with the assent of the will most often, tho' often too vainly because weakly opposed by it, I inevitably by some link or other return to you, or (say rather) bring some fuel of thought to the ceaseless yearning for you at my Inmost, which like a steady fire attracts constantly the air which constantly feeds it / I began strictly and as matter of fact to examine that subtle Vulcanian Spider-web Net of Steel—strong as Steel yet subtle as the Ether, in which my soul flutters inclosed with the Idea of your's—to pass rapidly as in a catalogue thro' the Images only, exclusive of the thousand Thoughts that possess the same force, which never fail instantly to awake into vivider flame the forever and ever Feeling of you—The fire / Mary, you, & I at Gallow-Hill / —or if flamy, reflected in children's round faces—ah whose children?—a dog—that dog whose restless eyes oft catching the light of the fire used to watch your face, as you leaned with your head on your hand and arm, & your feet on the *fender* / the fender thence / —Fowls at Table—the last dinner at Gallow Hill, when you drest the two fowls in that delicious white Sauce which when very ill is the only idea of food that does not make me *sicker* / all natural Scenery—ten thousand links, and if it please me, the very spasm & drawing-back of a pleasure which is half-pain you not being there—Cheese, at Middleham, too salt / horses, my ride to Scarborough—asses, to that large living 2 or 3 miles from Middleham / All Books—my study at Keswick / —the Ceiling or Head of a Bed—the green watered Mazarine!—A Candle in it's socket, with its alternate fits & dying flashes of lingering Light—O God! O God! —Books of abstruse Knowledge—the Thomas Aquinas & Suarez from the Durham Library.[1]

From such experiences Coleridge became convinced that the 're-currence of resembling states of *Feeling*' is far more important in providing a focus-point for the reflective associating memory than any mechanical associative principles,[2] a fact which has considerable bearing on the chronology of his development and upon the interpretation of *Dejection: an Ode*. Unfortunately, it was not only Asra who provided a focus-point for feeling, but also

[1] Quoted in HH, 146–7.   [2] CL, II, 961.

his wife and children. The states of feeling associated with them had now become painful to him, and possibly it was his inability to break this circle of ideas and feelings which prevented him from finishing *Christabel*:

> O Heaven when I think how perishable Things, how imperishable Thoughts seem to be!—For what is Forgetfulness? Renew the state of affection or bodily Feeling, same or similar—sometimes dimly similar / and instantly the trains of forgotten Thought rise, from their living Catacombs![1]

It was mainly to avoid the thoughts associated with these 'living Catacombs' that Coleridge pursued abstruse metaphysical researches, a device which, finally, only exacerbated his neurosis.

Since experience showed that thought and feeling must go together it followed that to differentiate and isolate them was merely inviting trouble. It led to what he called 'the thinking disease', on which 'no moral being ever becomes healthy'.[2] Though metaphysics provided incidental compensation (it being a salve for his wounded self-esteem that here was a sphere in which he outshone all rivals), because it was basically a neurotic activity it could afford no final anodyne. Coleridge admitted eventually that three years of austere speculations had failed to achieve their object—the realization of 'Quietness and Unity of Heart';[3] in fact, they had served only to bring home to him the full hopelessness of his predicament. An entry in a Malta notebook indicates that neither by metaphysics, nor even by putting the sea between him and Asra, could he forget the 'forever and ever' feelings at his heart:

> What change of place, Country, climate, company, situation, health of Shrubs, Flowers, Trees / —moving Seasons / & ever is that one Feeling at my Heart / felt like a faint Pain, a spot which it seems I could lay my finger on / —I talk loud or eager, or I read or meditate the abstrusest Researches, or I laugh, jest, tell tales of mirth / & ever as it were, within & behind I think, & image you.[4]

As Miss Coburn puts it, Coleridge's abstruse researches were not the 'destroyer' of his imagination, but rather a means (quite ineffectual, as it turned out) of sublimating 'the old Adam'.

---

[1] KC, I, 1575.

[2] See Stephen Potter, *Coleridge and S. T. C.* (London, 1935), 206.

[3] CL, II, 1008.   [4] KC, II, 2036.

The years 1801–4 were a period above all when Coleridge needed the support of a sympathetic 'sheet-anchor'. He recorded this need (in characteristic 'life-as-voyage' imagery) both in 1801—

> [My] Mind, shipwrecked by storms of doubt, now mastless, rudderless, shattered,—pulling in the dead swell of a dark & windless Sea.[1]

—and again in 1804, when he was about to take ship for Malta:

> ... I own myself no self-subsisting Mind—I know, I feel, that I am weak—apt to faint away inwardly, self-deserted & bereft of the confidence in my own powers—and that the approbation & Sympathy of good & intelligent men is my Sea-breeze, without which I should languish from Morn to evening; a very Trade-wind to me, in which my Bark drives on regularly & lightly.[2]

But by deciding to leave Stowey in July 1800, in order to be closer to Asra and the Wordsworths, Coleridge had unfortunately cut himself off from the one person who might have sustained him through this difficult period, for neither Wordsworth nor Southey gave him the same degree of understanding and sympathy that Tom Poole did. A notebook entry of 1801, written soon after Coleridge's arrival in the north, sadly reflected his sense of loss:

> The unspeakable Comfort to a good man's mind—nay, even to a criminal to be *understood*—to have some one that understands one —& who does not feel, that on earth no one does. The Hope of this —always more or less disappointed, gives the *passion* to Friendship.[3]

Poole was deeply hurt by Coleridge's decision to go north, believing (correctly) that it implied a preference for Wordsworth's society to his own.[4]

Coleridge had at first fought shy of breaking to Poole the news that he intended leaving Stowey, pretending that the pressure on him to do so was coming from Wordsworth:

> —Finally, I told him plainly, that *you* had been the man in whom *first* and in whom alone, I had felt an *anchor*! With all my other Connections I felt a dim sense of insecurity & uncertainty, terribly uncomfortable / —W. was affected to tears, very much affected;

---

[1] ibid, I, 932.   [2] CL, II, 1054–5.   [3] KC, I, 1082.

[4] Poole, like Charles Lamb, was always jealous of Wordsworth's ascendancy over Coleridge. Both had rejoiced to hear that Coleridge parted so quickly from the Wordsworths on the German tour, though the separation had been perfectly amicable (CL, I, 419n).

but he deemed the vicinity of a Library absolutely *necessary* to his health, nay to his existence. It is painful to me too to think of not living near him; for he is a *good* and *kind* man, & the only one whom in *all* things I feel my Superior—& you will believe me when I say, that I have few feelings more pleasurable than to find myself in intellectual Faculties an Inferior /. But my Resolve is fixed, *not to leave you till you leave me!*[1]

Unable to repress his jealousy Poole charged Coleridge with 'prostrating' himself before Wordsworth, an accusation Coleridge could hardly refute. He was convinced that Wordsworth would become the greatest English poet since Milton, and Wordsworth had already shown that he had much more to give than Poole in the way of inspiration and intellectual stimulation. However, he insisted that his feelings for Poole had not changed, and found further pretexts for justifying the move to Keswick:

Do not, my dearest Poole, deem me cold, or finical, or indifferent to Stowey, full and fretful in objection; but on so important an affair to a man who has, and is likely to have, a family, and who *must* have silence and a *retired study*, as a house is, it were folly not to consult one's own feelings, folly not to let them speak audibly, and having heard them, hypocrisy not to utter them... My dearest friend, when I have written to you lately, I have written with a mind and heart completely worn out with the fag of the day. I trust in God you have not misinterpreted this into a change of character. I was a little jealous at an expression in your last letter—'I am happy you begin to feel your power.' Truly and in simple verity, my dear Tom, I feel not an atom more power than I have ever done, except the power of gaining a few more paltry guineas than I had supposed.[2]

In his impatience to be nearer Asra and Wordsworth, he tended to forget Poole's reliable attributes, and the staunch support Poole had given Sara while he and Wordsworth were in Germany.

It was only a few months after moving to Keswick however that Coleridge began to feel the loss of Poole's society, for which nothing at Greta Hall could quite compensate:

My situation here is indeed a delightful situation; but I feel what I have lost—feel it deeply—it recurs more often & more painfully, than I had anticipated—indeed, so much so that I scarcely ever feel myself impelled, that is to say, *pleasurably* impelled to write to Poole. I used to feel myself more at home in his great windy Parlour, than

[1] CL, I, 491.   [2] ibid, I, 584–5.

in my own cottage. We were well suited for each other—my animal
Spirits corrected his inclinations to melancholy; and there was some
thing both in his understanding & in his affection so healthy
& manly, that my mind freshened in his company, and my
ideas & habits of thinking acquired day after day more of substance & reality.[1]

In February 1801, as Coleridge felt his creative power ebbing
away (notwithstanding Wordsworth's proximity), he expressed
his need for Poole in terms which bear closely on *Dejection: an
Ode*:

> O my dear dear Friend! that you were with me by the fireside
> of my Study here, that I might talk it over with you to the Tune of
> this Night Wind that pipes it's thin doleful climbing sinking Notes
> like a child that has lost it's way and is crying aloud, half in grief
> and half in the hope to be heard by it's Mother.[2]

Poole, unfortunately, was estranged by both distance and resentment, and no one else was capable of averting the approaching
crisis.

As troubles piled up, Coleridge maintained contact with Poole
by letter, seeking sympathy because of his illness and financial
problems. Poole's replies however were terse and unfeeling, implying that the former would not have arisen had he stayed at
Stowey and sharply reminding him that the Wedgwood annuity
should solve the latter:

> In God's name, why do you not think yourself independent? You
> have, after deducting Mrs. Fricker's £20 a year, £130 a year clear,
> besides what your own labours may produce.[3]

The tone of these rejoinders was not to Coleridge's taste, and,
when a further misunderstanding arose over money-matters,
something like an open quarrel developed just when Coleridge,
at the nadir of his fortunes, was writing *Dejection: an Ode*. Wordsworth, believing Coleridge really was about to die, asked Poole
(without mentioning it to Coleridge) to advance a sum of £50
or £100 to enable Coleridge to winter in the Azores. Unfortunately, Poole replied direct to Coleridge, declining to offer more

---

[1] ibid, I, 643–4.   [2] ibid, II, 669; cf. "Dejection: an Ode", ll. 121–5.
[3] Sandford, II, 44–5. Coleridge had been in receipt of the Wedgwood
annuity, value £150, since January 1798 (see CL, I, 373–4n for the terms of
the annuity). Despite constant financial difficulties of his own he helped to
support his mother-in-law over many years.

Q

than £20, a refusal which Coleridge interpreted as unfriendly. He wrote to Poole reproving his meanness and disaffection.[1]

Coleridge felt let down and Poole's unaccustomed lack of sympathy distressed him. Though Poole knew nothing of Asra and the real nature of Coleridge's troubles, his sharp questions cut so near to the quick that they must have stung Coleridge's conscience: 'What have you to do with the poverty, and misery, and sufferings around you? Have *you* caused the havock?'[2] Words which, spoken in friendliness over Poole's garden-gate, might have left no impression, set down thus on paper gave cause for deep resentment. Yet, shrewd as Poole's insight was, he had no inkling of the real nature of the problem. His offhanded advice that Coleridge should 'throw aside' metaphysics and poetry for the time being, and occupy himself instead with 'a humorous philosophical novel' or a 'farce', shows how wide of the mark his understanding was.[3] Poole had little to offer Coleridge now, and the estrangement widened at a critical period.

Coleridge first drafted *Dejection: an Ode* on 4 April 1802, and Poole's letter to him of 2 May indicates how wide the gulf between them had by then become:

> My dear Coleridge—Why is there so little communication between us? I suppose this letter will reach you, but I certainly do not know where you are by any information which you have given me. Can you suppose me uninterested in your welfare, and in your happiness in every point? Then wherefore this silence?[4]

Coleridge's reply, a 'dreary and vacant' epistle, instead of confiding in Poole as in former days, hedged and covered over his feelings: 'I have written to no human being. . . I have neither been very well, nor very happy.'[5] He had in fact dropped Poole in favour of Wordsworth, reconciled himself again to Southey, and made new friends in Sotheby and Tom Wedgwood. In February 1803 Coleridge went back to Stowey for a few days, to the immediate improvement of his health and 'tranquillity',[6] but by then it was too late. They remained distant friends for years afterwards (Poole maintaining a correspondence with Mrs Coleridge long after the separation), but the old intimacy had gone and— except possibly in James Gillman—Coleridge never found an adequate substitute for the man 'in whom alone I felt an anchor'.

[1] CL, II, 765–6; see Sandford, II, 52.   [2] Sandford, II, 45.
[3] ibid, II, 46.   [4] ibid, II, 78.   [5] CL, II, 799.   [6] ibid, II, 927.

It was Coleridge's wife probably who, on his return from Germany, had insisted that he must mend his quarrel with Southey. Her brother-in-law had been her mainstay during the shock of Berkeley's death, looking after the funeral arrangements, and inviting her to stay with Edith and him till she recovered. Since their original quarrel at the time of his marriage moreover Coleridge had had a further tiff with Southey over the publication of his 'Nehemiah Higginbottom sonnets,[1] and his nervousness in re-approaching Southey was apparent in the awkwardness of this letter with its embarrassed allusions to their former relationship:

> July 29th, 1799
> Nether Stowey
> I am doubtful, Southey, whether the circumstances which impel me to write to you, ought not to keep me silent— / & if it were only a feeling of delicacy, I should remain silent—for it is good to do all things in faith.—But I have been absent, Southey! ten months, & little Hartley prattles about you / and if *you* knew, that domestic affliction was hard upon me, and that my own health was declining, would you not have shootings within you of an affection, which ('tho' fall'n, tho' chang'd') has played too important a part in the events of our lives & the formation of our characters, ever to be *forgotten*? I am perplexed what to write, or how to state the object of my writing—/—Any participation in each other's moral Being I do not *wish*, simply because I know enough of the mind of man to know that is impossible. But, Southey, we have similar Talents, Sentiments nearly similar, & kindred pursuits—we have likewise in more than one instance common objects of our esteem and love —I pray and intreat you, if we should meet at any time, let us not withhold from each other the outward Expressions of daily Kindliness; and if it not be no [any] longer in your power to soften your opinions, make your feelings at least more tolerant towards me. . .
>
> God bless you & your's—
> S. T. Coleridge.[2]

At first Southey had hung back and, ironically, it was Poole's diplomacy that had finally brought them together again.[3] It was however a reconciliation with the Fricker circle at a time when Coleridge least wanted it and it is not surprising perhaps that shortly afterwards Coleridge had decided to move his family away from Bristol.

[1] See CL, I, 358–9n.   [2] ibid, I, 523–4.   [3] ibid, I, 524n.

Neither Southey nor Wordsworth gave Coleridge the sort of bolstering which he needed, nor anything like Poole's warmth of praise and encouragement. Both were apt to be damagingly critical of his work, their aspersions on *The Ancient Mariner* and Wordsworth's opposition to *Christabel* doing much to increase his sense of failure. He would rather have written *Ruth*, he said, 'than a million such poems' as *Christabel*[1]—'I do nothing, but almost instantly it's defects & sillinesses come upon my mind, and haunt me, till I am completely disgusted with my performance, & wish myself a Tanner, or a Printer, or any thing but an Author.'[2] He talked of abandoning poetry altogether, and of becoming merely the advocate of his rivals' works:

> I abandon Poetry altogether—I leave the higher & deeper Kinds to Wordsworth, the delightful, popular & simply dignified to Southey; & reserve for myself the honorable attempt to make others feel and understand their writings, as they deserve to be felt & understood.[3]

He accepted as final their adverse judgements on his own poetry, despite Lamb's challenging of Wordsworth's criticism, and only years afterwards did he begin to suspect that the Wordsworths' 'cold praise and effective discouragement' might conceivably have been ill-natured.[4]

He was depressed, too, by his rivals' industry and greater successfulness, especially as his wife never ceased tormenting him with this. Young Sara subsequently attributed her mother's peevishness to her father's 'non-success', and 'the unfavourable comparison Coleridge as a literary man made with Southey, who was luckily successful in his ventures while Coleridge was always unfortunate'.[5] While Coleridge was struggling to finish *Christabel*, Southey's *Madoc*, *Thalaba*, and the *History of Portugal* were paving his way to the laureateship. Coleridge found his rival's industry 'stupendous'—he 'is the most industrious man I know or have ever known'.[6] A comment by Longman, their joint publisher, is illuminating: '. . . there is no comparison as to Genius / Let it be one sheet or two Volumes, Mr. Southey brings it or sends it

[1] CL, I, 632.   [2] ibid, I, 629.   [3] ibid, I, 623.

[4] ibid, I, 631n. For details of Wordsworth's criticism of "The Ancient Mariner" and Lamb's defence of the poem, see CL, I, 602n.

[5] See A. Turnbull, *Biographia Epistolaris* (London, 1911), II, 102.

[6] CL, II, 1004.

to the *very hour* / whereas Mr. Coleridge &c &c'.[1] Coleridge admitted to Southey that he could not keep pace with him:

> Depend on it, no living Poet possesses the *general* reputation, which you possess. . . W. Wordsworth's reputation is hitherto *sectarian*—my *name* is perhaps nearly as well known & as much talked of as your's—but I am talked of, as the man of Talents, the splendid Talker, & as a Poet too—but not, as you are, as a Poet, κατ' ἔμφασιν—[2]

Wordsworth, meanwhile, was almost equally industrious, thirty-nine of the poems he published in 1807 being written between December 1801 and December 1803—the period of Coleridge's crisis.

Southey never showed any real insight into the nature of the psychological complications that were destroying Coleridge, all hints about these 'private afflictions' being lost upon him.[3] Wordsworth, though aware that Asra was the real cause of Coleridge's sufferings, offered only the blunt advice (expressed through the meaningful title *Resolution and Independence*) that Coleridge should look to himself for help:

> But how can He expect that others should
> Build for him, sow for him, and at his call
> Love him, who for himself will take no heed at all?

But Coleridge's neurotic state of mind was beyond the reach of self-help now and, chilled by Wordsworth's advice, he became so despondent as to prepare his own 'obituary' notice:

> Wordsworth descended on him [i.e. Coleridge], like the Γνῶθι σεαυτόν from Heaven; by shewing to him what true Poetry was, he made him know, that he himself was no Poet.[4]

He could scarcely take his troubles to Southey, who would have been disgusted by his liaison with Asra and probably more concerned in any case with Sara's welfare than Coleridge's. Coleridge's hint that it is a 'gross mistake' to suppose that a man must confine his affections to 'one woman' was entirely lost on Southey. It would have been easier to confide such thoughts to a bachelor like Poole than to Southey or Wordsworth, whose domestic routines were provincially narrow.

Indeed the apparent stability and happiness of his rivals' domestic lives may have been a more potent source of envy in Coleridge, and a greater barrier between them finally, than his

[1] ibid, II, 1052. [2] ibid, II, 912–13. [3] ibid, II, 831. [4] ibid, II, 714.

jealousy of their literary success. A revealing self-comparison runs through the substance of this letter to Southey:

> You are happy in your marriage Life; & greatly to the honour of your moral self-government. Qualities & manners are pleasant to, & sufficient for, you, to which my Nature is utterly unsuited: for I am so weak, that warmth of manner in a female House mate is as necessary to me, as warmth of internal attachment.[1]

Since his own creative peak had coincided with the best years of his marriage Coleridge was prepared to think that a virtuous family life was highly propitious to artistic achievement. By the time he wrote *Biographia Literaria* this belief had hardened into firm conviction:

> . . . it is SOUTHEY's almost unexampled felicity, to possess the best gifts of talent and genius free from all their characteristic defects . . . it will appear no ordinary praise in any man to have passed from innocence into virtue, not only free from all vicious habit, but unstained by one act of intemperance, or the degradations akin to intemperance.[2]

Southey had been lucky, Coleridge went on to say in this en-comium, in being able to 'act aright', not in obedience to any moral law, 'but by the necessity of a happy nature, which could not act otherwise'. Because he had escaped the emotional com-plications which 'irregular men scatter about them', he had not had to wrestle with the conflicting feelings which so divided Cole-ridge's moral being. This radical difference was reflected in their poetry: 'duty' and 'pleasure' seemed synonymous for Southey and Wordsworth, whereas in Coleridge's poetry they co-existed in continual tension. Life had been no less kind to Wordsworth, Coleridge felt:

> . . . Mortal Life seems destined for no continuous Happiness save that which results from the exact performance of Duty—and blessed are you, dear William! whose Path of Duty lies thro' vine-trellised Elm-groves, thro' Love and Joy & Grandeur.[3]

If tensions as acute as his own existed beneath the surface of Wordsworth's happiness, Coleridge seems never to have guessed it.

A leading theme of the original version of *Dejection: an Ode* is the contrast it draws between Wordsworth's blissful domestic

---

[1] CL, II, 929.   [2] BL, I, 47–8.   [3] CL, II, 1060.

circumstances and the household wretchedness which was Coleridge's 'own peculiar Lot'. Wordsworth 'deserves to be, and *is*, a happy man', said Coleridge, not only because of the extraordinary single-mindedness of purpose with which he pursued his literary vocation, but because he had arranged his private life so carefully. His friends and intimates had not arrived by 'accidental confluence', everyone near to his heart having been 'placed there by Choice and after Knowledge and Deliberation'.[1] This observation speaks volumes on the differences between Wordsworth's and Coleridge's temperament. Wordsworth once said that Coleridge would never understand him fully—'He is not happy enough. I am myself one of the happiest of men.'[2] Certainly, Wordsworth's happy childhood, his affectionate relationship with his mother, his close-knit family ties, all stood in direct contrast to the loneliness of Coleridge's youth. The profusion of family images in Wordsworth's poetry indicates how much he drew upon this reservoir of family affection. *The Brothers, Michael, The White Doe, The Borderers*, and *The Prelude* all have family themes, while parent and child metaphors, brotherhood and sister metaphors, household metaphors are abundant in his work.[3] Coleridge's Kubla Khan, Cain, and the Mariner, conversely, are all great lonely figures, while in poems like *Christabel* and *The Old Man of the Alps* family relationships tend to be brittle and easily destroyed. Above all, Dorothy's selfless devotion to William, her sympathy, her love, her care of him, her very presence and inspiration awoke Coleridge's envy—'What? tho' the World praise me, I have no dear Heart that loves *my* Verses.'[4]

The years at Grasmere (1799–1805) were years of happiness for the Wordsworths—'the very happiest of my life', according to Dorothy.[5] From his window at Keswick Coleridge looked towards Dove Cottage with unconcealed envy:

> While *Ye* are *well* and *happy*, 'twould but wrong you
> If I should fondly yearn to be among you.

[1] ibid, II, 1033. Elsewhere Coleridge remarked: 'Wordsworth is by nature incapable of being in Love, tho' no man more tenderly attached' (CL, III, xxix).

[2] See Herbert Read, *Wordsworth* (London, 1932), 225.

[3] See H. J. F. Jones, *The Egotistical Sublime* (London, 1954), 47–8.

[4] KC, I, 1463.

[5] E. de Selincourt, *The Early Letters of William and Dorothy Wordsworth, 1787–1805* (Oxford, 1935), 555.

He sought constant pretexts for visiting them, frequently 'developing' illnesses while he was there as a means of gaining sympathy and of enjoying, vicariously, a sense of security he could not find at home:

> I was at Grasmere a whole month—so ill, as that till the last week I was unable to read your [Richard Sharp's] letters—not that my inner Being was disturbed—on the contrary, it seemed more than usually serene and self-sufficing. . . I had only just strength enough to smile gratefully on my kind Nurses, who tended me with Sister's and Mother's Love, and often, I well know, wept for me in their sleep, and watched for me even in their Dreams. O dear Sir! it does a man's heart good, I will not say, to know such a Family, but even—to know, that there *is* such a Family. In spite of Wordsworth's occasional Fits of Hypochondriacal Uncomfortableness. . . his is the happiest Family, I ever saw—and *were* it not in too great Sympathy with my Ill health—*were* I in good Health and their Neighbour—I verily believe, that the Cottage in Grasmere Vale would be a proud sight for Philosophy.[1]

The phrase 'in spite of Wordsworth's . . . Hypochondriacal Uncomfortableness' suggests that it was the attentive sympathy of Wordsworth's womenfolk as much as anything which drew Coleridge to Grasmere. In Dorothy and the Hutchinson sisters he found his chief solace, all three of his main 'sheet-anchors' being for one reason or another insensitive to his sufferings.

That capacity for detachment which was Wordsworth's strength as a poet, enabling him to adopt the contemplative standpoint of a 'Spectator ab extra', was the very last quality Coleridge desired in a 'sheet-anchor'. The dissimilarity between Wordsworth's temperament and his own was forcefully illustrated by their different responses to the case of poor Rogers (a poet with psychological complications not unlike Coleridge's):

> Wordsworth's mind & body are both of a stronger texture than mine; & he was amused with the envy, the jealousy, & the other miserable Passions, that have made their Pandaemonium in the crazy Hovel of that poor Man's Heart—but I was downright melancholy at the sight. If to be a Poet or a Man of Genius entailed on us the necessity of housing such company in our bosoms, I would pray the very flesh off my knees to have a head as dark and unfurnished as Wordsworth's Old Molly has, if only I might have a heart as careless & as loving.[2]

[1] CL, II, 1032.   [2] ibid, II, 964.

This incident did much to confirm Coleridge's suspicion of the underlying hardness in Wordsworth's disposition. When on the Scottish tour of 1803, Wordsworth and Coleridge decided it was best to separate, Coleridge's notebook showed how much he regretted having made himself so dependent upon Wordsworth:

> ... am to make my own way alone to Edinburgh—⟨O Esteesee! [S.T.C. = himself] that thou hadst from thy 22nd year indeed made *thy own* way & *alone*!

Over this entry he later superimposed the words: 'My Friend'— ⟨'O me! what a word to give permanence to the mistake of a Life.'⟩[1] A further 1803 entry throws more light on this basic antipathy: in this passage A. = Coleridge and B. = Wordsworth:

> I have had some *Lights* lately respecting Envy. A. thought himself unkindly used by B.—he had exerted himself for B. with what warmth! honoring, praising B. beyond himself.—&c &c—B. selfish —feeling all Fire respecting every Trifle of his own—quite backward to poor A.—The *up*, askance, pig look, in the Boat &c. Soon after this A. felt distinctly little ugly Touchlets of Pain & little Shrinkings Back at the Heart, at the report that B. had written a new Poem / an excellent one!—& he saw the faults of B & all that belonged to B. & detested himself dwelling upon them—&c. What was all this?—Evidently, the instinct of all fine minds to *totalize*— to make a *perfectly congruous whole* of every character—& a pain at the being obliged to admit incongruities—This must be *plus'd* + by all the foregoing Pains which were self-referent, & by their combination introduce a selfish Brooding into this latter Pain.—This is a very, very dim Sketch / but the *Fact* is stated.—Then, A. took himself to Task respecting B.—It is very true, that B. is not so zealous as he might be, in some things—and overzealous for himself— But what is he on the whole? What compared with the mass of men?—It is astonishing how powerfully this Medicine acted—how instantly it effected a cure / one wakeful Hour's serious Analysis— & the Light thrown upon the former Subject had a great Share in this—for one important part of the Process in the growth of Envy is the Self-degradation (a painful self-referent Feeling) consequent on the first consciousness of the pang—the Obscurity & Darkness of mind from ignorance of the Cause—dim notion that our nature is suddenly altered for the worse. &c &c.—Deeplier than ever do I see the necessity of understanding the whole complex mixed character of our Friend—as well as our own / of frequently, in our kind-

[1] KC, I, 1471.

est moods, reviewing it—intensifying our Love of the Good in it, & making up our mind to the Faulty—it would be a good Exercise to imagine & anticipate some painful Result of the faulty part of our Friend's character—fancy him acting thus & thus to you— when it would most wound you / then to see how much of the wound might not be attributed to some lingering Selfishness in one's self—and at all events to fancy yourself forgiving it, passing it over, turning the attention forcibly to the valuable Parts of the character, & connecting a feeling of Respect & love with the *Person*, the visual Form—even during the manifestation of this unpleasant part of the Character.

Question is, whether I have not mistaken for Envy a very differ- ent Feeling. The same sort of Pain I have distinctly felt, at Mr. Pitt's being the Author of the Irish Union, deemed by me a great & wise measure / & introducing a subversion of my *Theory* of Pitt's Con- temptibility. Yet it would be strange to say, I envied Mr. Pitt?— This however is a mere Tenant of the Understanding—not con- nected with my Person in any way.—Take this Feeling, namely, as Pain at the excellence of another, and add to it other pains purely personal—will it be Envy then?—But it is not Pain at the excellence of another, but pain that that particular Person whom I had habi- tually despised, should have that excellence, which if he really have, I must be forced to give him a share of my Esteem & Love—. This seems a Vice of personal Uncharitableness, not Envy.—I am by no means satisfied with the analysis: & yet I think, that Envy might gradually rise out of this primary Pain of Incongruity / tho' it would be only a Sort of Envy—& no doubt different from Envy excited by the possession of Excellence—the more of it, the more Envy—Let me re-ennumerate. A. had been dwelling on the faulty parts of B.'s character = L. These views of A's understanding were *just* on this point, only that they had been *exclusive*: occasioned by A. having been himself deeply wounded by B.'s selfishness. = M. —A. had been long, long idle owing perhaps in part to his Idolatry of B. = N. 4. A. hears of some new Poems of B.—& feels little pain- ful shrinking back at the Heart = .O.—&, 5. a disposition to do something to surpass B. = P.—on the whole I suspect the Feeling to have been mere Resentment.—[1]

For all Coleridge's honesty of self-analysis and charitableness of disposition, and despite the recognition that he had expected the impossible of his 'sheet-anchor', the final resolution to 'do some- thing to surpass B' indicates some smouldering resentfulness—a

[1] KC, I, 1606.

feeling perhaps which underlies the *Dejection* line, 'I too will crown me with a Coronal'. However much Coleridge admired Wordsworth's poetic talent, the '*up*, askance, pig look' alluded to here was not the description of a man Coleridge could confide in, or identify his own happiness with.

Southey, too, lacked genuine warmth of feeling, for all his bland virtuousness (a point Dorothy Wordsworth mentions also[1]). Southey was the last person to understand Coleridge's neuroticism, which found its full expression in this rancorous private notebook entry:

> The character of Australis [Southey] . . . never once stumbling Temperance, his unstained Chastity . . . the simplicity of his daily Life, the Industry, & vigorous Perseverance in his Pursuit, the worthiness & dignity of these Pursuits. . . All this Australis *does*, & if all Goodness consists in definite, observable, & rememberable *Actions*, Australis is only not perfect, his good Actions so many, his unad[mirable] ones so few, & (with one or two exceptions) so venial. But now what is Australis? I can tell you, what he is *NOT*. He is not a man of warmth, or delicacy of Feeling . . . not incapable of doing base actions. . . The smiles, the emanations, the perpetual Sea-like Sound & Motion of Virtuousness, which is Love, is wanting— / He is a clear handsome piece of Water in a Park, moved from without—or at best, a ⟨smooth⟩ stream with one current, & tideless, & of which you can only avail yourself to one purpose.[2]

Paradoxically, Southey proved in one sense the most dependable of all Coleridge's 'sheet-anchors' (by caring for his neglected family), but one feels that in this matter Coleridge exploited Southey's attachment to Sara, just as Southey had once exploited him. He appears to have inveigled Southey to Greta Hall with the deliberate intention of shelving his domestic responsibilities and, once Southey was installed there, Coleridge promptly decamped, with the remark that his return to Keswick was 'not to be calculated on'.[3]

Concerning the quarrel of 1812, which brought to an end Coleridge's partnership with Wordsworth, Mr Griggs has this to say:

> On the whole the separation from Wordsworth proved to be beneficial to Coleridge. It freed him from servile idolatry and an unhealthy dependence, and put an end to his association with Sara

---

[1] *Early Letters*, 481; and cf. 196.   [2] KC, I, 1815.   [3] CL, II, 926, 1105.

Hutchinson. No one, it is true, ever laid hold of his affections with the same intensity as Wordsworth; nevertheless, other friends—the Morgans, R. H. Brabant, Byron, the Gillmans, J. H. Frere, J. H. Green, C. A. Tulk, and H. F. Cary—brought him the devotion and sympathy so necessary to him.[1]

These 'other friends', the Morgans and Gillmans especially, became 'sheet-anchor' supports in the generous, self-effacing sense that Poole had been, a rôle for which the egotistical Wordsworth was not well fitted. There was too much unhealthy dependence on Coleridge's part for that fruitful collaboration of the glorious Quantock summer to endure; too much self-abasement before his 'god' to constitute the friendship Coleridge needed.

Wordsworth's very excellence served only to magnify Coleridge's shortcomings, accentuating his sense of personal inferiority and provoking self-disgust with his own productions. At the heart of Coleridge's admiration of Wordsworth's work was his recognition of a mind moving with obvious assurance through country in which he was himself losing all sense of direction.[2] Critics since Arnold have been sceptical of Wordsworth's right to the title of 'the first and greatest philosophical Poet' which Coleridge conferred upon him, but it is important to distinguish the special quality Coleridge admired in Wordsworth's work. Not from virtue of any superior metaphysical standpoint did Coleridge venerate Wordsworth, but because Wordsworth had no peer in synthesizing thought and feeling (that synthesis which so constantly eluded Coleridge):

> Wordsworth is a Poet, a most original Poet . . . and I dare affirm that he will hereafter be admitted as the first & greatest philosophical Poet—the only man who has effected a compleat and constant synthesis of Thought & Feeling and combined them with Poetic Forms, with the music of pleasurable passion and with Imagination. . .[3]

'You were a thinking feeling Philosopher habitually', he told Wordsworth in 1803, by which time '*not* to think of what I needs must feel' but 'by abstruse Research to steal / From my own Nature, all the Natural man' had become the self-disintegratory habit of Coleridge's soul.[4] Hence, Wordsworth, the 'Friend of the wise! and Teacher of the Good' (as Coleridge called him),

[1] CL, III, Introduction, xliii.   [2] See Jones, op. cit., 28.
[3] CL, II, 1034.   [4] ibid, II, 957.

spoke to the hearts of the 'pure', whereas Coleridge, relinquishing now all claim to Philosopher-Poet status, wrote verses like
The Pains of Sleep, full of private griefs he dare not publish.[1]

The integrity and rich emotional harmony of Wordsworth's
domestic life was, as we have seen, a further cause of Coleridge's
envy. If, as Sir Herbert Read and Mr Bateson allege, there were
guilty secrets in Wordsworth's cupboard—concerning Annette
Vallon or some 'incestuous' relationship with Dorothy—Coleridge evidently attached little importance to them.[2] Wordsworth
seemed to him a model of purity and he would have concurred
quite literally with Shelley's encomium (disregarding, probably,
its wicked irony):

> He was a man, too great to scan;—
> A planet lost in truth's keen rays:—
> His virtue, awful and prodigious;—
> He was the most sublime, religious,
> Pure-minded Poet of these days.[3]

The corollary to this god-like excellence was unfortunately an
inflated sense of moral superiority, an egotism and lofty condes-
cension which (besides almost ruining his poetry eventually)
made the later Wordsworth a quite impossible friend for Coleridge. Indeed, much as Coleridge envied Wordsworth his bevy
of female housemates, he guessed (accurately as it proved) that
this living wholly among 'Devotees' who indulged his 'hypochon-

---

[1] PW 403, 389. "The Pains of Sleep", written about 1803, was not published until 1816, along with "Kubla Khan" and "Christabel".

[2] The years 1793–1802 were 'years of remorse and guilt' for Wordsworth,
according to Herbert Read. Wordsworth, he argues, denied his instinctive
love for Annette Vallon, the mother of his illegitimate child, and contracted
a loveless, conventional marriage with Mary Hutchinson, whom he never
really loved (op. cit., 95-6, 118, 164).

F. W. Bateson argues, in *Wordsworth: a Re-Interpretation* (London, 1954),
that "Tintern Abbey" and the Lucy poems suggest a love-relationship with
Dorothy (pp. 151 ff).

[3] "Peter Bell the Third", Part VI, xxxiv. Elsewhere in the poem Shelley
questions that very integrity which Coleridge admired in Wordsworth, ac-
cusing him of a want of moral commitment:

> But from the first 'twas Peter's drift
> To be a kind of moral eunuch,
> He touched the hem of Nature's shift,
> Felt faint—and never dared uplift
> The closest, all-concealing tunic (Pt IV, xi).

driacal Fancies' and fed his 'Self-involution' would eventually cause a 'Film [to] thicken on his moral Eye'.[1]

For one reason or another, therefore, Coleridge was deprived of the 'sheet-anchor' support which he badly needed while his home was breaking up and his conflicting loyalties to Asra and his children were undermining his mental health. It was a sad commentary on the ruin he had made of his life that when he fled the country to escape his intolerable predicament, not a friend was present to see him off. He set sail with sour recollections of his recent quarrel with Poole still rankling in his mind. Ungenerously, he confided these thoughts to Southey:

> Poole wrote me a Letter / Good God! to believe & to profess that I have been so & so to him, & yet to have behaved as he has done —denied me once a Loan of £50 when I was on a Sickbed—I never dreamt of asking him. Wordsworth did it without my knowledge— & it would have been against my Consent. Poole *answered* not W. but me, and proposed to have a subscription of £50 raised for me, to which *he* would contribute £5; but wondered, that I had not applied to my Brothers!!!—and 3 years long did I give my mind to this man / exclusive of introductions &c &c—.
> . . . God bless you, DEAR Southey.[2]

Southey himself came under similar censure for, though he was generously caring for Coleridge's neglected family, he was at the same time pointedly reminded that the *sole* responsibility for Coleridge's unhappy marriage lay with him:

> . . . I was blasted in my only absolute wish, having married for honor & not for love! Southey! that I think & feel so kindly & lovingly of *you*, who were [the] sole cause of my marriage, this is a proof to me that my nature is not ignoble.[3]

Thus Coleridge wilfully obliterated all memories of the earlier happiness he had known at Nether Stowey with Poole and Sara and his family, repudiating his past in the chimerical belief that his future happiness was bound up with the Dove Cottage circle. On returning from Malta he imagined, with characteristic naïveté, that Sara would allow him to take the children from her and set up home with Asra and the Wordsworths. Southey's 1807 comment on these later developments conveys the depth of animosity which by then prevailed between the Fricker and the Wordsworth circle:

[1] CL, II, 1013.   [2] ibid, II, 1124.   [3] ibid, II, 1156.

What you have heard of Coleridge is true, he is about to separate from his wife. . . His present scheme is to live with Wordsworth—it is from his idolatry of that family that this has begun,—they have always humoured him in all his follies,—listened to his complaints of his wife,—& when he has complained of the itch, helped him to scratch, instead of covering him with brimstone ointment, & shutting him up by himself. Wordsworth & his sister who pride themselves upon having no selfishness, are of all human beings whom I have ever known the most intensely selfish. The one thing to which W. would sacrifice all others is his own reputation, concerning which his anxiety is perfectly childish—like a woman of her beauty: & so he can get Coleridge to talk over his own writings with him, & criticise them & (without amending them) teach him how to do it,—to be in fact the very rain & air & sunshine of his intellect, he thinks Coleridge is very well employed & this arrangement a very good one.[1]

This sorry state of general recrimination was the unhappy point to which the great 'sheet-anchor' friendships of 1797 finally came. In consequence, when the major crisis arrived, Coleridge (like his own Ancient Mariner, self-alienated from the sympathy he needed) was forced to cope from his own inadequate resources with a psychoneurosis no self-help *could* cure.

Since his summer visit to the Hutchinsons in 1801 the mental strain upon Coleridge had been increasing. Prior to that visit he had already undergone a three-month period of 'intellectual exsiccation' which, as the famous letter to Godwin shows, had brought him to the verge of breakdown:

You would not know me—! all sounds of similitude keep at such a distance from each other in my mind, that I have *forgotten* how to make a rhyme—I look at the Mountains (that visible God Almighty that looks in at all my windows) I look at the Mountains only for the Curves of their outlines; the Stars, as I behold them, form themselves into Triangles—and my hands are scarred with scratches from a Cat, whose back I was rubbing in the Dark in order to see whether the sparks from it were refrangible by a Prism. The Poet is dead in me—my imagination (or rather the Somewhat that had been imaginative) lies, like a Cold Snuff on the circular Rim of a Brass Candle-Stick, without even a stink of Tallow to remind you that it was once cloathed & mitred with Flame.[2]

[1] ibid, III, 4n.   [2] ibid, II, 714.

By morbid introspectiveness and a 'multitude' of experiments ('too often repeated') which he conducted upon himself he 'did injury', as he put it, to his own nervous system.[1] He developed the classic symptoms of a nervous breakdown: pausing hours before he dare open a letter, avoiding all company unless braced by alcohol, trembling at unexpected sounds, confining himself indoors, avoiding emotional situations generally, and being overwhelmed by a sense of inferiority and personal inadequacy.[2] His susceptibility to bouts of hysterical weeping, to skin eruptions and bowel disorders made him 'an object of moral Disgust' to himself. Lacking a psychiatric terminology to describe his symptoms he attributed them to 'Scrofula', by which he meant a general physiological deterioration 'accompanied with an undue sensibility of the nervous system'.[3]

One should be chary perhaps of applying a blanket-term like 'psychoneurosis' to the complex convolutions of a mind like Coleridge's. It is a term which, 'explaining' everything, clarifies nothing, particularly since psychiatrists and psychologists themselves are not agreed upon what a 'neurosis' represents. One should be even more chary of making diagnostic inferences about a man who died in 1834. Yet, paradoxically, we know more about Coleridge's 'case-history' than we *could* know, probably, of any living author's. A living writer could furnish fuller data for psychiatric diagnosis only if he were prepared to collaborate in the investigation with utter fearlessness of self-exposure (and provided that his associates would talk about him with total frankness). Such naked self-honesty is not easily come by, however, for as Santayana says: 'Nothing requires a rarer intellectual heroism than willingness to see one's equation written out.' Coleridge's poems, his recently published letters and private notebooks reveal the fearless courage he possessed for writing out his own equation honestly. These documents contain a comprehensive and graphic record of a poet's introspective self-analysis which is virtually unique in literary annals.

Without making too much of the psychological aspect, it is evident that in Coleridge's case (far more than Wordsworth's) there *is* a great deal of maladjustment which can be explained if use is made of the extensive data now available. In the light of

[1] CL, II, 731.   [2] ibid, II, 1075, 1077, 1099, 1100, 1102.
[3] ibid, II, 726, 736, 897.

this evidence the 'Philosopher-killed-the-Poet' and 'Opium' explanations of his breakdown seem less than adequate. There is a
strong prima facie case for inferring that Coleridge suffered from
an obsessional neurosis, though disagreement might exist as to
its ultimate source—whether it originated in a repressed craving
for love owing to childhood feelings of deprivation, in a sense of
inferiority arising from frustrated power, or in an inability to
grapple successfully with life's moral demands. Undoubtedly,
he had the sensitive, highly-strung temperament which an unstable upbringing might predispose towards neurosis, while his
tendencies to invent illness and towards escapism, to showing off
and self-pity, were typical love-deprivation reactions. Some of
the defensive mechanisms he adopted may have served partly as
excuses for his failure, partly as a demand to be judged more
leniently, and partly as an attempt to avoid the complete dissociation of personality which (as *Dejection: an Ode* clearly shows)
he felt was imminent.

It remains to discover the actual precipitating cause of his
neurosis. The mental strain he subjected himself to could in itself
have been the cause, especially if accompanied by a severe emotional shock. At this distance of time one can only guess at what
particular contingency it was (amid the general emotional disturbances of 1800–3) which precipitated the crisis. Almost certainly this was linked with Asra, together with either the alienation from his children which his guilty love-affair produced, or
the sudden realization that, since Sara would not grant a separation, no release was possible from his predicament. A mysterious
letter he wrote to Asra, which made her ill with grief and hence
roused bitter self-reproach in him, may also have been a precipitating factor.[1] Or, finally, it may have been the shock of hearing
that Wordsworth was about to marry Asra's sister. This event,
which has hitherto eluded critical attention, may have been the
principal spur to the writing of *Dejection: an Ode*.

Coleridge was quite unaware apparently, when he commenced
his love-affair with Asra, that a similar relationship sprang up at
the same time between Wordsworth and Asra's sister, Mary
Hutchinson.[2] The news that they were to be married reached
Coleridge on or about 24 February 1802, the day on which he
communicated it to his wife. 'Wordsworth will marry soon after

[1] See pp. 254–6 below.   [2] See KC, I, 576n.

R

my return,' he wrote, evidently expecting that the ceremony would take place in March or April. After telling Sara this news, Coleridge wrote no further letters for eleven weeks until, in reply to Poole's anxious inquiries, he wrote back on 7 May saying that he had written to 'no human being', having 'neither been very well, nor very happy'.[1] In the interval he had visited Gallow Hill (Asra's home) and had written, on or about 4 April, the first draft of *Dejection: an Ode*. In other words he began writing his farewell to poetry soon after the announcement of Wordsworth's wedding and in the April when it was originally intended that this wedding should take place. Actually, the ceremony was postponed until 4 October, because the negotiations over Annette's settlement took longer than anticipated and were not concluded until August. The 4 October 1802 was also the date on which *Dejection: an Ode* (in its revised form) appeared in the *Morning Post*, its first publication thus coinciding with Wordsworth's wedding-day (and, ironically, with the seventh anniversary of Coleridge's own marriage).

Was it coincidence that Coleridge published the poem on Wordsworth's wedding-day, or a theatrical means of endowing his poetic renunciation of Asra (the original subject of the poem) with all possible significance? The Wordsworths had heard him read the original draft of the poem on 21 April and must have understood its significance and 'the full extent of the calamity' which was causing his 'Distress'.[2] By publishing on the wedding-day Coleridge may have been giving them and Asra a poignant reminder that Wordsworth had everything now—honour, love, obedience, troops of friends—all which he could not look to have.

[1] CL, II, 788, 799.
[2] Dorothy's Journal, 21 April 1802, records: 'Wednesday. William and I sauntered a little in the garden. Coleridge came to us, and repeated the verses he wrote to [Asra]. I was affected with them, and was on the whole, not being well, in miserable spirits. The sunshine, the green fields, and the fair sky made me sadder; even the little happy, sporting lambs seemed but sorrowful to me.'
On 1 February 1804, Coleridge wrote to Sir George Beaumont explaining that on medical advice he was about to go abroad. He continued: 'I was hardly used from infancy to Boyhood; & from Boyhood to Youth, most, MOST cruelly / yet "the Joy within me", which is indeed my own Life and my very Self, was creating me anew to the first purpose of Nature, when other & deeper Distress supervened—which many have guessed, but Wordsworth alone knows to the full extent of the Calamity' (CL, II, 1053; and cf. pp. 245-7 below on the 1802 'dialogue' between Coleridge and Wordsworth).

Wordsworth would henceforth be served by the three women dearer to Coleridge than all else, his path of duty lying open before him 'thro' vine-trellised Elm-groves'. The circle was complete and in *Dejection: an Ode* Coleridge, recognizing that ' 'twould but wrong you / If I should fondly yearn to be among you', accepted his exclusion from this circle and took poetic leave of it.

9

Dejection

The earliest draft of *Dejection: an Ode* was addressed to Asra on 4 April 1802 in the form of a verse-letter. Coleridge had returned home a few days before, having prior to that been living away from his wife since early November 1801. During this absence he had begun to think seriously about a separation. Immediately before returning home he had spent a fortnight (3–13 March) with Asra at Gallow Hill during which period some sharp unhappiness arose between them, which is alluded to in the verse-letter. We do not know the exact cause of this, but probably Wordsworth was informed of it between 19 and 21 March.[1] There is evidence that because of what had occurred Asra was in as distraught a state as Coleridge was.[2]

On 28 March the Wordsworths came to Keswick to stay with Coleridge for a week, Wordsworth having just written the first four stanzas of his *Ode on Intimations of Immortality*. While they were staying with him Coleridge wrote the first draft of *Dejection: an Ode*, though he did not show it to the Wordsworths until 21 April.[3] Wordsworth's Ode commences:

> There was a time when meadow, grove, and stream,
> The earth, and every common sight,
>   To me did seem
>   Apparelled in celestial light,
> The glory and the freshness of a dream.
> It is not now as it hath been of yore;—
>   Turn wheresoe'er I may,
>   By night or day,
> The things which I have seen I now can see no more.

[1] Whalley, 42.

[2] CL, II, 909; Whalley, 69.

[3] Chambers suggests that Dorothy Wordsworth may have seen part of the poem on 13 April 1802 (Life, 150).

244

'There hath past away a glory from the earth', it goes on to say, and the fourth stanza ends:

> Whither is fled, the visionary gleam?
> Where is it now, the glory and the dream?

This was the point Wordsworth's poem had reached when he came to stay with Coleridge.

Coleridge's *Dejection: an Ode* was written partly in response to Wordsworth's poem, and announced simultaneously that the poetic faculty was dying in him, too. It contained deliberate echoes of Wordsworth's Ode:

> There was a time when, though my path was rough,
>   This joy within me dallied with distress,
> And all misfortunes were but as the stuff
>   Whence Fancy made me dreams of happiness:
> For hope grew round me, like the twining vine,
> And fruits, and foliage, not my own, seemed mine.
> But now afflictions bow me down to earth:
> Nor care I that they rob me of my mirth;
>   But oh! each visitation
> Suspends what nature gave me at my birth,
>   My shaping spirit of Imagination. (76–86)

These two poems, with Wordsworth's *Resolution and Independence* (which was begun on 3 May 1802 in 'answer' to Coleridge's Ode), together form 'a kind of dialogue'.[1] Coleridge's *The Mad Monk* makes a fourth contribution to the 'dialogue', a fact which is not generally known since E. H. Coleridge assigned this latter poem to 1800, whereas its verbal echoes of Wordsworth's Ode show that it must have been written *after* April 1802:

> There was a time when earth, and sea, and skies,
>   The bright green vale, and forest's dark recess,
> With all things, lay before mine eyes
>   In steady loveliness:
> But now I feel, on earth's uneasy scene,
>   Such sorrows as will never cease;—
>   I only ask for peace;
> If I must live to know that such a time has been![2]

[1] See L. G. Salingar, "Coleridge: Poet and Philosopher", in *The Pelican Guide to English Literature*, ed. Boris Ford (1957), Vol. 5, 195; and cf. CL, II, 966–74.

[2] PW 348, ll. 9–16. The place of "The Mad Monk" in this 'dialogue' between Coleridge and Wordsworth is pointed out by Mr Whalley (128–9).

The full significance of this poetic 'dialogue' between Wordsworth and Coleridge in 1802 has still to be uncovered; here, we
are concerned only with Coleridge's part in it. As regards the two
Odes the important difference between them lies in the greater
objectivity Wordsworth's achieves. While regretting the loss of
the perceptive insight he had formerly possessed, Wordsworth
willed himself finally into philosophic acceptance of the change
within himself, drawing upon his personal resources to find comfort in 'what remains behind':

> Though nothing can bring back the hour
> Of splendour in the grass, of glory in the flower;
> We will grieve not, rather find
> Strength in what remains behind;
> In the primal sympathy
> Which having been must ever be;
> In the soothing thoughts that spring
> Out of human suffering;
> In the faith that looks through death,
> In years that bring the philosophic mind. (stanza 10)

Coleridge's failure of imagination was too much bound up with
tragic personal circumstances for him to contemplate it with a
like detachment.

Doubtless he discussed these circumstances with Wordsworth
during the latter's stay at Keswick, complaining that (as the
verse-letter put it) his might have been 'a most blessed Lot' had
the existence of his children not turned his 'Error' in marrying
Sara Fricker to 'Necessity'. We do not know how Wordsworth
replied to this, but it is noticeable that when he returned to work
upon his own poem he developed it as though consciously cham-
pioning Coleridge's children's cause. Wordsworth's lines about
the 'six years Darling' child were written with Hartley Coleridge
(then five and a half years old) in mind:

> Behold the Child among his new-born blisses,
> A six years' Darling of a pigmy size!
> See, where 'mid work of his own hand he lies,
> Fretted by sallies of his mother's kisses,
> With light upon him from his father's eyes! (stanza 7)

This final line seems like a pointed reminder to Coleridge of his
former affection for Hartley, as expressed, say, in the concluding

lines of *The Nightingale*.[1] The claims the *Immortality Ode* makes for
the sanctity of childhood, and its didactic insistence that childhood instincts are the 'master-light of all our seeing', must have
come as an uncomfortable rebuff to Coleridge's thoughts. Wordsworth was very fond of Hartley, and his poem, *To H.C.: Six Years
Old* (another element in the 1802 'dialogue'), reveals this affection fully. It reveals something else—Wordsworth's apprehensions regarding Hartley's future:

> O blessed vision! happy child!
> Thou art so exquisitely wild,
> I think of thee with many fears
> For what may be thy lot in future years.

Though these 'apprehensions' are linked with the philosophical
theme of the *Immortality Ode*—fears lest Hartley 'be trailed along
the soiling earth'—they may well have had a biographical significance too, since Wordsworth must by now have appreciated the
insecurity of Hartley's situation.

Coleridge's verse-letter to Asra, amounting to 340 lines, became the basis of *Dejection: an Ode*, which consists of 139 lines and
is divided into eight stanzas. It may be seen from a crude diagrammatic representation of the two versions of the poem how
drastically Coleridge re-arranged his material after deleting the
two hundred largely autobiographical lines which were unsuit-
able for publication:

	Ode	*Original*
Stanza	I	I
	II	II
	III	III
	—	ll. 52–183 (later deleted)
	IV	VII
	V	VIII (a)—first 9 lines only
	VI	VI including ll. 243–64 (later deleted)
	—	ll. 272–95 (later deleted)
	VII	IV
	VIII	V including ll. 325–33 (later deleted)
		VIII (b)—last 5 lines
Lines	139	340

[1] PW 266–7; see p. 122 above.

Originally, the poem constituted a poetic leave-taking of Asra and the Wordsworth circle, an act of *renunciation* which Coleridge believed (for reasons that will appear) might revitalize his 'suspended' imagination. Before publishing the poem he suppressed most of the material relating to this private theme, attempting to assimilate what remained into a poem about the failure of his imagination. Because its original intention was truncated therefore, and material relating to a private theme had now to be objectified, the published Ode presents a number of almost ineluctable problems. Chief among these are the ambivalence of the storm-wind's function and the uncertainty we are left in as to what finally becomes of Coleridge's despair. (Is his imagination reborn, or does his despair continue?) Also, what is meant by 'And may this storm be but a mountain birth', and why should Asra *need* 'wings of healing' when nowhere in the Ode is the possibility developed that her experience in any way corresponds to his?[1] This is not to imply that the verse-letter is a 'better' poem than the Ode; indeed, judged by the highest standards, both are poems of uneven quality. It is not a matter of which is the better, but that they are virtually *different* poems. Our concern is less with qualitative evaluations however, than with trying to get at the real (rather than the ostensible) cause of Coleridge's breakdown as a poet. For this purpose the autobiographical verse-letter is all-important, since in the Ode the original self-revelation has been camouflaged. Consequently, the discussion which follows is based mainly on the text of the verse-letter and, since this is still not readily accessible, most of the passages deleted from the textus receptus are here supplied in full.[2]

The first three of the original stanzas were carried over almost intact into *Dejection: an Ode*—not surprisingly, since they represent one of Coleridge's supreme achievements in the conversational style. Their tone is urbane and self-assured, the dry humour of this colloquial opening capturing perfectly the rhythm and diction of ordinary speech:

[1] See Schulz, 206. The line 'Ours is her wedding garment, ours her shroud!' (49) presents some problems both in the Ode and in the original stanzas (see HH, 135–6; also Suther, 137 ff.).

[2] The full text of the original verse-letter may be found in Griggs, CL, II, 790–8, and HH, Appendix I. The line references in this chapter refer to the verse-letter, unless otherwise stated.

Well! If the Bard was weather-wise, who made
  The grand old ballad of Sir Patrick Spence,
  This night, so tranquil now, will not go hence
Unroused by winds, that ply a busier trade
Than those which mould yon cloud in lazy flakes . . .

(Ode, 1–5)

Considering what is to come, this appearance of cool detachment
is remarkable, yet the key images which follow at once belie the
poet's self-assurance. Stock emblems of the creative imagination
(Eolian harp, moon, wind) are presented now in sinister and
unaccustomed form. Thus, the Eolian harp 'moans and rakes'
disagreeably (it 'better far were mute') under the 'dull sobbing
draft' which troubles it. The moon, juxtaposing the young and
promising (a 'New-moon winter-bright') with the old, wasted,
and worn ('the old Moon in her lap'), foretells squally blast and,
as the allusion to *Sir Patrick Spens* suggests, is heavily portentous.[1]
The poet yearns for the old afflatus, the revivifying wind which
will dispel his lethargy and send his soul 'abroad':

  . . . oh! that even now the gust were swelling,
    And the slant night-shower driving loud and fast!
  Those sounds which oft have raised me, whilst they awed,
      And sent my soul abroad,
  Might now perhaps their wonted impulse give,
  Might startle this dull pain, and make it move and live!

(Ode, 15–20)

But the wind that finally comes is a 'Mad Lutanist', a disintegratory, frenzied thing that makes 'Devil's yule with worse than
wintry song'. Lute, wintry moon, and unbridled wind all join
together finally in a distempered frenzy which makes mockery of
the poet's initial self-assurance.

  Coleridge's Ode (like Wordsworth's) conveys powerfully a
sense of stifling imprisonment.[2] The 'prisoner' this time is no
fictitious creature but the poet himself, experiencing personally
the Mariner-like, life-in-death acedia:

  These lifeless Shapes, around, below, Above,
    O what can they impart? (52–3)

[1] cf. Suther, 120.
[2] cf. Wordsworth: 'Shades of the prison-house begin to close / Upon the
growing Boy' (stanza 5). Mr Schulz notes that 'freedom-restriction' is a 'sup-
plementary motif' of "Dejection: an Ode", and points to the powerful light–
dark symbolism in both Coleridge's and Wordsworth's Ode (Schulz, 33, 40).

His is not a prison of walls and towers but a private, self-created hell, resulting from a wilful betrayal of his own sensibility. Deliberate repression of his feelings (a stealing from his 'own nature all the natural man') has induced a suspension of his 'shaping spirit of Imagination'. His mind, inert and passive, resembles that of *The Dungeon* prisoner, except that in this case it is beyond the reach of nature's healthful ministrations. He stands outside the kinship which exists between the things of nature, unable to participate:

> A grief without a pang, void, dark, and drear,
> A stifled, drowsy, unimpassioned grief,
> Which finds no natural outlet, no relief,
> In word, or sigh, or tear—
> O Lady! in this wan and heartless mood,
> To other thoughts by yonder throstle woo'd,
> All this long eve, so balmy and serene,
> Have I been gazing on the western sky,
> And its peculiar tint of yellow green:
> And still I gaze—and with how blank an eye!
> And those thin clouds above, in flakes and bars,
> That give away their motion to the stars;
> Those stars, that glide behind them or between,
> Now sparkling, now bedimmed, but always seen:
> Yon crescent Moon, as fixed as if it grew
> In its own cloudless, starless lake of blue;
> I see them all so excellently fair,
> I see, not feel, how beautiful they are![1]

Unable to feel the joy of interpenetration, Coleridge attributes his loss to an *emotional* blockage, not (as Wordsworth does) to a filming over of youthful intuitiveness. He cannot project his soul 'abroad', because of a 'smothering weight' that lies upon his heart (hence the appeal to the wind to do it for him):

> My genial spirits fail;
> And what can these avail
> To lift the smothering weight from off my breast?
> It were a vain endeavour,
> Though I should gaze for ever
> On that green light that lingers in the west:

---

[1] "Ode", stanza 2. Coleridge's letter to Godwin (quoted p. 239 above) describing how he looked at the mountains only for the curves of their outlines might almost be taken as a gloss upon this stanza.

> I may not hope from outward forms to win
> The passion and the life, whose fountains are within.
>
> (stanza 3)

Apart from the emotional and philosophical implications here (the swing to a 'projectivist' philosophy, about which more will be said later), there are moral ones of equal importance. As the poem goes on to state, only the 'pure in heart' are capable of interfusion with the spirit-life of nature, indicating that a moral as well as an emotional harmony is requisite before the poet can *feel* earth's loveliness. By this token Coleridge's Mad Monk is likewise committed to dissonance, because he also had 'murdered' his sensibility.[1]

After stanza 3 the two versions of the poem develop along quite different lines, the verse-letter proceeding next to a long autobiographical section, the whole of which was later excised. Immediately this personal matter intrudes in the original version of the poem there is a dislocation of the earlier urbanity: detachment crumbles, taut control gives way to rambling discursiveness, and the confident rhythms of the earlier meditative stanzas are broken by weak repetitions and lax parentheses. Yet in these disjointed lines we witness in fact the re-awakening of Coleridge's imagination. His mind now begins to free itself from the 'prison' his disordered sensibility has produced, moving *outwards* and back in time to the recollection of another 'prison' (the 'barr'd' window of Christ's Hospital). He recalls that it required the influence of a visionary 'Abyssinian maid' to release him from *that* 'jail':

> These lifeless Shapes, around, below, Above,
>   O what can they impart?
> When even the gentle Thought, that thou, my Love!
> Art gazing, now, like me,   55
> And see'st the Heaven, I see—
> Sweet Thought it is—yet feebly stirs my Heart!
>
> Feebly! O feebly!—Yet
> (I well remember it)
> In my first Dawn of Youth that Fancy stole   60
> With many secret Yearnings on my Soul.
> At eve, sky-gazing in "ecstatic fit"
> (Alas! for cloister'd in a city School

---

[1] cf. especially ll. 38–45 (PW 348–9).

The Sky was all, I knew, of Beautiful)
At the barr'd window often did I sit,   65
And oft upon the leaded School-roof lay,
And to myself would say—
There does not live the Man so stripp'd of good affections
As not to love to see a Maiden's quiet Eyes
Uprais'd, and linking on sweet Dreams by dim Connections
To Moon, or Evening Star, or glorious western Skies— 71
While yet a Boy, this Thought would so pursue me,
That often it became a kind of Vision to me!

Sweet Thought! and dear of old
To Hearts of finer Mould!   75
Ten thousand times by Friends and Lovers blest!
I spake with rash Despair,
And ere I was aware,
The Weight was somewhat lifted from my Breast!
O Sara! [Asra] in the weather-fended Wood,   80
Thy lov'd haunt! where the Stock-doves coo at Noon
I guess, that thou hast stood
And watch'd yon Crescent, and it's ghost-like Moon.
And yet, far rather in my present Mood
I would, that thou'dst been sitting all this while   85
Upon the sod-built Seat of Camomile—
And tho' thy Robin may have ceas'd to sing,
Yet needs for *my* sake must thou love to hear
The Bee-hive murmuring near,
That ever-busy and most quiet Thing   90
Which I have heard at Midnight murmuring.

I feel my spirit moved.
And whereso'er thou be,
O Sister! O Beloved!
Those dear mild Eyes, that see   95
Even now the Heaven, *I* see—
There is a Prayer in them! It is for *me*—
And I, dear Sara, *I* am blessing *thee*!

It was as calm as this, that happy night
When Mary, thou, and I together were,   100
The low decaying Fire our only Light,
And listen'd to the Stillness of the Air!
O that affectionate and blameless Maid,

Dear Mary! on her Lap my head she lay'd—
Her Hand was on my Brow,   105
Even as my own is now;
And on my Cheek I felt the eye-lash play.
Such joy I had, that I may truly say,
My spirit was awe-striken with the Excess
And trance-like Depth of it's brief Happiness.   110
Ah fair Remembrances, that so revive
The Heart, and fill it with a living Power.

In this section the gradual shift from 'Thought' to feeling (so characteristic of Coleridge's conversational poems) is attributable wholly to Asra's influence, and not (as the published Ode implies) to the stimulus of the wind.

Asra is thirteen miles distant and, at first, his only link with her is the 'gentle Thought' that she, like him, may be looking at the self-same sky. Yet it is this thought which, albeit weakly, first begins to dispel the dreary torpor from which there had been 'no natural outlet': 'Sweet Thought it is—yet feebly stirs my Heart'. As always, it takes a strong personal attachment to activate feeling and imagination, Asra doing for Coleridge here what his 'cradled infant' had done in *Frost at Midnight*, and his 'dear home' in *Fears in Solitude*. Whereas 'outward Forms' had availed nothing to lift the 'smoth'ring weight' from off his breast, a 'sweet thought' such as this, 'Ten thousand times by Friends and Lovers blest', is instantly cathartic:

And ere I was aware
The Weight was somewhat lifted from my Breast!
(78–9)

As awakening feeling provides a new focus for ideas, his imagination begins to range more widely, centring next on two of Asra's favourite haunts, places rich with vivid, recent associations. The feeling at once intensifies, and imaginative activity becomes fully conscious: 'I feel my spirit moved.' His torpor forgotten, his mind projects itself into outgoing, self-forgetful concern for Asra —'And I, dear [Asra], *I* am blessing *thee*!'[1] Finally, the recollection of recent happiness at Gallow Hill 'revives' his heart completely, filling it with 'a living Power'. All this time the wind in the background has lain completely dormant:

[1] The parallel here with "The Ancient Mariner" is interesting.

> It was as calm as this, that happy night
> When Mary, thou, and I together were, . . . (99–100)

In the original version of the poem therefore it was the strength of feeling associated with Asra, and *not* the wind, which freed Coleridge's imagination and provided the stimulus under which the deepest self-analysis occurred. Because this autobiographical material was deleted subsequently, we are forced in the Ode to explain the poet's re-awakening creativity (somewhat awkwardly) as a function of the wind.

This suppressed autobiographical passage then went on to explain why Asra needed 'wings of healing', so clarifying another point on which the Ode is puzzling. The living power of pleasurable feeling which Asra has evoked soon gives way to more painful feelings of self-reproach, remorse, and grief. In this section particularly, the private renunciatory theme comes right into the foreground of the poem:

> Ah fair Remembrances, that so revive
> The Heart, and fill it with a living Power,
> Where were they, Sara?—or did I not strive
> To win them to me?—on the fretting Hour
> Then when I wrote thee that complaining Scroll,   115
> Which even to bodily Sickness bruis'd thy Soul!
> And yet thou blam'st thyself alone! And yet
> Forbidd'st me all Regret!
>
> And must I not regret, that I distress'd
> Thee, best belov'd, who lovest me the best?   120
> My better mind had fled, I know not whither,
> For O! was this an absent Friend's Employ
> To send from far both Pain and Sorrow thither
> Where still his Blessings should have call'd down Joy!
> I read thy guileless Letter o'er again—   125
> I hear thee of thy blameless Self complain—
> And only this I learn—and this, alas! I know—
> That thou art weak and pale with Sickness, Grief, and Pain—
> And *I*,—*I* made thee so!
>
> O for my own sake I regret perforce   130
> Whatever turns thee, Sara, from the course
> Of calm Well-being and a Heart at rest!
> When thou, and with thee those, whom thou lov'st best,
> Shall dwell together in one happy Home,

One House, the dear *abiding* Home of All,   135
I too will crown me with a Coronal—
Nor shall this Heart in idle Wishes roam
    Morbidly soft!
No! let me trust, that I shall wear away
In no inglorious Toils the manly Day,   140
And only now and then, and not too oft,
Some dear and memorable Eve will bless
Dreaming of all your Loves and Quietness.
Be happy, and I need thee not in sight.
Peace in thy Heart, and Quiet in thy Dwelling,   145
Health in thy Limbs, and in thine eyes the Light
Of Love and Hope and honorable Feeling—
Where e'er I am, I shall be well content!
Not near thee, haply shall be more content!
To all things I prefer the Permanent.   150
And better seems it, for a Heart, like mine,
Always to *know*, than sometimes to behold,
    Their Happiness and thine—
For Change doth trouble me with pangs untold!
To see thee, hear thee, feel thee—then to part   155
    Oh! it weighs down the heart!
To *visit* those, I love, as I love thee,
Mary, and William, and dear Dorothy,
It is but a temptation to repine—
The transientness is Poison in the Wine,   160
Eats out the pith of Joy, makes all Joy hollow,
All Pleasure a dim Dream of Pain to follow!
My own peculiar Lot, my house-hold Life
It is, and will remain, Indifference or Strife.
While *Ye* are *well* and *happy*, 'twould but wrong you   165
If I should fondly yearn to be among you—
Wherefore, O wherefore! should I wish to be
A wither'd branch upon a blossoming Tree?

But (let me say it! for I vainly strive
To beat away the Thought), but if thou pin'd   170
Whate'er the Cause, in body or in mind,
I were the miserablest Man alive
To know it and be absent! Thy Delights
Far off, or near, alike I may partake—
But O! to mourn for thee, and to forsake   175
All power, all hope, of giving comfort to thee—
To know that thou art weak and worn with pain,

> And not to hear thee, Sara! not to view thee—
> Not sit beside thy Bed,
> Not press thy aching Head,   180
> Not bring thee Health again—
> At least to hope, to try—
> By this Voice, which thou lov'st, and by this earnest Eye—

If we knew the contents of the 'complaining Scroll' Coleridge
had written to Asra, which evidently had shocked her deeply, we
might have the key to everything that lies so tantalizingly hidden. Did it express resentment that she was going to live with
William and Mary after their wedding? Did it inform her that
he was ready to abandon his children and family commitments
for her sake? Did it threaten her that he must go abroad to quell
his passion? Whatever it was, it distressed her and made her
realize probably the havoc his love for her was causing in his
domestic life.[1] Sensing perhaps that Coleridge was about to break
under the strain, Asra had taken upon herself the entire guilt and
responsibility for the suffering that had been caused—'And yet
thou blam'st thyself alone! And yet / Forbidd'st me all Regret!'
Appalled by Asra's own distress, however, and touched by her
charitableness, Coleridge was angry with himself for having
placed her in such a situation:

> I hear thee of thy blameless Self complain—
> And only this I learn—and this, alas! I know—
> That thou art weak and pale with Sickness, Grief,
>   and Pain—
> And *I*,—*I* made thee so![2]

Belatedly, he now insisted that after the wedding she must continue to remain within the permanent gladness of the Wordsworth circle ('When thou, and with thee those, whom thou lov'st
best / Shall dwell together in one happy Home'); for only by
breaking free of this guilty liaison could she recover her peace
of mind and 'honour'—

> Peace in thy Heart, and Quiet in thy Dwelling,
> Health in thy Limbs, and in thine eyes the Light
> Of Love and Hope and honorable Feeling. (145–7)

---

[1] One recalls Tom Poole's sharp question: 'What have you to do with the
poverty, and misery, and sufferings around you. Have *you* caused the havock?'
(see p. 226 above).
[2] ll. 126–9. See p. 259, note.

Because Asra had now become alarmed at the serious implications of what had seemed a harmless flirtation, Coleridge himself was forced at last to face the realities of the situation.[1]

Two notebook entries made during Coleridge's recent stay at Gallow Hill are indications possibly of the trend of his thoughts during this unsettled time. The writing of the first is difficult to decipher, perhaps because of the feelings it aroused (or because of the opium used to alleviate these feelings?):

> Wordsworth & [? M]—S & Coler.—Little Boy seeking me—
> N.B. poems—.[2]

Assuming that 'S' stands for Sara Hutchinson, as seems likely from the circumstance of its having been written at Gallow Hill and from 'M' and 'S' being sisters, the entry conceivably means that if Asra and Coleridge were to pursue a love-relationship like that existing between Wordsworth and Mary Hutchinson, then there would be the problem of a 'Little Boy [Hartley] seeking me', i.e. seeking a father. (The 'poems' may refer to *Christabel*, *A Day-Dream*, and *Dejection: an Ode* itself.) The second entry, even more enigmatical, is a very large clear entry, obviously marking something of immense importance:

> Gallow Hill, Thursday, March 11th, 1802.
> S.T. Coleridge
> Sara
>   SarHa

Miss Coburn conjectures that the playing with the 'H' in Sar-Ha may be related to Lamb's stammer or to calling out names to hear an echo, or to Coleridge's preference for 'Sara' spelt without a final 'h'. None of these surmises seems quite commensurate

---

[1] Shortly before embarking for Malta, Coleridge wrote in a notebook: '⟨... Tuesday Night, Feb. 21. 1804, 11°clock / the day of the Receipt of that heart-wringing letter from [Asra], that put Despair into my Heart, and not merely as a Lodger, I fear, but as a Tenant for life.⟩' (KC, II, 1912).

Miss Coburn comments: 'Sara Hutchinson must have known as well as Coleridge did that any journey in search of his health would be ineffectual unless he resolved the emotional conflict connected with her; apparently she took steps to further the process.'

Was Coleridge alluding to the 1802 correspondence referred to in in ll. 115–25 of the poem above? If Coleridge's memory is accurate then this correspondence must have passed between them shortly before his visit to Gallow Hill during 3–13 March.

[2] KC, I, 1144.

S

however with the extreme importance which (as Miss Coburn herself points out) Coleridge evidently attached to this particular entry.[1] Could 'SarHa' be a cryptogram for Sara and Hartley, in which case the key figures in Coleridge's dilemma are all represented: S.T.C., Asra, his wife, and favourite child? Such guesses are admittedly inconclusive, yet they would interpret these enigmatical passages in what certainly seems to have been the mood of Coleridge's mind at this particular time. In coupling the little lost boy (Hartley) with both his love for Asra and his 'poems' they would be consonant with the whole sequence of lost or orphan-child images which had been prevalent in Coleridge's poems and notebooks since the time of writing *Christabel*.[2]

Returning then to the autobiographical passage under discussion, we can see that Coleridge's gesture of renunciation (suppressed from the published Ode) was originally an essential link between the private and the public themes. This act of altruism, by releasing Asra from a painful imbroglio and so restoring her peace of mind, was the best possible means of recovering his own integrity and—once he recovered his moral and emotional harmony—he would be fitted to seek a 'Coronal' again.[3] There is a deliberate echo here of Wordsworth's resolution, though the manner and context of it are entirely different. When Wordsworth came to stay with Coleridge his Ode had reached the point of declaring that a consolatory 'coronal' might yet be won:

> Ye blessèd Creatures, I have heard the call
>   Ye to each other make; I see
> The heavens laugh with you in your jubilee;
>   My heart is at your festival,
>   My head hath its coronal,
> The fulness of your bliss, I feel—I feel it all. (stanza 4)

Wordsworth refused to let 'grief of mine the season wrong'; 'I again am strong', he discovered, and went on to fortify his acceptance of the change within himself by *willing* creativity to continue. There is a resolute firmness in the tone and syntax of Wordsworth's stanza ('My heart *is* at . . . My head *hath* its . . .)

---

[1] KC, I, 1150.   [2] ibid, II, 1991n.

[3] cf. Coleridge's letter to Cottle in early April 1797 (at the commencement of his 'annus mirabilis'): 'So I would write haply not unhearing of that divine and rightly-whispering Voice, which speaks to mighty minds of predestinated Garlands, starry and unwithering' (CL, I, 321).

which is quite lacking in Coleridge's.[1] Coleridge's affirmation,
'I *too* will crown me with a Coronal', seemed threatened from
the start by 'morbidly soft' counter-desires:

> I too will crown me with a Coronal—
> Nor shall this Heart in idle Wishes roam
>   Morbidly soft!
> No! let me trust, that I shall wear away
> In no inglorious Toils the manly Day,
> And only now and then, and not too oft,
> Some dear and memorable Eve will bless
> Dreaming of all your Loves and Quietness.
> Be happy, and I need thee not in sight. (136–44)

The diffidence with which Coleridge expresses his vow to seek a
'Coronal' ('*let me trust*, that I shall wear away / In *no inglorious*
toils the manly Day') is not reassuring. Within thirty lines indeed
it is forgotten in this painful self-comparison with Wordsworth's
fruitfulness:

> While *Ye* are *well* and *happy*, 'twould but wrong you
> If I should fondly yearn to be among you—
> Wherefore, O wherefore! should I wish to be
> A wither'd branch upon a blossoming Tree? (165–8)

In the published Ode even this weakly resolution disappears,
leaving the reader to speculate whether Coleridge's imagination
will be reborn. It seems that all along, in fact, Coleridge's re-
dedication of his life to poetry was secondary to his promise to
stay away from Asra and do nothing to disturb the happiness of
her circle.

And yet the *private* resolution is scarcely more convincing:
'Only now and then, and not too oft' will he repine for Asra. His
claim above all things to 'prefer the Permanent' (150), because
'Change' troubles him 'with pangs untold' (154), encourages no
expectation that he has resigned himself to permanent exclusion
from the Wordsworth circle. He says it would be better for him
not to visit Grasmere again, which would be 'but a temptation
to repine' (159), yet within ten lines a fresh pretext for visiting
Asra is contrived—a concession demanded which drastically
qualifies his resolution:

---

[1] The rhythm of Wordsworth's 'I feel—I feel it all' seems to have been
mirrored sadly (even bitterly) in Coleridge's 'And *I*,—*I* made thee so' (129),
where all hope of 'bliss', so far as he was concerned, had been destroyed.

But (let me say it! for I vainly strive
To beat away the Thought), but if thou pin'd
Whate'er the Cause, in body or in mind,
I were the miserablest Man alive
To know it and be absent! Thy Delights
Far off, or near, alike I may partake—
But O! to mourn for thee, and to forsake
All power, all hope, of giving comfort to thee—
To know that thou art weak and worn with pain,
And not to hear thee, Sara! not to view thee—
 Not sit beside thy Bed,
 Not press thy aching Head,
 Not bring thee Health again—
 At least to hope, to try—
By this Voice, which thou lov'st, and by this earnest Eye—
             (169–83)

The 'Voice' tails off finally in ambiguous incompleteness. Probably the sick-room pathos inverts the basic motivation here; it is really a device, one suspects, for ensuring that Asra will comfort *him* again, if his resolve should falter.[1] Thus the resolution associated with *both* the poetic themes was invalidated from the outset by Coleridge's temperamental limitations. It was little use Wordsworth exhorting him to evince 'resolution and independence' when Coleridge was so utterly dependent on Asra's sympathy.

It is noticeable that whereas Wordsworth believed his to be a permanent loss of power, for which some compensation must be found, Coleridge regarded his as a temporary, contingent loss, believing that his 'shaping spirit' of imagination was only momentarily 'suspended'. And indeed, through the medium of his prose-writings, letters and notebooks chiefly, the flow of imagination continued fitfully yet strongly till his death.[2] The *Dejection* poem laments not a drying-up of imagination therefore, so much as a loss of *moral* confidence which had temporarily afflicted the 'shaping spirit'. Hence, of all Coleridge's Odes, this is the least didactic and assertive; it has no palpable design on the reader because the confident prophet of the 1790's has ended in self-disillusionment.[3] Only a year earlier Coleridge had been confi-

---

[1] As subsequently it *did* falter. From 20 December 1803 to 14 January 1804 Coleridge was ill and back again at Grasmere, enjoying the propinquity of 'dear Dorothy, in the Parlour' and 'O dear Sara Hutchinson' (KC, 1, 1820).
[2] cf. Chapter 10, p. 289, note 1.   [3] See Schulz, 33.

dent that the creative wind could 'attune' his heart by fusing thought and feeling into a whole man 'unity'.[1] But, by 1802, feeling had become repressed and imagination torpid. Though Asra could still stimulate his feelings, the feelings associated with her were painful, no longer of a sort to send his soul 'abroad' for interpenetration with the forms of nature. Thus, when in response to re-awakened feeling the creative wind at last appeared in the poem, its activity gave no reassurance that the poet's mind would be restored to wholeness and wholesomeness again.

Originally the storm-wind stanza came immediately after this long autobiographical section we have been discussing, the 'dark distressful Dream' following naturally upon the imagined scene of Asra's sick-bed.[2] In the Ode, where the wind stanza follows the announcement that the poet's imagination is 'suspended', there is some awkwardness in accounting for the precise connection between his own inertness and the vigour of the wind. If, however, this wind represents the *distempered* imaginative activity which is all his guilty feelings can now generate, the problem is overcome. The difficulty arises in the published Ode because Coleridge took material with a bearing on both the private and the public (imagination) themes, applying it with minor modifications to the public theme only. Yet one cannot interpret the imagery of this stanza adequately, except by reference to its personal implications. This suggestion may be reinforced if we examine now the version of this stanza as it appeared not in the verse-letter but in the final Ode:

> Hence, viper thoughts, that coil around my mind,
>   Reality's dark dream!
> I turn from you, and listen to the wind,
>   Which long has raved unnoticed. What a scream

---

[1]   And when the gust of Autumn crowds,
                And breaks the busy moonlight clouds,
             Thou best the thought canst raise, the heart attune,
             Light as the busy clouds, calm as the gliding moon.

             The feeling heart, the searching soul,
             To thee I dedicate the whole!
                —"Ode to Tranquillity" (1801), ll. 21–6, PW 361.

[2] Curiously enough, he had parted from Asra in a violent storm following his recent visit to her: 'Friday, March 12th / "& wept aloud"—you made me feel uncomfortable / Saturday, March 13th, left Gallow Hill on the Mail, in a violent storm of snow & Wind . . .' (KC, i, 1151).

Of agony by torture lengthened out
That lute sent forth! Thou Wind, that rav'st without,
    Bare crag, or mountain-tairn, or blasted tree,
Or pine-grove whither woodman never clomb,
Or lonely house, long held the witches' home,
    Methinks were fitter instruments for thee,
Mad Lutanist! who in this month of showers,
Of dark-brown gardens, and of peeping flowers,
Mak'st Devil's yule, with worse than wintry song,
The blossoms, buds, and timorous leaves among.
    Thou Actor, perfect in all tragic sounds!
Thou mighty Poet, e'en to frenzy bold!
    What tell'st thou now about?
    'Tis of the rushing of an host in rout,
  With groans, of trampled men, with smarting wounds—
At once they groan with pain, and shudder with the cold!
But hush! there is a pause of deepest silence!
    And all that noise, as of a rushing crowd,
With groans, and tremulous shudderings—all is over—
    It tells another tale, with sounds less deep and loud!
      A tale of less affright,
      And tempered with delight,
As Otway's self had framed the tender lay,—
      'Tis of a little child
      Upon a lonesome wild,
Not far from home, but she hath lost her way:
And now moans low in bitter grief and fear,
And now screams loud, and hopes to make her mother hear.

                         (stanza 7)

Though, earlier, Coleridge had besought the wind to project his 'soul' abroad, it was the thought of Asra which had in fact stimulated feeling and imagination.[1] The wind indeed had 'rav'd *unnoticed*'. Asra failed to secure for him full attunement with the forms of nature, and the wind is equally unsuccessful. It comes not as a fusing, but as a disintegratory, force, merely corroborating his melancholy by translating 'a grief without a pang' into 'viper thoughts'. He had invoked the wind originally, hoping perhaps for something like the old afflatus described in poems like *Shurton Bars* and the *Chatterton Monody*, where wild storm-winds had been associated with the sweetness of melancholic self-abandonment, with 'Inspiration's eager hour / When most the big

---

[1] But see p. 225 above, where a possible connection with Poole is traced.

soul feels the mastering power'. *Lines in a Concert Room* had described how, when the 'midnight wind careers' and 'the gust
[pelts] on the out-house shed' an 'Abyssinian maid' would attune
her voice to the tone 'the things of Nature utter'.[1] But this is a
maniacal onslaught which, in the 'sweet Primrose-month' of
April, makes 'Devil's yule, with worse than wintry Song'. It tells
of clashing armies, of groans, of trampled men and smarting
wounds, a tale conducive to anything but sweetness. The wind's
second tale moreover is only relatively 'a tale of less affright', for
it ends in the terrified screams of a child who feels insecure and
lost. This 'tale' (likened to Otway's) was ascribed to Wordsworth
in the original version, and referred probably to the tragedy of
Lucy Gray, the lost child who died in a wintry storm unable to
find her parents' door. Thus, the wished-for wind, instead of re-
viving the old afflatus, may have signified by its destructive hos-
tility towards kindred things of nature, the disorganized un-
wholesomeness of Coleridge's own imagination.[2] Instead of send-
ing his soul 'abroad' and producing the 'Joy' and wholeness of
spirit he anticipated, it turned his soul inwards to gloomy and
viperish introspection.

Mr House's change of thought on the subject of this wind bears
interestingly on my argument. Originally, he was inclined to
regard it as at once 'destroyer and creator'—a destructive wind
from which regeneration might follow. It was under the stimulus
of this strong 'creative' wind, he suggested, that the deepest self-
analysis occurs, and also the fullest realization of the power of
joy, as it is actually achieved in Asra herself. But later he revised
this standpoint, still holding to the view that the wind's vigour
acts as the stimulus to the lines on the Imagination ('in that Coleridge's insight has been deepened by his response to it and by his
development of the idea of its creativeness'), but deciding that
in stanza 7 of the Ode the emphasis is not so much upon the
creativeness of the wind, 'as upon the evils, torments and sorrows
which it appears to create'. He felt also that the stanza 'involved
the wish' that Coleridge would not intrude with *his* 'worse than
wintry Song' upon the blossoms and buds of Wordsworth's
spring-like creativeness.[3] I agree that the emphasis is upon the

[1] See p. 90 above.
[2] I am following here Mr Schulz's interpretation of the poem (Schulz,
203–4). [3] HH, 137, 165–6.

sorrows which the wind creates, but am doubtful about its relevance to Wordsworth. This storm-wind, which belongs with
desolate crags and inaccessible pine-groves, with the home of
witches rather than the trim 'dark-brown gardens and peeping
flowers' of domesticity, seems more like an emblem of the romantic furore, of the turbulent spirit associated with the Chatterton
cult and 'poète maudit' genius (a 'mighty Poet, e'en to *frenzy*
bold'), which, as we have seen, was always unfavourably disposed
towards the blossoms of the 'dell'.[1] This antipathy is reinforced
by the effect the wind produces on the Eolian harp—an emblem
once for the delights of sexual union with Sara (in addition to
being a One Life symbol). Now it produces 'a scream of agony
by torture lengthened out', and acts as an oblique reminder, possibly, of the domestic discord which was the background to the
poem. The frightful tales told by this 'Actor, perfect in all tragic
sounds' seem scarcely intelligible, except as representing the
shattering effect on Coleridge's domestic life of the disruptive
inclination of his thoughts.

After the nightmare thoughts of the child screaming in grief
and fear, the tone of the verse-letter drops to a lower register, as
Coleridge invokes 'gentle Sleep' to cover Asra with 'wings of
healing':

> 'Tis Midnight! and small Thoughts have I of Sleep.
> Full seldom may my Friend such Vigils keep—
> O breathe She softly in her gentle Sleep!
> Cover her, gentle sleep! with wings of Healing.
> And be this Tempest but a Mountain Birth!
> May all the Stars hang bright above her Dwelling,
> Silent, as though they *watch'd* the sleeping Earth!
> Healthful and light, my Darling! may'st thou rise
> With clear and chearful Eyes—
> And of the same good Tidings to me send! (216–25)

Placed as it is here, in contrast to the painful 'Vigils' which are
at present keeping Coleridge awake, the relevance of the passage
is obvious; we understand his reason for hoping that this tempest
may be 'but a mountain birth'. The problems posed by this particular line arise mainly because in the Ode the whole stanza in
which it appears has been moved from its original place in the
poem and stripped of its former context. Several leading theories

---

[1] See p. 151, note 1 above.

about this line are discussed by Mr Schulz, who offers a further explanation of his own—that Coleridge hoped that the storm might prove a very local disturbance, limited to his own side of Dunmail Raise and not extending to the Dove Cottage side where Asra is.[1] The interpretation of the passage may be arrived at with considerably less ingenuity, however, once the line is restored to its original context. It expresses the hope that now renunciation has been determined on Asra's honour may be restored and that he, on recovering the integratedness of his personality, will discover that his present discord (emblematized by the wind's destructiveness) will soon pass.[2]

Then in the verse-letter came more autobiographical material, enclosing some lines which were retained in the Ode, though greatly re-arranged.[3] Here it is the failure-of-imagination theme which comes to the fore, though now embedded in its proper context:

> And of the same good Tidings to me send! 225
> For oh! beloved Friend!
> I am not the buoyant Thing I was of yore
> When like an own Child, I to Joy belong'd:
> For others mourning oft, myself oft sorely wrong'd,
> Yet bearing all things then, as if I nothing bore! 230
>
> Yes, dearest Sara, yes!
> There *was* a time when tho' my path was rough,
> The Joy within me dallied with Distress;
> And all Misfortunes were but as the Stuff
> Whence Fancy made me Dreams of Happiness; 235
> For Hope grew round me, like the climbing Vine,
> And Leaves and Fruitage, not my own, seem'd mine!
> But now Ill Tidings bow me down to earth,
> Nor care I that they rob me of my Mirth—
> But Oh! each Visitation 240
> Suspends what nature gave me at my Birth,
> My shaping spirit of Imagination!

[1] Schulz, 201–6.

[2] I agree therefore with Humphry House and Florence Marsh (though on different grounds) that the line 'And may this storm be but a mountain-birth' ("Ode", 129) expresses Coleridge's hope that what seems terrible may prove to be a trifle. See "Coleridge: 'A Mountain-Birth'", *Notes and Queries*, II (1955), 261–2.

[3] See table, p. 247 above.

I speak not now of those habitual Ills
That wear out Life, when two unequal Minds
Meet in one House and two discordant Wills—   245
   This leaves me, where it finds,
Past Cure, and past Complaint,—a fate austere
Too fix'd and hopeless to partake of Fear!
But thou, dear Sara! (dear indeed thou art,
My Comforter, a Heart within my Heart!)   250
Thou, and the Few, we love, tho' few ye be,
Make up a World of Hopes and Fears for me.
And if Affliction, or distemp'ring Pain,
Or wayward Chance befall you, I complain
Not that I mourn—O Friends, most dear! most true!   255
   Methinks to weep with you
Were better far than to rejoice alone—
But that my coarse domestic Life has known
No Habits of heart-nursing Sympathy,
No Griefs but such as dull and deaden me,   260
No mutual mild Enjoyments of it's own,
No Hopes of its own Vintage, None O! none—
Whence when I mourn'd for you, my Heart might borrow
Fair forms and living Motions for it's Sorrow.
For not to think of what I needs must feel,   265
But to be still and patient all I can;
And haply by abstruse Research to steal
From my own Nature, all the Natural man—
This was my sole Resource, my wisest plan!
And that, which suits a part, infects the whole,   270
And now is almost grown the Temper of my Soul.

My little Children are a Joy, a Love,
   A good Gift from above!
But what is Bliss, that still calls up a Woe,
   And makes it doubly keen   275
Compelling me to *feel*, as well as *know*,
What a most blessed Lot mine might have been.
Those little Angel Children (woe is me!)
There have been hours when feeling how they bind
And pluck out the Wing-feathers of my Mind,   280
Turning my Error to Necessity,
I have half-wish'd they never had been born!
That seldom! but sad Thoughts they always bring,
And like the Poet's Philomel, I sing
My Love-song, with my breast against a Thorn.   285

With no unthankful Spirit I confess,
This clinging Grief, too, in it's turn, awakes
That Love, and Father's Joy; but O! it makes
The Love the greater, and the Joy far less.
These Mountains too, these Vales, these Woods, these
  Lakes,   290
Scenes full of Beauty and of Loftiness
Where all my Life I fondly hop'd to live—
I were sunk low indeed, did they *no* solace give;
But oft I seem to feel, and evermore I fear,
They are not to me now the Things, which once they were.

O Sara! we receive but what we give,   296
And in *our* life alone does Nature live . . .

It is difficult to make out a case for the full coherence of these
lines, Coleridge's attempt to analyse his problem being, for all its
honesty, self-contradictory and inconsistent. The wonder is, of
course, that he succeeded at all in diagnosing a condition which
by its very nature was an obstacle to detached analysis.[1] The
main difficulty lies in Coleridge's contention that his 'coarse
domestic Life' has known—

No Habits of heart-nursing Sympathy,
No Griefs but such as dull and deaden me,
No mutual mild Enjoyments of it's own,
No Hopes of its own Vintage, None O! none—
Whence when I mourn'd for you, my Heart might borrow
Fair forms and living Motions for it's Sorrow. (259–64)

This is to suggest that his married life had been an emotional
blank, a claim against which Mr Suther advances three objections. The subsequent lines about his children (272–85), Suther
argues, show that it had produced griefs which Coleridge felt
keenly ('Compelling me to *feel*'); the most obvious meaning of
lines 265–71 is that he was trying (by diverting himself into abstruse research) not to feel things he was forced by circumstances
to feel; and finally Coleridge contradicts himself in any case in
that 'he is repeatedly telling [Asra] in this letter that he cannot
feel what he ought to feel towards her'.[2]

[1] John Stuart Mill, who suffered a nervous breakdown not unlike Coleridge's, said in his *Autobiography* that parts of "Dejection: an Ode" 'exactly
describe my case' (see F. A. Cavenagh, *James and John Stuart Mill on Education*
(Cambridge, 1931), 120).
[2] Suther, 132 ff.

But is Coleridge's self-analysis quite so inconsistent as this suggests? It is true that the notion of *borrowing* 'fair forms' with which to express his feelings for Asra creates an unfortunate appearance of insincerity, while the line 'No Griefs but such as dull and deaden me' seems a complete self-contradiction, yet apart from this the general argument holds together. Mr Suther's last point, that Coleridge repeatedly tells Asra he cannot feel what he *ought* to feel towards her, may be confusing two different things. As I have shown, there is no mistaking the intensity of Coleridge's feelings for Asra, who he says is the 'Heart within my Heart' and whose small circle makes up 'a World of Hopes and Fears for me'. Admittedly, the 'living power' she has revived in him still does not enable him to feel the beauty of natural things, because his feelings are too much bound up with guilt. But his wish that Asra shall recover Joy seems a genuine example of feeling what he ought to feel for her.

This leads incidentally to a further important difference between the two versions of the poem. Originally, it was not 'afflictions' but 'Ill Tidings' that had suspended Coleridge's shaping spirit of Imagination (ll. 238–42). By 'Ill Tidings' he meant bad news concerning Asra, this phrase being closely linked with his earlier wish that once Asra had recovered peace of mind she would 'the same *good* Tidings to me send'. In the original poem therefore it was his realization of the injury he had done to Asra which had temporarily dislocated Coleridge's powers of creativity, whereas in the Ode the 'afflictions' which bow him down to earth have been transferred from Asra to himself and made to seem a permanent condition. Coleridge himself stressed that this temporary suspension of imaginative power was *not* connected with his unhappy married life, since he had been long accustomed to household discord:

> *I speak not* now of those habitual Ills
> That wear out Life, when two unequal Minds
> Meet in one House and two discordant Wills—
>   This leaves me, where it finds,
> Past Cure, and past Complaint. (243–7)

So far as his wife is concerned his married life *is* an emotional blank, whereas his relationships with Asra and his children provoke a maelstrom of tormented feelings—and it is these which have affected his creative powers.

Turning to the details of Coleridge's 'coarse, domestic life' it can be seen that the negation of feeling must apply solely to his relationship with his wife ('Coarse' could hardly include his 'Angel Children' who, as he admits, are still a source of love and joy). Lines 258–62 give a fairly accurate description of the Coleridges' day-to-day relationship in 1802. 'Heart-nursing' tenderness had long since died between them, they no longer had any 'mutual' pleasures or interests, and there seemed no prospect of any future improvement. A notebook entry written a year earlier indicates the sort of emotional impasse they had reached:

> Nothing affects her [his wife] with pain or pleasure as it is but only as other people will *say it is*—nay by an habitual absence of *reality* in her affections I have had an hundred instances that the being beloved, or the not being beloved, is a thing indifferent. . .
> I have dressed, perhaps washed, with her, & no one with us—all as cold & calm as a deep Frost . . .
> . . . Sara is uncommonly *cold* in her feelings of animal Love.[1]

It was true therefore that his relationship with Sara was an emotional blank; even their quarrels produced only apathy—'habitual Ills / That wear out Life . . . past Cure, and past Complaint'.

The repression of his feelings, begun as a temporary defensive mechanism, had become a chronic, almost unalterable habit. Consequently when (as now) Coleridge sought 'fair forms' as an objective correlative for private feelings, his coarse domestic life could provide no stimulus. Old stand-bys (like the Eolian harp, moon, and creative wind) all failed him, while outward forms could provide no satisfactory 'natural outlet' either. The feelings which the thought of Asra and his children had awakened in him since he settled down to write this poem however were genuine '*living* Motions', and because his heart has come alive to such feelings again there has been a notable advance from the dissonance described at the outset of the poem. His outward-turning concern for Asra and his children has proved therapeutic; he can now draw *some* solace from the natural beauties surrounding him, whereas earlier he had given up all hope of doing so:

> With no unthankful Spirit I confess,
> This clinging Grief, too, in it's turn, awakes
> That Love, and Father's Joy; but O! it makes
> The Love the greater, and the Joy far less.

[1] KC, 1, 979; cf. 1816, also p. 152 above.

> These Mountains too, these Vales, these Woods, these Lakes,
> Scenes full of Beauty and of Loftiness
> Where all my Life I fondly hop'd to live—
> I were sunk low indeed, did they *no* solace give;
> But oft I seem to feel, and evermore I fear,
> They are not to me now the Things, which once they were.
>
> (286–95)

There cannot be a full re-attunement yet, because the renunciation has still to be *enacted*—over a period of time and without repining or backsliding.

At present, the self-destructive guilt which has been inwardly corroding Coleridge, deadening his sensibility, is too ingrained to be easily obliterated. The lines about his alienation from his children, among the most terrible Coleridge ever wrote, show why even now he must doubt the return of creative power:

> My little Children are a Joy, a Love
>   A good Gift from above!
> But what is Bliss, that still calls up a Woe,
>   And makes it doubly keen
> Compelling me to *feel*, as well as *know*,
> What a most blessed Lot mine might have been.
> Those little Angel Children (woe is me!)
> There have been hours when feeling how they bind
> And pluck out the Wing-feathers of my Mind,
> Turning my Error to Necessity,
> I have half-wish'd they never had been born!
> *That* seldom! but sad Thoughts they always bring,
> And like the Poet's Philomel, I sing
> My Love-song, with my breast against a Thorn. (272–85)

This self-revelation, combined with the no less painful guilt for the injury he had done to Asra, provides the real clue surely to the present 'suspension' of Coleridge's creative powers. In these factors (carefully suppressed from the Ode) reside the emotional and moral disturbances which had precipitated his mental breakdown.

In the original version of the poem the great hymn to Joy came immediately after these lines about his children, thus emphasizing why the 'Grief' associated with them had put Joy beyond his own reach. By this earlier arrangement we could perceive more readily the full significance of the statement: 'Joy, that ne'er was given / *Save to the pure*, and in their purest Hour':

O Sara! we receive but what we give,   296
And in *our* life alone does Nature live
Our's is her Wedding Garment, our's her Shroud—
And would we aught behold of higher Worth
Than that inanimate cold World allow'd   300
To that poor loveless ever anxious Crowd,
Ah! from the Soul itself must issue forth
A Light, a Glory, and a luminous Cloud
Enveloping the Earth!
And from the Soul itself must there be sent   305
A sweet and potent Voice, of it's own Birth,
Of all sweet Sounds, the Life and Element.
O pure of Heart! thou need'st not ask of me
What this strong music in the Soul may be,
What and wherein it doth exist,   310
This Light, this Glory, this fair luminous Mist,
This beautiful and beauty-making Power!
Joy, innocent Sara! Joy, that ne'er was given
Save to the pure, and in their purest Hour,
Joy, Sara! is the Spirit and the Power,   315
That wedding Nature to us gives in Dower
    A new Earth and new Heaven,
Undreamt of by the Sensual and the Proud!
Joy is that strong Voice, Joy that luminous Cloud—
    We, we ourselves rejoice!   320
And thence flows all that charms or ear or sight,
All melodies, the Echoes of that Voice,
All Colors a Suffusion of that Light.

The philosophical implications of these lines, which were incor-
porated into stanzas 4 and 5 of the published Ode, have been
over-emphasized possibly at the expense of their autobiographical significance.

They are taken generally to express the opposition of the
imaginative reaching towards organic wholeness and the deep
delight at the centre of creative happiness (all of which I accept)
as against that inanimate cold world of those 'who regulate their
lives by the ruling mechanistic theology of eighteenth-century
society and its self-centred, utilitarian ethics'.[1] They have been
linked to the mechanist/vitalist controversy and seen as a counter-
blast to the influence of Descartes, Hobbes, Locke, Hume, and
David Hartley. They may also constitute, as I. A. Richards and

[1] See, for example, L. G. Salingar, op. cit., 200.

Marshall Suther have explained, a 'recantation' of Coleridge's earlier poetic beliefs, representing a protest on behalf of the 'projective' view to the exclusion of the 'realist' view of nature. Here Coleridge appears to repudiate his former faith in the influxes of nature, stressing now that 'in *our* life alone does Nature live', demanding activity on our part rather than mere receptivity as a prerequisite for interpenetration with nature.[1] There is evidence certainly of a swing towards projectivism, and yet there is an important sense in which these lines are entirely consistent with Coleridge's general thesis. He had always insisted that receptivity is not by itself sufficient for the influx of nature's spirit: man must also be 'wise and *pure*' for nature not to desert him. Only while integrity lasted could the heart be kept 'awake to Love and Beauty'.[2] The 'projective' theory in the *Dejection Ode* rests on the same assumption, demanding that the soul must be *morally* as well as emotionally integrated before it can be 'sent abroad'. Hence Joy is unattainable to the 'loveless ever anxious' crowd, and to the 'Sensual and the Proud'; it is given solely to the '*innocent*' and '*pure*', and to them only in their 'purest hour'.

In the original version of the poem this hymn to Joy served another function also, which is not apparent in the Ode. It showed Asra why, for his sake (as well as hers), renunciation was necessary. To recover creativity he must free himself from the guilt which was destroying his fitness to be a poet. As he put it later in the *Lay Sermon*, creativity demands a spontaneous exertion of *all* the poet's faculties, which a healthful 'wholeness' can alone promote:

> . . . that pleasurable emotion, that peculiar state and degree of excitement, which arises in the poet himself in the act of composition; —and in order to understand this, we must combine a more than ordinary sympathy with the objects, emotions, or incidents contemplated by the poet, consequent on a more than common sensibility, with a more than ordinary activity of the mind in respect of the fancy and the imagination. Hence is produced a more vivid reflection of the truths of nature and of the human heart, united with a constant activity modifying and correcting these truths by that sort of pleasurable emotion, which the exertion of all our faculties gives

[1] cf. Suther, 148 ff.
[2] cf. "This Lime-tree Bower My Prison", ll. 59–64, PW 181.

in a certain degree; but which can only be felt in perfection under the full play of those powers of mind, which are spontaneous rather than voluntary, and in which the effort required bears no proportion to the activity enjoyed.[1]

This is a clear statement of Coleridge's 'whole man' theory which, as my final chapter seeks to show, grew directly out of the personality disintegration he had himself experienced in 1802.

Originally, then, the poem was saying that not even Asra's inspiration could help him any longer. She could still activate his feelings, producing 'that peculiar state and degree of excitement' needed before creativity could begin, but the final effect of it all was hardly satisfying. When the storm-wind arrived it came in its other guise of moral chastiser,[2] demonstrating the impossibility at present of any real fusion with nature, and confronting Coleridge also with a dramatic representation of the injury he had done his child.[3] He might repine endlessly for what *might* have been had his children never been born, but in the end must accept his obligations to them as 'Necessity'. It is Asra therefore, not Hartley, whom he finally relinquishes (as formerly he had relinquished Mary Evans, his other Abyssinian maid), and thus he sings his love-song, like the Poet's Philomel, with his 'breast against a Thorn'. The unalterable 'Necessity' of repudiating his love for Sara is the sad personal theme masked over in *Dejection: an Ode*.

Finally, this hymn to Joy was intended to give Asra comforting reassurance. It led into the final verses where she is imagined as wholly exculpated from guilt and reinstated within the security of the Wordsworth circle. The stress upon her 'innocence' and 'sisterly' qualities and the complete identifying of her with the Grasmere circle, all reinforce this intention, thus atoning for the pain Coleridge had previously caused her when his 'Blessings *should* have call'd down Joy'. Now he calls down Joy for her, encouraging her to go to Wordsworth and find her happiness at Grasmere:

> Thou being innocent and full of love,   325
> And nested with the Darlings of thy Love,
> And feeling in thy Soul, Heart, Lips, and Arms
> Even what the conjugal and mother Dove,
> That borrows genial Warmth from those, she warms,

[1] LS, 10.   [2] See p. 90 above.   [3] See Schulz, 202.

T

Feels in the thrill'd wings, blessedly outspread—   330
Thou free'd awhile from Cares and human Dread
By the Immenseness of the Good and Fair
   Which thou seest everywhere—
Thus, thus, should'st thou rejoice!
To thee would all things live from Pole to Pole;   335
Their Life the Eddying of thy living Soul—
O dear! O Innocent! O full of Love!
A very Friend! A Sister of my Choice—
O dear, as Light and Impulse from above,
Thus may'st thou ever, evermore rejoice!   340

As Mr House remarked, the loss of the first part of this passage from inside the praise of 'joy' is perhaps the worst the Ode has suffered. It unites 'the physical and emotional in the mood of joy more concrete[ly] than anything retained in the public poem', and stands as a poignant contrast to his unhappiness about his own marriage.[1]

Both themes thus converged originally to end upon a note of Joy. Coleridge's decision to break with Sara Hutchinson was the only possible means of restoring 'Joy' to both of them. The question was: could he sustain his resolution? He tried hard to do so, making a genuine effort to improve his relationship with his wife. By July 1802 he was able to claim: '*At home all is Peace and Love*'.[2] He quoted the 'For not to think of what I needs must feel' stanza of the poem in a letter to Southey a few days later, and went on:

Having written these Lines, I rejoice for you as well as for myself, that I am able to inform you, that now for a long time there has been more Love & Concord in my House, than I have known for years before. I had made up my mind to a very aweful Step—tho' the struggles of my mind were so violent, that my sleep became the valley of the Shadows of Death / & my health was in a state truly alarming. It did alarm Mrs Coleridge—the thought of separation wounded her Pride—she was fully persuaded, that deprived of the Society of my children & living abroad without any friends, I should pine away—& the fears of widowhood came upon her— And tho' these feelings were wholly selfish, yet they made her *serious* —and that was a great point gained—[Coleridge digresses here into a discussion of their temperamental incompatibilities,[3] then continues:]—But as I said—Mrs Coleridge was made *serious*—and for the first time since our marriage she felt and acted, as beseemed

[1] HH, 135-6.   [2] CL, II, 820.   [3] Quoted, in part, p. 206 above.

a Wife & a Mother to a Husband, & the Father of her children—
She promised to set about an alteration in her external manners &
looks & language, & to fight against her inveterate habits of puny
Thwarting & unintermitting Dyspathy—this immediately—and to
do her best endeavors to cherish other *feelings*. I on my part promised to be more attentive to all her feelings of Pride, &c &c and
to try to correct my habits of impetuous & bitter censure—. We
have both kept our Promises—& she has found herself so much
more happy, than she had been for years before, that I have the
most confident Hopes, that this happy Revolution in our domestic
affairs will be permanent, & that this external Conformity will
gradually generate a greater inward Likeness of thoughts, & attachments, than has hitherto existed between us . . .[1]

The fragmentary remains of a recently-discovered letter which
Coleridge wrote to Asra in the following month indicate that he
was sticking to his resolution:

. . . —the black thick Cloud indeed is still over my head, and all the
Landscape around me is dark & gloomy with it's shadow—but the
wind has risen, Darling! it blows this way a strong & steady gale,
& I see already with the eye of confident anticipation the laughing
blue sky, & no black thick Cloud!—.[2]

The creative wind had indeed arisen again, for on 11 September
1802 Coleridge published his *Hymn Before Sunrise, in the Vale of
Chamouni*, a poem which, though partially plagiarized, suggests
that a return of moral confidence had led to a rediscovery of Joy:

O dread and silent Mount! I gazed upon thee,
Till thou, still present to the bodily sense,
Didst vanish from my thought: entranced in prayer
I worshipped the Invisible alone.

Yet, like some sweet beguiling melody,
So sweet, we know not we are listening to it,
Thou, the meanwhile, wast blending with my Thought,
Yea, with my Life and Life's own secret joy:
Till the dilating Soul, enrapt, transfused,
Into the mighty vision passing—there
As in her natural form, swelled vast to Heaven![3]

Unfortunately Coleridge could not sustain his resolution; it
was never remotely likely that he would. In the same week that

[1] CL, ii, 832–3.   [2] ibid, ii, 851.   [3] PW 377.

Hymn Before Sunrise, in the Vale of Chamouni appeared he also published *The Picture, or the Lover's Resolution,* a poem which, as we have seen, shows how a lover's resolution failed.[1] There were no more 'Joy' poems in 1803–4, only poems of anguish and self-pity. As he contemplated his unproductiveness he recalled, ironically, his resolve to win a 'Coronal':

> All Nature seems at work. Slugs leave their lair—
> The bees are stirring—birds are on the wing—
> And Winter slumbering in the open air,
> Wears on his smiling face a dream of Spring!
> And I the while, the sole unbusy thing,
> Nor honey make, nor pair, nor build, nor sing.
>
> Yet well I ken the banks where amaranths blow,
> Have traced the fount whence streams of nectar flow.
> Bloom, O ye amaranths! bloom for whom ye may,
> For me ye bloom not! Glide, rich streams, away!
> With lips unbrightened, wreathless brow, I stroll:
> And would you learn the spells that drowse my soul?
> Work without Hope draws nectar in a sieve,
> And Hope without an object cannot live.[2]

This sonnet was assigned by E. H. Coleridge to 1825, but its melancholy resignation surely belongs somewhere nearer to 1804.[3]

The 'happy Revolution' in Coleridge's domestic life did not prove permanent; hence his conviction grew that only a separation or the death of his wife could 'emancipate' his faculties.[4] After two years' exile in Malta he came back resolved on a separation, which Sara finally agreed to. Having secured this he turned at once to Asra, demanding:

> I know, you love me!—My reason knows it, my heart feels it / yet still let your eyes / your hands tell me / still say, o often & often say, My beloved! I love you / indeed I love you / for why should not my ears, and all my outward Being share in the Joy—the fuller my

---

[1] See pp. 39–40 above.

[2] PW 447. The parallels between this sonnet and Hopkins's "Thou art indeed just, Lord" were pointed out by Mr House. Hopkins's 'birds build—but not I build' (and 'send my roots rain') contrasts the fertility and life of nature with his own eunuch-like unproductiveness in a way that suggests he knew Coleridge's poem (HH, 139–40).

In a draft of this sonnet Coleridge wrote: I lost my object and my inmost All— / Faith *in* the Faith of THE ALONE MOST DEAR! (see Whalley, 134).

[3] cf. KC, II, 2070n.   [4] See p. 214 above.

inner Being is of the sense, the more my outward organs yearn &
crave for it / O bring my whole nature into balance and harmony.[1]

But he was now the husk of the man Asra had once loved: his
hair had turned white, and he was so ravaged by opium and
dropsy as to be scarcely recognizable—'alas! you will find me the
wretched wreck of what you knew me, rolling, rudderless'.[2] By
a strange twist of fate he met Mary Evans again in 1808, and each
was appalled at the change in the other.[3]

It was Asra who engrossed his thoughts however in 1806 and,
freed at last from family commitments, he set off for Coleorton,
where she was staying with the Wordsworths, his mind full of
ideas for a poem on the pleasures of sleeping 'cum amatâ'—with
the beloved.[4] But he found Asra's attitude changed and soon
became jealous of Wordsworth's ascendancy over her. His feelings, warped by repression, opium, and illness, induced morbid
delusions, so that he imagined on one occasion that he discovered
Asra in bed with Wordsworth.[5] Though he realized it must be
a delusion, he continued to brood on it, jealously imputing Asra's
change of heart to Wordsworth's influence:

W. [would instruct her] to withdraw herself from my affections.
Whither?—O agony! O the vision of that Saturday Morning—of
the Bed / —O cruel! is he not beloved, adored by two—& two such
Beings— / and must I not be beloved *near* him except as a Satellite?
—But O mercy mercy! is he not better, greater, more *manly*, &
altogether more attractive to any the purest Woman? . . .
W. is greater, better, manlier, more dear, by nature, to Woman,
than I—I—miserable I!—but does he—O No! no! no! no! he does
not—he does not pretend, he does not wish, to love you as I love
you, Sara! . . . I alone love you so devotedly, & therefore, therefore,
love me [Sara!—Sara!] love me![6]

This was the desperate pitch to which Coleridge's infatuation
finally brought him.

[1] KC, II, 2938. Sara finally agreed to a separation on 15 November 1806
(cf. KC, II, 2935); the above entreaty to Asra was written on 28 November
1806.

[2] CL, III, 22. Again, the voyage-image was peculiarly appropriate.

[3] Mary was upset by Coleridge's altered appearance, while he saw in her
'a counterpart of the very worst parts of my own Fate, in an exaggerated
Form' (her marriage was about to end as disastrously as his own). See CL,
III, 85–6, 91. Compare the 1795 and 1814 portraits of Coleridge on the end
papers of this book.

[4] KC, II, 2953.   [5] ibid, II, 2975.   [6] ibid, II, 3148; 2975n.

It was too late now for Asra to help Coleridge. Though, once, her love had stimulated his creative powers, the guilt and neurosis it subsequently induced had left scars which could not be erased. Coleridge and Asra came together in 1810 for one final venture—*The Friend*—she stimulating him to a scale of industry which overshadowed for a time even Southey's output. But, significantly, it was a work of *prose*. When this venture broke up it marked the end. Dorothy Wordsworth's comment on this parting, though lacking in insight into the true nature of Coleridge's feelings, showed that the relationship between Coleridge and Asra was finally ruptured. Dorothy confided to Mrs Clarkson:

> . . . I need not tell you how sadly we miss Sara [Asra], but I must add the truth that we are all glad she is gone. True it is she was the cause of the continuance of *The Friend* so long; but I am far from believing that it would have gone on if she had stayed. He was tired, and she had at last no power to drive him on; and now I really believe that *he* also is glad that she is not here, because he has nobody to teize him. His spirits have certainly been more equable, and much better. *Our* gladness proceeds from a different cause. He harassed and agitated her mind continually, and we saw that he was doing her health perpetual injury. I tell you this, that you may no longer lament her departure. As to Coleridge, if I thought I should distress you, I would say nothing about him; but I hope that you are sufficiently prepared for the worst. We have no hope of him. None that he will ever do anything more than he has already done. If he were not under our roof, he would be just as much the slave of stimulants as ever; and his whole time and thoughts, (except when he is reading and he reads a great deal), are employed in deceiving himself, and seeking to deceive others. He will tell me that he has been writing, that he *has* written, half a Friend; when I *know* that he has not written a single line. This Habit pervades all his words and actions, and you feel perpetually new hollowness and emptiness. Burn this letter, I entreat you. I am loath to say it, but it is the truth. He lies in bed, always till after 12 o'clock, sometimes much later; and never walks out. Even the finest spring day does not tempt him to seek the fresh air; and this beautiful valley seems a blank to him. He never leaves his own parlour except at dinner and tea, and sometimes supper, and then he always seems impatient to get back to his solitude. He goes the moment his food is swallowed. Sometimes he does not speak a word, and when he does talk it is always very much upon subjects as far aloof from himself, or his friends, as possible. The boys come every week, and he talks to them,

especially to Hartley, but he never examines them in their books.
He speaks of *The Friend* always as if it were going on, and would go
on; therefore, of course, you will drop no hint of my opinion. I
heartily wish I may be mistaken . . .

. . . do not think that it is his love for Sara which has stopped him
in his work. Do not believe it; his love for her is no more than a
fanciful dream. Otherwise he would prove it by a desire to make
her happy. No! He likes to have her about him as his own, as one
devoted to him, but when she stood in the way of other gratifica-
tions it was all over. I speak this very unwillingly and again I beg,
burn this letter. I need not add, keep its contents to yourself alone.[1]

Soon afterwards Coleridge separated from the Wordsworths too,
thus freeing himself from what Mr Griggs has called his 'servile
idolatry'.

The years that followed were years of anguish and broken
spirit. It is true that Coleridge's achievements as lecturer, literary
critic, philosopher, and historian of ideas during these latter years
hardly suggest that his later literary career was a failure, and
entitle him to a better image than the 'poor Coleridge' of legend.[2]
But after the crisis of 1802 the sap went out of his poetry. Perhaps,
as Mr Boulger suggests, this was due partly to Coleridge's 'failure
of emotional commitment' to the Christian doctrine which replaced the One Life philosophy.[3] It was due also to his recognition that he could not keep his private feelings aloof from poetry
as Wordsworth did. In December 1818 Coleridge wrote (and it
points, I think, to the true cause of his 'failure' as a poet):

—Poetry is out of the question. The attempt would only hurry
me into that sphere of acute feelings, from which abstruse research,
the mother of self-oblivion, presents an asylum.[4]

[1] E. de Selincourt, *The Letters of William and Dorothy Wordsworth, The Middle
Years, 1806–June 1811* (Oxford, 1937), I, 365–6.
[2] See G. Watson, "On Patronising Coleridge", *The Listener*, 24 October
1957.
[3] Boulger, 199.   [4] CL, IV, 893.

10

The Whole Man

Coleridge's theory that art and religious experience involve the 'whole soul of man' permeated his critical writings, and works like *Aids to Reflection* and *The Statesman's Manual*. In the theological studies published after his death[1] and in the scattered elements of his 'theory' of education, the 'whole man' concept is everywhere implicit.[2] *Biographia Literaria* contains perhaps the best-known formulation of the 'whole man' theory:

> The poet, described in *ideal* perfection, brings the whole soul of man into activity, with the subordination of its faculties to each other, according to their relative worth and dignity. He diffuses a tone and spirit of unity, that blends, and (as it were) *fuses*, each into each, by that synthetic and magical power, to which we have exclusively appropriated the name of imagination. This power, first put in action by the will and understanding, and retained under their irremissive, though gentle and unnoticed, controul (laxis effertur habenis) reveals itself in the balance or reconciliation of opposite or discordant qualities: of sameness, with difference; of the general, with the concrete; the idea, with the image; the individual, with the representative; the sense of novelty and freshness, with old and familiar objects; a more than usual state of emotion, with more than usual order; judgement ever awake and steady self-possession, with enthusiasm and feeling profound or vehement; and while it blends and harmonizes the natural and the artificial, still subordinates art to nature; the manner to the matter; and our admiration of the poet to our sympathy with the poetry...
>
> Finally, GOOD SENSE is the BODY of poetic genius, FANCY its DRAPERY, MOTION its LIFE, and IMAGINATION the SOUL that is every-

[1] S. T. Coleridge, *Confessions of an Inquiring Spirit*, edited from the Author's MS. by Henry Nelson Coleridge (London, 1840); S. T. Coleridge, *Notes on English Divines*, edited by the Rev. Derwent Coleridge, 2 vols. (London, 1853).
[2] See W. Walsh, *The Use of Imagination*, Ch. 3, "Coleridge and the Education of Teachers" (London, 1959).

where, and in each; and forms all into one graceful and intelligent whole.[1]

This notion of 'wholeness' is found in Coleridge's definition of poetry—

A mode of composition that calls into action and gratifies the largest number of the human Faculties in Harmony with each other, & in just proportions.[2]

—and also in his account of literary appreciation, in which he suggested that poetry should involve (what D. H. Lawrence later called) 'the whole man alive'. A writer should always be clear, said Coleridge, which 'faculties, or passions, or habits of mind' in the reader he intends to gratify,[3] but the greatest writers are those—like Shakespeare, Milton, Wordsworth, Jeremy Taylor, and Archbishop Leighton—who can compel the reader's whole being into sympathy:

The writer who makes me sympathise with his presentations with the *whole* of my being, is more estimable than the writer who calls forth and appeals to but a part of my being.[4]

This 'whole man' theory owed more, probably, to years of patient self-analysis on Coleridge's part than to anything he learnt from Schelling or Schlegel. Indeed, it is not too much to say that all that is most valuable and fruitful in Coleridge's theory had its roots in this private introspection, while its most characteristic defects—its rhapsodic, gnomic features and the puzzling switches from psychological to metaphysical premises—were the outcome either of Idealistic influences or of the difficulty he had in avoiding out-dated 'faculty' terminology.

Coleridge's claim, in the opening chapter of *Biographia Literaria*, that his critical theory had evolved only after a prolonged and intensive study of 'the component faculties of the human mind' was fully justified. As early as March 1798 he stated that he had 'for some time past' been patiently investigating 'Quid sumus, et quidnam victuri gignimur—What our faculties are and what they are capable of becoming'.[5] It was during the grave intellectual crisis of 1801, however, that the foundations of his later theory were laid. By the spring of that year he was criticizing

[1] BL, II, 12–13.   [2] MS. Notebook No. 18; quoted HH, 150.
[3] CL, II, 830.   [4] MC, 293; L, II, 640.
[5] CL, I, 397; and see BL, I, 14; CL, III, 30.

Locke for having failed to provide for the marriage of mind and emotion.[1] In September 1801 he rejected Hume's notion that our whole being consists of an aggregate of isolated sensations ('Who ever *felt* a *single* sensation?'), arguing that every sensation involves a 'blending & unifying of the sensations that inhere in the manifold goings on of the Life of *the whole man*'.[2] As early as October 1802 he deplored the 'Great Injury that has resulted [in neoclassic literary theory] from the supposed Incompatibility of one talent with another / Judgment with Imagination, & Taste— Good sense with strong feeling &c'.[3] In October 1803, mainly as the result of painful private experiences, he repudiated the Associationist psychology—holding that ideas are linked as much by recurrent states of feeling as by the mechanical principles favoured by Aristotle or David Hartley. With this discovery the basis of the 'whole man' theory was laid.

A word needs to be said about Coleridge's employment of faculty terms, on which he has been attacked somewhat unfairly.[4] He never underestimated the complexities of personality, but found himself severely limited by the crudity of the terminology available to him. He stated his problem thus:

> Consciousness, εἰμί, mind, life, will, body, organ)(machine, nature, spirit, sin, habit, sense, understanding, reason: here are fourteen words. Have you ever reflectively and quietly asked yourself the meaning of any one of these, and tasked yourself to return the answer in *distinct* terms, not applicable to any of the other words? . . . [If not] . . . can you wonder that the *Aids to Reflection* are clouds and darkness for you?—S.T.C.[5]

Coleridge spoke in terms of mental faculties because in that way it was easier for him to be understood; but the whole trend of his

---

[1] See KC, I, 921n.   [2] ibid, I, 979 (my italics); and cf. ibid, II, 2370.

[3] ibid, I, 1255. It will be noticed, however, that at the conclusion of the famous account in *Biographia Literaria* of what constitutes the 'whole soul of man' (quoted at the start of this chapter) Coleridge himself resorted to eighteenth-century neoclassic terminology.

[4] See J. V. Baker, *The Sacred River* (Louisiana State University Press, 1957), 215–17. Mr Baker, while agreeing that Coleridge's criticism was grounded in a 'whole man' psychology, yet holds that 'Coleridge remained old-fashioned in his attempt to retain *separate and sharply-defined* faculties' (my italics). Baker overlooks, I believe, the necessity imposed upon Coleridge to employ a familiar terminology by which he could more readily be understood.

[5] IS, 205–6.

thinking was, in reality, away from faculty psychology and towards a principle of totality of mind. Only trouble can result, he
maintained, from dividing the intellectual faculties. He ridiculed

> . . . the exquisite absurdity involved in the very notion of splitting
> the intellectual faculties, and subdividing the business of thought,
> almost as curiously as that of a pin factory—[1]

and was greatly amused when Spurzheim, the celebrated 'cranio-
logist', decided after examining the configuration of his skull that
Coleridge was deficient in imagination![2] A passage in *Table Talk*
best illustrates Coleridge's opposition to faculty psychology:

> . . . every intellectual act, however you may distinguish it by name
> in respect of the originating faculties, is truly the act of the entire
> man; the notion of distinct material organs, therefore, in the brain
> itself, is plainly absurd.[3]

He would have agreed with Jung that we are forced to use terms
like 'reason', 'memory', and 'feeling' because, however difficult
it may be to define these scientifically, they are nevertheless
current ideas in daily speech, perfectly accessible and compre-
hensible to everyone.[4]

It needs emphasizing that in laying the psychological foundations of his 'whole man' theory during 1801–4, Coleridge was
motivated primarily by anxieties about his own health, and that
initially this theory was not a matter of aesthetic or philosophical
concern. Even had Coleridge known at this time that John
Cooper's *Letters Concerning Taste* (1757) had made aesthetics a
matter for the whole man, or that the German *Bildungsroman*—
the novel concerned with the development of the entire, integral
personality—was already being developed in Goethe's *Wilhelm*

---

[1] S. T. Coleridge, *Essays on his Own Times*, ed. Sara Coleridge, 3 vols. (1850),
I, 188.

[2] IS, 416, note 27.

[3] *Table Talk*, 29 July 1830; cf. McDougall: 'All those specialised highly
developed forms of mental activity which are usually treated in text-books in
separate chapters on imagination, memory, conation, affection, association,
conception, judgment, comparing, reasoning, and so forth . . . all these functions are involved in the simplest mental acts' (William McDougall, *An Outline of Psychology* (London, 1926), 309).

[4] C. G. Jung, *Modern Man in Search of a Soul* (London, 1943), 102–3. Jung
adds: 'We can be sure that these expressions coincide with perfectly definite
psychic facts, no matter what the scientific definitions of these complex facts
may be.'

Meisters Lehrjahr (1786–1830), it is doubtful if he would have been more than mildly interested.[1] He knew of Abraham Tucker's *Light of Reason Pursued* (1768), another tentative 'whole man' formulation, and of the principle of the reconciliation of opposites developed by Jacob Boehme, but was less influenced by these probably than by Erasmus Darwin's *Zoonomia* (1794–6) because this bore specifically upon the question of the body–mind relationship.[2] One may infer Coleridge's unreadiness at this stage for philosophical or literary applications of the 'whole man' concept from his genuine astonishment in 1803 on encountering Kant's notion of mind as an organized manifold (in *Grundlegung zur Metaphysick der Sitten*):

> On the simplicity or manifoldness of the human Being? In what sense is it one? Sense, Appetite, Passion, Fancy, Imagination, Understanding, & lastly the Reason & Will?[3]

Yet the Kantian attempt to resolve the body–mind dualism undoubtedly stimulated Coleridge to widen the scope of his own inquiry. Characteristically, he attacked a philosophical standpoint with arguments furnished from his private psychological experience. Against Kant's notion that Will is synonymous with moral reason, Coleridge postulated (somewhat uncertainly) that moral evil originates in the sickly imaginings which 'denaturalised' feelings may produce in us. Kant's stringent conception of

---

[1] 'For taste does not wholly depend upon the natural strength and acquired improvement of the intellectual powers, nor wholly upon a fine construction of the organs of the body, nor wholly upon the intermediate powers of the imagination, but upon a union of them all happily blended, without too great prevalency in either' (sic)—John Gilbert Cooper, *Letters Concerning Taste*, 3rd edn. (London, 1757), 27.

In *Wilhelm Meister* Goethe traces one man's inward development and education. Meister says that his aim is 'to develop myself, exactly as I am' and to achieve the 'harmonious development of my nature'. Mignon, another character in the novel, represents the madness of discordant relationships. Cf. Roy Pascall, *The German Novel* (University of Manchester, 1956). Coleridge knew of Goethe's novel in 1818, by which time he had certainly become interested in its theme (see MC, 335).

[2] For further discussion of these and other possible influences upon Coleridge's theory see Baker, 90, 130; Alice D. Snyder, "The Critical Principle of the Reconciliation of Opposites as Employed by Coleridge", in *Contributions to Rhetorical Theory*, ed. F. N. Scott, Vol. IX (Ann Arbor, 1918); also Elisabeth Schneider, *Coleridge, Opium and Kubla Khan* (Chicago, 1953), 91–103.

[3] KC, I, 1712.

'Duty', Coleridge decided, had little relevance for a personality like his own, which seemed to exist wholly in 'streamy' imaginings. He thought Kant had underestimated the power of imagination, because of his inadequate grasp of psychology:—'Again and again, he is a wretched Psychologist'.[1]

After writing *Dejection: an Ode* (which had dealt with his own lack of 'wholeness') Coleridge became interested in the psychology of personality, hoping thereby to recover his own mental health. He was not thinking at this stage of poets like Shakespeare who bring the 'whole soul of man' into activity, but rather of the enviable self-integration of a personality like Poole's. His immediate need was to achieve, so far as was possible, 'that full possession of all our moral & bodily faculties' which makes for self-reliance and dignity.[2] Sometimes he doubted whether regeneration was possible, since his 'cowardice of all deep Feeling', his 'habit of bedrugging the feelings' with opium, and the ravages of psychosomatic illness had brought him to the edge of despair:

> . . . What is to be done—o what a question! Is then regeneration a mechanical or chemical process that can be performed by a direction / or a medicine that can be made by a Recipe? Even Prayer, the only external means, requires half the conquest to have been attained / Quere? does not the Soul repeat the *Vices* which it knows to be degrading & destructive, and really detests, in consequence of clinging to some *Passion*, which Reason—nay, of which it dreads to question its reason?[3]

Then, too, there was still the matter of Asra and his children. While his passion for Asra continued to consume him there seemed little hope of his acquiring that 'unity of Feeling' needed before he could exist 'wholly & as a whole man'.[4] His feelings needed to be 'co-adunated', not repressed and isolated.[5]

In spite of the resolution he had made in 1802 to break free from Asra he persisted in the hope that her love might regenerate him. He sought to convince himself, as we have seen, that in physical union with her he might find a spiritual exaltation.[6] But at bottom he knew that this was self-delusion:

> Würde, Worthiness, VIRTUE consist in the mastery over the sensuous & sensual Impulses—but Love requires INNOCENCE . . .

[1] ibid, I, 1770, 1833, and 1717.   [2] ibid, II, 1880, 2471.
[3] ibid, II, 2458; and cf. ibid, I, 1737; II, 2237; I, 1651.
[4] ibid, II, 2026, f. 6.   [5] ibid, II, 2357.   [6] See pp. 207–8 above.

Love in short requires an absolute Peace & Harmony between all parts of human Nature, such as it is; & it is offended by any War, tho' the Battle should be decided in favor of the worthier. This is perhaps the final cause of the *rarity* of true Love, and the efficient and immediate cause of its Difficulty. Ours is a life of Probation / we are to contemplate and obey *Duty* for its own sake, and in order to this we—in our present imperfect state of Being—must see it not merely abstracted from, but in direct opposition to the *Wish*, the *Inclination* / having perfected this the highest possibility of human nature, he may then with safety harmonize *all* his Being with this —he may love.

This notebook entry concluded with a beautiful sentence in which, sadly, Coleridge again resigned himself to his unalterable lot:

O [Asra]! gladly if my miserable Destiny would relax, gladly would I think of thee and of me, as of two Birds of Passage, reciprocaly [sic] resting on each other in order to support the long flight, the awful Journey.[1]

The thought of his children still lay heavily upon him, too:

June 7th 1806. O my Children!—Whether, and which of you are dead, whether any, & which among you, are alive, I know not / and were a Letter to arrive this moment from Keswick . . . I fear, that I should be unable to open it, so deep and black is my Despair —O my Children, my Children! I gave you life once, unconscious of the Life I was giving / and you as unconsciously have given Life to me. / . . . Even this moment I could commit Suicide but for you, my Darlings (of Wordsworths—of Sara Hutchinson / that is *passed* —or of remembered thoughts to make a Hell of /) O me! now racked with pain, now fallen abroad & suffocated with a sense of intolerable Despair / & no other Refuge than Poisons that degrade the Being, while they suspend the torment, and which suspend only to make the Blow fall heavier /.[2]

Coleridge's mind was now so 'fallen abroad' and disorganized that it was incapable of sustaining *any* resolution, his conduct being shaped entirely by expediency and circumstance. On returning to England from Malta he implored Asra to bring his '*whole nature* into balance and harmony'—still insisting that 'My hope and my joy on earth is Asra'.[3] The subsequent dashing of

[1] KC, ii, 2556. This passage throws further light on Coleridge's envy of Southey and Wordsworth (see p. 230 above).

[2] ibid, ii, 2860.   [3] ibid, ii, 2938, 3068 (my italics).

his hopes at Coleorton (discussed in my previous chapter) reduced him to despair again, showing once for all that Asra could
never be the means of restoring 'wholeness':

> My path becomes daily more rugged and mazy, a cloud dwells
> upon my eyes, my heart is sick, and hope is dead & ⟨yet⟩ the deep
> Yearning will not die, but lives & grows as in a charnel house—and
> all my Vitals are possessed by an unremitting Poison.[1]

That unity of feeling which constituted mental health seemed as
unattainable as ever. Again he felt self-imprisoned while, physically, his condition deteriorated:

> O tis a crazy tenement, this Body, a ruinous Hovel . . . My Fetters
> have eat in / the vital flesh Has grown up o'er them / the unwilling
> Gaoler Leaves with a scornful Laugh the fruitless Task To the per
> plex'd Chirurgeon.[2]

Long after it had become apparent that his love for Asra was not
reciprocated he was still powerless to do anything about it. Incapable of reasoning it away, he could only wait until it resolved
itself.[3]

During the Malta exile of 1804–6 Coleridge still nourished
hopes that 'nature' might somehow heal him; that natural restoratives would prove as beneficial as his pre-1802 poetry had
affirmed them to be. On the voyage out, consciously identifying
himself with his own Ancient Mariner (who 'in his loneliness and
fixedness yearneth towards the journeying Moon, and the stars
that still sojourn'), Coleridge discovered in the heavens above a
visible paradigm of the unity he craved for himself:

> O that Sky, that soft blue mighty Arch, resting on the mountains
> or solid Sea-like plain / what an aweful adorable omneity in unity.
> I know no other perfect union of the sublime with the beautiful,
> that is, so that they should both be felt at the same moment tho' by
> different faculties yet each faculty predisposed by itself to receive
> the specific modification from the other . . .[4]

But the old spontaneous attunement had gone for ever, and there
were clear signs now that his former joyous communion with
nature was breaking apart. The truth of his intuition that only
the souls of the 'pure in heart' may interfuse with outward forms
was being painfully corroborated. Now, when opportunities

---

[1] ibid, II, 3075; cf. 3149.   [2] ibid, II, 3189.   [3] ibid, II, 3231, f. 15v.
[4] ibid, II, 2346, and cf. 2344, 2045, f. 15.

arose for projective interpenetration, he could not take them:

Friday—Saturday 12—1 °clock / What a sky, the not yet orbed moon, the spotted oval, blue at one edge from the deep utter Blue of the Sky, a *mass* of *pearl*-white Cloud below, distant, and travelling to the Horizon, but all the upper part of the Ascent, and all the Height, such *profound* Blue, *deep* as a deep river, and deep in color... Unconsciously I stretched forth my arms as to embrace the Sky, and in a trance I had worshipped God in the Moon / the Spirit not the Form / I felt in how innocent a feeling Sabeism might have begun / O not only the Moon, but the depth of Sky!—the Moon was the *Idea*; but deep Sky is of all visual impressions the nearest akin to a Feeling / it is more a Feeling than a Sight / or rather it is the melting away and entire union of Feeling & Sight / And did I not groan at my unworthiness, & be miserable at my state of Health, its effects, and effect-trebling Causes? O yes!—Me miserable! O yes!—Have Mercy on me, O something *out* of me! For there is no *power*, (and if that *can* be, less *strength*) in aught *within* me! Mercy! Mercy!

Sat. Morn. 2 °clock, S.T.C.[1]

Again the obsessional nature of Coleridge's neurosis asserts itself in the conviction that he has no 'strength' to overcome it. This complaint was reiterated constantly: 'Who that thus lives with a continually divided Being can remain healthy!'[2] Yet few people can be cured of such a condition except with outside assistance. From the psychiatric point of view Coleridge was right to seek his cure in love or some larger concern outside himself. The truth was, unfortunately, that neither love, nature, nor least of all exile, could provide the cure he needed, which required a recovery of moral self-confidence and emotional security. His sole relief at this time was the consolatory pleasure he found in unburdening his mind to his private notebooks.[3] He was forced to accept in the end that (in his case, at any rate) nature was not the soothing healer he had formerly imagined, but a 'tough old witch' impervious to the appeals of the distempered mind:

In youth and early manhood the mind and nature are, as it were, two rival artists both potent magicians, and engaged, like the King's daughter and the rebel genii in the Arabian Nights' Entertainments, in sharp conflict of conjuration, each having for its object

[1] KC, II, 2453.   [2] See p. 293 below (my italics).
[3] cf. *Macbeth:* 'Give sorrow words: the grief that does not speak / Whispers the o'erfraught heart, and bids it break' (IV, 3).

to turn the other into canvas to paint on, clay to mould, or cabinet to contain. For a while the mind seems to have the better in the contest, and makes of Nature what it likes, takes her lichens and weather-stains for types and printers' ink, and prints maps and facsimiles of Arabic and Sanscrit MSS. on her rocks; composes country dances on her moonshiny ripples, fandangos on her waves, and waltzes on her eddy-pools, transforms her summer gales into harps and harpers, lovers' sighs and sighing lovers, and her winter blasts into Pindaric Odes, Christabels, and Ancient Mariners set to music by Beethoven, and in the insolence of triumph conjures her clouds into whales and walruses with palanquins on their backs, and chases the dodging stars in a sky-hunt! But alas! alas! that Nature is a wary wily long-breathed old witch, tough-lived as a turtle and divisible as the polyp, repullulative in a thousand snips and cuttings, integra et in toto. She is sure to get the better of Lady Mind in the long run and to take her revenge too; transforms our to-day into a canvas dead-coloured to receive the dull, featureless portrait of yesterday: not alone turns the mimic mind, the ci-devant sculptress with all her kaleidoscopic freaks and symmetries! into clay, but leaves it such a clay to cast dumps or bullets in; and lastly (to end with that which suggested the beginning) she mocks the mind with its own metaphor, metamorphosing the memory into a lignum vitae escritoire to keep unpaid bills and dun's letters in, with outlines that had never been filled up, MSS. that never went further than the title-pages, and proof sheets, and foul copies of Watchmen, Friends, Aids to Reflection, and other *stationary* wares that have kissed the publishers' shelf with all the tender intimacy of inosculation! Finis![1]

Finally, Coleridge turned to Spiritus Sanctus to give him the solace which neither love nor nature had provided. Religion, he decided, might be as much a 'friend' to the poet as philosophy is, by producing those two prime requisites—'tranquillity, & the attachment of the affections to *generalizations*'.[2] In God he might find the ultimate source of all unity—in 'Him, from whose absolute Unity all Union derives its possibility, existence, and meaning'.[3] He repudiated his passion for Asra therefore and committed himself wholly to God:

Father of Heaven . . . I loved, I deny it not, fleeting and fragile beauty, and abandoned that which is immortal. Heal, oh Lord,

[1] L, II, 742–3. Such a passage, incidentally, gives ample demonstration that Coleridge's imagination had not been 'destroyed' by the crisis of 1802.
[2] KC, II, 2194.   [3] ibid, II, 2600.

U

with loving affection, my fault of love! Listen to my prayers; Thou who art a Father, do not deny me pity.[1]

Nature was similarly dispensed with, since experience had shown its inadequacy as a source of moral regeneration: 'Life *begins* in detachment from Nature and ends in union with God.' Such union implied not a mystic annihilation of personality, he said, but, on the contrary, 'an *intension*, a perfecting of our Personality'.[2] Thus, Coleridge turned to faith and prayer as a means of regenerating 'the whole man', but in so doing he acknowledged the true motivation behind it, confessing himself to be

> ... neither fair nor saintly, but [one] who—groaning under a deep sense of infirmity and manifold imperfection—feels the want, the necessity, of religious support;—[one] who cannot afford to lose any the smallest buttress . . .[3]

In fact he subsequently recovered something like the inner harmony he yearned for, but not wholly nor even primarily (one suspects) as the result of the religious and philosophical studies he undertook during the latter years of his life. The 'whole Spiritual Man' which emerged as the goal of his speculations was almost entirely an intellectual abstraction.

As his interest shifted from literature to religion Coleridge tried for a time to reconcile imagination with reason. In *The Lay Sermon* (1816) and *Biographia Literaria* (1817) he postulated the need for a synthesis of the higher reason and imagination in the construction of suprasensible ideas.[4] But, gradually, he alluded less and less to the possibility of synthesizing these, and began to separate their functions, drastically reducing in the process the rôle he had formerly given to the creative imagination. Similarly, the emotional aspect of his 'whole man' theory was increasingly discounted while the pre-eminent alliance of reason, understanding, and will became a matter of bewildering intellectual complexity:

> Faith, that is, fidelity—the fealty of the finite will and the understanding to the reason, the light that lighteth every man that

[1] KC, II, 2871. This is a translation (supplied by Miss Coburn) of the original entry, which was a transcription of G. B. Guarini's *Cristiana compunzione*. As Miss Coburn points out, the selection of these lines for transcription was surely related to Coleridge's recent resolution in regard to Asra in KC, 2860 (see p. 286 above).

[2] MS. Notebook No. 36, f. 65; see Boulger, 150.

[3] S. T. C., *Confessions of an Inquiring Spirit*, pp. 3–4; Boulger, 171.

[4] Boulger, 105.

cometh into the world, as one with, and representative of, the absolute will, and to the ideas or truths of the pure reason, the super-
sensuous truths, which in relation to the finite will, and as meant to
determine the will, are moral laws, the voice and dictates of the
conscience;—this faith is properly a state and disposition of the
will, or *rather of the whole man*, the I, or finite will, self-affirmed.[1]

It was not this highly intellectualized 'faith' probably (any more
than Asra or nature) which promoted Coleridge's eventual recovery, but rather that under Dr Gillman's hospitable roof in
Highgate he at last found the security which had for so long
eluded him. He lived with this last of his 'sheet-anchors' from
1816 until his death in 1834, enjoying, apart from a regular
medical attention, the sympathy and affection which were more
important to his personal well-being than anything else.

Though Coleridge was doubtless grateful for whatever relief
physicians like James Gillman, Thomas Beddoes, or Joseph
Adams could provide for the effects of his opium-addiction and
his psychosomatic disorders, his real need was for a psychiatrist:

> . . . the habit of inward Brooding daily makes it harder to confess
> the Thing, I am, to any one—least of all to those, whom I most
> love & who most love me—& thereby introduces and fosters a habit
> of negative falsehood, & multiplies the Temptations to positive,
> Insincerity. O God! let me bare my whole Heart to Dr. B. or some
> other Medical Philosopher—.[2]

His own diagnosis of his condition was possibly more accurate
than, and his understanding of the psychology of personality
probably far in advance of, those of a 'Medical Philosopher' like
Dr Beddoes. Without the help of laboratory experimentation
Coleridge achieved an insight into personality-organization
which anticipated the modern Gestalt psychology, and which
bore interesting affinities with the homeostatic model upon which
a good deal of modern Adjustment Psychology is based.[3] Today,
'wholeness' or internal consistency of development is regarded
either as the characteristic norm of mental health, or as an un-

[1] S. T. C., *Notes on English Divines*, p. 90 (my italics); cf. S. T. C., *Confessions of an Inquiring Spirit*, p. ix.

[2] KC, II, 3078: 'Dr. B.' was probably Dr Thomas Beddoes (1760–1818) who is chiefly remembered now for his fostering of Humphry Davy's genius and his vivid presentation of the phenomena of disease.

[3] See G. W. Allport, *Personality, a Psychological Interpretation* (London, 1949), Ch. XIII; also Shaffer and Shoben, *The Psychology of Adjustment*.

realizable ideal. Psychologists are still not agreed upon this point. The former viewpoint is occasionally expressed in terms which seem like an up-to-date rendering of Coleridge's theory:

> If a branch of a tree is cut, new shoots spring out; if starfish are cut into two, each half will turn into a complete fish; if you injure your hand, all the forces of the blood are mobilized until that wound is healed and you are made whole. It is a law of nature. So it is psychologically, every individual has potentialities in his nature, all of which are not merely seeking their own individual ends, but each and all of which subserve the functions of the personality as a whole. Our personality as a whole, like every organism, is working towards its own fulfilment. That indeed is what we mean by mental health, which may be defined as the fulfilment of the whole personality by the release and co-ordination of all its potentialities.[1]

The second school holds that optimum 'wholeness' is unattainable because, inevitably, we develop certain qualities at the expense of others.[2] The point to notice here is that though the concept of 'wholeness' has long stood in the foreground of modern personality studies, it is still regarded as 'a new and poorly formulated problem in psychology . . . a many-sided issue whose solution lies yet in the future'.[3] Perhaps, after all, this is a matter in which literary insight may prove as valuable as experimentation.

We may turn now to Coleridge's theory of poetry itself, which seems to have evolved originally as a by-product of his search for mental health. During the period in which Coleridge was looking to Asra and nature for regeneration insights occurred from time to time by means of which the later literary theory was developed. In a notebook entry recorded during the voyage to Malta we discover an actual instance of how the later theory may have had its birth-pangs in the course of a sad analysis by the poet of his own condition:

> This Evening, or rather night, from $\frac{1}{2}$ past 8 to 11 I had genial feelings tho' not without an alloy of old Languor. But this is not the time—the barren sea, no related Mind, and a wearisome fickle Voyage / my limbs deprived of their natural motion, & my Stomach & Bowels controlled by an unkind influence—this is not the Time

[1] J. A. Hadfield, *Dreams and Nightmares* (Pelican, 1954), 109, 103.

[2] C. G. Jung, op. cit., 106, 127.

[3] See G. W. Allport, op. cit., 365, 562; also H. J. Eysenck, *Experiments in Motivation* (Oxford, 1964), 9.

for me to begin my aweful Duty of considering & investigating the
real state of my Health—what I have to hope, what to fear. Yet
my Voyage in rough weather from Hamburgh forces itself upon my
recollections painfully! Whither have my Animal Spirits departed?
My Hopes—O me! that they which once I had to check . . . should
now be an effort / Royals & Studding Sails & the whole Canvas
stretched to catch the feeble breeze!—I have many thoughts, many
images; large Stores of the unwrought materials; scarcely a day
passes but something new in fact or in illustration, rises up in me,
like Herbs and Flowers in a Garden in early Spring; but the combining Power, the power to do, the manly effective *Will*, that is
dead or slumbers most diseasedly—.[1]

Here his breakdown as a poet is expressly related to the state of
his mental health. The discovery that his 'diseased' condition has
impaired the 'genial' impulse leads on to the perception that art
demands a transcending of the personal, requiring some objective
correlative for the poet's private feelings:

Poetry a rationalized dream dealing [?] to manifold Forms our
own Feelings, that never perhaps were attached by us consciously to
our own personal Selves.—What is the Lear, the Othello, but a
divine Dream / all Shakespere, & nothing Shakespere . . .[2]

In this passage the germ of the later critical theory takes shape.
In a further entry of the same year (1804) there are signs of its
developing:

Idly talk they who speak of Poets as mere Indulgers of Fancy,
Imagination, Superstition, &c—They are the Bridlers by Delight,
the Purifiers, they that combine them with *reason* & order, the true
Protoplasts, Gods of Love who tame the Chaos.[3]

The 'Chaos' to be tamed by reason and order was, for Coleridge,
chiefly an internal matter. Despairingly, in 1805, he compared
his own failure as an artist with that of 'sots' like Henderson,
Collins, and Boyse, whose sensibilities, he alleged, had been destroyed by dissipation:

. . . all the realities about me lose their natural *healing* powers . . .
Who that thus lives with a continually divided Being can remain
healthy! ⟨And who can long remain body-crazed, and not at times
use unworthy means of making his Body the fit instrument of his
mind? Pain is easily subdued compared with continual uncomfort-

---

[1] KC, II, 2086 (and cf. II, 2279).   [2] ibid, and cf. ibid, II, 2194.
[3] ibid, II, 2355.

ableness—and the sense of stifled Power!—O this is that which made poor Henderson, Collins, Boyce, &c &c &c—*Sots!*—awful Thought—O it is horrid!—Die, my Soul, die!—Suicide—rather than this, the worst state of Degradation! It is less a suicide! S.T.C.⟩ —I work hard, I do the duties of common Life from morn to night / but verily—I raise my limbs "like lifeless Tools"—The organs of motion & outward action perform their functions at the stimulus of a galvanic fluid applied by the *Will*, not by the Spirit of Life that makes Soul and Body one . . .[1]

Coleridge's notion of the poet in '*ideal* perfection' who brings the 'whole soul of man' into activity, was thus the exact antithesis of Coleridge himself at this time—'body-crazed' and continually 'divided', as he was.

During the next two years the notebooks were devoted largely to intimate, personal items, and the development of the critical theory seems to have been suspended until, late in 1807, the following entry appeared in which the thesis of the 1818 essay *On Poesy or Art* is embryonically detectable. In the manuscript this passage is tortured with corrections, indicating the struggle Coleridge had at this time to formulate the matter accurately:

> Love will vent his inmost and veriest Griefs in sweet and mea-sured [sounds] is it that—a divine Joy being its end it will not utter even its woes and weaknesses, sorrows & sicknesses, except in some form of pleasure? pleasure the shadow & sacramental Type of that Joy (which by union fit et facit et creat et creatur) or is it rather, that its essence being a divine synthesis of highest reason—and ve-hementest Impulse, it must needs the soul in its two faculties, or perhaps of the two souls, vital power of Heat, & Light of Intel-lect—attract & combine with poesy, whose essence is passionate order.[2]

Coleridge never adduced his own poetry in support of his critical theory yet, as we have seen, he had himself always attempted to objectify his private 'woes and weaknesses' in pleasing aesthetic form. His revisions of the original draft of *Dejection: an Ode* are a case in point—a poem in which he was 'able to derive, and to

---

[1] KC, II, 2557. For fuller biographical details concerning John Henderson (1757–88), William Collins (1721–59), and Samuel Boyse (1708–49), each of whom, Coleridge alleged, died prematurely from dissolute causes, see KC, II, 2557n. (The allusion here to "The Ancient Mariner" is a further indication of Coleridge's self-identification with his Mariner during 1804.)

[2] ibid, II, 3092.

impart, aesthetic pleasure from the very emotion aroused by his *own* inability to experience aesthetic pleasure'.[1]

Coleridge's account in *Biographia Literaria* of what ideally constitutes the 'whole soul' of the poet gives little indication unfortunately of the detailed psychological scheme which lay behind it. He nowhere elaborated this scheme comprehensively, but left various clues to its elements scattered about in miscellaneous contexts. A notebook entry gives the clearest single formulation of these elements, holding that reason, judgment, fancy, imagination, the senses and sensations are the chief constituents of the poetic genius,[2] but it is clear from what is said elsewhere that 'will' and the unconscious mind were intrinsic elements too. Coleridge's famous distinction between fancy and imagination was, by the way, never intended to dissever these 'faculties', but designed purely to differentiate two distinct modes of mental activity. In the last analysis fancy and imagination have a *complementary* function in creative activity.[3] For purposes of philosophical analysis we *must* separate and distinguish the components of mind, but having done so, he said, 'we must then restore them in our conceptions to the unity, in which they actually co-exist'.[4]

Within the totality of the 'whole man' organization the basic relationship between imagination and feeling is all-important. Will is, so to speak, the self-starter in the processes of artistic creativity, that which originates activity by summoning the forces of personality and directing them to a common aim,[5] but, thereafter, feeling becomes the dynamic, sustaining force. The 'property' of passion is not to create (which is the work of the imagination) 'but to set in increased activity'.[6] We have seen how, in poems like *Frost at Midnight* and the original version of *Dejection: an Ode*, feeling provided the stimulus for the imaginative activity. It is feeling above all which energizes fresh associations of ideas and, consequently, 'the blending, *fusing* power of Imagination and Passion' has paramount status in Coleridge's theory of poetry.[7] He interpreted 'feeling' in the widest sense, including bodily sensation as well as emotional states within the

---

[1] See A. O. Lovejoy, "Coleridge and Kant's Two Worlds", *Journal of English Literary History*, VII (1940), 350.

[2] See HH, 150.   [3] See BL, I, 194; *Table Talk*, 20 August 1833.

[4] BL, II, 8.   [5] IS, 131.   [6] BL, II, 42.   [7] ibid, II, 123.

synthesis of imagination and feeling. It is strange that Coleridge should have been accused of having neglected the importance of the body–mind relationship when, as we have seen, he was almost fatally obsessed with it. His view was that there is 'a mutual action of the imagination upon the nervous system and [of] the nervous system upon the imagination'.[1] It was precisely because his own creative imagination lay so much at the mercy of every vicissitude of emotion and sensation that Coleridge was so concerned about their general relationship: 'O strange is the self-power of the imagination—when painful sensations have made it their interpreter'.[2]

Hardly less important to Coleridge's theory of creative activity is the part played by the unconscious mind, another matter on which he has been seriously misrepresented.[3] Against Hobbes's claim that imagination and memory are but '*decaying* sense' Coleridge postulated that all thoughts are 'imperishable', so that the unconscious contains 'the collective experience of our whole past existence'—a view which closely resembles Freud's.[4] All our past images and ideas survive, he said, in a state of 'shadowy half-being', having a 'nascent Existence in the Twilight of Imagination, and just on the vestibule of Consciousness'.[5] Unlike so many of his predecessors, Coleridge did not regard the unconscious simply as a storage tank, but recognized that within the 'deep well' the forces of the unconscious themselves actively engage in modifying, re-arranging, and reshaping their materials:

> For a Thing at the moment is but a Thing of the moment / it must be taken up into the mind, diffuse itself through the whole

---

[1] PL, 239–40; and see pp. 221–2 above. J. V. Baker remarks that Coleridge's 'high-flying transcendental theory of imagination failed sufficiently to, though it did partly, take account of the physiological basis of the mind' (op. cit., 225). The weakness of this view is that it ignores all the evidence to the contrary which may be found in Coleridge's notebooks and private correspondence.

[2] MC, 199.

[3] I refer again to Mr Baker's examination of Coleridge's 'whole man' psychology which, it seems to me, gravely misrepresents the facts. Baker alleges that Coleridge 'seriously underestimated the power of memory and the "deep well" to effect a sea change. For a man who profited by it so much, [Coleridge] was strangely ungracious concerning the alchemy of the unconscious' (op. cit., 227).

[4] BL, I, 79–80.   [5] CL, II, 814.

multitude of Shapes and Thoughts, not one of which it leaves un-
tinged, between [not one of] which and it some new Thought is
not engendered.[1]

This unconscious activity is an essential part of artistic creativity
—'there is in genius itself an unconscious activity; nay, that is
the genius in the man of genius'.[2] After the conscious will takes a
hand, therefore, it builds upon processes already initiated, establishing a purposive '*centre*' for them, 'a sort of nucleus in the reservoir of the soul', towards which various clusters of images are
drawn from all sides.[3] With the intervention of the conscious will,
the creative imagination and judgment are likewise summoned
into action, and reason and order are imposed upon chaos as the
poetic imagination goes to work—idealizing and unifying; dis-
solving, diffusing, and dissipating in order to re-create. Thus,
conscious and unconscious imaginative activity are complementary and are both indispensable in artistic creation, just as fancy
and imagination, reason and understanding, are.

Perhaps the main source of difficulty in Coleridge's theory is
the uncertainty we are left in regarding the precise relationship
between imagination and reason. Sometimes imagination is
made to appear altogether inferior to reason (*The Statesman's
Manual* suggests, for instance, that reason *comprises* sense, understanding, and imagination[4]), whereas in *Biographia Literaria* the
'synthetic and magical power' of imagination seems all-important. This confusion may have arisen because, as we have seen,
Coleridge himself seemed uncertain whether art or religion constituted the higher end of the 'whole man's' endeavour. Broadly,
he tended to make art a matter more of emotion, imagination,
and judgment than of the higher reason (which he reserved on
the whole for ethical and religious matters). He retained, for
example, the supervisory function of 'judgement' in poetry much
as the neoclassicists had done, insisting that poetry is a matter
of 'studied selection and artificial arrangement', that imagery
must never be disproportionate to the matter, and that metaphors ('tricksy companions') should always be examined 'by the
stronger light of reflection'. He was fond of drawing attention to
Shakespeare's and Milton's excellent judgment, arguing very

[1] KC, I, 1597. [2] *On Poesy or Art*, in BL, II, 258.
[3] See A. Turnbull, *Biographia Epistolaris*, II, 182.
[4] *The Statesman's Manual*, Appendix C, xii.

much in the eighteenth-century manner.[1] He was never prepared to make quite the claims for imagination that, say, Blake or Shelley did. Nevertheless, his was a much more exalted view of creative imagination than anything to be found in neoclassical theory. Precisely because of the 'wild and lawless' overtones which imagination had acquired from the work of writers like Dryden (and the medieval schoolmen), and because he himself associated it so closely with the vicissitudes of ordinary feeling, Coleridge was concerned to discover general principles, or laws, for governing its operations.

The laws which he specified for the imagination were not laws imposed authoritatively from *without*, but such as the stringent self-discipline entailed in realizing inchoate ideas in poetic form necessitates:

—The spirit of poetry, like all other living powers, must of necessity circumscribe itself by rules, were it only to unite power with beauty. It must embody in order to reveal itself; but a living body is of necessity an organized one; and what is organization but the connection of parts in and for a whole, so that each part is at once end and means? . . .

No work of true genius dares want its appropriate form, neither indeed is there any danger of this. As it must not, so genius cannot, be lawless; for it is even this that constitutes its genius—the power of acting creatively under laws of its own origination.[2]

In Coleridge's theory, therefore, imagination is both inner-directed (by the laws of its own constitution) and other-directed (by being kept under the supervision of the poet's judgment). In practice, these processes occur almost simultaneously, as part of the totality of action by which the 'whole soul' of man is brought into activity.

Essentially, the function of imagination is to modify ideas and images, a function it performs in close collaboration with feeling:

It has been before observed that images, however beautiful, though faithfully copied from nature, and as accurately represented in words, do not of themselves characterise the poet. They become proofs of original genius only as far as they are modified by a predominant passion; or by associated thoughts or images awakened by that passion . . .[3]

---

[1] BL, II, 11, 109; IS, 403; *Table Talk*, 5 April 1833.   [2] LS, 45–6.
[3] BL, II, 16.

Coleridge gave clues as to the various modes of modification: for example, one image or feeling can be made to modify several others, and by a sort of fusion to force many into one; in drama especially, many circumstances may be combined in one moment of consciousness; a succession of images may be reduced to a 'oneness'; inanimate objects may have impressed upon them the 'stamp of humanity' and human feelings; or the power may act in such a way that the reader loses all consciousness of the words of a poem, while their over-all meaning flashes upon his inward eye.[1] Whatever mode it employs, the imagination always modifies so as to give unity to variety, for to unify and to create are its essential functions. This is *'the great law'* of the imagination— 'that a likeness in part tends to become a likeness of the whole'.[2] The new unities it forms are original in the sense that they idealize the details of common experience, restoring these as the objects of wonder they are to the eyes of a child. Thus, the imaginative activity consists in

—spreading the tone, the *atmosphere*, and with it the depth and height of the ideal world around forms, incidents, and situations, of which, for the common view, custom had bedimmed all the lustre, had dried up the sparkle and the dew drops.[3]

This presupposes an exceptional sensibility in the poet, a Wordsworthian (or child-like) capacity for participating in the universal:

. . . all genius exists in a participation of a common spirit. In joy individuality is lost and it therefore is liveliest in youth, not from any principle in organization, but simply from this that the hardships of life, that the circumstances that have forced a man in upon his little unthinking contemptible self, have lessened his power of existing universally.[4]

This passage provides apt comment on the theme of *Dejection: an Ode*, explaining both why Coleridge's own children were a 'joy' to him and why the 'circumstances' which had forced him 'in upon' himself had lessened his own power for existing universally. It indicates yet again how closely Coleridge's theory of poetry was tied to his own past experience. Many of his exemplifications of how the 'great law' of imagination operates had their origins in the speculations he had made about 'the One and the Many' during the voyage to Malta.[5]

[1] LS, 39–40.   [2] *The Friend*, I, 247–8.   [3] BL, I, 59.   [4] PL, 179.
[5] e.g. KC, II, 2151, 2344, 2356, et alia.

To be capable of universalizing its materials thus, imagination must fuse not just with feeling but also with reason, and conversely, without imagination, the intellect is limited:

> The completing power which unites clearness with depth, the plenitude of the sense with the comprehensibility of the understanding, is the imagination, impregnated with which the understanding itself becomes intuitive, and a living power.[1]

The highest truths, Coleridge argued, can be presented only through images or symbols; indeed, without such symbols the apprehension of suprasensible ideas would be impossible.[2] Thus, in the highest genius imagination and reason are interdependent and, though all of us think to some extent by symbols, 'the strongest minds possess the most vivid Symbols in the Imagination'.[3] God is known to us only by symbols, a theory Coleridge had propounded in early poems like *Religious Musings* and *The Destiny of Nations*:

> For what is Freedom, but the unfettered use
> Of all the powers which God for use had given?
> But chiefly this, him First, him Last to view
> Through meaner powers and secondary things
> Effulgent, as through clouds that veil his blaze.
> For all that meets the bodily sense I deem
> Symbolical, one mighty alphabet
> For infant minds; and we in this low world
> Placed with our backs to bright Reality,
> That we may learn with young unwounded ken
> The substance from its shadow.[4]

The poet therefore seeks his symbols in nature, and the finding of some appropriate 'outward' symbol brings relief to the labouring mind as it struggles to idealize and unify—'a relief, which the spirit of man asks and demands to contemplate in some outward symbol of what it is inwardly solemnizing'.[5] In its original version *Dejection: an Ode* showed how, once neurosis had disrupted the alliance of imagination and reason by forcing the intellect too much 'in upon' itself, the poet wooed outward symbols in vain for some 'fair form' in which to express his needs.

Because his own breakdown as a poet had coincided with a

---

[1] *The Statesman's Manual*, Appendix C, xi–xii.   [2] PL, 169; BL, I, 100.
[3] Notebook 21½, p. 19; Add. MSS. 47519.
[4] "The Destiny of Nations", ll. 13–23, PW 132.   [5] L, II, 721.

partial disintegration of his personality it was natural perhaps that Coleridge should esteem 'wholeness' as indispensable to creativity. In later life he was fond of distinguishing 'genius' from 'talent' in terms of a psychological distinction between 'whole' and what he called 'pollarded', personalities. Thus, Don Quixote personified for him reason and moral sense divested of judgment and understanding, whereas Sancha Panza exemplified common sense without reason or imagination.[1] Southey, Cowley, Landor, Crabbe, Gray, and Scott, because deficient in 'high imagination', were pollarded poets in Coleridge's view.[2] A person like Archbishop Leighton, on the other hand, possessed a basic 'wholeness' of character, which was reflected in the quality of his writing:

> Leighton had by nature a quick and pregnant fancy, and the august objects of his habitual contemplation, and their remoteness from the outward senses, his constant endeavour to see or to bring all things under some point of unity, but, above all, the rare and vital union of head and heart, of light and love, in his own character,—all these working conjointly could not fail to form and nourish in him the highest power, and more akin to reason, the power, I mean, of imagination.[3]

This is not to say that *any* balanced personality is capable of creative work for, in Coleridge's view, genius is always given, never acquired. Poole, for all his balanced integrity of being, could never have written literary work of any consequence. Nevertheless, it is implicit in Coleridge's theory that the writer who has 'by nature' a well-adjusted personality starts at a distinct advantage. It was partly because Wordsworth's was naturally a 'homogeneous' character that Coleridge expected so much of him:

> . . . [Wordsworth] is a happy man, because he is a Philosopher— because he knows the intrinsic value of the Different objects of human Pursuit, and regulates his Wishes in Subordination to that Knowledge—because he feels, and with a *practical* Faith . . . that we can do but one thing well, & that therefore we must make a choice—he has made that choice from his early youth, has pursued

[1] MC, 102.
[2] These, and similar judgments on various genres of literature which Coleridge felt to be deficient in 'high imagination', are repeated almost ad nauseam in *Table Talk* and the *Miscellaneous Criticism*.
[3] L, II, 718–19.

& is pursuing it—and certainly no small part of his happiness is owing to this Unity of Interest, & that Homogeneity of character which is the natural consequence of it—& which that excellent man, the Poet Sotheby, noticed to me as the characteristic of Wordsworth. Wordsworth is a Poet, a most original Poet . . . and I dare affirm that he will hereafter be admitted as the first & greatest philosophical Poet—the only man who has effected a compleat and constant synthesis of Thought & Feeling and combined them with Poetic Forms, with the music of pleasurable passion and with Imagination or the *modifying* Power . . .[1]

When Wordsworth's eagerly awaited *Excursion* failed to live up to these expectations Coleridge criticized it, but not altogether fairly. He measured the poem against a preconceived ideal of what he thought it *should* have contained, and was disappointed that it had not achieved a synthesis and reconciliation of philosophy and religion such as he himself was seeking.[2] Such a task was beyond Wordsworth's scope and belonged more properly to Coleridge's province. It was from this time onwards however that Coleridge began to find defects in Wordsworth's work—never deviating from his admiration for Wordsworth's over-all pre-eminence among contemporary writers, but obviously feeling that Wordsworth had failed to achieve his full potentialities. His work did not reveal the 'whole man' in action as consistently as Shakespeare's did.[3]

This change of attitude with regard to Wordsworth prompts some important questions concerning Coleridge's theory. If even philosopher-poets are not always 'whole', then who are the poets who 'in ideal perfection' bring the 'whole soul of man' into activity? Were 'pollarded' poets like Southey, Cowley, Crabbe, and Gray never 'whole' at any time? Gray, after all, took ten years to write his *Elegy*. Since Coleridge speaks exclusively of poets in this connection what would he have made of D. H. Lawrence's contention that only *novelists* 'can make the whole man alive tremble'? Lawrence argued:

> The novel is the one bright book of life. Books are not life. They are only tremulations on the ether. But the novel as a tremulation can make the whole man alive tremble. Which is more than poetry,

---

[1] CL, II, 1033–4.   [2] ibid, IV, 574–5.

[3] For further discussion of this point, see R. H. Fogle, *The Idea of Coleridge's Criticism* (University of California Press, 1962), Chapters 5, 6.

philosophy, science or any other book-tremulation can do. . . Plato makes the perfect ideal being tremble in me. But that's only a bit of me. Perfection is only a bit in the strange make-up of man alive. The Sermon on the Mount makes the selfless spirit of me quiver. But that too is only a bit of me. The Ten Commandments set the old Adam shivering in me, warning me that I am a thief and a murderer, unless I watch it. But even the old Adam is only a bit of me. I very much like all these bits of me to be set trembling with life and the wisdom of life. But I do ask that the whole of me shall tremble in its wholeness some time or other. . . [Novels] in their wholeness affect the whole man alive, which is the man himself beyond any part of him. They set the whole tree trembling with a new access of life, they do not just stimulate growth in one direction.[1]

Lawrence's belief that 'whole man' integration comes only *intermittently* is extremely important (though here it has to do more with 'response' than actual creative writing). It leads us to ask whether the artist's 'wholeness' is, or need be, a static equilibrium (like Poole's), or whether it is not the act of creativity itself which makes a man 'whole'. Is 'wholeness' a mark of maturity, in other words, or is it achieved only during the excitement of creativity?

Coleridge touches on this question in Chapter xv of *Biographia Literaria*, where he analyses Shakespeare's *Venus and Adonis* and *The Rape of Lucrece* with a view to discovering what these early works reveal of Shakespeare's potentialities. The point is made incidentally that genius is always in some sense given ('poeta nascitur non fit'). Both poems, Coleridge decided, were proofs of the present '*immaturity* of Shakespeare's genius'. Yet, already, a powerful synthesis of imagination, passion, depth and energy of thought was evident, suggesting that at the actual time of composition Shakespeare's imagination was functioning within a fully integrated personality. The conclusion arrived at is that, though eventually Shakespeare matured as a 'whole man', he could from the beginning bend all his potentialities to the achievement of one common purpose in the act of creativity:

. . . No man was ever yet a great poet, without being at the same time a profound philosopher. For poetry is the blossom and the fragrancy of all human knowledge, human thoughts, human passions, emotions, language. In Shakespeare's *poems* the creative power and the intellectual energy wrestle as in a war embrace.

[1] D. H. Lawrence, *Selected Literary Criticism*, ed. Anthony Beale (1955), 105.

Each in its excess of strength seems to threaten the extinction of the other. . . The *Venus and Adonis* did not perhaps allow the display of the deeper passions. But the story of Lucretia seems to favor and even demand their intensest workings. And yet we find in Shakespeare's management of the tale neither pathos, nor any other *dramatic* quality. There is the same minute and faithful imagery as in the former poem, in the same vivid colors, inspirited by the same impetuous vigor of thought, and diverging and contracting with the same activity of the assimilative and of the modifying faculties; and with a yet larger display, a yet wider range of knowledge and reflection; and lastly, with the same perfect dominion, often *domination*, over the whole world of language. What then shall we say? even this; that Shakespeare, no mere child of nature; no automaton of genius; no passive vehicle of inspiration possessed by the spirit, not possessing it; first studied patiently, meditated deeply, understood minutely, till knowledge, become habitual and intuitive, wedded itself to his habitual feelings, and at length gave birth to that stupendous power, by which he stands alone . . .[1]

It appears from this that Coleridge would have agreed substantially with T. S. Eliot that 'maturing as a poet means maturing as the whole man'.[2] We recall his earlier contention that 'there is no profession on earth, which requires an attention so early, so long, or so unintermitting as that of poetry'; twenty years' preparation would be needed, he said, before one could begin to write an epic poem. He laid great emphasis always on the essential depth of Shakespeare's thinking:

The body and substance of his works came out of the unfathomable depths of his own oceanic mind: his observation and reading, which was considerable, supplied him with the drapery of his figures.[3]

Nevertheless, as the analysis of Shakespeare's early work had shown, the act of creativity could itself induce a momentary 'wholeness', even before the personality had matured. This point is important, as otherwise we are left with the discouraging thought that 'wholeness' exists only as a static, and somewhat implausible, ideal.

In all Coleridge's major 'whole man' pronouncements the

[1] BL, II, 19–20.
[2] T. S. Eliot, "The Poetry of W. B. Yeats", in *Selected Prose* (Penguin, 1953), 199.
[3] BL, I, 32; *Table Talk*, 15 March 1834; LS, 37.

poet's need actually to *bring* his 'whole soul' into activity is emphasized, as here:

> Give to a subtle man fancy, and he is a wit; to a deep man imagination, and he is a philosopher. Add, again, pleasurable sensibility in the threefold form of sympathy with the interesting in morals, the impressive in form, and the harmonious in sound,— and you have the poet.

> But combine all,—wit, subtlety, and fancy, with profundity, imagination, and moral and physical susceptibility of the pleasurable,—*and let the object of action be man universal*; and we shall have— O, rash prophecy! say, rather, we have—a SHAKESPEARE![1]

That is to say, it is the poet's actual response to the challenge of artistic purpose which produces the harmonious inner balance. Though art demands finally an aloofness of the poet's own feelings (expressed in his choosing subjects 'very remote' from his private circumstances), yet in the act of composition itself a pleasurable emotion and excitement are generated from the *spontaneous* exertion of all the faculties.[2] Even in the most rigidly metaphysical of Coleridge's statements concerning genius this emphasis on the spontaneity of the 'whole man' fusion may be found.[3] Coleridge would have agreed not only with T. S. Eliot's concept of 'wholeness' (as 'maturity') therefore but, still more, with the Yeatsian view that it is at the flash-point of creativity that we find 'the whole man, blood, imagination, intellect, running together'.

A man may to some extent *mature* into 'wholeness', but a perfectly stable harmony must be regarded as something of an ideal; it is the 'conatus' or 'harmony of striving' itself which serves as the prime condition of unity.[4] Few artists, probably, have been 'whole men' habitually, while many have paid a high price (sometimes a tragic one, in terms of their personal happiness) for the inner creative force which monopolized their capital of energy. Dostoievsky, Beethoven, Lawrence, Coleridge himself, are cases in point. It seems to be a law of nature that a heavy expenditure of energy in one direction entails a consequent drain from some other side of life.[5] It is the paradox of *Dejection: an Ode* that in the course of writing the poem Coleridge probably achieved momentarily that 'wholeness' the loss of which, in

---

[1] LS, 177—my italics.   [2] ibid. 10 (quoted pp. 272–3 above).
[3] ibid, 12.   [4] See G. W. Allport, op. cit., 351.
[5] Cf. C. G. Jung, op. cit. 194–6.

V

broader, general terms, the poem was lamenting. Because he felt at that time that he might never again achieve such self-integration, his theory of what constitutes a poet in ideal perfection represents an ironic commentary upon his own case. The germ of this theory can be traced back to Coleridge's early awareness of his own insufficiency—to that sense of possessing 'power' but not 'strength' which permeates his letters, notebooks, and poems. This is a matter finally in which ideas and theory are inseparable from the poetry and biographical details, since the formulating of the theory of the poet as a 'whole man' seems to have begun when Coleridge's own breakdown as a poet occurred. It began to emerge during the emotional crisis of 1802, when Coleridge realized that the neurotic habit of stealing from his 'own nature all the natural man' had become

> . . . my sole resource, my only plan:
> Till that which suits a part *infects the whole*,
> And now is almost grown the habit of my soul.

'Meek Daughter in the Family of Christ'

Against the view that Sara's reproof in *The Eolian Harp* was dictated by her 'extremely narrow and governessy' Christian orthodoxy must be set the fact that in 1795 her 'orthodoxy' appears to have been singularly elastic. For example, she readily married Coleridge though she must have known (as Mary Evans, Poole, Southey, and the Rev. George Coleridge knew) his reputation for being an 'infidel'. The knowledge did not deter her, any more than it would have deterred her sisters from accepting an otherwise promising offer of marriage. Edith Fricker married Southey, despite his propensity for attacking the Church and his denial of the necessity for an *established* faith, while the eldest sister, Mary, married Robert Lovell, a self-confessed atheist.

In none of his letters, so far as I have been able to discover, does Coleridge mention any radical *religious* differences between Sara and himself. In the long letter to Sir George Beaumont of 1 October 1803 in which he traced his earlier political development Coleridge admitted that his unconventional religious opinions had offended his own family in 1794–5, but there was no mention of their having offended Sara too. One feels he would have mentioned it in this particular letter had there been grounds for so doing. It is true that in 1806 Sara's brother, George Fricker, quarrelled with Coleridge over religious points, but this arose mainly from the fact that young Fricker had very recently become a militant convert to Methodism.

The possibility cannot be ruled out that Coleridge's show of penitence before the 'Meek Daughter in the family of Christ' was put on, perhaps half-consciously, to gain kudos at Southey's expense. Southey, the man of '*perpendicular Virtue*' and the dominant figure in this Bristol circle, had been exposed as a perjuror —a man who, despite his professed antipathy to the established Church, was for the sake of a benefice prepared to take holy orders (particularly as his uncle had access to the bishop's ear).

Coleridge took it upon himself to point out to Southey the 'enormous Guilt' of this 'doughty Sophistry'.

> 'But your Joan of Arc—the sentiments in it are of the boldest Order. What if the Suspicions of the Bishop be raised, and he particularly questions you concerning your opinions of the Trinity, and the Redemption?' O (you replied) I am pretty well up to their Jargon and shall answer them accordingly. In fine, you left me fully persuaded, that you would enter into holy Orders . . . Southey! I am not besotted, that I should not know nor hypocrite enough not to tell you, that you were diverted from being a Priest—only by the weight of Infamy which you perceived coming towards you, like a Rush of Waters![1]

Southey admitted the charge in a letter of 22 August 1795: 'My uncle urges me to enter the church; but the gate is perjury.' It was in August 1795 that Southey was tempted to enter the Church, the month when *The Eolian Harp* was written, and when Coleridge was still smarting under Southey's abandonment of the Pantisocratic scheme and his interference in the Mary Evans affair. As Mr Boulger points out, Coleridge was always prepared at this time 'to use the Christian religion to facilitate a pose',[2] and it is conceivable, therefore, that his recantation in *The Eolian Harp* was designed, partly at any rate, to enable him to appear in a more favourable light than Southey in Sara's eyes. This is the more credible in view of Miss Coburn's surmise that originally Southey was more attracted to Sara than to Edith Fricker.[3] It helps also to explain that jibe which was frequently thrown at Coleridge by Southey—'my home is flung in my face with "I know your Sara, I know that Meek Sister in the Family of Christ"'.[4] In any event, Southey's taunt sounds like a denouncement of Sara, though whether of her supposed orthodoxy or her meekness one cannot be certain.

Shurton Bars, which followed *The Eolian Harp*, in September 1795, reinforces the suspicion that Coleridge was seeking at this time to oust his rival from the hegemony of the Fricker circle. There Southey is made the scapegoat for the quarrel between Sara and Edith:

> I see you all oppressed with gloom
> Sit lonely in that cheerless room—
> Ah me! You are in tears!

[1] CL, i, 166.   [2] Boulger, 175n.   [3] KC, i, 1815n.   [4] ibid.

> Belovéd Woman! did you fly
> Chill'd Friendship's dark disliking eye . . .? (10–14)

Spiteful and malicious though it seems, such behaviour was not incompatible with what we know of Coleridge's character.

The Abyssinian Maid

As a generic symbol of woman the inspirer, the Abyssinian maid was a composite, doubtless, of many women in Coleridge's life. She represented the qualities he admired in Dorothy Words-worth (Wordsworth's Abyssinian maid), and those which in later years he discovered in, say, Catherine Clarkson or the sisters, Mary Morgan and Charlotte Brent, of whom he wrote: 'Me did you soothe . . . as on unthaw'd ice the winter sun. . . You have been to me / At once a vision and reality' (PW 411). Asra pos-sessed all the requisite qualities too, but *Kubla Khan* was written before he met her. Circumstantial evidence suggests that it was chiefly Mary Evans whose persistent image lay behind the Abys-sinian maid, and this evidence may be found in the poem *Lewti*. Since this poem was written about the same time as *Kubla Khan*, and since it reveals a continuing infatuation with Mary Evans ('Lewti' being a pseudonym for Mary) it is possible that the Abyssinian maid was also a pseudonym for his former mistress. *Lewti* was composed in April 1798 and *Kubla Khan* in either Oc-tober 1797 or May 1798.

There is ample evidence that 'Lewti' was a cover for Mary Evans. There is, first, *Lewti's* close resemblance to *The Sigh* (1794), the poem in which, while yielding to the 'stern decree,' Coleridge had revealed his hopeless infatuation with Mary Evans:

> Thy Image may not banish'd be—
> Still, Mary! still I sigh for thee.

The affinity between these lines and the *Lewti* theme is unmistak-able:

> At midnight by the stream I roved,
> To forget the form I loved.
> Image of Lewti! from my mind
> Depart; for Lewti is not kind.

Secondly, a well-known notebook entry on the impossibility of quelling a deep infatuation suggests that 'Lewti' in fact described a true-life predicament ('Many of my Instances recalled to my mind my little poem on *Lewti*, the Circassian'—see p. 221 above). Thirdly, it seems likely that the discreet reticence in which Coleridge shrouded the poem may have been dictated by delicate consideration for Sara's feelings. He first published *Lewti* in the *Morning Post* under the pseudonym of 'Nicias Erythraeus' (much as his personal attacks on Lloyd and Lamb had been disguised under the cover of 'Nehemiah Higginbottom's' signature) and, for reasons not disclosed, he withdrew the poem from the *Lyrical Ballads* of 1798, not allowing it to appear again until 1817, years after he had separated from his wife. Finally, there is the conclusive fact that in an unpublished variant of *Lewti*, Coleridge forgot himself and actually substituted Mary's name for 'Lewti':

> High o'er the silver rocks I roved
> To forget the form I loved
> In hopes fond fancy would be kind
> And steal my *Mary* from my mind. (See PW 547)

Either the cipher slipped or, because these lines were not for publication, he allowed his fantasy free rein. 'Lewti' then was Mary Evans, with whom Coleridge was probably still in love when he wrote *Kubla Khan*. It is important to note how 'Lewti's' qualities resembled those of the Abyssinian maid, and how different they were from Sara's.

An erotic picture in *Lewti* of the loved one's bed serves to remind us of the strong physical attraction which Mary Evans possessed for Coleridge. This bed, more inflammatory of feeling than ever Sara's was, differs from the Clevedon rose-leaf beds in being associated with both the 'breeze' and the 'nightingale', two symbols for free-ranging creative originality which in Sara's presence Coleridge was obliged to suppress. The symbolization in the following description suggests that Mary Evans could have given Coleridge not only sexual, but also creative, fulfilment:

> I know the place where Lewti lies,
> When silent night has closed her eyes:
> It is a breezy jasmine-bower,
> The nightingale sings o'er her head:
> Voice of the Night! had I the power
> That leafy labyrinth to thread,
> And creep, like thee, with soundless tread,

> I then might view her bosom white
> Heaving lovely to my sight,
> As these two swans together heave
> On the gently-swelling wave. (65–75)

A variant reading of these lines suggests even more forcibly the strength of sexual desire that lay behind them:

> Haste Haste, some God indulgent prove
> And bear me, bear me to my love
> Then might—for yet the sultry hour
> Glows from the sun's oppressive power
> Then might her bosom soft and white
> Heave upon my swimming sight
> As yon two swans together heave
> Upon the gently-swelling wave
> Haste—haste some God indulgent prove
> And bear—oh bear me to my love. (PW 548)

Rarely did Coleridge's wife evoke such sexual intensity, and never such promise of imaginative empathy. *Could* he find Lewti again, the poem states, he would rediscover the deep delights of 'joy' (PW 549), whereas without her life was 'joyless' (ll. 15–41).

In *Kubla Khan* this wistful yearning was sublimated into a splendid description of the effect her wished-for inspiration would have upon him; in *Lewti* Coleridge fell back unfortunately on self-pity and something of his former theatricality:

> Oh! that she saw me in a dream,
>   And dreamt that I had died for care;
> All pale and wasted I would seem,
>   Yet fair withal, as spirits are!
> I'd die indeed, if I might see
> Her bosom heave, and heave for me!
> Soothe, gentle image! soothe my mind!
> To-morrow Lewti may be kind. (76–83)

'Motive' in The Ancient Mariner

Professor J. T. Boulton, in an unpublished paper to which he has generously given me access, suggests that Coleridge's discussion of the function of the 'Will' (in *The Statesman's Manual*, Appendix C) may be central to the interpretation of *The Ancient Mariner*. In this passage Coleridge argued that reason and religion exist and 'co-exist' only in so far as they are actuated by the Will. He continued:

> ... In its state of immanence (or indwelling) in reason and religion, the Will appears indifferently, as wisdom or as love: two names of the same power, the former more intelligential, the latter more spiritual, the former more frequent in the Old, the latter in the New Testament. But in its utmost abstraction and consequent state of reprobation, the Will becomes satanic pride and rebellious self-idolatry in the relations of the spirit to itself, and remorseless despotism relatively to others; the more hopeless as the more obdurate by its subjugation of sensual impulses, by its superiority to toil and pain and pleasure; in short, by the fearful resolve to find in itself alone the one absolute motive of action, under which all other motives from within and from without must be either subordinated or crushed.

This seems a fruitful suggestion, particularly as *The Statesman's Manual* (1816) was written while Coleridge was revising *The Ancient Mariner* for *Sybilline Leaves* (1817).

It is possible, too, that Wordsworth's *The Borderers* (1795–6) had an important bearing on Coleridge's poem. Consider, for example, the discussion among the Borderers concerning Oswald's 'motive':

Wallace   Natures such as his
          Spin motives out of their own bowels, Lacy!
          I learn'd this when I was a Confessor.
          I know him well; there needs no other motive
          Than that most strange incontinence in crime
          Which haunts this Oswald. Power is life to him

And breath and being; where he cannot govern,
He will destroy.

Lacy   To have been trapped like moles!—
Yes, you are right, we need not hunt for motives:
There is no crime from which this man would shrink;
He recks not human law; and I have noticed
That often, when the name of God is uttered,
A sudden blankness overspreads his face.

Lennox Yet, reasoner, as he is, his pride has built
Some uncouth superstition of its own.

(Act III, 1427–41)

Here, as in the passage from *The Statesman's Manual*, we have a description of a state of mind impervious to the importance of the individual being, of universal harmony, or of the individual as representative of the universal; a mind to which the individual being is of no consequence, whatever its intrinsic worth; a mind indifferent to its own participation in the general life; but one which is motivated by the egocentric will. Bearing in mind that *The Ancient Mariner* is a poem in which New Testament religion is prominent, we note that according to *The Statesman's Manual* 'love' is the outward proof of an integrated and balanced personality; when the Will is in the ascendant, however, self-love, remorselessness, and 'wilfulness' denote a lack of balance. These passages, taken in conjunction, provide surely a description of the Mariner himself at the beginning of the poem. He found 'in [himself] alone the one absolute motive of action, under which all other motives from without [were] either subordinated or crushed'. This being so, Coleridge was perfectly right to omit an explicit motive from the account of the Mariner's killing of the Albatross; he was right to give him, initially, a contemptuous attitude towards the sea-snakes. The Mariner's self-assurance, resolve, and remorselessness at the beginning of the poem are all in place, as are the matter-of-fact manner in which he tells of the cross being removed from his neck and his lack of understanding of the significance of this act. Experience leads the Mariner finally to a full awareness of the prime importance of love; it produces in him a recognition of the wholeness of life and of the significance of the individual life. He is motivated finally by love, proof of his new spiritual integration, and at this stage his will is in a state of 'immanence in reason and religion'.

Yet, as the poem makes clear, the Mariner needs *help* before
he can achieve a full awareness of the principle of love that permeates the universe. His individual will has to be acted *upon* by
the beneficent powers of the universe in which he lives. As *Aids
to Reflection* puts it:

> Is nothing to be attributed to the harmony of the system to which
> he belongs, and to the pre-established Fitness of the Objects and
> Agents, known and unknown that surround him, as acting *on* the
> will, though, doubtless, *with* it likewise?[1]

Coleridge went on to postulate here that the harmony of external
nature presupposes 'a Universal Power, as the cause and pre-
condition of the harmony of all particular Wholes'. If this is true
of the world of '*objects*', he asked, is it unreasonable

> . . . to entertain a similar Belief in relation to the System of intelli-
> gent and self-conscious Beings, to the moral and personal World?
> But if in *this*, too, in the great Community of *Persons*, it is rational
> to infer One universal Presence, a One present to all and in all, is
> it not most irrational to suppose that a finite Will can exclude it?

Thus, when the Mariner is induced to act in harmony with the
undivided life, his change of attitude is in part attributable to
'this all-present power as acting *in* the Will'. Here, we have surely
an indirect comment on *The Ancient Mariner*—an amplification
of what is referred to in my interpretation of the poem as 'grace'.
One further passage from *Aids to Reflection* serves to illustrate the
point. It is a passage with obvious bearing, I think, upon *The
Ancient Mariner*:

> Though the mariner sees not the *pole-star*, yet the needle of the
> compass which points to it, tells him which way he sails; thus the
> heart that is touched with the loadstone of divine love, trembling
> with godly fear, and yet still looking towards God by fixed believ-
> ing, interprets the fear by the love *in* the fear, and tells the soul that
> its course is heavenward, towards the haven of eternal rest. He that
> loves may be sure he was loved first; and he that chooses God for
> his delight and portion, may conclude confidently, that God has
> chosen him to be one of those that shall enjoy him, and be happy
> in him for ever; for that our love and electing of him is but the
> return and repercussion of the beams of his love shining upon us.[2]

A final comment on the last stanzas of the poem is provided
by a further passage from *The Statesman's Manual*. It is noticeable

---

[1] AR, 42–3.   [2] ibid, 39.

that the Mariner is not satisfied merely by giving an account of his experiences (the tale is completed 35 lines before the end of the poem); but he has a kind of missionary zeal to impart what is sometimes denounced as the too-obtrusive 'moral' of the poem. In this context the following passage is illuminating:

> Even so doth religion finitely express the Unity of the Infinite Spirit by being a total act of the soul... Nor doth it express only the fulness of the Spirit. It likewise represents His overflowing by its communicativeness, budding and blossoming forth in all earnestness of persuasion, and in all words of sound doctrine... The love of God, and therefore God himself, who is love, religion strives to express by love, and measures its growth by the increase and activity of its love. For Christian love is the last and divinest birth, the harmony, unity, and god-like transfiguration of all the vital, intellectual, moral, and spiritual powers. Now it manifests itself as the sparkling and ebullient spring of well-doing in gifts and in labours; and now as a silent fountain of patience and long-suffering . . .

> From God's love through His Son, crucified for us from the beginning of the world, religion begins; and in love towards God and the creatures of God it hath its end and completion.

Assuming that this is relevant to *The Ancient Mariner* one may observe now the difference between the ending of Coleridge's poem and that of *The Borderers*. Wordsworth's poem concludes with this speech of Marmaduke's:

> . . . in silence hear my doom:
> A hermitage has furnished fit relief
> To some offenders; other penitents,
> Less patient in their wretchedness, have fallen,
> Like the old Roman, on their own sword's point.
> They had their choice: a wanderer *must I* go,
> The Spectre of that innocent Man, my guide.
> No human ear shall ever hear me speak;
> No human dwelling ever give me food,
> Or sleep, or rest: but over waste and wild,
> In search of nothing that this earth can give,
> But expiation, will I wander on—
> A Man by pain and thought compelled to live,
> Yet loathing life—till anger is appeased
> In Heaven, and Mercy gives me leave to die.
>   (Act v, 2339–53)

Coleridge's poem ends with the Mariner suffering evermore the 'penance of life', yet at the same time treasuring within himself a recognition of the principle of love that binds the universe in harmony. When he has told his tale it leaves him 'free'. Marmaduke, conversely, sees no respite from endless suffering; because he has not been vouchsafed (by 'grace') an insight into perfect love, his universe remains a world of death.

Though it seems to me certain that Coleridge's poem was influenced by *The Borderers*, and that *The Statesman's Manual* may have sought to express in philosophical terms the intuitive truths which at the time of writing *The Ancient Mariner* Coleridge had arrived at by experience, I have placed this material in an appendix rather than in the text because, in accordance with the general principle of this book, I wish to consider the poem so far as possible without reference to the later events in Coleridge's chronology. I have however included some references to the Malta voyage of 1804 for reasons that will be obvious.

Geraldine and Genevieve

Love, first published in the *Morning Post*, 21 December 1799, was written less than two months after Coleridge's first meeting with Asra (26 October 1799) and six months *before* he began Part II of *Christabel*. Originally, he called the poem *Introduction to the Tale of the Dark Ladie* and like its 'sister tale', *The Ballad of the Dark Ladie*, it is a poem about a guilty love-affair (see PW 557, stanza 33; also PW 294, ll. 29–32, 41–8). Coleridge obviously borrowed details from this poem, *Love*, for Part II of *Christabel* and the parallels between these poems reinforce the suggestion that the Geraldine/Sir Leoline relationship may have been a projection of Coleridge's own relationship with Asra.

Love opens with what seems like a defiant vindication of promiscuity:

> All thoughts, all passions, all delights,
> Whatever stirs this mortal frame,
> All are but ministers of Love,
>   And feed his sacred flame. (1–4)

It goes on to recall the pleasure of Coleridge's first meeting with Asra at Sockburn, idealizing the setting considerably so that it resembles the moonlit Gothic landscape in which Geraldine first appeared:

> Oft in my waking dreams do I
> Live o'er again that happy hour,
> When midway on the mount I lay,
>   Beside the ruined tower.
> The moonshine, stealing o'er the scene
>   Had blended with the lights of eve;
> And she was there, my hope, my joy,
>   My own dear Genevieve! (5–12)

In the poem Coleridge tells 'Genevieve' (a 'Geraldine'-like pseudonym for Asra by the way), a doleful story which, he admits, could be applied to himself:

> I told her, how he pin'd: and ah!
>   The deep, the low, the pleading tone
> With which I sang another's love,
>   Interpreted my own. (33–6)

It is a tragic story of romantic love (the model, possibly, for Keats's *La Belle Dame Sans Merci*), though marred occasionally by sentimentality.

Briefly, it concerns a Knight, 'crazed with madness' (cf. Sir Leoline) because he has been rejected by his mistress, who saves a Lady from outrage at the hands of a murderous band (from a danger, that is, similar to that which threatened Geraldine). In gratitude, the Lady 'wept, and clasped his knees', just as Geraldine, on promise of Sir Leoline's assistance

> . . . fell, and clasped his knees
> Her face upraised, her eyes o'erflowing. (519–20)

The Knight dies shortly afterwards, dying in the Lady's arms (in a typically Coleridgean sick-room situation) while she seeks to nurse away his madness. At this point the interior story is abruptly discontinued; it has had the wished-for effect on 'Genevieve' (Asra), who has recognized its implications:

> —but when I reach'd
> That tenderest strain of all the ditty,
> My faultering voice and pausing harp
> Disturbed her soul with pity! (65–8)

All through the story 'Genevieve' has been listening intently. Twice in the poem Coleridge remarks:

> She listened with a flitting blush,
> With downcast eyes and modest grace . . .
>   (25–6, 37–8)

Six months later he described Geraldine's demeanour while listening to Sir Leoline in almost similar terms:

> And Geraldine *in maiden wise*
> Casting down her large bright eyes
> With blushing cheeks and *courtesy fine* . . . (573–5)

But Geraldine's modesty was merely feigned, as the phrases I have italicized indicate. Nevertheless, these parallels suggest that 'Genevieve' (Asra) was never far from Coleridge's thoughts when a few months later he developed Geraldine's character in Part II of *Christabel*.

'Genevieve' is drawn much more sympathetically than 'Geraldine', as though to represent the more tender, ingenuous aspects of Coleridge's love for Asra. Yet, despite the poem's bold opening assertion that *all* passions feed the sacred flame of love, a weight of guilt hangs over it. It may be significant that in revising the poem for *Lyrical Ballads* (1800) Coleridge amended the phrase 'my *guiltless* Genevieve' to 'my guileless Genevieve' (70), the meaning of which is subtly different. This sense of guilt can best be shown by extended quotation:

> All impulses of soul and sense
> Had thrilled my guileless Genevieve;   70
> The music and the doleful tale,
>   The rich and balmy eve;
>
> And hopes, and fears that kindle hope,
> An undistinguishable throng,
> And gentle wishes long subdued,   75
>   Subdued and cherished long!
>
> She wept with pity and delight,
> She blushed with love, and virgin-shame;
> And like the murmur of a dream,
>   I heard her breathe my name.   80
>
> Her bosom heaved—she stepped aside,
> As conscious of my look she stepped—
> Then suddenly, with timorous eye
>   She fled to me and wept.
>
> She half enclosed me with her arms,   85
> She pressed me with a meek embrace;
> And bending back her head, looked up,
>   And gazed upon my face.
>
> 'Twas partly love, and partly fear,
> And partly 'twas a bashful art,   90
> That I might rather feel, than see,
>   The swelling of her heart.
>
> I calmed her fears, and she was calm,
> And told her love with virgin pride;
> And so I won my Genevieve,   95
>   My bright and beauteous Bride.

Despite Asra's guilelessness and 'virgin-shame' it is evident from lines 85–92 that sexual passions had been roused during the recent meeting at Sockburn, passions which were more guilt-inducing than 'sacred'. The phrase 'gentle wishes' long subdued (ll. 75–6) was a euphemism for sexual desires, which needed to be 'subdued' for obvious reasons. The poem reveals Coleridge's vivid awareness of Asra's physical presence and possibly some wish-fulfilment in his imagining that she would take the initiative in love-making and eventually become his 'Bride'.

The parallels between *Love* and *Christabel* suggest that 'Genevieve' and 'Geraldine' are closely related characters. We know that 'Genevieve' was based on Asra, and a link is suggested therefore between 'Geraldine' and Asra. Whereas 'Genevieve' was used to heighten Asra's innocence, 'Geraldine' seemed more like a creature of the id, an image of adultery from which Coleridge's better mind recoiled. It is entirely consistent with Coleridge's general attitude to women that he should be able to regard Asra in both these ways.

GENERAL INDEX

(Poems and works of primary importance referred to in this book appear under their titles in a separate index. Contents of footnotes are not distinguished from entries concerning the text.)

INDEX OF TITLES